ASPECTS
OF
LANGUAGE

ASPECTS

OF

LANGUAGE

DWIGHT BOLINGER
Harvard University

HARCOURT, BRACE & WORLD, INC.
New York / Chicago / San Francisco / Atlanta

TO MY SON BRUCE, IN ADMIRATION AND AFFECTION

ISBN: 0-15-503865-6

LIBRARY OF CONGRESS CATALOG CARD NUMBER: 68–15946

PRINTED IN THE UNITED STATES OF AMERICA

FOREWORD

L INGUISTS have long complained that the Wonder of Words approach to language has been almost their only contact with the outside world, but to date they have done very little about it. A number of good books have been issued or reissued in low-priced editions in the past few years: some are general outlines by scholars of a generation or two ago, but most are technical or semi-technical works on specialized topics: origins of writing, development of speech, linguistics in the nineteenth century, anthropological linguistics, and the like. One looks in vain for the book that will maintain a proper balance of readability, informativeness, and fidelity to the interests, goals, and trials of linguists as linguists see them, to give the average reader an appreciation of what modern linguistics is about. Other sciences have been able to describe themselves to the general public and to the unspecialized student. The same should be possible for linguistics. At least it is time to try.

What makes the attempt all the more imperative is that the reader of the typical book on the wonderful world of words sees in the spectacle no particular relevance to himself. Yet there is no science that is closer to the humanness of humanity than linguistics, for its field is the means by which our personalities are defined to others and by which our thoughts are formed and gain continuity and acceptance. Until linguists can bring their point of view clearly and palatably before the reader at large and the student in the language classroom, they will have only themselves to blame for what one linguist has called the towering failure of the schools to inform ordinary citizens about language. Of no other scientific field is so much fervently believed that isn't so. And not only believed but taught.

We do not need to travel abroad nor back in time to discover the facts of language. They lie all about us, in the tablets of our handwriting and the potsherds of our own speech. Almost nothing of interest to the linguist goes on anywhere that does not go on in our communication here and now. This book is an invitation to the reader to see within him and around him the objects of a science, and to glimpse how the scientist interprets them. It is not intended to teach linguistics but to help ordinary people divine themselves as the creators and perpetuators of the most wonderful invention of all time.

There are no directions for reading this book beyond one mild word of caution. To follow the plays in a game one must first learn the rules. This demands a willingness to submit to certain initiatory rites. The beginning chapters, in particular Chapters 4 and 5, carry the heaviest burden of terms and concepts. They ask a measure of patience from the reader. After that he should find the going fairly easy.

To recognize individually all those whose scholarship was drawn upon in this volume would be impossible, and to settle on a few is to risk unintentionally slighting others to whom the debt may be just as great. I can only thank my intellectual mentors and creditors in a general way and assure them that the gratitude is not less for not being more specific.

Nevertheless a few must indeed be singled out—those who have criticized the manuscript in whole or in part: John Algeo, Fred W. Householder, Jr., George Lakoff, William G. Moulton, Thomas Pyles, John R. Ross, and James Sledd. Without their help this book could not have kept true to its aim, and if even so it has fallen short, the author is all the more to be blamed.

CONTENTS

ASPECTS
OF
LANGUAGE

BORN TO SPEAK

THOMAS A. EDISON is supposed to have parried the question of a skeptic who wanted to know what one of his fledgling inventions was good for by asking "What good is a baby?" Appearances suggest that a baby is good for very little, least of all to itself. Completely helpless, absolutely dependent on the adults around it, seemingly unable to do much more than kick and crawl for the greater part of nine or ten months, it would seem better off in the womb a little longer until ready to make a respectable debut and scratch for itself.

Yet if the premature birth of human young is an accident, it is a fortunate one. No other living form has so much to learn about the external world and so little chance of preparing for it in advance. An eaglet has the pattern of its life laid out before it hatches from the egg. Its long evolution has equipped it to contend with definite foes, search for definite foods, mate, and rear its young according to a definite ritual. The environment is predictable enough to make the responses predictable too, and they are built into the genetic design. With human beings this is impossible. The main reason for its impossibility is language.

We know little about animal communication but enough to say that nowhere does it even approach the complexity of human language. By the time he is six or eight years old a child can watch a playmate carry out an intricate series of actions and give a running account of it afterward. The most that a bee can do is perform a dance that is related analogously to

1

the direction and distance of a find of nectar, much like what we do in pointing a direction to a stranger. The content of the message is slight and highly stereotyped. With the child, the playmate's actions can be as unpredictable as you please; he will verbalize them somehow. Attaining this skill requires the mastery of a system that takes literally years to learn. An early start is essential, and it cannot be in the womb. Practice must go on in the open air where sounds are freely transmitted, for language is sound. And if language is to be socially effective, it cannot be acquired within a month or two of birth when the environment is limited to parents and crib but must continue to grow as the child becomes stronger and widens his contacts. Human evolution has insured that this will happen by providing for a brain in which the speech areas are the last to reach their full development.[1] So we might say to Edison's question that a baby is good for learning language.

All that a child can be born with is an instinct for language, not for any particular language, just as he is born with an instinct for walking but not for walking in a given direction. This is another reason why an early beginning is necessary: languages differ and even the same language changes through time, so that an infant born with patterns already set would be at a disadvantage. One still hears the foolish claim that a child of German ancestry ought to be able to learn German more easily than some other language. Our experience discredits this. An infant of whatever race learns whatever language it hears, one about as easily as another. Complete adaptability confers the gift of survival. Children do not depend on a particular culture but fit themselves to the one into which they are born, and that culture in turn is one that is maintaining itself in a not always friendly universe. Whatever success it has is largely due to the understanding and cooperation that language makes possible.

Another reason for an early beginning and a gradual growth is *permeation*. The running account that a child is able to give of a series of actions that he performs or sees performed betokens an organized activity that is not enclosed within itself but relates at all times to something else. It would seem absurd to us to be told that every time we stood up, sat down, reached for a chocolate, turned on a light, pushed a baby carriage, or started the car we should, at the same time, be twitching in a particular way the big toe of our left foot. But just such an incessant accompaniment of everything else by our speech organs does not surprise us at all. Other activities are self-contained. That of language penetrates them and almost never stops. It must be developed not separately, like walking, but as part of whatever we do. So it must be on hand from the start.

---

[1] Leonard Carmichael, "The Early Growth of Language Capacity in the Individual," in Eric H. Lenneberg (ed.), *New Directions in the Study of Language* (Cambridge, Mass.: M.I.T. Press, 1966), pp. 1–22, especially pp. 17–19.

The idea that there is an instinct for language has been recently revived by psychologists and linguists working in the field of child learning. For a long time language was thought to be a part of external culture and nothing more. Even the physiology of speech was seen as more or less accidental: our speech organs were really organs of digestion which happened to be utilized to satisfy a social need. A child in a languageless society, deprived of speech but permitted to chew and swallow, would not feel that he was missing anything. That view has been almost reversed. Now it is felt that the organs of speech in their present form were shaped as much for sound production as for nourishment. The human tongue is far more agile than it needs to be for purposes of eating. On the receiving end, the sensitivity of the human ear has been sharpened to the point that we can detect a movement of the eardrum that does not exceed one tenth of the diameter of a hydrogen molecule.

So there are three ingredients in the consummation of language:

1. an *instinct* in the shape of mental and physical capacities developed through countless centuries of natural selection;

2. a preexisting language *system,* any one of the many produced by the cultures of the world;

3. a *competence* that comes from applying the instinct to the system through the relatively long period during which the child learns both to manipulate the physical elements of the system, such as sounds and words and syntactic rules, and to permeate them with meaning.

The development of so finely graded a specialization of our organs of speech and hearing and of the nervous system to which they are attached is not surprising if we assume that society cannot survive without language and individual human beings cannot survive without society. Natural selection will take care of it.[2] And natural selection unquestionably has. Language is species-specific. It is a uniquely human trait, shared by cultures so diverse and by individuals physically and mentally so unlike one another—from Watusi tribesmen to nanocephalic dwarfs—that the notion of its being purely a socially transmitted skill is not to be credited.[3]

An instinct for language implies that a child does more than echo what he hears. The older notion of mere plasticity has been abandoned. The first months are a preparation for language in which babbling, a com-

---

[2] See Charles F. Hockett and Robert Ascher, "The Human Revolution," *American Scientist* 52.71–92 (1964).

[3] Eric H. Lenneberg, "A Biological Perspective of Language," in Lenneberg, *op. cit.,* pp. 65–88.

pletely self-directed exercise, is the main activity. Imitation begins to play a part, of course, but it too is experimental and hence creative. We see how this must be if we imagine a child already motivated to imitate and being told by his mother to say *papa.* This sounds simple to us because we already know what features to heed and what ones to ignore, but the child must learn to tell them apart. Shall he imitate his mother's look, her gesture, the way she shapes her lips, the breathiness of the first consonant, the voice melody, the moving of the tongue? Even assuming that he can focus on certain things to the exclusion of others, he has no way of knowing which ones to select. He cannot then purely imitate. He must experiment and wait for approval. Imitation is an activity that is shaped creatively.

PROGRESS

We do not know the extent to which children are taught and the extent to which they learn on their own. If learning is instinctive, then children will learn whether or not adults appoint themselves to be their teachers. But if there is an instinct to learn, for all we know there may be an instinct to teach. It is possible that parents unconsciously adopt special modes of speaking to very young children, to help them learn the important things first, impelled by the desire not so much to teach the child as to communicate with him, but with teaching a by-product.

One psychologist noted the following ways in which she simplified her own speech when talking to her child:

1. the use of a more striking variant of a speech sound when there is a choice, for example using the /t/ of *table* when saying the word *butter* in place of the more usual flapped sound (almost like *budder*);

2. exaggerated intonation, with greater ups and downs of pitch;

3. slower rate;

4. simple sentence structure, as, for example, avoidance of the passive voice;

5. avoidance of substitute words like *it,* as, for example, *Where's your milk? Show me your milk* instead of *Where's your milk? Show it to me.*[4]

Most parents would probably add *repetition* to this list.

---

[4] Lila R. Gleitman and Elizabeth F. Shipley, "A Proposal for the Study of the Acquisition of English Syntax," grant proposal submitted March 1, 1963, to National Institutes of Health, p. 24.

Whatever the technique, the child does not seem to follow any particular sequence, learning first to pronounce all the sounds perfectly, then to manage words, then sentences, then "correct expression." A child of twelve to eighteen months with no sentences at all will be heard using sentence intonations on separate words in a perfectly normal way—*Doggie?* with rising pitch, meaning 'Is that a doggie?' or *Doggie,* with falling pitch, to comment on the dog's presence. The child's program seems to call for a developing complexity rather than doing all of one thing before taking up the next.

The first stage of communication, when parents feel that their children have really begun to speak, is reached when individual words are being pronounced intelligibly—that is, so that parents can match them with words in their own speech—and related to things and events. This is the *holophrastic* stage, when utterance and thing are related one to one. The thing named may be a single object called *mama* or a whole situation called *mapank.* The parents will interpret the latter as a sentence—*Mama spank*—but to the child it is a word. He has no basis for dividing it. A thing or situation has a proper name. There is no syntax.

The second stage is *analytic:* the child begins to divide his proper names into true sentences. Besides *mapank* the vocabulary probably includes additional words like *mama, papa,* and *baby.* The day comes when Papa spanks, and the uniqueness of *mapank* is broken up—the different elements in the situation are recognized for who they are and *ma* is properly attached to *mama.* Now *mapank* is a sentence and will probably be modified to *Mama pank.* Before long the child begins to *look* for parts within wholes and to play with them: *Baby spank.* Words become playthings. When a two-and-a-half-year-old runs to his parents and says *House eat baby*—the sort of expression that unimaginative adults brush aside as preposterous or even punish as "untrue"—he is only exulting over the discovery that he can do the same with his words as with his building blocks, put them together in fascinating ways. Much of learning a language is a pattern-flexing game. Children's monologs sometimes sound like students practicing in a language lab.[5]

To make a sentence a child must recognize certain things as the same and certain things as different, must have names for them, and must combine the names. (This achievement is simply the *collocation.*) The third stage calls for noticing more subtle kinds of samenesses in the connections. It can be called the *syntactic* stage. When *mama* and *spank* are recognized as recurring sames, their presence in both *Mama spank* and *Spank mama* (the latter accompanying a playful situation in which the mother makes the baby hit her for some real or pretended misdemeanor) is recognized and

---

[5] See Lenneberg, *op. cit.,* p. 181 for a child's substitution drill: *what color blanket, what color mop, what color glass.*

the difference in the two situations is assigned to the reversal of the order. *Kiss mama, Come-to mama, See mama* then constitute a different kind of same—verb plus object noun—that recurs like all the others and that the child will invent or reinvent using old material to see how far he can go.

The product of the syntactic stage is a variety of sentence types, all simple but distinguished by the number and arrangement of their parts— *Get Daddy, Baby go-play, Mama eat cereal.* The component parts too are simple. There are no morphological complications like articles or verb inflections. But the syntactic stage also offers combinations like *that doggie, baby chair* ('Baby's chair'), *more cereal,* which are used as verb-less sentences but are the raw material for the fourth stage in which arrangements are added to arrangements: *Daddy sit chair* contains a simple arrangement; *Daddy sit baby chair* contains an arrangement within an arrangement. This can be called the *structural* stage. Parts are made up of other parts. When the child discovers this he is in a position to make up his own "words." If, as happened with one child, he lacks the verb *to cross,* he can say *I'm going to the other side of the whole lake,* using *go-to-the-other-side-of* as a substitute (an adult will interpret the sentence as a mistake for *I'm going all the way to the other side,* a more complex structure). As a culmination of his structural stage the child learns how to treat whole sentences as if they were elements, to insert them in larger sentences. A statement like *I go* and a question like *Will you stay?* are combined: *If I go will you stay?*

The step-by-step increase in complexity is illustrated in the responses given by one child at various ages to the command *Ask your daddy what he did at work today.* At two years and five months it was *What he did at work today,* which shows enough understanding to separate the inner question from the command as a whole (*Ask your daddy* is not repeated), but no more. At the age of three, the response was *What you did at work today?,* with the right change of intonation and with *you* for *he.* The child is now really asking a question but has "optimized" its form—that is, he has fitted a newly acquired expression into the mold of an old one that resembles it and is familiar and easy, in this case making the word order of statements serve also for questions. Finally, at three years and five months, he made the right transformation of the verb and produced *What did you do at work today?*[6]

Optimizing occurs at all stages. It may replace a difficult sound with an easy one, as when children say *woof* for *roof.* It may result in a correct sentence or an incorrect one. *What you did at work today?* is incorrect. Correct optimizing occurs when the language offers two different con-

---

[6] Gleitman and Shipley, *op. cit.,* p. 14.

structions, both correct, but one more frequent or more in harmony with familiar constructions. When four-year-olds are given a sentence like *I gave the dog the bone* they will repeat it and understand it, but if they are asked to report the same event themselves they will say *I gave the bone to the dog.*[7] The construction without *to* is less general (for instance, it seldom occurs in the question *Who(m) did you give the money?*—the more normal form is *Who(m) did you give the money to?*) and is not like the related constructions in which prepositions are required: *I got the money from Dad, I got the present for Dad and then I gave it to him*, etc.

The final stage is *stylistic*. The child now has a repertory of constructions among which he can choose. Choice makes for flexibility. He is no longer restricted to conveying just the primary information but is able to show a certain way in which the message is to be taken. *Give the bone to Dingo* and *Give Dingo the bone* "mean the same," but if there is also a cat named Tillie who gets raw liver and both pets are about to be fed, *Give Dingo the bone* is the choice to make when Dingo was about to be given Tillie's ration; it puts the emphasis in the right place.

ATTAINMENT

A favorite generalization of one school of linguists used to be that every child has complete control of his language by the age of five or six. Without disparaging the truly phenomenal control of an enormously complex system that six-year-olds do achieve, we must realize that no limit can be set and that learning by the same old processes continues through life, though at a rate that diminishes so rapidly that well before adolescence it seems almost to have come to a stop. It might be described as a curve that starts by virtually touching infinity and ends by approaching zero (see table).

If learning never ceases, it follows that a language is never completely learned. There is always someone who knows a bit of it that we do not know.[8] In part this is because with the experimental and inventive way in

---

[7] Colin Fraser, Ursula Bellugi, and Roger Brown, "Control of Grammar in Imitation, Comprehension, and Production," *Journal of Verbal Learning and Verbal Behavior* 2.133 (1963).

[8] Some linguists tend to retort, "This may be true of vocabulary—we obviously keep on learning new words all our lives—but it is not true of grammar." Yet one investigation, which studied the sentences written by ninth and tenth graders, after noting that by rigorous standards of sentence formation "almost half of the sentences written by the ninth graders were mal-formed," concluded that it is probably true that "the grammar of English is never fully mastered." Abstract of dissertation by Donald Ray Bateman, *The Effects of a Study of a Generative Grammar upon the Structure of Written Sentences of Ninth and Tenth Graders*, Ohio State University, 1965, in *Linguistics* 26.21–22 (1966).

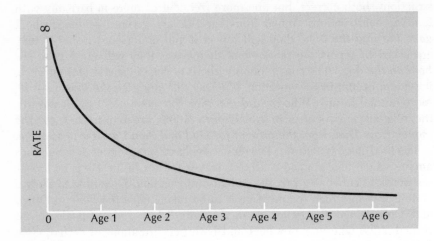

Rate of learning expressed as a proportion of new to old over equal intervals of time

which learning is done, no two people ever carry exactly the same network of shapes and patterns in their heads. A perfect command eludes us because as we catch up it moves off—"the" language exists only as imperfect copies, with original touches, in individual minds; it never stays exactly the same. All we can say is that interplay is so fast, frequent, and vital that great differences are not tolerated, networks are forced to acquire a similar weave, and all within cooperating distance are said to "speak the same language."

ADDITIONAL REMARKS
AND APPLICATIONS

1. What advantages does the younger child learning his first language have over the older child or adult learning a second language? Consider such factors as permeation, time for practice, and instinct for play.

2. Tests show that children apparently develop skill in imitating what they are told to say before they fully understand the meaning.[9] There seems to be enjoyment in saying something just to be saying it. Does this support the theory of an instinct for language?

3. Observe a mother speaking to her child and see what modifications she makes in her speech. Does she say *Give Mummy the shoe* rather than *Give me the shoe,* thus helping to identify *Mummy?* Does she pronounce the important words in an especially distinct way, for example the noun *shoe* in this same sentence? Explain how the need to do this for very young children might have a stabilizing effect on language. (Do adults have a style of speech that is clear and deliberate in addition to other styles in which things are run together?)

4. Observe the vocal sounds of a very young child to see whether he is communicating in any sense at all. Even though his speech may be unintelligible, is he using intonation appropriately? A study of one child showed that at as early as four months he was using a basic sound of *m* as a sort of carrier for intonations when pointing at objects, varying the intonation according to whether the object was desired or merely wondered about.[10] Can you think of any reason why intonation should be the first of the subsystems of language to develop?

5. Would you expect a child to give up its holophrastic stage immediately once it discovers that there are significant parts, or would the stages probably continue to exist side by side? Consider a sentence like *Another thing is is that . . . ,* spoken by an adolescent. Does this point to *another thing is* as an unanalyzed unit? When you say *by the way,*

---

[9] Fraser, Bellugi, and Brown, *op. cit.,* p. 134.

[10] Walburga von Raffler Engel, *Il Prelinguaggio Infantile* (Brescia: Paideia Editrice, 1964), p. 115.

meaning 'incidentally,' do you think of separate meanings for the words ('This is something that stands by the wayside, off the main track')?

6. At the language-learning stage, which is more important for a child, truth or syntax?

7. There are dictionaries that enumerate the words in a language. What about the sentences? Is there something about the way sentences are put together that makes a sentence dictionary impossible? Is this an important difference between animal communication and human language?

8. Discuss the sentence *She went back and told the queen it* (spoken by a nine-year-old) as an example of optimizing. Compare it with *She went back and told the queen the story.* What does it suggest about which of the two word forms, nouns or pronouns, is learned first?

9. What is the main difference between a ten-year-old's command of his language and a twenty-year-old's? Consider the ability to handle the distinctive sounds, the sentence structure, and the range of vocabulary.

SOME TRAITS
OF LANGUAGE

ONE ESTIMATE puts the number of languages in active use in the world today somewhere between three and four thousand. Another makes it five thousand or more. The latter is probably closer to the truth, for many languages are spoken by only a few hundred persons, and many areas of the world are still not fully surveyed. In one subdistrict of New Guinea, for example, there are sixteen languages spoken by an average of fewer than a thousand persons each.[1] Also, it is impossible to be exact, for no one knows just what constitutes "one language." Danish and Norwegian have a high degree of mutual intelligibility; this makes them almost by definition dialects of a single language. Do we count them as two? Cantonese and Mandarin, in spite of both being "Chinese," are about as dissimilar as Portuguese and Italian. Do we count mainland Chinese as one language? To be scientific we have to ignore politics and forget that Denmark and Norway have separate flags and mainland China one. But even then, since differences are quantitative, we would have to know how much to allow before graduating X from "a dialect of Y" to "a language, distinct from Y."

However that may be, the number of different languages is formidable

---

[1] Richard Loving and Jack Bass, "Languages of the Amanab Sub-district," report published by the Department of Information and Extension Services, Territory of Papua and New Guinea, Port Moresby, April, 1964.

and is quite awesome if we include the tongues once spoken but now dead. Languages are like people: for all their underlying similarities, great numbers mean great variety. Variety confronts us with this question: Do we know enough about languages to be able to describe language? Can we penetrate the differences to arrive at the samenesses underneath?

The more languages we study—and previously unexplored ones give up their secrets each year by the score—the more the answer seems to be *yes*. Learning a new language is always in some measure repeating an old experience. Variety may be enormous but similarities abound, and one can even attempt a definition, perhaps something like "Human language is a system of vocal-auditory communication using conventional signs composed of arbitrary patterned sound units and assembled according to set rules, interacting with the experiences of its users." However we word it— and obviously no one-sentence definition will ever be adequate—there is enough homogeneity to make some sort of definition possible. Languages are alike because people are alike in their capacities for communicating in a uniquely human way.

LANGUAGE IS PATTERNED BEHAVIOR

Our five-hundred-year romance with printer's ink tempts us to forget that a language can disappear without leaving a trace when its last speaker dies and that this is still true of the majority of the world's languages in spite of the spread of presses and tape recorders. Written records and tape recordings are embodiments of language, but language itself is a way of acting. Our habit of viewing it as a *thing* is probably unavoidable, even for the linguist, but in a sense it is false.

What is somewhat thing-like, in that it persists through time and from speaker to speaker, is the system that underlies the behavior. This is what makes language so special. Breathing, grasping, and crying are also ways of acting, but we come already equipped to do them. Language is *skilled* behavior and has to be learned. Probably as the child acquires it the system is engraved somehow on the brain, and if we had the means to make it visible we could "read" it. For the present all we can see is the way people act, and linguists are useful precisely because, not being able to look into the brain, we need specialists to study the behavior and infer the system.

THE MEDIUM OF LANGUAGE IS SOUND

All languages use the same channel for sending and receiving: the vibrations of the atmosphere. All set the vibrations going in the same way, by the activity of the speech organs. And all organize the vibrations in essentially the same way, into small units of sound that can be combined and recombined in distinctive ways. Except for the last, human communication is the same as that of most other warm-blooded creatures that move on the earth's surface: the most effective way of reaching another member of one's kind seems to be through disturbances of the air that envelops us.

Paradoxically, what sets human speech apart also sets it above dependence on any particular medium: the capacity for intricate organization. The science of phonetics, whose domain is the sounds of speech, is to linguistics what numismatics is to finance: it makes no difference to a financial transaction what alloys are used in a coin, and it makes no difference to the brain what bits of substance are used as triggers for language—they could be pebbles graded for color or size, or, if we had a dog's olfactory sense, a scheme of discriminated smells. The choice of sound is part of our pre-human heritage, probably for good reason. We do not have to look at or touch the signaler to catch the signal, and we do not depend on wind direction as with smell—nor, as with smell, are we unable to turn it off once it is emitted.[2]

Language is sound in the same sense that a given house is wood. We can conceive of other materials, but it is as if the only tools we had were woodworking ones. If we learn a language we must learn to produce sounds. We are unable to use any other medium except as an incidental help. So part of the description of language must read as if the sound that entered into the organization of language were as indispensable as the organization itself.

SOUND IS EMBEDDED IN GESTURE

If language is an activity, we cannot say that it stops short at the boundaries of *speech* activity, for human actions are not so easily compartmentalized. It is true that we can communicate over the telephone, which seems to prove that everything is carried by the sound wave; but we can also communicate pretty efficiently in writing, and we know that writing leaves out a great deal—intonation, for example. No communication is quite so effective as face-to-face communication, for some part of the communicative act is always contained in the expression and posture of the communicators. We call this *gesture*.

Not all gestures are equally important to language. Three kinds can be distinguished: *instinctive, semiotic,* and *paralinguistic.* The third is closest to language proper.

---

[2] Thomas A. Sebeok, "Coding in the Evolution of Signaling Behavior," *Behavioral Science* 7.435 (1962).

Instinctive gestures are automatic reactions to a stimulus. They are not learned. Dodging a blow, widening the eyes in astonishment, leaning forward to catch a sound, bowing in submission, smiling with pleasure, and others of the kind either are instincts or are based on instinct in such a way that, like the flight of a young bird, it takes no more than a slight parental or social push to set them going. Of course all such gestures give information to anyone observing them, and this is soon noted by the one performing the gesture, who then puts it on as a disguise: he smiles to please rather than to show pleasure, bows when he would rather hurl insults, and weeps when he feels no pain. In the long run all gestures acquire a social significance and take on local modifications, which is one reason why members of one culture behave awkwardly when transplanted to another.

Whereas instinctive gestures tell something—true or false—about the person making them, *semiotic* gestures are free to mean anything. They are not like distinctive sounds, because they do have their own meanings (semaphoric signs, which are just ways of signaling the alphabet, are not included here); they are more like words or even whole sentences. Thus a waving hand means 'good-bye,' both hands held palm up and outstretched with shoulders raised means 'I don't know,' the thumb and forefinger held close together means 'small'—that is, these are the meanings in our culture. Being arbitrary, semiotic gestures are not the same everywhere. In some places the gesture for 'come here' is to hold out the hand cupped palm up with the fingers beckoning; in other places it is the same except that the hand is cupped palm down, and to an outsider it may appear to be a greeting rather than a summons. Semiotic gestures are independent of language. Cooperation between the two is only incidental—a 'come-hither' gesture accompanied by the words *come here* is like a red light at a railroad crossing accompanied by a sign reading *Stop, look, and listen.*

Paralinguistic gestures are not really an independent class but a subclass of instinctive gestures, more or less systematized, much as intonation was perhaps systematized out of a set of instinctive cries and calls. They cooperate with sound as part of a larger communicative act. In the following utterance,

You don't mean it.

everything else can remain the same, yet with one's head held slightly forward, eyes widened, and mouth left open after the last word, the result is a question ('You surely don't mean it, do you?'), while with head erect, eyes not widened, and mouth closed afterward, it is a confident assertion.

Facial gestures are sometimes the only way to tell a question from a statement.

Gestures of the hands and head are used to reinforce the syllables on which the accent falls. A person too far away to hear a speaker can often tell what syllables he is emphasizing by the way he hammers with his fist or jabs downward with his jaw. How closely the two are related can be shown by a simple test: reversing the movement of the head, going up instead of down on each accent, in a sentence like *I wíll nót dó it.* It is hard to manage on the first attempt.

At the outer fringes of the system we call language is a scattering of gestural effects on speech, more curious than important. The [m] of *ho-hum* and the [p] of *yep* and *nope* come from closing the mouth as a gesture of completion: "He was the last juror and quite unconsciously smacked his lips as he finished the oath."[3] Certain gestures get tangled with sets of words and serve as a kind of semantic cohesive. The kinship of *vicious, venomous, vituperative, violent, vehement, vindictive, vitriolic, vile* (and indirectly *vital, vigorous, vim*) is helped by the suggestion of a snarl in the initial [v]. Similarly there is a suggestion of lip-smacking in the last syllable of *delicious, voluptuous, salacious, luscious* that results in a new slang alteration or coinage every now and then—*scrumptious* in the early 1800's, *galuptious* about 1850, *crematious* in the 1940's, the trade name *Stillicious* at about the same time, *scruptillicious* in teen-age talk in the 1960's.[4]

LANGUAGE IS LARGELY ARBITRARY

It is exceptional to find words as alike as *meow* in English and *miaou* in French. Identical meanings in different languages are almost never expressed by the same combination of sounds (the fact that the same *spellings* are often encountered is another matter). If there were a real connection between the sound of a word and its meaning, a person who did not know the language would be able to guess the word if he knew the meaning and guess the meaning if he heard the word. This almost never happens, even with words that imitate sounds: *to caw* in English is *croasser* in French; *to giggle* in English is *kichern* in German. Elsewhere it does not happen at all. *Square* and *box-shaped* mean the same but have no resemblance in sound.

---

[3] Raymond Postgate, *Verdict of Twelve* (New York: Simon and Schuster, Pocket Books, 1946), p. 70.

[4] *Boulder Camera* (Boulder, Colorado), June 10, 1963.

Arbitrariness comes from having to code a whole universe of meanings. The main problem with such vast quantities is to find not resemblances but differences, to make a given combination of sounds sufficiently unlike every other combination so that no two will be mistaken for each other.[5] It is more important to make *wheat* and *barley* sound different than to use the names to express a family relationship as a botanist might do. Our brain can associate them if the need arises more easily than it can help us if we hear one when the other was intended.

Syntax is no less arbitrary than words. Take the order of elements. *Ground parched corn* has *first* been parched and *then* ground—the syntactic rule calls for reversing the order in which the events occur. Often the same meanings can be conveyed by quite different sequences of elements which may themselves be the same or different: *nonsensical,* which contains a prefix and a suffix, means the same as *senseless,* which has only a suffix; *more handsome* and *handsomer* are mere variants. Here and there one detects a hint of kinship between form and function—in *He came in and sat down* the phrases are in the same sequence as the actions; but other syntactic devices quickly override it: *He sat down after he came in.*

The most rigidly arbitrary level of language is that of the distinctive units of sound by which we can distinguish between *skin* and *skim* or *spare* and *scare* the moment we hear the words. It was noted earlier that the very choice of sound itself for this purpose was, while practical, not at all necessary to the system built up from it. And once it was determined that sound was to be the medium, the particular sounds did not matter so long as they could be told apart. What distinguishes *skin* from *skim* is the sound of [n] versus the sound of [m], but could just as well be [b] versus [g]—there is nothing in the nature of skin that decrees it shall be called *skin* and not *skib.* The only "natural" fact is that human beings are limited by their speech organs to certain dimensions of sound—we do not, for example, normally make the sound that would result from turning the tip of the tongue all the way back to the soft palate; it is too hard to reach. But given the sets of sounds we *can* make (not identical, of course, from one language to another, but highly similar), arbitrariness frees us to combine them at will—the combinations do not have to match anything in nature, and their number is therefore unlimited.

Arbitrariness is the rule throughout the central part of language, the part that codes sounds into words, words into phrases, and phrases into sentences. To use computer terminology, language is *digital,* not *analog:* its units function by being either present or absent, not by being present in varying degrees. If a man is asked how many feet tall a friend is and answers *six,* he gives a digital answer; for a lower height he will no longer

---

[5] What happens when two words come to sound the same is treated in Chapter 7.

say *six*. If words were coded analogically he might, to express 'six,' take half of the word *twelve*, say *twe*. We actually do communicate analogically in situations like this, not using words but holding up our hand to the desired height; the height of the hand is "analogous" to the height of the person.

But the digital island floats on an analog sea. If one is tired, the feebleness of the voice will show how tired one is—degrees of sound correspond to degrees of fatigue. If one is angry and not controlling oneself, the loudness of the voice will tell how angry. And wrapped around everything that is spoken is a layer of intonation which in many languages comprises an analog system that is highly formalized; for example, varying degrees of finality can be expressed by deeper and deeper lowering of the pitch at the end of an utterance.

It would not be surprising if now and then a bit of the analog sea washed over the digital island. There seems to be a connection, transcending individual languages, between the sounds of the vowels produced with the tongue high in the mouth and to the front, especially [i] (the vowel sound in *wee, teeny)*, and the meaning of 'smallness,' while those with tongue low suggest 'largeness.' The size of the mouth cavity—[i] has the smallest opening of all—is matched with the meaning. We *chip* a small piece but *chop* a large one; a *slip* is smaller than a *slab* and a *nib* is smaller than a *knob*. Examples crop up spontaneously—"A *freep* is a baby *frope*," said a popular entertainer in a game of Scrabble—or in modifications of existing words, for example *least* with an exaggeratedly high [i], or the following:

> "That's about the price I had in mind," said Joe Peel. "Eight to ten thousand, but of course, it would depend on the place. I might even go a *leetle* higher."[6]

But mostly the digital island stays pretty dry.

LANGUAGES ARE SIMILARLY STRUCTURED

The average learner of a foreign language is surprised and annoyed when the new language does not express things in the same way as the old. The average linguist, after years of struggling with differences between languages, is more surprised at similarities. But at bottom the naive learner is right: there are differences in detail, but in broad outline languages are put together in similar ways. A study on universals in language reached these conclusions about syntax:

---

[6] Frank Gruber, *The Silver Jackass* (New York: Penguin Books, 1947), p. 45.

1. All languages use nominal phrases and verbal phrases, corresponding to the two major classes of noun and verb, and in all of them
   the number of nouns far exceeds the number of verbs. One can be
   fairly sure that a noun in one language translates a noun in another.

2. All languages have modifiers of these two classes, corresponding
   to adjectives and adverbs.

3. All languages have ways of turning verbal phrases into nounal
   phrases *(He went—*I know *that he went).*

4. All languages have ways of making adjective-like phrases out of
   other kinds of phrases *(The man went—*The man *who went).*

5. All languages have ways of turning sentences into interrogatives,
   negatives, and commands.

6. All languages show at least two forms of interaction between verbal
   and nominal, typically "intransitive" (the verbal is involved with
   only one nominal, as in *Boys play)* and "transitive" (the verbal is
   involved with two nominals, as in *Boys like girls).*[7]

A more recent study views nouns as the one category of syntax that can
be assumed for all languages, with the other elements being defined (differently, from language to language) by how they combine with nouns.[8]
One of the promising developments of transformational-generative
grammar[9] is the hypothesis that all languages are fundamentally alike in
their "deep grammar," an underlying domain of universal grammatical
relationships and universal semantic features, and different only on the
surface, in the more or less accidental paths along which inner forms link
themselves and make their way to the top. One is reminded of what is so
often said about sexual behavior—that it can be modified by social restrictions but never seriously changed. If the hypothesis is true then our bent
for language is as much a part of us as our mating instincts and our hunger
drives.

Describing the complexities of distinctive sound and its buildup into
ever higher structures imbued with meaning are the two subjects that
linguistics is mostly about. They require chapters to themselves.

---

[7] Paraphrased from Samuel E. Martin's review of J. H. Greenberg (ed.), *Universals
of Language, Harvard Educational Review* 34.353–55 (1964).

[8] John Lyons, "Towards a 'Notional' Theory of the 'Parts of Speech,'" *Journal of
Linguistics* 2.209–36 (1966).

[9] See Chapter 11, pp. 201–04.

ADDITIONAL REMARKS
AND APPLICATIONS

1. Name three countries in which at least three mutually unintelligible languages are spoken. (The USSR is publishing in more than seventy non-Slavic languages, in addition to Slavic.)

2. Since a page of writing requires a living reader to interpret it, can a dead language be said to live on in its written records, or has the reader somehow managed to revive it in himself? Is understanding even the writings of one's own language a matter of activating its symbols, say by a form of inner speech?

3. Can the sense of touch be used for communication in language? Consider the reading of Braille. Can the temperature sense be so used? Why?

4. Herman Melville in *Typee* described an incident in which his hero, an American sailor, almost got himself in serious trouble by passing something over the head of one of his native hosts in the South Seas. What type of gesture do you think was involved?

5. What type of gesture is a handshake? Could you be sure, if you held out your hand to a member of some completely unknown culture, that he would not take it as a challenge to a wrestling match?

6. Would you say that the gesture of tilting the head slightly to one side and looking at your interlocutor out of the corner of your eye is appropriate or inappropriate to saying the following words with the intonation shown?

Don't push him too fa r.

7. If we think of families of words that are related in meaning as being less arbitrary if the relationship shows somehow in their form, how do

the two families represented by *inch, foot, yard, rod, mile* and *millimeter, centimeter, meter,* and *kilometer* compare? List two other opposing series like these (say, the popular versus the scientific names for a family of plants).

8. Does length have analog significance in English? Experiment with *long* in *It's a long road,* with *way* in *They went way out to California,* and with the syllable *de-* in *It's delicious.* Comment on *I won't, I won't, I won't, I won't!*

THE PHONETIC 3
ELEMENTS

$\mathbb{L}$ANGUAGE COMES in a kind of envelope of speech sounds; it is wrapped in other disturbances of the air that convey such information as whether the speaker has a cold or has been eating or feels angry or is a long way off or is a man rather than a child. Only part of the sound wave corresponds to the central organization, a narrow and precisely limited set of contrasts between various combinations of pitches, durations, loudnesses, and voice and whisper, which are the audible results of the ways we exercise our speech organs. Though no two languages are identical, these ways are similar enough to generalize about them.

ARTICULATIONS

All languages use certain articulations that shut off or constrict the breath stream and others that let it flow freely through the mouth cavity. The first are the consonants, the second the vowels. This alternate checking and releasing is essential for getting the variety of sounds that we need in order to have a large set of signaling units. The two kinds of articulations depend on each other: the consonants separate the vowels and the vowels allow the speech organs to get from one consonant position to the next. (It is possible to have vowels side by side, but such combinations tend to

21

be unstable, resulting in some kind of loss or change, as when *pro-te-in*
with three vowels was reduced to *pro-tein* with two. Certain consonants
can also stand side by side, but again separation is the rule.) Furthermore,
we are partly dependent on the vowels to hear the consonants—it is largely
the effect of a given consonant on the vowel or vowels next to it that
makes the consonant audible, for the vowels, produced with the breath
stream unimpeded, are by definition the sounds that carry best. Each
consonant distorts the portion of a vowel that lies next to it in its own
peculiar way.

In making a consonant we either shut off the air completely or narrow
the passage at some point so that it comes through noisily. The first kind
is called a *stop*, the second a *fricative*. The stopping or narrowing can be
at any point that our speech organs permit, and this of course makes for a
good deal of variety in the particular consonants that different languages
create. In English we use the following:

1. The lips. The [p] and [b] in *pane* and *bane* are stops: the lips are
   closed completely and then abruptly parted. The [f] and [v] in
   feign and *vane* are fricatives: the air keeps coming through, but
   with friction. We call [p b] *bilabials*, because both lips are
   involved; [f v] are *labiodentals*, involving the lower lip and the
   upper teeth. English has no bilabial fricatives (unless the exclamation variously spelled *whew!* and *phew!* is counted as a word),
   but many languages do.

2. The tongue tip on the upper front teeth. English makes no stops
   this way, but it has two fricatives for which the symbols [θ] and
   [ð] are used—the initial sounds in *thin* and *that*. Since the tongue
   is involved in all consonants made in the interior of the mouth, we
   name the sound just by the position that the tongue touches or
   approaches. Accordingly, these two sounds are *dentals*.

3. The tongue tip on the ridge back of the upper front teeth. The
   [t] and [d] of *to* and *do* are stops. The [s z] of *seal* and *zeal* are
   fricatives. As the ridge in question is known as the alveolar ridge,
   these sounds are called *alveolar*.

4. The whole fore part of the tongue on the roof of the mouth, or
   palate. English has no stops made with this contact, but has other
   sounds including the two fricatives symbolized [š ž], which occur
   at the ends of the words *ash* and *rouge*. Sounds made on the palate
   are called *palatal*.

5. The rear of the tongue backed against the velum or soft palate, the

fleshy part of the roof of the mouth at the rear. English has two stops, [k g]; examples, *caw* and *go.* These sounds are *velar.* The Scottish dialect of English has a velar fricative, for example in *loch,* and many other languages, including German, use this sound.

Of course, other positions and tongue contacts are possible. In a number of languages, typically those of India, there are sounds made on the palate not with the whole front part of the tongue, including the blade or broad central part, but only with the turned-back tip. There is a stop sound that is used freely in many languages but is not generally counted among our distinctive sounds in English, although we use it in two peculiar ways. This is the glottal stop, symbolized [?], which many people put between *the* and a following word that begins with a vowel. Most of us use it in the warning *oh-oh!* (meaning 'Look out, you're about to make a mistake') and in the negative *hunh-uh.* Some languages, of which a number in Africa are typical, produce certain of their stops by an intake of air such as one hears in the smack of a kiss or in the sound spelled *tsk! tsk!* which to us is a sign of disapproval.

The stops and fricatives are the two chief "manners" of manipulating the air at the various contact points. But there are others, one of which is simply a combination of a stop and a fricative. If instead of breaking the contact crisply and cleanly at the end of a [t] the tongue is withdrawn gradually, the result is the initial sound in the foreign borrowings *Tsar* and *tsetse.* Such sounds are called *affricates.* English has two palatal affricates in its native stock of words, the initial sounds in *chump* and *jump,* symbolized [č ǰ]. Another manner consists in the direction in which the air is allowed to escape. If it is diverted through the nose, the result is a *nasal* sound, of which English has three: the labial [m] in *ram,* the alveolar [n] in *ran,* and the velar [ŋ] in *rang.* If it is diverted around the sides of the tongue instead of along the median line, the result is a lateral sound, typified in English by [l], as in *Lee.*

The most fundamental difference of all is that of voice and voicelessness. If the vocal cords are vibrating the result is a voiced sound, as in [v] (if we prolong a [v] and hold a finger on our Adam's apple, we can feel the vibration); if the air moves past the vocal cords without causing them to vibrate, the result is a voiceless sound, as in [f]. Voiced and voiceless consonants generally come in pairs for each position and manner: [b-p v-f ð-θ d-t z-s ž-š ǰ-č g-k]. Vowels are typically voiced, but English has a consonant that is simply a vowel without voice: in the words *heat, hope, hail, hoot,* and so on the [h] is made by starting the sound of the vowel without voice.

The descriptions that have been given apply to English. It does not follow that other languages, even when they have closely similar sounds, necessarily make them in exactly the same way. This should cause no surprise, since English speakers themselves have different ways sometimes of producing the "same" sound. Take the sound of [s]. Many people do not make it with the tip of the tongue but get the tip out of the way by curling it slightly downward so that it is more or less directly behind the lower front teeth, and instead use the blade or flat part of the tongue by bunching it up against the alveolar ridge. In French a stop such as [p] is followed so quickly by the vowel that it sounds almost like [b] to a speaker of English (English does the same with a [p] after an [s], so that it is hard to hear any difference between *Monk Spread* and *Monk's Bread*); in English the vowel is delayed somewhat after a voiceless stop at the beginning of a word and we hear a puff of voiceless air in between, called an aspiration. It is enough to blow out a match held close to the lips when we say a word like *pin*. In English the tongue-tip is generally up for the sound [č] as in *cheek*, but in Spanish it is down and only the blade touches the palate, as in *chico* 'boy.' The ways of making [r] are so different that if it were not for the common origin of many words containing it we would not consider it to be the same at all from one language to another. To show how widely it can vary even in one language it is enough to mention the Bostonian's *paahk* and the Midwesterner's *parrk,* for *park.*

With the vowels it might seem that since the air comes through unimpeded they should all sound alike. But as it happens more things can be done with the breath stream, especially when it is voiced, than merely obstructing it. The *shape* of the mouth cavity makes a difference: for example, whether it is narrow, wide, or elongated as when we purse our lips for the word *coo.* It is mostly the tongue and lips that produce these shapes. Notice how the tongue is pushed well forward in the mouth for the word *key* but drawn back for the word *coo.* English vowels can be described thus by noting whether the tongue is *front* as in *key, back* as in *coo,* or *central* as in *cut,* and by whether it is *high* (close to the palate) as in *key* and *coo, low* (lowered away from the palate by dropping the jaw) as in *bat* and *tot,* or *mid* as in *bet* and *tote.* (In making these comparisons the vowels must be abstracted from the neighboring consonants, which of course have their own positions.) In addition we have to note whether the lips are *spread* as in *key* or *rounded* as in *coo.* Ordinarily it is assumed that they are spread unless rounding is mentioned. The "vowel quadrilateral" below shows the positions of the tongue for the English full vowels. Except for [a], rounding does not need to be mentioned because all the vowels on the right-hand side, that is, all the back vowels, are automatically accompanied by rounding of the lips. The vowel [a] usually has little or no rounding. (In French, rounding would have to be indicated in such a diagram, for there are front vowels with rounding and front vowels without.)

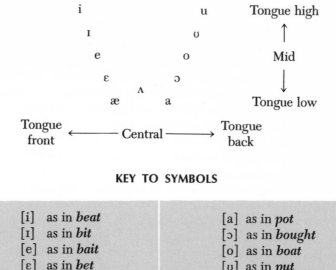

KEY TO SYMBOLS

[i]	as in *beat*	[a]	as in *pot*
[ɪ]	as in *bit*	[ɔ]	as in *bought*
[e]	as in *bait*	[o]	as in *boat*
[ɛ]	as in *bet*	[ʊ]	as in *put*
[æ]	as in *bat*	[u]	as in *boot*
[ʌ]	as in *butt*		

Diphthongs—two vowels or vowel-like sounds in combination—are treated by some phoneticians as two separable elements, by others as indivisible units. The simplest way of transcribing them is with double symbols, as if they were divisible. The tongue glides in producing a diphthong, usually toward either a high front position or a high back position, symbolized [y] and [w] respectively: *Roy* is [rɔy] and *now* is [naw]. Or the glide may be in the opposite direction, from rather than to the high front or high back position: *yore* [yɔr], *wan* [wan]—in fact, if *Roy* and *now* are played backward on a tape recorder they will sound like *yore* and *wan.* For reasons that are not very important here, the [y] or [w] element is generally called a semivowel when it comes after the main vowel and a semiconsonant when it comes before. There may of course be additional consonants bordering the diphthong on either side: *coin* [kɔyn], *proud* [prawd], *fiord* [fyɔrd], *swan* [swan].

To complete the picture of the vowels we should include three others, called *reduced* to distinguish them from the *full* ones just diagrammed. They are the vowels in the last syllables of the words *hairy, Harrah,* and *harrow,* and can be symbolized [ɨ ə ɵ]. The second of these—[ə]—is often called *schwa* and is the most frequent vowel in English; for example, it occupies all but the first syllable of the word *formidableness* [fɔrmədəbəlnəs]. The contrast between full and reduced vowels is what produces the

choppy rhythm that speakers of many other languages find so characteristic of English. Where syllables with full vowels succeed one another, as
in *Irene Carstairs' pet chimpanzee Nimrod dotes on fresh horehound
drops,* the syllables are spaced out with a fairly even beat; but where
syllables with reduced vowels intervene, the reduced vowels borrow
their time from the preceding full vowels, producing an irregular beat:
Minnie Abbott's little kitten Missie's fond of liverwurst. The vowel [ɨ]
has a tongue height anywhere from about that of [e] to about that of [i],
but the tongue is not pushed forward as far. Similarly, [ə] has a range
close to that of [ʌ] but the mouth is less open, and [ɵ] ranges close to [o]
and [ɔ] but the tongue is less drawn back. Because of the less extreme
positions of the tongue, reduced vowels are often called *centralized.*[1]

The vowels show more clearly than the consonants how readily one may
find differences within a single language. The fact that the tongue moves
smoothly backward and forward and up and down enables it to take not
only the positions shown in the vowels of the quadrilateral but also any
position between. A consonant is an easy target as a rule—the teeth, for
example, occupy a discontinuous part of the mouth and the tongue knows
exactly what to aim for; but with the continuum of the mouth cavity as a
whole there are no definite targets and it is not so easy to aim true. So we
find many speakers whose vowels would disagree here and there with
those of the chart, in their position and even sometimes in how many of
them there are. In some dialects of American English no distinction is
made between [a] and [ɔ]—the pairs *bot-bought, cot-caught, tot-taught,*
and others like them are pronounced the same. Other speakers may make
a distinction sometimes, for example between [ɪ] and [ɛ] in *bit* and *bet,*
but disregard it at other times, as in *pin* and *pen.* This is apt to happen in
a language, like English or French, that crowds a large number of vowels
into the mouth-cavity continuum—they tend to interfere with one another.
In a language with few vowels—as few as three is possible and five is
commonplace—this is not so apt to happen.

All languages make their vowels in much the same way by carving up
the continuum, but the number of slices varies, as does the position of
each slice. Some languages multiply their vowels by adding another
dimension. The potentiality for adding dimensions is universal, though not
all languages make use of the same ones. We can note three:

The first is *rounding.* As was mentioned earlier, this does not really
count in English because it automatically accompanies all the back vowels,
but French uses it for front vowels as well so that there is a rounded series
and an unrounded series. The word pairs *fée* 'fairy' and *feu* 'fire,' *père*

---

[1] Dwight Bolinger, "Length, Vowel, Juncture," *Linguistics* 1.5–29 (1963); Robert
P. Stockwell and J. Donald Bowen, *The Sounds of English and Spanish* (Chicago:
University of Chicago Press, 1965), pp. 90–92.

'father' and *peur* 'fear' differ only in that the first member has the lips spread and the second has them rounded.

The second is *nasalization.* English disregards this as a feature of vowels—in saying **Did he go?** the nasal passage can be left loosely open for all three vowels without affecting the meaning. But—to use French again—the word pairs *beauté* 'beauty' and *bonté* 'goodness,' *seau* 'pail' and *son* 'sound' differ only in that the second member of each pair is nasalized.

The third is *length.* The Classical Latin *mēto,* with its *e* lengthened, meant 'to measure'; *meto,* without the extra length, meant 'to reap.' (Consonants are sometimes lengthened too—Italian has this feature. It is often hard to decide whether a lengthened sound ought to be regarded as a single sound with extra length, or as two identical sounds side by side. The latter could be shown by writing *meeto* instead of *mēto.*)

A possible fourth is *tone.* In many languages a higher or lower pitch on a vowel can make each one count for more than one. In Ticuna, a language of the upper Amazon, five steps of pitch are observed; the "word" *čanamu* is actually four words depending on the combination of tones that go with it: numbering 1 for highest tone and 5 for lowest, *ča₃na₃mu₃* means 'I weave it,' *ča₃na₃mu₄* means 'I send it,' *ča₃na₃mu₅* means 'I eat it,' and *ča₃na₃mu₃₋₅* means 'I spear it.'[2] In situations where the words and meanings apt to be appropriate are fairly familiar and predictable, it is sometimes possible just to transmit the series of tones and be understood—the hearer can guess at the rest. This in stylized form is the basis of African drum signaling as well as of the "whistle speech" of Mazatec in Oaxaca, Mexico. Following is Dr. George M. Cowan's description of a whistled conversation:

> Eusebio Martínez was observed one day standing in front of his hut, whistling to a man a considerable distance away. The man was passing on the trail below, going to market to sell a load of corn leaves which he was carrying. The man answered Eusebio's whistle with a whistle. The interchange was repeated several times with different whistles. Finally the man turned around, retraced his steps a short way and came up the footpath to Eusebio's hut. Without saying a word he dumped his load on the ground. Eusebio looked the load over, went into his hut, returned with some money, and paid the man his price. Not a word had been spoken. . . .[3]

The use of tone is extremely complex, and it is not always easy to say that it is added and subtracted just to get a bigger percentage out of the vowels. Often it has a kind of marking function: a negative statement, for

---

[2] Lambert Anderson, "Ticuna Vowels with Special Regard to the System of Five Tonemes," *Serie Lingüistica Especial,* No. 1 (Rio de Janeiro: Museu Nacional, 1959), pp. 76–127.

[3] "Mazateco Whistle Speech," *Language* 24.280–86 (1948).

example, may have a different tone from an affirmative one, or an active sentence from a passive.[4] The over-all effect is similar to certain effects of speech melody or intonation—in marking the difference between questions and statements, for example—and is one reason why certain British linguists group such phenomena together as "prosodies."

DISTINCTIVE FEATURES

Adding "dimensions" like rounding, nasalization, and tone suggests the possibility of describing not just certain characteristics of vowels but all speech sounds in terms of them. We have already noted that all sounds divide according to whether they are voiced or voiceless, and of course they also divide according to whether they are consonants or vowels. Are there other equally general dimensions, or "distinctive features" as those who work with this kind of description call them, that would enable us to analyze each sound into its components, to "split the atom of phonology," as one writer puts it?[5] If we could find them we not only would reduce the number of units but also could make more scientific comparisons; for example, between one sound and another: "Sound A differs from Sound B by x number of features" or "Sound A does not occur next to Sound B because both contain y feature, which in that language cannot be repeated"; or between one language and another: "Language A has a series of consonants like a similar series in Language B, but differing by one particular feature." Keeping the number of features small would call for the ability to see an underlying sameness in two or more superficially different manifestations.

The samenesses are not strictly in the way sounds are *made*, though this is a factor. Rather they are samenesses in *sound*. Usually a similar articulation produces a similar sound, and classifying the features by articulations is easier to grasp. Otherwise, to see the kinships in exact acoustic terms would call for a certain amount of acoustic analysis. But certain of the kinships in sound are quite easy to see. The quality of "nasal" is obvious and ties together the sounds [n m ŋ] in *bun, bum,* and *bung.* Another that is slightly less obvious but easy to hear is "stridency," which is simply the harsh noise by which we associate the eight consonants [f v s z č ǰ š ž], for example in *laugh, love, loss, buzz, rich, pledge, plush, rouge.* Thus [f] has the feature of stridency and in addition that of diffuseness (a quality of

---

[4] Petr Zima, "On the Functions of Tones in African Languages," *Travaux Linguistiques de Prague,* 2.154 (1966).

[5] Pavle Ivić, "Roman Jakobson and the Growth of Phonology," *Linguistics* 18.35–78 (1965). This article contains, on pp. 53–64, an account of the origins and development of the distinctive-feature theory.

sound produced by a rather tight narrowing at the front of the mouth) and that of continuation (the sound can be emitted steadily as long as the breath holds out), plus a few others. Grouping sounds by features is useful in describing various things that happen when sounds occur together. The feature of stridency, for instance, helps to explain how English forms the plural of nouns: it is always pronounced -[əz] following a strident sound other than [f v]. If we try to state this rule without referring to distinctive features we have to list all six sounds.[6]

By eliminating redundancies in this way, feature analysts have arrived at a set of about fifteen features and their opposites with which all sounds of all languages can theoretically be defined. Viewed in this light the differences between one language and another sink to the same unimportance as that of the two ways of saying English [s] or the difference between French and English [p]—all languages draw from the same pool of features but do not use exactly the same number or the same combinations.

The table on page 30 analyzes English consonants in terms of distinctive features.[7]

---

[6] See Chapter 5, p. 59.

[7] A "consonant" for feature analysis means a sound that is both "consonantal" and "nonvocalic," as defined below. That is why the sounds [r l h] are missing. The reason for the absence of [ŋ] is too complex to discuss here.

The features are made to do double service by interpreting their *absence* to signify the *presence* of an opposite feature. For that reason both the feature proper and its "non-" or opposite have to be described:

Vocalic: The sound has a distinctive pitch or set of pitches (such as all vowels have, whether voiced or whispered) and the mouth is relatively open—there is no narrowing anywhere greater than approximately that suitable for the sound of [i]. *Nonvocalic* means either that there is a greater narrowing or that the sound does not have a clearly defined pitch or pitches.

Consonantal: There is a tight enough narrowing at some point in the mouth cavity either to stop the flow of air completely or to let it through with friction. *Nonconsonantal* sounds have lesser degrees of narrowing.

Grave: There is a narrowing at the extreme front (lips) or extreme back of the mouth cavity; *nongrave* sounds are narrowed at the middle of the cavity—for example, at the teeth or palate.

Diffuse: There is a narrowing at least as tight as that of the sound of [i], at the front of the mouth. *Nondiffuse* sounds are located in the back part of the mouth cavity.

Strident: The air stream has enough of an obstacle in its path to create a noisy turbulence but not enough to check the flow of air completely. *Nonstrident* sounds lack this turbulence.

Continuant: The air passes through without being completely shut off. *Noncontinuant* or *interrupted* means the same as *stop*.

Nasal-nonnasal and voiced-voiceless have already been defined.

DISTINCTIVE-FEATURE REPRESENTATION OF THE
CONSONANTS OF ENGLISH

	p	b	m	f	v	k	g	t	d	θ	ð	n	s	z	č	ǰ	š	ž
VOCALIC	−	−	−	−	−	−	−	−	−	−	−	−	−	−	−	−	−	−
CONSONANTAL	+	+	+	+	+	+	+	+	+	+	+	+	+	+	+	+	+	+
GRAVE	+	+	+	+	+	+	+	−	−	−	−	−	−	−	−	−	−	−
DIFFUSE	+	+	+	+	+	−	−	+	+	+	+	+	+	+	−	−	−	−
STRIDENT	−	−	−	+	+	−	−	−	−	−	−	−	+	+	+	+	+	+
NASAL	−	−	+	−	−	−	−	−	−	−	−	+	−	−	−	−	−	−
CONTINUANT	−	−	−	+	+	−	−	−	−	+	+	−	+	+	−	−	+	+
VOICED	−	+	+	−	+	−	+	−	+	−	+	+	−	+	−	+	−	+

FROM Morris Halle, "On the Bases of Phonology," in Jerry A. Fodor and Jerrold J. Katz (eds.), *The Structure of Language: Readings in the Philosophy of Language* (Englewood Cliffs, N.J.: Prentice-Hall, Inc., 1964), pp. 324–33.

INTONATION

Language resembles music in making use of both the musical and the unmusical qualities of sound. The unmusical qualities—noises—we have seen as components of certain consonants, for example, the hissing stridency of an [s] or the sudden explosion of a [p]; in music, noise is characteristic of the percussion section of an orchestra. But the musical qualities—pitches or tones—are equally important. Just as in music, two kinds of musical quality are used: the singing or tune-carrying quality and the quality of timbre or depth. In music if we think of the "message" as being carried by the tune, i.e. the succession of sounds that are written as notes on a musical score, and the "mood" as contributed by the richness or depth of the particular instrument on which the notes are played, we see the two-dimensional nature of musical communication. The organ makes a good example because it is many instruments combined in one.

The organist can play the tune and in addition can vary the mood by manipulating the stops, which imitate various musical instruments. Putting this acoustically, the tune is a succession of *fundamental* pitches and the depth is the *overtones* which are controlled by the stops. (Another kind of "depth," of course, is harmony, achieved by playing two or more notes at the same time; but the depth referred to here is the richness of a single tone, which varies according to the stops.) Most instruments, including the organ (but not the tuning fork, which is made intentionally to get "pure" tones), when played at a given pitch produce not only that pitch, known as the fundamental, but an infinite series of higher pitches each an even multiple of the number of vibrations in the fundamental. If the organ is emitting a middle A at 440 vibrations per second, it also gives out a pitch exactly an octave higher at 880, another three times as high at 1320, and so on up. The higher pitches are the overtones and the depth they contribute depends on how well we hear them. This is determined by the stops. A given stop may make the overtone at 880 practically inaudible while building up the one at 1320, with the fundamental or singing pitch going on unabated all the while. In a violin it is mainly the combination of the size and the shape of the body of the instrument that cuts out certain overtones and reinforces others, giving the quality of sound that we associate with violins.

The human vocal cords when they are set vibrating are just another musical instrument and are so used when we sing. Depth is controlled when we vary the shape of the mouth cavity. Each shape checks certain overtones and reinforces others.

Here the resemblance to music ends. For if in music the fundamental gives the message and the overtones the mood, in language the overtones are crucial to the message and the fundamental is mostly used for mood and punctuating effects. Varying the shape of the mouth cavity affects the overtones, and that is precisely what we do to make the difference between the [u] of *fool* and the [i] of *feel*. Whether we say the words at a low or a high singing pitch makes no difference to their meaning.

The overtones, not the fundamental, are the chief musical ingredients of language. Only in tone languages is the fundamental used to a limited extent as an ingredient of distinctive sound. As we have seen, Ticuna— like Chinese and a number of other languages from all parts of the world— adds fundamental pitch at varying heights as an extra dimension to vowels.

But all languages, including tone languages, use the fundamental for mood and punctuating effects over longer stretches of speech. We call these "intonations"—speech melody—as distinguished from the "tones" of tone languages. They have several characteristics. The main ones are range, direction, height, abruptness, and pattern.

Probably all languages use the *range* of intonation to show emotion.

When we are excited our voice extends its pitch upward; when we are depressed we speak almost in a monotone. Displaying emotion in this way is probably instinctive.

Probably all languages use the *direction* of intonation to show where major divisions of utterances start and stop. One effect that is found everywhere is a running down, a tendency to drift toward a low pitch when the speaker nears the point where he intends to stop. He starts full of energy but deflates at the end like a bagpipe running out of wind. But if he is unsatisfied—as he normally would be in asking a question—his pitch goes up. As with excitement and depression these tensions and relaxations may be instinctive, but we seem to have learned how to use them intentionally. The following is a typical intentional use:

$$\text{If you're read}^{\text{y}}\text{ let's }\underset{\text{o}_.}{\text{g}}$$

The pitch follows a generally upward movement in *If you're ready* and switches to a downward movement in *let's go.* The separation between the clauses is marked by the change in direction.

Probably all languages use relative *height* as a sign of importance. If in an example like the one just given there happen to be two separations instead of one, it may be necessary to show which is major and which is minor:

$$\text{If you're }^{\text{ready}}\text{ when I get }^{\text{the}^{\text{re}}}\text{ we'll }\underset{\text{o}_.}{\text{g}}$$

$$\text{If you're }^{\text{read}^{\text{y}}}\text{ when I get there we'll }\underset{\text{o}_.}{\text{g}}$$

The first says 'If you're ready when I get there'—the extra-high rise in pitch puts the major break between *there* and *we'll.* The second says 'when I get there we'll go'—the extra-high pitch puts the major break between *ready* and *when.*

Many languages use abrupt jumps in pitch to make certain elements stand out. This is *accent.* Usually it is combined with a slight lengthening and a certain extra loudness, but the main element is the sudden change in pitch. Usually it involves highlighting one word as more important than the words that surround it. Children learning to speak catch the important words in this way and reproduce them first: *Mama spank* culls the words that really count from the sentence *Mama is going to spank you.* It makes little difference whether the jump in pitch is up or down. In the sentence *His brother was the one who cheated him, brother* can be emphasized by raising it,

$$\text{His} \quad {}^{\text{bro}}\text{ther} \ {}^{\text{was}} \ \text{the} \ {}_{\text{one}} \ {}_{\text{who}} \ {}_{\text{cheated}} \ {}_{\text{him}}.$$

or by lowering it,

$$\text{His} \quad {}_{\text{bro}}\text{ther} \ \text{was} \ \text{the} \ \text{one} \ \text{who} \ \text{cheated} \ {}^{\text{him?}}$$

But in either case the stressed syllable of the important word is pushed out of the intonational line.[8] (In these examples accent is marked by the jump, question versus statement by the direction.)

Probably all languages use *patterns* of successive pitches to distinguish different kinds of utterances. In English one can usually tell a command regardless of the syntactic form of the sentence:

$$\text{On} \ \ \text{your} \quad {}_{\text{fe}}{}_{\text{e}}{}_{\text{t}}.$$

makes a good command, but would be unusual as a statement, while

$$\text{On} \ \ \text{your} \quad {}^{\text{fe}}{}_{\text{et}}.$$

makes a good answer to *How am I supposed to get there?* but not a good command (though it might do for a repetition of a command). Since patterns involve directions with their punctuating functions, the two cannot be clearly distinguished. The ambiguity of the word *finality* itself—with which the falling pitch at the end is associated—tells us this: there is a finality or decisiveness about a command and a finality or conclusiveness about the end of a statement.

How general any individual pattern may be is hard to say, but close similarities crop up in out-of-the-way places. In the Kunimaipa language of New Guinea, for example, there are several patterns that resemble

---

[8] Dwight Bolinger, "Around the Edge of Language: Intonation," *Harvard Educational Review* 34.282–96 (1964).

those in English quite closely, even including one that is like the mid-high-low curve that we use for intensification in expressions like

$$o^o \qquad ple^a \qquad so^o$$
$$\quad oh \qquad \quad se \qquad \quad oo$$

—for example in *So! you didn't keep your word after all!*[9] The distinction in English between questions introduced by interrogative words *(Why did you go?, Where is she?, What's the difference?)*, usually with a falling pitch at the end, and yes-no questions *(Is he ready?, Will it work?, Have you met them?)*, usually with a rising pitch at the end, is shared by many languages of varied parentage.

---

[9] See Alan Pence, "Intonation in Kunimaipa (New Guinea)," *Linguistic Circle of Canberra Publications*, Series A, Occasional Papers, No. 3, 1964.

ADDITIONAL REMARKS

AND APPLICATIONS

1. One of the values of distinctive-feature analysis is its recognition that there is no sharp distinction between consonants and vowels. A sound that is "plus consonantal" and "minus vocalic" has no characteristics of vowels. One that is "plus consonantal" and "plus vocalic" is consonant-like and vowel-like at the same time. Is this true of [r] and [l]? Consider the words *bottle* and *butter*. How many syllables do they contain? If we say that each has two syllables and that every syllable must contain a vowel (this is part of the usual definition), what is the vowel element in the second syllables of these two words?

2. The sentence *They can't reason with such people* can be transcribed [ðe kænt rizn wɪθ sʌč pipl]. Identify

   a. the stop consonants

   b. the voiced consonants

   c. the voiceless fricatives

   d. the voiced fricatives

   e. the affricate

   f. the lateral.

3. Do you hear a glide—a kind of sliding change in the quality of the sound—at the end of [i e o u] that is lacking in the other vowels? Try saying *beet, bait, boat, boot* and contrast them with *bit, bet, bat,* and *but,* to detect this difference. (Some phoneticians prefer to think of such words as *beet, bait, boat,* and *boot* as containing diphthongs and transcribe them [biyt], [beyt], [bowt], and [buwt].) What is the significance of the fact that the glided sounds and the unglided sounds alternate with each other on the right and left sides of the quadrilateral? Consider the problem of crowding and the need to make one vowel as different as possible from the next.

4. Among the dimensions in the distinctive-feature system the one called *stridency* refers to a marked amount of noise as against little or none. Which are strident, stops or affricates?

5. Old-time phoneticians had no machines to analyze sounds for them, but some were observant enough to detect the reinforced overtones that make up the vowels. Try this experiment: *whisper* the vowels [i e æ], slowly, in that order, and see if you can hear in each of them two pitches, one very high and one very low for [i], closer together for [e], and still closer for [æ]. (It is less confusing with a whisper, which cuts out the fundamental.) Try this easier experiment: produce the sounds of [s] and [š] and decide which is higher in pitch.

6. Does English have anything resembling whistle speech? Think of the pitches used with the greeting *yoo-hoo* or the exclamation *oh, boy (gee whiz, my gosh,* and so on)—are they sometimes whistled with the general meaning that they have with these words? Is this an example of whistled *tones* (as in Ticuna) or of whistled *intonation?*

7. The type of intonation to mark separation illustrated on page 32 is the most usual one in Western languages, but another type is somewhat more common in English. Say the following over to yourself and decide

   a. whether the intonation still performs the function of separating the parts of the sentence

   b. whether you can detect a difference of some other kind (say, of mood or feeling) that distinguishes this type from the other:

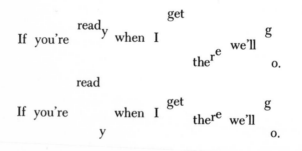

If you had to attach the label 'matter of fact' to one of the two pairs (the pair above and the pair on page 32) and the label 'I don't care, it's up to you' to the other, where would the labels go?

8. The syllable of a word to which an accent is applied when the word is accented is the *stressed syllable.* It seldom varies—knowing where the stress is is part of knowing the word. Mark the stressed syllables in the following words: *amiableness, intentionally, conversationalist, interconversion, contravene.*

9. When written, a sentence like *Was he more or less courteous* is ambiguous. Is it ambiguous in speech? If not, why not?

10. In what way does

$$\text{When did he } rea^{li^{ze \ it^?}}$$

differ from

$$\text{When did he } {}^{re}_{}{}_{a^{li}{}_{ze \ it?}}$$

Would you conclude from this that intonation is helpful in distinguishing one kind of question from another? Can you think of another example? (See if you can make an important change by saying the *don't you* in *You want to marry her, don't you?* in two different ways.)

11. The trilled [R] (sometimes heard in an exaggerated pronunciation of *thr-r-ree*) has been a distinctive sound in a number of European languages, but has tended to give way to other *r*-like sounds. In languages where the tongue-tip trill is still required, as in Czech and Latvian, it is usually the last sound that a child learns.[10] Can you think of a reason for this?

---

[10] See Velta Rūķe-Draviņa, "The Process of Acquisition of Apical and Uvular *r* in the Speech of Children," *Linguistics* 17.58–68 (1965).

STRUCTURE IN LANGUAGE: THE UNITS OF SOUND

VERY THEME OF HUMAN BEHAVIOR is cohesive. One can find the elements of a system in sports, religion, fraternity life, cocktail parties, and the etiquette of the telephone, not to mention really formalized systems like the legal code: wherever people might say, "No, you don't do it that way, do it like this" or "No, that is wrong" or "That is unfair," we can be sure that certain standards are involved and that the standards fit together coherently and can be learned. If this were not true, life in society would be impossible. But nowhere is the system so elaborate, interlocked, and luxuriant as it is in language. It represents the human capacity for system raised to the nth degree.

LEVELS OF STRUCTURE

As with geological formations, the visible mass of linguistic structure forms itself into layers. We saw this in Chapter 2 (pages 15–17), where we examined the arbitrariness of language on three levels: sound, word, and syntax. This three-part division is as old as the study of language; almost every textbook for teaching a foreign language is organized around it, and where parts of language are treated in separate books, they usually divide the field in the same way: phonetics manuals for sound, dictionaries for words, and grammars for syntax. (The term *grammar* is ambiguous, for it is sometimes restricted to syntax and sometimes used to cover all organized study of language. Historically it meant learning of any kind.)

It is obvious that words are "made up of" sounds (or at least that they contain sounds) and that sentences are "made up of" words. Most linguistic business is that of defining the levels and determining their inter-relationships, getting a more precise understanding of what "made up of" signifies.

One can choose among several descriptions of what the levels are and how they are related. Some linguists start with the top or syntactic level and work down; others start with the bottom or phonetic level and work up. Since the levels are tied together and can only be understood as a whole, either approach is possible and picking one rather than the other is a more or less arbitrary decision.

One suggestive point of view is that held by members of the Summer Institute of Linguistics, the largest group of field workers among the languages of the world.[1] It describes the levels more or less as follows.[2]

Language has roughly the three levels already noted: sounds, words, and syntax. In turn each level is manifested in three ways. One is simply the existence of *units* at each level, of elements or "particles" that populate it. Another is the *affinities* that particles show when speakers combine them—how they assort themselves in "strings" in which only certain ones are used with certain others, with limitations on how many can go together or which ones precede and which ones follow. The third is the *"field" relationships* among the particles—the way each fits into the grammatical system of particles at its own level.

Language is not unique in this respect. Other forms of activity have the same three-way organization. A good analogy is that of the roles of players in a baseball game. Each role is a "particle"—pitcher, catcher, outfielder, third baseman. The ways in which the roles interact in a game are its "strings": the catcher at a given moment interacts with the pitcher, and he regularly interacts more with the pitcher than with any other player. The abstract relationships among the players are the "field": a treatise on baseball might compare the function of shortstop with that of catcher on the one hand and second baseman on the other, explaining how the three roles are alike and how they differ.

Similarly with the three levels in language. At the level of *sound* we find first the sound particles themselves, such as /a f t m/. Next are the

---

[1] See Chapter 11, p. 192.

[2] The material that follows is paraphrased from the article by Robert E. Longacre, "Prolegomena to Lexical Structure," *Linguistics* 5.5–24 (1964). See also Kenneth L. Pike, "Language as Particle, Wave, and Field," *Texas Quarterly* 2.37–54 (1959).

strings—syllables and parts of syllables—within which the particles combine in characteristic ways. One trait of the particle /s/, for example, is that it can join with a following /l/ but not with a following /r/ to form the beginning of a syllable. Last are the contrastive field relationships among the particles; one such relationship is displayed in the vowel diagram in Chapter 3 on page 25.

At the level of *words* there are first the words themselves. Then there are the compatibility relationships among words which permit us to say **The dog bites the man** or **The man is bitten by the dog** but not ***The man is swallowed by the peanut**.[3] Finally there are the semantic fields that envelop "color words," "kinship words," "food-and-digestion words," and so on.

At the level of *syntax* we find words again, but now we find them as representatives of word classes (noun, verb, adjective, and so on) rather than of meanings. Then come syntactic strings, in which classes are allowed to occur in particular positions (noun-as-subject plus verb plus noun-as-object, for instance, gives a simple declarative string like **Monkeys love bananas**). Lastly, there is the syntactic field, in which syntactic elements are ranged according to similar functions—for example, **with gratitude** alongside of **gratefully** (that is, prepositional phrase = adverb).

We will now take the side road to each level and on the way, in this chapter and the next, will look more narrowly at such loose terms as *sound, word,* and *sentence.*

DISTINCTIVENESS IN SOUND

The earlier discussion of sound was concerned with how sounds are produced and how languages make use of different parts of the sound wave to carry a message. We saw that sound is not important in itself; it is only one kind of raw material for creating distinctive shapes that can be used to convey meaning. The distinctiveness of the shapes is no more dependent on sound than the distinctiveness of letters is dependent on ink, pencil, or chalk. Therefore "distinctive sound" must now be said with the emphasis on "distinctive." We are no longer interested in it as sound except to note here and there some trivial problem created by the fact that sound is sound—**East meets West** is hard to say because of interference among the consonants, just as the words **myself** and **Egypt** are hard to write because of interferences among the successive longhand loops.

---

[3] In syntax the asterisk marks utterances regarded as wrong.

THE PHONEME

The particles at the level of distinctive sound are called *phonemes*. Ideally, each phoneme is a set combination of distinctive features such as voicing, stoppage, nasalization, and friction. A phoneme is like a chord in music. A distinctive feature is like one of the notes that make up the chord. The notes in the chord, and the distinctive features in the phoneme, are sounded simultaneously; hearers react to the complex sound as a unit. The chords themselves—the phonemes—occur in succession. It is these successive bits of complex sound that constitute the apparatus for making syllables and words. The linguist's first job is to catalog them.

This is carried out by comparing utterances that are partly alike and finding out what it is that makes them different. If the analyst is working with his own language he has a head start since all speakers have a feel for the system of sounds they use, even though it may not be scientific. The person who makes a pun like *The undertaker said he was going to buy his little boy a rocking hearse* is aware—and expects his hearer to be aware—of a minimal or near-minimal contrast between *hearse* and *horse.* To speak pig Latin—*Arymay antsway ouyay otay aitway orfay erhay* for *Mary wants you to wait for her*—children have to sense the consonant-plus-vowel structure of the syllable. This makes it fairly easy for the native speaker to hit upon *minimal pairs:* items that differ by only one element and that rather quickly reveal the phonemes when enough of them are accumulated. In English one can quickly list a riming set like *bay-day-Fay-gay-hay-jay-Kay-lay-may-nay-pay-ray-say-shay-way* which gives a strong hint of distinctive consonants /b d f g h ǰ k l m n p r s š w/, and it takes only a moment more to confirm them by other sets like *robe-rode-rogue-roam-roan-rope-roar.* (The square brackets used up to this point—for example, see page 22—are the usual way of designating a *sound;* the analyst may use them to mean that he is not ready to commit himself as to whether the sound is a phoneme, or to mean that the symbol stands for some variant manifestation of the phoneme. Slant lines are used to mark *phonemes.* Thus, in the words *top* and *pot* there are two varieties of the phoneme /t/, an aspirated sound [tʰ] in the first and an unaspirated [t] in the second. Normally, speakers of English do not notice the difference; their intuitive reaction confirms the linguist in grouping both sounds together in the same phoneme /t/.)

The analyst confronting a new language has a rougher time, for he lacks both a feel and a folklore to fall back on. Or rather he has a folklore—that of his native language—which misleads him. If he were a foreigner analyzing English he might, for instance, hear the words *vial* and *phial* and be told that they mean the same, and conclude, erroneously, that the difference between the sounds [v] and [f] is only accidental—that English has a labiodental consonant phoneme (which might be represented by some such symbol as /ꬵ/) that is indifferently voiced or voiceless. But eventually he would discover that the feature of voice is significant, in pairs like *vary-fairy, leave-leaf, shelve-shelf,* and hence /v/ and /f/ are phonemes, independent of each other.

Nor is it all smooth sailing even in one's native language. Since a phoneme consumes a certain length of time, however short, there is always the question of where the borders are and of whether a given span of time should be assigned to just one phoneme or split down the middle and assigned to two; this is the problem of *unit phoneme* versus *cluster.* The analogy with music is appropriate again. While it is true that the notes in a chord are heard simultaneously, sometimes chords appear as arpeggios, in which the notes are played one after the other—notes in this kind of arrangement are both simultaneous and successive: the chord changes in the course of its production. Language too has sounds that fluctuate, and just as the succession CEGCE on a piano might be thought of either as a single arpeggio or as one arpeggio consisting of CEG followed by another consisting of CE, so with the phonemic "chord" in a language: one can often choose between regarding the clustered sound as one unit or two.

Some clusters are fairly easy to deal with. One might hesitate briefly over words like *play-spay-sway-stay-splay-spray-clay-cray-flay-fray-gray-dray.* Are the consonant sounds preceding the vowels in these words units or clusters? If they are unit phonemes, then *sway* differs from *way* in that one starts with / ṣ̌ / and the other with /w/; if they are clusters, then the difference is that *sway* has one more phoneme than *way,* the initial /s/. But it would soon be clear that by splitting /s/ from /w/ the total number of phonemes could be reduced—instead of three phonemes, /s/, /w/, and / ṣ̌ /, to account for *say, way,* and *sway,* only two would be needed; and by splitting /r/ from /d/ one could account not only for *dray* in addition to *day* and *ray* but also, by recognizing /dr/ as distinct from /rd/, for part of the contrast between *dry* and *yard.*

Other clusters are more troublesome. There are still a few phoneticians who think of the vowel glides in words like *oil, shy,* and *frown* as consisting of just one vowel phoneme each. Most would regard them as two, transcribing these three words /ɔyl/, /šay/, and /frawn/. One argument in favor of counting just one is the nature of the glide itself: the transition is smooth, without the clearly perceptible break that one finds in a consonant cluster such as /st/. One bit of evidence for doing the opposite is that playing a tape recording of a word such as *nigh* backwards makes it sound as *yon,* suggesting that the /y/ already identified in *yet-bet, young-tongue, yell-fell, yes-guess* and other such pairs is the same as the last phoneme in *nigh.* This would mean that sounds containing glides—that is, *diphthongs*—can be split up.

Such technical problems put a fringe of uncertainty around the catalog of phonemes, but it is not a wide fringe. Linguists agree on the main points.

ALLOPHONES

What happens to phonemes when they stand next to other phonemes or when they occur at different locations in an utterance? Do they keep their identities intact like a row of bullets laid end to end? If not, do traits of one somehow get mixed with others and do given positions—say, at the beginning or end of the utterance—have some strengthening or weakening effect?

Phonemes are indeed affected by the company they keep, much as letters are affected in ordinary handwriting. When a letter that normally ends with a stroke above the bottom of the line, like a *b* or a *v* , is followed by one that normally starts at the bottom, such as an *i* or an *r* , the latter starts instead where the former leaves off: *bi*, *vi*, *br*. This is called *assimilation* of one shape to the other. Assimilation of one sound to another is equally common. Between vowels an English /n/ is generally alveolar, but in the word *tenth,* where it stands before an interdental /θ/, it too becomes interdental. English /r/ is normally fully voiced, but in a cluster after a voiceless /t/, as in *tree,* it is partially unvoiced.

Different positions in a word bring different influences to bear. The pairs *intent-indent, satin-sadden,* and *sat-sad* illustrate what happens to /t/ and /d/. We have no trouble hearing the difference between the two sounds. They are produced with the same position of the tongue in all three pairs, and we seem to "hear" voicelessness as the feature of the /t/, but it is actually manifested in three different ways. In *intent* it appears as a strong puff of breath, or aspiration. In *satin* it appears as a brief interval of silence right after the tongue makes contact—with *sadden* the sound flows on. In *sat* it appears as a sharp cut-off of sound, and the burden of the difference shifts to what happens to the vowel: it is drawled in *sad* but not in *sat.* In point of actual sound, *sad* is longer. But our ear interprets both words as having about the same length, and this means adding a little bit of nothing—silence—at the end of *sat,* the same silence that was manifested in *satin.* All these phenomena are read back into our minds as the voicelessness characteristic of /t/.

Noting these modifications and classifying the environments that cause them make it possible to define the materialization of a phoneme in sound. Each such different physical manifestation of a phoneme is called an *allophone.* The allophones of /t/ thus include one that is aspirated (any /t/ standing before a full vowel), one that is combined with an interval of silence (a /t/ before most consonants), and one that is *un*like the /d/ that has a lengthened vowel before it (a /t/ in final position). The allophones of /n/ include one that is interdental *(tenth)*, one that is palatal *(inch)*, and one that is alveolar *(tint)*, among others.

For the linguist the problem of identifying and classifying allophones is harder because he has to approach it in reverse. He cannot decide beforehand what the phonemes are and then look for what makes them different. His starting point is the sounds themselves, tumbled together, never repeated in exactly the same way, undifferentiated in their similarities and contrasts. At this stage they are *phones*—not allophones, for with no phonemes yet determined one cannot tell what they are allophones of. Instead of saying "Here I have phoneme *a*" and asking "What causes the variants *a′* and *a″*?" the linguist must say "Here I have phones *x* and *y*" and ask "Do they belong together as two allophones of one phoneme or are they distinct phonemes?"

The answer depends on criteria that are varied and complex. The most obvious one is similarity in sound; no matter how strong the other reasons may be for regarding two phones as allophones of a single phoneme, the linguist is reluctant to do so unless they are at least partially alike. Ideally, each should resemble the other more than either resembles any sound that is classed with some other phoneme. Another criterion is that the difference between the two must never contribute to any difference in meaning. A speaker might be heard to say the word *probably* in rapid speech with his lips not quite closed for the first [b] sound, then later when talking more slowly or emphatically be heard to make the [b] as a firmly closed stop. If the linguist can then ask, "Is there any difference between pro—ably and pro—ably?" filling in with the two sounds he has heard, the answer "No difference" given by a native speaker is usually a safe sign that both sounds belong to a single phoneme. A third criterion is that of spotting some predictable cause for whatever difference there is. The interdental [n] noted in the word **tenth** is always associated with a following sound that is also interdental. Given other [n]-like sounds that are identical in all other respects, one can safely assume that the interdental [n] is conditioned by the sound that follows it and therefore belongs with other [n]s as a member of the same phoneme.

A few uncertainties always remain. The English /t/ can be cited again. In words like **butter, totter, matter, pewter, bitter, atom, sputum, motto, grotto, pity,** and **duty,** for most speakers of American English, the /t/ (if we can beg the question by calling it a phoneme in advance) is reduced to a bare tap which picks up the voicing of the surrounding sounds and becomes almost if not completely indistinguishable from /d/. The result is that **bitter** sounds like **bidder, latter** like **ladder, He hit 'er** like **He hid 'er, let 'em** like **led 'em,** and so on. How is one to deal with this kind of fickleness? There are several possibilities, of which three are worth noting:

1. Continue to call it /t/. This is what most dictionaries do. The justification is that in some dialects /t/ and /d/ are still quite distinct, and it is better to assume that even among those speakers who make them sound alike some trace of a difference may remain. After all, a person who produces a clear /t/ in *atomic* is not apt to be "thinking" of a /d/ when he says *atom* even if he does make it sound like *Adam*—especially if, when he slows down and says *atom* emphatically, he makes a clear /t/. Following the criterion "a word is a word," one therefore transcribes *atom* with the same symbols wherever possible. (It is not always possible: *insert* also has a /t/ but by no stretch of the ear can we find one in *insertion*.)[4]

2. Call it /d/ whenever /d/ is heard. This is what the Merriam-Webster *Third New International Dictionary* does, and it is justified by phonetic realism: "a sound is a sound."

3. Call it something between the two, using a neutral symbol such as /d̶/ that implies "in this environment the distinction between /t/ and /d/ is lost." This neutral symbol is sometimes called an *archiphoneme*. Another example is the contrast between /ɪ/ and /ɛ/ which most speakers of American English make in pairs like *bit-bet, trick-trek, slipped-slept,* but which many speakers disregard before /n/ with the result that *pin-pen, Min-men, din-den,* and so on, sound the same. One could say that for these speakers the intermediate sound is an /ɪ/, an /ɛ/, or an archiphoneme /E̶/.

In situations like these no solution is perfectly satisfactory. They are uncertainties to be tolerated, areas of vagueness in the language itself. But the noteworthy and comforting fact is that vagueness in phonemes is the exception rather than the rule. Languages are remarkably efficient in keeping these signaling units clear and distinct.

Linguists who use the distinctive-feature approach to phonology feel that the level of phonemes is superfluous. Instead of saying, for example, that the segment of sound symbolized by /d/ has independent status, they prefer to view it as "represented directly by the features which make it up."[5] One reason for this preference is that it simplifies the

---

[4] But by stretching the imagination we can. In order to respect the "word is a word" principle and preserve the way a word or a recurring part of a word is written, the generative grammarians (about whom more will be said in Chapter 11) assume a kind of abstract phoneme /T/ which, by the rules of English phonology, "generates" a [t] in *insert* and a [š] in *insertion*.

[5] Robert D. Wilson, "A Criticism of Distinctive Features," *Journal of Linguistics* 2.201 (1966).

description of morphemes, where the features (voice, nasalization, stridency, and so on) have to be mentioned anyway and can just as well be used in place of phonemes.

But the distinctive-feature approach has itself been criticized as too phonetic, for using acoustic and articulatory features directly instead of treating them as the mere physical manifestations of underlying units. Too often we are compelled to ignore some articulatory or acoustic feature when we find that even though it is present the language disregards it. In Hungarian, for example, there is a phonetically rounded vowel (short /a/) which is used in such a way that it has to be classed as unrounded.[6] The distinctive feature of roundedness thus becomes awkward as a device for setting up a phonological unit. It still seems useful to assume a set of underlying abstractions—phonemes, or something very much like them—which take on different manifestations under different conditions.

THE SYLLABLE

If puns and pig Latin prove a dim awareness of phonemes, verse proves a full awareness of syllables: syllable-counting is as old as poets and poetry. Young children are aware of them too; they exploit the effect of spaced-out syllables in their jeering chants (*Fred-die-is-a-fraid-y-cat*) and emphatic warnings like this one from a four-year-old, with each syllable separately accented: *You-bet-ter-not-say-that-to-mo-ther!* The syllable has not always received the attention that it deserves from linguists. One of them has called it "the stepchild of linguistic analysis."[7] In part this has been due to its fuzzy borders. One can distinguish *Ben Tover* from *bent over* by the aspirated /t/ in the first which shows that the division is /bɛn-tovər/ rather than /bɛnt-ovər/; but often the separation is impossible to locate precisely. In ordinary speech *one's own* sounds like *one zone, an ungodly* like *a nun godly, palisades* like *palace aides,* and so on. Linguists have preferred to work with units that have sharper edges.

Syllables have a typical internal structure consisting of a *nucleus*, which is a vowel or a vowel-like consonant (/r/ or /l/, for example), plus one or more *satellites* in the form of consonants before or after the nucleus.

---

[6] The problem is one of vowel harmony, too complex to be detailed here. Consult the criticism of distinctive features, on which these remarks are based, in E. C. Fudge, "The Nature of Phonological Primes," *Journal of Linguistics* 3.9–10 (1967).

[7] Kenneth L. Pike, "Grammemic Theory," *General Linguistics* 2.38 (1957).

Probably the most striking thing about any language, in the impression it makes on listeners who do not understand it and notice sounds rather than meanings, is the way its syllables are built. The main difference is between harmonic and inharmonic sounds, between music and noise. A language in which the satellites are few sounds musical; one with numerous satellites, especially voiceless ones, is noisy. English stands about midway. It has syllables consisting of a nucleus alone, as in the words *oh* and *ah,* and syllables in which the nucleus is flanked by two or more satellites on each side, as in *splashed* and *sprints.*

The syllable exists mainly because language is speech. If speakers did not have to *say* their phonemes we might be able to dispense with the syllable; but the sounds of most phonemes cannot be uttered effectively by themselves. One can barely produce the sound of /g/ without a vowel before it or after it—that is, without putting it in a syllable. One can manage the sound of a /t/ by itself but too faintly for it to be heard very far away. (The effect a consonant has on the neighboring vowels—noted in Chapter 3—is generally a sure way to tell what consonant it is; a /t/, for example, affects a neighboring vowel in a way that sets it off clearly from a /p/—more clearly than the particular noises that we usually think of as the chief characteristics of particular consonants.) In the syllable the phoneme comes to life. To describe the syllable we have to tell how phonemes make it up, and an essential part of the description of phonemes is how they arrange themselves in syllables.

Not all arrangements are possible. The permitted combinations can be seen by building consonants one by one around a nucleus. Starting with *oh,* for example, and adding successively to the left, one may get *row, crow,* and *scrow;* with *a* (that is, the sound /e/) might come *lay, play,* and *splay;* or with *ill* the words *will* and *twill.* Studying many such examples would reveal something about the possible arrangements of consonants to the left of the nucleus. If there is only one it can be any consonant in the language except /ŋ/. If there are two, /l/ and /r/ occur pretty freely as the second and the stops and voiceless fricatives as the first: *truce, pry, plea, sly, free.* If there are three the first will be /s/: *splurge, stray.* But there are restrictions: no /tl-/, no /sb-/, no /sfl-/, and so on. A similar build-up will reveal the situation at the end of the syllable—for example, *oh-own-owned, bur-Bearse-burst-bursts.* The entire structure of English syllables can be stated in a rather complex set of rules embodying classes of consonants and positions relative to the nucleus and to one another.

Not all the combinations of sounds that speakers fail to use are avoided because they are hard to say or confusing to hear, given the speech habits of the language in question. Some have just never happened to develop. No language uses all the combinations that would be possible with its phonemes. English speakers have no trouble with initial clusters like /vl/- and /šp/- —we can easily say *Vladimir,* and *He shpilled his drink* is not unknown when under the influence; but they are not put to any use worth mentioning. Some day they may be. We could easily grow accustomed to /vl/- if we adopted a few more words like *Vladimir* and *Vladivostok,* as we have grown accustomed to /šl šn šm/ by borrowing words from German and Yiddish: *schlemiel, schnook, schmo,* and so forth.

The inner structure of the syllable is only half its story. The other half is the role it plays in the phonetic description of words. No word can contain fewer than one syllable—it is the smallest unit that is normally pronounced by itself. And the syllable is the field of action for the three most important ways in which the sound of words is intentionally modified. The first of these is *accent:* when we say "The word *reverberate* is accented in this sentence" we mean, as far as physical sound is concerned, that just the syllable *-ver-* is accented. The second is *expressive length:* to make the word *awful* more emphatic we drawl just the first syllable, the accented one. The third is the rise and fall of *pitch:* normally, a marked change in the direction of the pitch curve coincides with the beginning of a syllable—*Do you have to spend your money so carelessly?* shows pitch rises on *have, mon-, care-,* and *-ly.*

Units of distinctive sound do not stop with the syllable, but they do become progressively vaguer so that it gets less and less profitable to try to single them out. Above the level of the syllable is the breath group— a series of syllables spoken with one expiration of breath. It generally coincides with a particular intonation shape. After the breath group comes the phonological sentence, which some linguists like to point out, marked by a pause. From there on it is next to impossible to decide on higher phonological divisions, though they must exist in a hazy kind of way—one can usually tell, for example, when someone reading a speech has come to the end of a paragraph because he makes an extra-long pause. One reason for ending the build-up of sound at the level of the syllable is that anything higher is almost necessarily related in some way to meaning. Meaningless syllables (syllables that are not already words by themselves) are common. Breath groups are almost always arranged by speakers to fit divisions of sense, and phonological sentences even more so.

For all their importance, units of sound are fundamentally meaningless. Meaningful units are on the higher levels of language.

ADDITIONAL REMARKS
AND APPLICATIONS

1. Take baseball again as an example of particle, string, and field, only this time consider the plays as the particles. Identify some of the particles, then describe some of the strings (definite sequences of plays) and some of the field relationships (for example, "all the ways to be put out").

2. Tongue twisters are examples of difficult articulations. The phrase *homeland of subversives* appeared in a newspaper column. The phrase *critical flicker fusion frequency* is used in psychology. Try saying them fast. What makes them difficult? (Sometimes just the repetition of a sound is bothersome. See Chapter 6, page 94.)

3. What phonemic contrasts do the following minimal pairs point to?— *gristly-grisly, confusion-Confucian, spite-spied, crutch-crush, luff-love, rode-roan, mutt-much, lean-dean.* Are the two members of each pair widely different from each other? If you could measure the difference in terms of the number of distinctive features that separate one phoneme from another, how many points of difference would you say there are in /f/-/v/? In /m/-/p/?

4. See if you have a contrast in the following: *fawned-fond, caught-cot, wrought-rot, cawed-cod.* (Speakers in some dialect areas have no contrast here.) If you do, does it carry over into *hornet-horrible, Laurie-sorry?* You almost certainly have a contrast in *mat-met, bat-bet, sad-said, shall-shell, sand-send;* see if this contrast carries over to *marry-merry, Barry-berry, arrow-error.* Do you observe anything here that suggests a blurring influence from a nearby /r/? Does something similar happen for you in *ferry-fairy* (compare *met-mate)?*

5. Compare the sound represented by the *s* of *pleasure* with the sound represented by the *dg* of *pledger.* Some phoneticians regard the latter as a cluster of two consonants of which the consonant in *pleasure* is the second. What would the other one be? Compare the words *shoes* and *choose.* Is there a similar possibility of regarding the second of the two compared sounds as a cluster of two consonants?

6. In the word *lapboard* there is little or no accommodation between

the /p/ and the /b/—both are articulated in almost the normal way. But the combination is a difficult one, and in the word *cupboard* it is possible to see what may some day happen to *lapboard.* Describe the steps that may bring it about.

7. In rapid speech a combination like /ptm/ is hard to negotiate. What do most speakers do in an utterance like **When I started to take it off they stopped me** with the words *stopped me?* Contrast this with **When I start to take it off they stop me.** Do you hear a difference? Can you explain *stopp' me* as a kind of assimilation?

8. Describe the allophones of /t/ in the following words: **shanties, Cervantes, mutton, pity.** Describe the allophones of /n/: **pawnshop, naughty, neat, wince, panther;** explain the effect of the environment that causes these changes in /n/.

9. The merging of /t/ and /d/ is not necessarily uniform even for speakers who have it fairly generally. If you have it in the pairs **latter-ladder, metal-meddle, pouter-powder,** see if you also have it in the pairs **traitor-trader, seater-cedar, (hoity-)toity-toidy.** If not, can you account for the difference? (There seem to be several factors.)

10. Does what happens in rapid speech with combinations like **white shoes, why choose; nitrate, night rate; Hiram, hire 'em,** and the like show why it is so hard to tell where the borders of a syllable are? Find a couple of additional pairs like these.

11. Are there phonetic reasons for English to reject the initial cluster /sb/? Relate your answer to assimilation and to the contrast, or lack of contrast, between /b/ and /p/ after /s/.

12. The most complex consonant clusters in English words occur at the ends of words—for example, /ksθs/ in **sixths,** /lkts/ in **mulcts.** Find two or three more examples of at least three consonants together. Is there a morphological reason for this? (Consider how often /s z t d/ are at the end, and why.)

13. The neighbors that a phoneme is permitted to have are its distribution in the string sense. There are also questions of distribution in the field sense. One is frequency: how widely a given phoneme is used by comparison with other phonemes. Some phonemic contrasts are not much exploited—for example, the contrast between /u/ and /ʊ/ as in **cooed-could, pool-pull, gooed-good, hood(lum)-hood, fool-full, Luke-look.** Can you find other pairs with these two phonemes? The extent to which a contrast is exploited is called its functional load: /u/ versus /ʊ/ obviously has a light functional load. Can you guess why? What is apt to happen eventually to this contrast?

STRUCTURE IN 5 LANGUAGE: THE HIGHER LEVELS

WHEN THE LABORATORY is supplied with subatomic particles in the form of distinctive features, atoms in the form of phonemes, and molecules in the form of syllables, what is to be done with them? One might say that the next step is to go from physics to biology, to find the cells that perform their specialized functions in the collection of muscular and other structures that make up the body.

THE LEVEL OF MORPHEMES AND WORDS

The organic function of language is to carry meaning. Meaning must therefore have something to do with the workings of the linguistic cell. Up to now we have spoken of words as if *they* were the cells of meaning. To be precisely that, the simplest meaning would have to stand in a one-to-one relationship with a word; but this is not always true. We would like to say that *roadblock* is "a word," yet it is made up of elements that are themselves words. And certainly *un-American* is a word, yet it is made up of an independent word, *America,* plus a prefix *un-* and a suffix *-an,* for each of which we seem to discern a kind of meaning—as is quickly confirmed by listing other places where they occur: *unhealthy, unwise,* *unsteady; Hawaiian, Alaskan, Russian.* It hardly seems that in our dissection of cells we can stop with the word.

→   The apparently meaningful bits that are smaller than words are termed *morphemes.* A sentence like *Every/one / admire/s / Bill/'s / man/li/ness* breaks up into nine morphemes bunched into four words: *everyone* is a compound containing the morphemes *every* and *one* (which also happen to be words when used separately), *admires* is a verb containing the stem *admire-* and the suffix *-s* meaning 'third person singular,' and so on. The word *morpheme* itself contains *morph-* and the suffix *-eme,* which also appears in *phoneme.*

If morphemes are the minimal units of meaning, one begins to wonder what words are good for—or even what words are. Is popular thinking about words an illusion? Do we only imagine that *roadblock* is one word but *road machinery* is two?

If it is only imagination, people are strangely consistent, for nearly everyone would make this distinction between these two examples. There is pretty general agreement on whether to regard a particular segment of speech as one word, two, or more. What is it that makes us feel that certain units are somehow distinct and separable?

Linguists sometimes answer this question by defining the word as 'the smallest unit of language that can be used by itself,' that is, used to form an utterance: *Go!, Henry* (in answer to *Who was it?*), *Tomorrow* (in answer to *When are you going?*), and *Nice* (in answer to *What do you think of it?*) qualify as words under this definition. But a good many forms that we like to regard as words don't qualify: one can't make an utterance with just *the* or *from* or *and.* Either they are not words, or the separateness of words does not always go so far as potentially complete independence.

Nevertheless, there is a mark of a lower degree of independence that does correlate very closely with our notion of what constitutes a word. This is our freedom to insert, between one word and the next, a vocalized hesitation—typically, the sound *uh: The—uh—workman—uh—who—uh —put up—uh—that—uh—roadblock—uh—didn't—uh—leave—uh—any —uh—warning-light.* Murder would be too merciful for a speaker who put in all these hesitations, but one or two, at any of the points indicated, would be perfectly normal for someone who must pause to gather his thoughts. The gaps agree remarkably well with our feel for separations between words.[1] No pause can be inserted between the morphemes in

---

[1] LeRoy Little, *The Syntax of Vocalized Pauses in Spontaneous Cultivated Speech.* Dissertation, George Peabody College for Teachers, 1963. Abstract in *Linguistics* 11.105–6 (1965). See also the studies that show audible changes in the phonemes (referred to as "junctural" changes) to be lacking between morpheme and morpheme but present between word and word—for example, Ilse Lehiste, "An Acoustic-phonetic Study of Internal Open Juncture," supplement to *Phonetica* 5.1–54 (1960).

workman, roadblock, didn't, or *warning-light.* A pause can be inserted between *the* and *workman.* The one apparent disagreement, the unlikelihood of a pause between *put* and *up,* coincides with our uncertainty about whether to regard such forms as one word or two—grammarians often call *put up, leave out, take off,* and so on "two-word verbs."

The possibility of hesitating most likely reflects the freedom we have to insert other words at the same point. Instead of separating the words of the example with repeated *uh's* we could separate them with other words: *The careless workman there who supposedly put up just that one roadblock surely didn't dutifully leave in view any red warning-light.*

This is the physical evidence, but it is less important in itself than as a symptom of the role that words play in a language. A word is evidently "something that is not to be broken up." Words are *prefabricated units.* Language in action is a process of fabrication that takes two forms: the fabrication of larger segments using words and the fabrication of the words themselves. The first we call syntax. It goes on whenever a speaker says anything: *I got Mary some buttered popcorn at the movies last night* is a sentence that the speaker may never have said before in his life; he throws it together out of the prefabricated units he has at hand, to fit a situation. Once said, that sentence may never again be repeated and it may well be forgotten, as if the parts were disassembled and returned to the stockroom. But the parts themselves, the prefabricated units, are not forgotten and will be used again.

But what about the fabrication of words? Obviously, this is not something that happens every time we speak. If it were, the Oxford Dictionary could not tell us that the word *frontage* appeared for the first time in English in the seventeenth century while the words *slippage* and *roughage* appeared in the latter part of the nineteenth century. It may be hard to decide sometimes who first used a word, or where and when it was first used, and many words are doubtless created independently by more than one speaker. But that is nothing new in the history of invention. The fact remains that a word is tied to its moment in history. If something is prefabricated there must have been a time when the job was done.

Words are not the only prefabricated units, of course. There are also idioms, platitudes, and proverbs. But words are the prefabricated units of syntax. The larger prefabs do not typically become parts of larger structures but are the complete structures themselves. They tend to be sentences, not parts of sentences.

The morpheme is now a bit easier to define. It is the semi-finished material from which words are made. Semi-finished means second-hand. The times when speakers set about constructing words out of the pure raw material of phonemes and syllables are few and far between—an occasional trade name such as *Kodak* or an acronym (word made up of initial letters) like *Unesco*—and these are almost always of one part of speech, nouns. Practically all words that are not imported bodily from some other language (this too is an abundant source) are made up of old words or their parts. Sometimes those parts are pretty well standardized, like the suffix *-ness* or the prefix *un-*. Other times they are only broken pieces that some inventive speaker manages to re-fit, like the *bumber-*, altered from *umbr-* in *umbrella*, and the *-shoot*, based on the *-chute* of *parachute*, that go to make up the word *bumbershoot*. In between are fragments of all degrees of standardized efficiency and junkyard irregularity. *Hamburger* yields *-burger*, which is reattached in *nutburger*, *Gainesburger*, and *cheeseburger*. *Cafeteria* yields *-teria*, which is reattached in *valeteria*, *groceteria*, and *washateria*. Trade names make easy use of almost any fragment, like the *-roni* of *macaroni* that is reattached in *Rice-a-Roni* and *Noodle-Roni*. The fabrication may re-use elements that have been re-used many times, or it may be a one-shot affair such as the punning reference to being a member of the *lowerarchy*, with *-archy* extracted from *hierarchy*. The principle is the same. Scientists and scholars may give themselves airs with high-bred affixes borrowed from classical languages, but they are linguistically no more sophisticated than the common speakers who are satisfied with leftovers from the vernacular. The only thing a morpheme is good for is to be melted down and recast in a word.

Word-making, for all its irregularity, has two fairly well defined processes. One process uses words themselves as raw material for new words. It is called *compounding*. The other attaches a lesser morpheme—an affix—to a major morpheme—a stem, frequently a word. It is called *derivation*. *Roadblock* and *warning-light* are compounds. *Worker* is a derivative (so, probably, is *workman*, since *-man*, pronounced *m'n*, has been reduced to an affix in English). *Troubleshooter* embodies both processes, derivation in *shoot* + *-er* and compounding in *trouble* + *shooter*. An affix that is rather freely used to make new derivatives is termed *active*. When one man referred to the occupants of flying saucers as *saucerians*, he was using the active suffix *-ian*.[2] An affix that is not freely used is *inactive*, though one can never pronounce any element completely dead. The suffix *-ate* is a Latinism that can hardly be used to make new words—until some wag comes forward with *discombobulate* and makes it stick. If a word fragment like *-burger* can be used as if it were an affix, nothing prevents any piece of a word, inactive or not, from being reused.

There are other processes. A fairly common one is *reduplication*, where the same morpheme is repeated in the same or slightly altered form: *hushhush, mishmash, helter-skelter, fiddle-faddle*.

The meanings of morphemes can vary as widely as their forms. This

---

[2] *Look*, March 21, 1967, p. 76.

is to be expected of second-hand materials. When an old dress is cut down to a skirt its former function may be partly remembered, but when a remnant of it becomes a dustcloth the old function is forgotten. Almost no morpheme is perfectly stable in meaning. The morpheme *-er* forms agentive nouns—a *builder* is one who builds, a *talker* one who talks, a *wrecker* one who wrecks; but an *undertaker* is no longer one who undertakes—the morpheme has been swallowed up in the word. The suffix *-able* suggests something on the order of 'facilitation,' but this would be hard to pin down in words as various as *charitable, likable, tangible, terrible, reputable,* and *sensible.* Language is not like arithmetic; numerical composites are strictly additive: the number 126 is an entity but it is also the exact sum of 100 + 20 + 6. When morphemes are put together to form new words, the meanings are almost never simply additive. This is because a word is coined *after* the speaker has the meaning before him. If he can lay hold of parts whose meanings suggest the one he had in mind, so much the better, but that is not essential. The speaker who first put together the word *escapee* was not bothered by the fact that he should have said *escaper,* since *-ee* is etymologically for persons acted upon, not for persons acting. He wanted something to suggest the same "set category of persons" idea that is carried by words like *employee* and *draftee,* and he twisted *-ee* to his purpose.

The high informality of word-making in English, the clutching at almost anything to nail up a new prefab, reflects the vast expansion of our culture. A supermarket that in 1966 stocked eight thousand items and by 1971 is expected to stock twelve thousand[3] is one ripple in a tide of growth that carries our vocabulary along with it. We have to have names for those new items. All cultures exhibit this to some extent: the list of content-carrying words—nouns, verbs, adjectives, and most adverbs—is the one list in the catalog that has no limit. Phonemes, syllable types, rules of syntax, and certain little "function words" that will be discussed later are "closed classes"—they are almost never added to; but the major lexicon is open-ended. The relationship of morphemes to words is therefore the hardest thing in language to analyze. Asking what morphemes a word contains and what they mean is asking what the coiner of the word had in mind when he coined it and possibly what unforeseen associations it may have built up since.[4] It is less an analytical question than a question about history.

---

[3] Estimate by American Paper Institute, *Consumer Reports,* September, 1966, p. 425.

[4] How we analyze a word into morphemes can change in the course of the word's history. A *wiseacre* is generally thought to be someone who acts wise but is not entitled to—*wise* is morphemicized by the speaker in spite of the fact that *wiseacre* originally meant 'soothsayer' and the *wise-* part is related to *witch.* More examples of such "folk etymology" will be given in Chapter 7, pp. 104–06.

The morpheme at best continues to live a parasitic life within the word. It remains half-alive for one speaker and dies for the next; or it may be revived by education. A child who calls a tricycle a *three-wheeled bike* and later discovers other words with the prefix *bi-* may reanalyze *bicycle* into two morphemes instead of one. Hundreds of morphemes lie half-buried in the junkheaps of the etymological past. A corner of the Latin *pre-* sticks out in words like *predict, prearrange, predetermine,* and maybe *prepare*—we sense that *pre-* here has something to do with 'before'; but in the verb *present* it is almost hidden and in *preserve, pregnant,* and *prelate* it is lost from sight. No one but an etymologist remembers what the *luke-* of *lukewarm* means (it originally signified 'lukewarm' by itself— *lukewarm* = 'lukewarmly warm'). The *re-* of *reduce* and the *di-* of *digest* are only meaningless syllables to speakers of English, even though their sources are the same as the *re-* of *readjust* and the *dis-* of *distrust.*

Still, in spite of the difficulties, looking for morphemes is a necessary part of linguistic analysis. This is true partly because not all languages are quite so unsystematic (or so burdened with conflicting systems, which comes to the same thing) as English; some of them have more regular habits of word formation. It is also true because even in English there is one class of morphemes that are more orderly in their behavior.

Source morphemes and system morphemes

Most morphemes are like the ones already described: bits of form and meaning that provide the stuff for an expanding lexicon. At the first moment one of them is pressed into service, we say that a new word has been created. As with other creative acts, we cannot be sure which way it is going to go. The person who first invented the expression *stir-crazy* might have said *jail-happy, cell-silly, pen-potty,* or anything else that came handy and was colorful. But once *stir-crazy* had made its bow, anyone wishing to compare two individuals in terms of this affliction was almost certain to do it in just one way: "Abe is *more stir-crazy* than Leo." The use of *more,* or of the suffix *-er* in *crazier,* is seen not as a way of making new words but as a way of doing something to the words we already have. It is manipulative, not creative. In the early part of World War II, someone might have said *The news is that Hitler threatens to blitz London* and someone else might have replied *I don't know what "blitz" means but if he ever blitzed that place he'd get blitzed right back.* The second speaker added *-ed* automatically to something he had never heard before. He did not create a "new word" but used the "same word" in a "different form."

Morphemes such as *more*, *-er*, and *-ed* are of the highest importance to the language as a system and may accordingly be called *system morphemes*. By and large they do two things: they signal relationships within language, and they signal certain meanings that are so vital in communication that they have to be expressed over and over. An example of the first function is the morpheme *than* (which also happens to be a word), which simply relates the terms of a comparison: *John is older than Mary.* An example of the second function is the morpheme that pluralizes nouns. We can say, without committing ourselves as to how many dogs there were, *John suffered several dog bites.* But if we mention *dog* in the usual way we are forced to reveal whether there was one or more than one: *John was bitten by his neighbor's dog(s).* English feels that "number" is important enough to be automatically tagged to the word. Languages do not always agree on the particular kinds of meanings that are given this sort of preferential treatment but certain ones are typical: number, tense, definiteness, animateness, possession—even, in certain languages, such things as size and shape.

The two uses of system morphemes just mentioned—to signal relationships within language and to signal certain favored meanings—are usually separated by linguists but are really impossible to keep apart. *Henry's book* uses the possessive morpheme *-'s* to describe ownership, a fact of the real world. *Henry's smoking* does not use it to say that Henry owns smoking but to show that *Henry* is the grammatical subject of the verb *smoke.* The word *that* in *That's the man!*, with a pointing gesture, singles out an object in the real world. In *I didn't mean that* it refers to something just said, something in language.

The last example with *that* and the earlier one with *than* reveal that system morphemes, like source morphemes, may be whole words as well as parts of words. Both the suffix *-ed* and the word *that* are system morphemes. When we attach them, system morphemes are called *inflections*. When we leave them outside they are called *function words*. The suffixes *-s*, *-ed*, *-'s*, and *-ing* are inflections (English likes to inflect by using suffixes, but other languages may incorporate their inflections at the beginning or in the middle of words). *That, the, my, he, and, when, than,* and numerous similar forms are function words.

The difference between inflections and function words is not in what they do with meanings and relationships. They are so similar in this respect that one occasionally finds an inflection and a function word both playing the same role or even alternating with each other, like *-er* and *more* in *quicker* and *more rapidly.* The difference between them lies in their behavior as physical entities. Function words share the freedom of words. Other words may be inserted between them and the items to which they belong. Thus *the man* can be split to give *the big man, the* *great big man, the wonderful great big man,* and so on; *more beautiful* can have additional *more's* inserted, giving *more and more beautiful* (we cannot say *prettier and -er*); *who* can be separated fore and aft by pauses: *the man—uh—who—uh—had to leave.* Function words may be contrastively accented, which is hardly possible with inflections: we can say *Mary is happier now,* but if someone asserts that she is less happy we cannot contradict him by saying *She is happiér—we have to say *She is móre happy.*

As mere appendages, inflections are more exposed than function words to influences from their environment. Their resistance to phonetic and analogical changes is lowered, with the result that they have many more irregularities than function words. The nature of these irregularities is the subject of the next section.

System morphemes are more stable in meaning than source morphemes. Almost always their meanings are simply additive: *dog* + *-s* gives the plural of *dog,* no more. As we have seen, this is not true of source morphemes. Take one as comparatively stable as the adverbial *-ly.* We can generally predict that when a word can be used as an adjective its adverbial counterpart in *-ly* will have only the meaning 'adverbiality' added: *an enveloping affection, She is so envelopingly affectionate.* But this is not true of *presently.* It is true of *hopefully* in *He looked at me hopefully* but not in *Hopefully there will be no more complaints.*

The distinctions among the various kinds of morphemes are summarized in the chart on the next page.

Allomorphs

System morphemes might be said to lack phonetic bulk. As a class, they are usually insignificant in terms of their small number of phonemes and their lack of stress. This leads to changes that resemble the ones already discussed in the section on allophones. We noted that the interdental [n] of *tenth* is an allophone of /n/ induced by the following interdental /θ/. Now we note that the voiceless -/s/ of *cats* and the voiced -/z/ of *dogs* are similarly induced by the preceding voiceless /t/ and voiced /g/. To state these changes calls for recognizing a new unit, the allomorph, which is to the morpheme what the allophone is to the phoneme. Obviously, it will not do to identify morphemes by their spellings, as we have done in a few instances just for convenience. A linguistic description must be in terms of sounds, and it happens that with system morphemes this can often be quite precise.

SUMMARY CHART OF MORPHEMES

TWO KINDS OF MORPHEMES	TWO DEGREES OF INDEPENDENCE	
	Words	Affixes
Source morphemes	Words incorporatable in new words by COMPOUNDING (*clam* + *bake* → *clambake*)	More or less active prefixes (*un-* in *un*denatured)
	Words incorporatable in new words by DERIVATION (*push* + *-y* → *pushy*) (*mis-* + *fire* → *misfire*)	Inactive prefixes (*di-* in *di*gest)
		More or less active suffixes (*-able* in orbit*able*)
		Inactive suffixes (*-ose* in verb*ose*)
		Word fragments (*-burger* in cheese*burger*)
System morphemes	Function words (*the, of, which, my, when, and, if . . .*)	Inflectional suffixes (*-s, -ed, -ing . . .*)

The 'plural' morpheme has three allomorphs:

1. After the strident consonants /s z š ž č ǰ/ it is -/əz/: *losses, roses, dishes, rouges, riches, edges, axes, adzes.*

2. After any other voiceless consonant it is -/s/: *rocks, rats, hips, cliffs, harps, runts, gulps, fists, parks.*

3. After any other voiced consonant and after any vowel it is -/z/: *tubs, rugs, heads, stoves, lathes, fools, rooms, tons, tongues, cars, elves, birds, barns, elms, toys, cows, shoes, bras.*

The allomorphs of the 'past' morpheme are also three:

1. After /t/ or /d/ it is -/əd/: *tooted, added, insisted, parted, funded, tilted, welded.*

2. After any other voiceless consonant it is -/t/: *raced, roughed,*

pitched, rushed, rapped, clicked, axed, rasped, parked, milked, helped, pumped, risked.

3. After any other voiced consonant and after any vowel it is -/d/: *hummed, planed, edged, rouged, felled, banged, purred, rubbed, rigged, loved, blazed, charmed, turned, delved, filmed, curbed, sowed, defied, plowed, weighed, booed, sawed, rah-rahed.*

Statements like these take care of system morphemes as living elements of speech. The first person who made *goofed* from *goof* knew exactly what to do: the 'past' morpheme had to be -/t/. But the same thing that sets system morphemes apart as a class—their importance to grammar— also makes it necessary to recognize forms that are no longer productive. The grammar of English has to include the past tense of all verbs in the language, not just of the ones that carry the active allomorphs -/əd t d/. How can forms like *took* from *take, sold* from *sell, blew* from *blow,* and *went* from *go* be included? Or, with the plural of nouns, how can *geese* from *goose, oxen* from *ox, insignia* from *insigne, umbones* from *umbo, sheep* from *sheep,* and *jinn* from *jinnee* be included? Many of these oddities result from a language dragging its past into its present—*oxen* is an older plural that is matched by just one other word in everyday use, *children.* Others result from foreign borrowings—for example, *data,* which is the Latin plural of *datum, stigmata,* the Greek plural of *stigma,* and *cherubim,* the Hebrew plural of *cherub.* No matter what the source, the grammar cannot overlook any form the inflections may take.

This naturally complicates the listing of allomorphs. Along with -/əz s z/, the plural morpheme must now include -/ən/ to account for *oxen,* -/ə/ to account for *insignia* (the singular is *insigne* /ɪnsɪgnɨ/), -/ɨm/ to account for *cherubim.* In cases like *jinn* and *data,* the plural represents a phonemic loss, which can be shown by representing the dropped element as "going to zero": /ɨ/ → /∅/, /m/ → /∅/. With *geese* the change to plural is internal: /u/ → /i/. With *sheep* it is nothing: /∅/. Along with each irregularity must go a list of the forms that take it, for there is no way to predict them; they are not conditioned by their neighboring sounds.

So the level of morphemes and words is different from that of distinctive sound. No such liberties are apt to be taken with allophones: phonetic similarity is a requirement. By what right, then, can it be said that a minus quantity /m/ → /∅/ for the plural *data* is the "same morpheme" as -/s/, -/z/, and -/əz/, which do resemble each other? Only the tight organization of the grammar permits it, the need to make inclusive statements about all the noun plurals in the language. It would seem unnecessary to go to such extremes anywhere else.

The one other area requiring similar measures is with some irregular forms to which the system morphemes themselves are attached. With very few exceptions (such as *wife* with its plural *wives* or *goose* with its *geese*), these irregularities are found in English only with verbs: *write-wrote, dig-dug, see-saw-seen, read-read* /rɛd/, *do-does-did-done,* and so forth.

Every language has a few such maverick stems and endings among its regular forms. As a rule, they are relics of older kinds of inflection which through extremely frequent use have managed to maintain themselves against the tendency of speakers to make things easy by leveling and regularizing everything. Thus, if the older form *fon* was regularized to its modern form *foes,* fewer people would notice the "mistake" than would notice it with a more frequently used word such as *oxen.* So one is regularized, just as children today regularize *did* to *doed,* and the other is kept in its old irregular form.

There are two ways of handling irregularities. One can simply view them as divisible semantically but not physically, saying that *dug* is *dig* + past and *children* is *child* + plural, or one can try to identify their parts, saying that *d-g* represents the stem and that /ɪ/ → /ʌ/, the change of /ɪ/ to /ʌ/, is an allomorph of the past morpheme. Such morpheme-chopping was once a popular pastime among linguists but is no longer in vogue. After all, if the word *decade* includes the meanings 'period,' 'ten,' and 'year' without making us feel compelled to identify each meaning with a physical segment of the word, it should be possible to regard *wrote* as a unit including 'to write' and 'past' without having to decide which part corresponds to which meaning.

What about the other set of system morphemes, the function words? They suffer from fewer irregularities, because they are less exposed to influences from their environment. What variations they undergo are mostly phonetic—predictable if we know the nature of the nearby sounds. Consider the allomorphs of the articles, definite and indefinite, outlined in the chart on page 62.

In *the man, the* is /ðə/; in *the ether* it is also sometimes /ðə/; in *the ox* it is /ði/; in *I don't want just any man, I want thé man for the job,* it is /ði/. There are thus three allomorphs, two of which are unaccented, with one, /ðə/, used before consonants and sometimes before the vowel /i/, and the other, /ði/, before vowels; the third, /ði/, is accented and used without regard for the following sound. (Some speakers have only two, /ðə/ and /ði/, unaccented and accented respectively; they then, as a rule, add a glottal stop after *the* whenever it appears before a vowel: *the otter* /ðəʔatər/, *the ax* /ðəʔæks/.)

The indefinite article has four allomorphs: /ə ən e æn/. The first two are unaccented, the second two accented; the first and third are used before consonants, the second and fourth before vowels: *He lives in a* /ə/ *big house; Give me an* /ən/ *orange; I don't want just á* /e/ *lawyer, I want the bést lawyer; I don't want just án* /æn/ *editor, I want the bést editor.*

ALLOMORPHS OF THE ARTICLES

the		
Unaccented	Before consonants and /i/	ðə
	Before other vowels	ði
Accented		ði
a, an		
Unaccented	Before consonants	ə
	Before vowels	ən
Accented	Before consonants	e
	Before vowels	æn

Most other function words have only two allomorphs, usually depending on whether they are accented. The normal thing is for the vowel—whatever it is—in the accented form to become schwa /ə/ in the unaccented form: *He works só-o-o* /so/ *hard!* versus *Don't work so* /sə/ *hard; It's all right, bút . . . !* /bʌt/ versus *Nobody went but* /bət/ *me; I don't know the place he went to* /tu/[5] versus *He went to* /tə/ *Chicago; What's he asking for?* /fɔr/ versus *He's asking for* /fər/ *bread; That's it!* /ɪt/ versus *Take it* /ət/ *off.* A few function words have somewhat more drastically altered allomorphs. The negative word *not* sometimes loses its vowel completely and becomes a consonant cluster attached to an auxiliary verb; the accented *I have nót* thus turns into *I haven't* /nt/. Some of the auxiliary verbs themselves, in combination with the /nt/ allomorph of *not,* take on a different allomorph even when accented: the

---

[5] Most function words at the end of a sentence take their full—non-schwa—form whether accented or not. Thus *I don't want to* has /tu/ as a rule, though sometimes schwa appears, and then a sentence like the example just quoted is often written *I do' wanna.*

/du/ of *do not* becomes the /do/ of *don't;* the /wɪl/ of *will not* becomes the /wo/ of *won't.* The verb *be* picks up the usual schwa in the *was* of *That was* /wəz/ *all right* when unaccented, but when the present-tense forms *am, is,* and *are* are unaccented they lose the vowel entirely, and this is usually shown by the spelling: *I'm ready, Mary's here, You're crazy.* The pronouns *he, him, his,* and *her* lose their /h/—for example, *he* has the allomorph /hi/ in *I'll bet hé never takes no for an answer* and the allomorph /ɨ/ in *I think he did.*[6]

Allomorphs with reduced vowels reflect the subordinate role of all system morphemes. Their job is to serve the main carriers of meaning, the "content words": to relate them, refer back to them, combine them or separate them, augment them or diminish them, substitute for them, and so on. (It is the content words that are everlastingly being added to, and they are the ones that draw on the source morphemes.) System morphemes, including function words, hover about the content words or groups of words, attaching themselves in front or behind and sometimes in the middle; they get less attention, are less clearly articulated and less frequently accented, and the reductions and losses of sounds are the consequence of their second-class citizenry.

Not that it is always easy to draw a line between content words and function words. We ordinarily think of the word *man* as a content word—certainly it is one in *Do you see that man over there?* But if in answer to *Why is he on trial?* someone says *Because he kílled a man,* de-accenting *man,* then *man* is little more than 'somebody'—it is a function word filling an otherwise empty grammatical slot, and the whole idea could just as well have been expressed with *Because he did a killing.* This is the process by which the word *body* became incorporated in *everybody, somebody,* and *nobody* and by which *-man* became an unstressed suffix in *workman.*

Dialect

If /ə ən e æn/ are just different ways of pronouncing the "same mor-pheme," then what about things like *either* pronounced /iðər/ or /ayðər/ and the word for 'dry spell' pronounced /drawθ/ and spelled *drouth* by some people but /drawt/ spelled *drought* by others? Should these variants be regarded as allomorphs too?

The answer is a matter of definition. If in describing a language a

---

[6] Function words containing diphthongs, for example *I* and *by,* are more resistant and less likely to have allophones with a reduced vowel; so for most speakers *They passed him by* and *It was written by me* both have /bay/.

linguist wants to include more than one variety of it, he can organize the variations in terms of dialectal allomorphs. (He would recognize dialectal allophones too—the ways of pronouncing or not pronouncing /r/ at the end of a syllable are a striking example.)

More will be said about dialect later. But the question of how much to include in a linguistic description calls for a bit of reflection. Every speaker has a few peculiarities of his own. These characterize his "idiolect." Every region has something that is not shared by other regions. And every age and mood has its style—a speaker may be old or young, emphatic, indifferent, domineering, subservient. Most languages have forms that differ from other forms in terms of these variables. The ideal language is a language spoken by just one person, in one frame of mind, at one time, in one place. But such a language could never be described, because some of the circumstances would change before the description was finished. Every description must be at a certain level of generality, and this is reflected in the number of variants that it embraces, whether or not they are explicitly acknowledged in the form of allo-this or allo-that. The "scale of delicacy," as British linguists term it, is infinite.

Downgrading

A language achieves near-immortality by wasting nothing, renewing and enriching itself constantly by re-using all its old material. The levels below are continually being fed by those above, somewhat like the process of decay whereby older, simpler organisms are fragmented and returned to serve as material for newer, more complex ones.

It was doubtless in this way, in some millennium long past, that a handful of once-meaningful sounds, embodying the limited repertory of ideas of a race on the threshold of multiplying its ideas and needing far more shapes of sounds to express them, were rendered meaningless in order to serve as distinctive units out of which more numerous complexes could be built: the birth first of syllables, perhaps, then of phonemes, with no sense of their own.

This reclaiming process, which can be called *downgrading*, may have happened just once in the creation of phonemes, but it goes on constantly in the sphere of source morphemes and content words. The resources for making new content words are unlimited because words themselves can be downgraded to serve as source morphemes.

Sometimes it happens accidentally. In producing sentences a speaker is not always fully conscious of the units that count as words for him. And even if he were capable of holding each one in the full glare of awareness, the same might not be true of his hearer—especially his hearer

who represents the next generation of speakers. An adult offers a child
some *little bits of* candies. For him, *little bits of* is analytically clear. For
the child, who sees merely some small candies, it is a unit, and soon the
adjective *little-bitty,* or *itty-bitty* or *itsy-bitsy* is on its way in as a synonym
of *tiny.* The words have unconsciously been downgraded to source morphemes. Goods are sold *as they are* or an article is sold *as it is,* meaning
'without guarantee,' but the practice and the name for it tend to become
set—*as is* enters as a new adverb, a single word that no longer changes
for singular and plural. It is unlikely that many speakers nowadays when
they say *old maid* think either of *old* or of *maid.* The two words that
make it up have sunk below the level of words; we no longer pause
between them unless we are deliberately being humorous: **She's an old
—uh—maid.*[7]

Often it happens intentionally. Old words are downgraded to make
new ones in a process that we have already identified as *compounding.*
It has a fairly well defined set of rules. One rule prescribes how verbs
and adverbs are joined, with a shift of stress, to make nouns: *flareup,
countdown, teach-in.* Another prescribes compounds of verb and noun,
like *killjoy, breakwater, scarecrow.* English is rich in devices for compounding. Here are some examples of compound adjectives made up in
various ways:

1. Noun plus adjective: *letter-perfect, garden-fresh, kissing-sweet.*

2. Adjective plus adjective: *icy-cold, red-hot, greenish-blue.*

3. Adjective or adverb plus participle: *low-slung, quick-frozen, easygoing, slow-running.*

4. Adjective plus noun plus -ed: *half-witted, one-eyed, old-fashioned.*

5. Adjective plus noun (related to 3 and 4 but without -ing and
   -ed): *bonehead(ed), high-class(ed), low-budget(ed), low-cost(ing),
   whole-grain(ed).*

6. Noun plus verb with -ing: *man-eating, truth-telling, heart-warming.*

7. Noun plus past participle of verb: *store-bought, heaven-sent,
   company-built.*

8. Noun plus noun plus -ed: *fish-faced, bull-headed, bow-legged.*

This does not exhaust the ways of making adjectives, and the resources
for building other compounds are just as rich.

---

[7] More examples of accidental source morphemes are given in the section on Fusion,
Chapter 7, pp. 106–07.

THE LEVEL OF SYNTAX

Speakers are rather free to apply the rules of compounding. It would cause no particular surprise to hear one person ask complainingly of another *When was his most recent goof-off?* making a noun out of what already exists as a two-word verb, *to goof off*. But if he does this very often, and particularly if he creates words for which the way has not in part already been paved, the result may sound abnormal: *The royal ship-off he got was a real emotional stir-up* might be understood but the speaker would be put down as someone with strenuous mannerisms. On the other hand *Their shipping him off so royally really stirred him up emotionally* would not surprise anyone nor would—as a third possibility—*The royal send-off he got was a real emotional shake-up.*

The difference in our reactions to these sentences stems from crossing the border between morphology and syntax. In making the first sentence the speaker was behaving as if compounds could be thrown together as freely as phrases. But compounds, like other coinages, are tied to a time and a place. When they are used again they are felt to be repeated—they are additions to our vocabulary; *send-off* and *shake-up* are now stock compounds.

Phrases, unlike words, are at the level of syntax: they can be assembled at will. None of the following contain a precise term for an astronautical landing, but any one of them is suitable for referring to it:

The astronauts touched down in the vicinity of Barbados.

The astronauts came down at 6 P.M.

The astronauts let themselves down from their capsule.

The astronauts plunged down.

The astronauts got down.

The astronauts splashed down.

The fact that other things or persons have been said to touch or slip or flop down does not bar these expressions from use with astronauts. But on the morphological side there is no such freedom. The astronauts may touch down, but this is not a *touchdown,* nor is it a *comedown* nor a *letdown.* These are *terms,* preempted for other uses. To find a term for the astronauts' landing it was necessary to look elsewhere. The splash was only incidental, but *splashdown* was chosen.

Of course, phrases and even whole sentences can be frozen and then come to resemble words, as we saw with accidental compounds like *as is.* This happens especially when an occasion is oft-repeated and its phrase or sentence keeps recurring, as with *How do you do?*, which has come to be scarcely more than a synonym of **Hello.** We would call this an idiom.

Nevertheless, the essence of syntax is freedom. It is the airiest stratum of language, where elements unite and separate in the white heat of communication. The speaker has almost unlimited means at his disposal for building sentences, provided he builds them according to certain expectations of his hearer—expectations in the form of syntactic rules. The connectedness within words is established once and then repeated. The connectedness within syntax is ad-libbed.

Relatedness

The first expectation is that things belonging together will be together. This is the concept that underlies all of syntax, which means etymologically 'a putting together.' The togetherness may be no more than a nearness in time if a message is spoken, a nearness in space if it is written; or it may be some kind of physical envelope, such as an intonation curve, that wraps one element up with another. Mere closeness in a series like **Sick John mad me** is enough to suggest a meaning—perhaps 'When John is sick I'm mad'—if the speakers know the separate meanings of the words and the meaning of the whole is a reasonable guess under the circumstances.

There is another form of relatedness which is even more fundamental, but is outside syntax. This is the relation between what is said and what it is said about. If one adolescent calls **Chicken!** to another adolescent, no syntax is needed to make the connection. Such connections are what language is mainly for. They will be discussed in Chapter 12, on Meaning.

Operators

Togetherness is a necessary but not a sufficient condition for syntax. Without something more, language would be intolerably ambiguous. Even with just three words side by side one needs to know how to rank them and group them, and as a rule we join more than three words, so that ranks over ranks and groups within groups become a necessity.

Among the traffic signals that give this information we find the familiar function words and other system morphemes, plus such other devices as characteristic types of emphasis or pause or pitch and characteristic arrangements. Together they can be called *operators*. They tell the hearer what goes with what, how close the connection is, what is subordinate to what, where an utterance begins and ends, and so on. They are language turned inward on itself.

As was noted earlier with the possessive *'s,* not all system morphemes are pure traffic signals. Some refer to facts in the real world. The same is true of other operators. Take intonation. A level span by itself at a low pitch in the middle of an utterance is an operator that marks the accompanying words as 'not belonging,' for instance the parenthetical *I wouldn't put it past him* in the sentence

If he ^{does} ^{it—}

and I ^{would}_{n't} ^{put} _{it} ^{past} _{hi}^m—he's ⁱⁿ for ^{trou} _{ble.}

But this is impure, because parentheses suggest 'unimportance' as well as grammatical 'incidentalness.' Similarly with word order: In *red brick* versus *brick red* the arrangement tells us which word is the modifier and which is the head. But in *A hundred dollars that mistake cost me!* the word order conveys an emotion; the matter-of-fact statement is *That mistake cost me a hundred dollars.*

How different operators play on different aspects of a sentence can be shown by two sets that get the same result by different means. In *I saw Mary and John together; the former was talking to the latter* the function words *former* and *latter* direct the hearer to select the first and second items just mentioned, in that order. In *I saw Mary and John together; she was talking to him* the function words *she* and *him* direct the hearer to select personal nouns with the semantic feature "female" and "male" respectively. The gross meaning of both sentences is the same.

The more complex a sentence is, the more we depend on the operators to tell us which way to go. If the operators are omitted or garbled, the total sense is lost no matter how clear the content words may be. But if the operators are preserved and nonsense words substituted for the content words, some intelligent guesses can still be made. John Algeo and Thomas Pyles illustrate both situations with the following sentences:

> Oll considerork meanork, ho mollop tharp fo concernesh bix shude largel philosophigar aspectem ith language phanse vulve increasorkrow de recent yearm engagesh sho attentuge ith scholarm.
>
> In prefarbing torming, we cannot here be pretolled with those murler dichytomical optophs of flemack which have demuggingly in arsell wems exbined the obburtion of maxans.[8]

---

[8] *Problems in the Origin and Development of the English Language* (New York: Harcourt, Brace & World, Inc., 1966), p. 244.

Though in the first sentence we recognize *consider, mean, concern,* and several other familiar words, we have no idea what to do with them. We might think of a foreign language that happened to share a number of cognates with English. But with the second we are back home; perhaps it is just from some scientific treatise in an unfamiliar field; if we met the writer on the street we could pass the time of day with him.

Word classes

Some words can replace others without changing the structure of the sentence. If A says *Joe went to Nevada* and B replies *Joe went to California,* B shows, by de-emphasizing everything except *California,* that he intends it to be the same except for that one item. Words treated in this fashion have the same function and belong in the same class. B could have replied *Joe went from Nevada,* de-emphasizing everything but *from* which belongs to the same class as *to.* Our acquaintance with word classes accounts for the half-familiar ring of the phrase *in arsell wems.* Knowing the operators, we can tell that it is a prepositional phrase and that *arsell* is probably an adjective and *wems* a plural noun. *Arsell* could be replaced by *special, inert, organic, selective,* or any one of thousands of members of its class; *wems* could be replaced by *substances, ingredients, programs, insertions,* and so on.

The traditional name for classes like these is *parts of speech,* and there would be no reason to call them anything else except that the classical parts of speech have been limited to a very few broad classes—noun, verb, adjective, adverb, pronoun, preposition, interjection, and conjunction—and the term is apt to suggest that classification stops there, when actually it must go farther.

The adverb is a good example of the over-inclusiveness of the traditional classes. It is defined in grammar books as a word that "modifies a verb, an adjective, or another adverb." Yet one can easily find adverbs that fit one form of modification and not others. Take *very: He came in very fast, It's very good,* but not *°He eats very; very* is obviously a modifier of other modifiers and not a modifier of verbs. Or consider *aside: He turned aside,* but not *°an aside tasty food; aside* modifies only verbs. Many adverbs do straddle: *He worked unnecessarily, It is unnecessarily elaborate, They stayed unnecessarily long.* But this no more justifies ignoring the differences than one can justify lumping nouns and verbs together in a single class of "nerbs," on the strength of words like *run, walk, reach, play,* and *strike,* which can belong to either part of speech.

Less obvious classes can be identified by refining the same procedures that led to identifying the obvious ones. The test is whether or not an utterance is "grammatical," and its crudest application is in terms of whether something can or cannot be said. No native speaker of English accepts a sentence like **I'm going to machinery the factory,* even though it would probably be understood to mean 'I'm going to supply the factory with machinery'; but *I'm going to equip the factory* is normal. The two sentences form a minimal pair, like the ones that were useful in testing for phonemes. They mean the same, which proves that neither is rejected because it is nonsense; and they are identical in all respects except the use of one word. The trouble must lie in the use of the word *machinery.* A test frame like this confirms the suspicion that there is at least one class of words, to which *machinery* belongs, that cannot be used in the same way as the class that includes words like *equip.* The two classes are, of course, noun and verb.

Native speakers reject many utterances that do not violate the norms of the familiar parts of speech, and these, contrasted with similar utterances that they accept, are the key to more refined classes. Most speakers of English would approve a sentence like *The truck collision damaged the cargo* but reject one like **The truck collision damaged the driver,* though both are normal in terms of the parts of speech, with a subject noun, a transitive (object-taking) verb, and an object. The rejection obviously has something to do with the verb *damage,* for one can replace it with almost any synonym and avoid trouble: *The collision hurt the cargo (the driver), The collision harmed the cargo (the driver), The cargo (The driver) suffered as a result of the collision,* and so forth. To take another example, on the surface it would appear that two verbs as closely related as *concert* and *disconcert* ought to be able to coexist in the same class, yet a similar difficulty crops up: one can say either *His uncooperative attitude disconcerted his friends* or *His uncooperative attitude disconcerted the plans,* but *They concerted their plans* is acceptable while **They concerted their friends* is not. A native speaker will soon detect what it is about *damage* and *concert* that makes them so temperamental. *Damage* is normally used with inanimate objects, not with animate ones. One can damage a car, a shipment, a reputation, a carcass, or a vital organ, but not a whole person or whole living animal: *It damaged the beef, *It damaged the cows. Concert* is normally used with abstract objects, not with concrete ones. One can concert a set of plans, arrangements, ideas, concepts, but not a set of chessmen, cartons of merchandise, or people. Since people are both animate and concrete, *damage* and *concert* are ruled out.

So it appears that there must be classes of animate nouns as distinguished from inanimate ones, and also, more than likely, classes of verbs that go only with animate or inanimate nouns, since the verb *damage* is not likely to be unique. It also appears that there must be classes of abstract and concrete nouns with their corresponding verbs. And there must be a good deal of overlapping between these classes, as the broader acceptability of *harm* and *hurt* seems to prove.

Unfortunately, what can or cannot be said, taken alone, is not a reliable test of grammatical classes. Speakers have more than one reason for rejecting utterances and it is often hard to tell them apart. Both *The eraser magnified the driver* and *The eraser magnified the cargo* are sure to be rejected. Is it because there is a class of nouns naming things that can be magnified, to which *driver* and *cargo* do not belong, or perhaps a class naming things that can magnify, to which *eraser* does not belong? Pursuing this line of reasoning might lead to a class of nouns including *microscope, reading glass, lens, beer bottle,* and a few more that could occupy the subject slot in *X magnified Y*—nouns that have nothing in common that is not shared by *eraser* except the fact that all can go with this one verb. Nothing much could be said about the object slot—one can magnify a picture, a tree, a star, a fear, or a passion. Such clues to classes are a blind alley. Apparently the basis for rejection here is different. It is *semantic incompatibility.* We chew with organs of mastication, kill with what is deadly, and magnify with what is capable of magnifying. *The eraser magnified* is rejected because the meanings—the semantic features —of *eraser* and *magnify* are not congruent with each other.

Semantic incompatibility is different from ungrammaticalness. The first depends on the meanings of individual words, the second on the behavior of classes of words. Every word has a set of features: *semantic* features, which are its individual meanings as a dictionary would define them, and *grammatical* features, which are the labels of the classes and subclasses to which it belongs. The word *boy* has "young" and "male" among its semantic features, "noun" and "countable" among its grammatical features ("countable" means that it can be pluralized: compare *poems* versus *poetries*).

If behaving as a class is what distinguishes classes, then grammatical features ought to be statements of how classes behave toward one another. One set of features of verbs should be the ways they relate to nouns. And since relationships are made explicit by system morphemes and other operators, these can be used in part to mark the classes.

So we find that the class "verb" is marked by the various ways in which its members react to system morphemes. If a word form is a verb, the following will be true, almost without exception:

1. Either it will carry no inflectional morpheme at all (this is true of the imperative or infinitive) or it will carry one of these four: past, perfective (usually *-ed* or *-en,* as in *has studied, had stolen*), third-singular present (*-s* in *works*), and *-ing* (*working*).

2. It accepts *to* and the auxiliaries *can, may, will*, and so on, before it when in the uninflected form *(to work, can work)*.

3. It has an emphatic form with *do* or *did (He does like it, He did go there)*.

More could be added, though additional hedging would be required.

Once the first class is established, others can be referred to it. Thus the features of nouns include, besides their own behavior toward system morphemes (being modified by *the* or *a*, taking as a rule some plural ending, being normally required as the last member of a prepositional phrase, and so on), a relationship of concordance with verbs: when a noun picks up a plural ending, the verb following it loses its third-singular ending if it had one: *The girl talks, The girls talk.* Adjectives in turn have their own acceptances of system morphemes plus a relation to nouns. The scheme interlocks so tightly that most classes can be identified in a variety of ways, which leaves no doubt that they exist in the language and in the minds of speakers.

Subordinate classes have fewer distinguishing marks. The class of verbs that take inanimate objects—including, besides *damage*, such verbs as *devalue, invest, publish, cash, leach, unfurl, prorogue*, and so on—reacts in a characteristic way with the function words called pronouns: *it* may be used as their object, but not *him, her, me*, or *us*. There is a class of "human" verbs, however, that can take these pronouns but not *it: convince, persuade, convict, amuse, anger, dishearten*.[9]

Other marks of classes

English almost never marks its classes by some peculiarity of internal form. To imagine what this would be like, we could think of some sound that always appeared with nouns but never with any other class of words—say, a doubling of the first vowel and insertion of a glottal stop, so that a verb *walk* would be matched by a noun *waʔalk*, a verb *interest* by a noun *iʔinterest*, an adjective *green* by a noun *greʔeen*, and so on. (Something like this happens in Neapolitan, where countable nouns may have single initial consonants after the word for 'the' but uncountable ones have double consonants: *o lupo* 'the wolf' but *o llate* 'the milk.'[10]

---

[9] An exception, referring to a baby, might be *I can't amuse it—see if you can.* But here *it* is replaceable by *him* or *her*.

[10] James E. Iannucci, *Lexical Number in Spanish Nouns* (Philadelphia: University of Pennsylvania Press, 1952), p. 15.

One would welcome this as proof that speakers have a genuine feel for the class. Instead, classes are marked only indirectly by the potential for combining with system morphemes or by their behavior toward one another. Nevertheless, there is at least one small tendency toward internal marking. Many verbs have final syllables that are more prominent than the final syllables of related nouns and adjectives—when the words have more than one syllable, that is. The last syllable of the adjective *intimate* has a reduced vowel, -/ət/; that of the verb *to intimate* is full, -/et/. The same change occurs in the noun-verb *prophecy* (verb spelled -*sy*) and the noun-verb *supplement*. With the noun-verb *discharge* and the noun-verb *address,* the complete shift of stress to the last syllable makes the difference all the more striking. Not all speakers agree on all items (with *graduate,* for example, some make the distinction noted here, others use -/et/ for both noun and verb), but for many of us there is a reshuffling whereby more and more nouns and verbs are distinguished in this way— a speaker who started out saying *to mánifest* may find himself saying *to manifést.* This tendency has become most entrenched in the *teach ín* (verb) versus *téach-in* (noun) contrast. In itself it is little more than a curiosity in the present stage of English, but it does prove the reality of the class—speakers seem to have a feel for "verbness."

Syntax and invention

If the traffic department of a large modern city wants to find out in the most painless way whether some proposed change in the direction, signaling, speed, number of lanes, and lane width of a flow of traffic will move the cars and trucks more smoothly or jam them up, it resorts to a simulation: the conditions are pre-set and a computer sends pretended vehicles along imaginary streets to reproduce the movements and interferences that would occur in reality. It is not necessary to erect the signals, re-route the lanes, and alter the face of the city to find out whether or not the new arrangement will work.

The mechanism of syntax is like the computer. In our advance scheming for good and bad ends, we try out alternatives in a simulated program to see how close we can come to predicting what the results would be if the plans were actually carried out. In part this is possible because we can pre-set the words in the program and then sit back and watch the fun. Will the semantic features clash or blend? Will they weave themselves into amusing or startling or suggestive patterns? What we think of as the free play of ideas is to some extent pure frolicking with the semantic features of words, which the syntax of our language permits us to do.

The bars to incompatibility then are let down—but not, as a rule, those of ungrammaticalness, which correspond to the built-in characteristics of the computer: you punch this button first and turn this crank last, because the machine is made that way; but within those limits you can go where you please.

Dreams are perhaps the extreme of this free-wheeling use of language—the restraints on semantic features are lowered but most of the grammatical ones remain intact. One attested dream sequence was the following: *How to write* (not *ride*) *a creeping doorcan bicycle.* Everything here is according to rule—*how to* is a normal beginning for a set of directions, *write* follows in the normal spot for a verb, the *-ing* form *creeping* is used in its normal way as a modifier, *doorcan* is a normal compound on the order of *doorway* or *ashcan* used normally as a modifier, and *bicycle* occupies the normal slot for the noun. The design of poetry is similar, except that it is contrived and not random. The poet may even alter some of the less secure grammatical features. He is not concerned that the verb *unfurl* takes inanimate objects when he describes a lanky and attitudinizing man as *unfurling himself.*

Being able to "think together" things that do not belong together is a first step to invention. The verb *to fly* has as one of its semantic features the possession of wings. Human beings have no wings, but that was no bar to simulating them verbally and in the end concretely.

Tagmemes and syntagmemes[11]

Classes of words exist to perform functions. Some classes perform only one. There is a class of correlative conjunctions, a very small class, including just the two words *and* and *or* (perhaps *either, neither, nor,* and *whether* should be added too), that serves just one purpose; to join together elements of equal rank. Usually the two things joined are themselves members of a single class: *Mary and John,* two nouns; *to be or not to be,* two verbs; *It's slimy and wet,* two adjectives.

More often, a class performs two or more functions. Then it becomes necessary to name the syntactic operations both in terms of the class that performs the function and the function that it performs. In a sentence like *The man saw the boy, the man* performs one function, that of subject, and *the boy* another, that of direct object. Both are nouns: an

---

[11] These terms are used here in a more restricted way—to apply just to grammar—than they are used by such writers as Pike and Longacre. See, for example, Robert E. Longacre, "Some Fundamental Insights of Tagmemics," *Language* 41.65–76 (1965), especially pp. 70–71.

equally correct sentence is *The boy saw the man.* To describe these sentences, it is necessary to recognize noun-as-subject and noun-as-direct-object. In the sentence *The father gave the man his daughter, father* is noun-as-subject, *daughter* is noun-as-direct-object, and *man* is noun-as-indirect-object.

The combination of class and function is sometimes called a slot-class correlation, and the term for it is *tagmeme.* Tagmemes are the particles of syntax. The adjective in *one sure thing, one thing sure,* and *The thing is sure* occurs in three different tagmemes, since each of those positions represents a different function—the meanings are not the same. The adverb *clearly* in *Clearly he can't see* and *He can't see clearly* occurs in two tagmemes: adverb-as-sentence-modifier and adverb-as-verb-modifier.

As with other levels, particles are ranged in strings. A typical string in syntax is noun-as-subject plus verb plus noun-as-object: *Monkeys love bananas.* Syntactic strings are called *syntagmemes,* that is, tagmemes taken together. Besides noun-as-subject plus verb plus noun-as-object, a number of other simple sentence syntagmemes can be mentioned: noun-as-subject plus verb *(The prisoners escaped)*; noun-as subject plus linking verb plus adjective-as-complement *(Lead is soft)*; interrogative-pronoun-as-complement plus linking verb plus noun-as-subject *(Who is that man?,* an inversion of *That man is John).*

Syntagmemes are the different syntactical patterns that a language provides for. Besides sentence syntagmemes there are subordinate syntagmemes, like noun phrases and prepositional phrases. In the prepositional phrase *by the author* we find an additional noun tagmeme: noun-as-prepositional-object. In the noun phrase *the visible stars* we find adjective-as-premodifier, whereas in the noun phrase *the stars visible* we find adjective-as-postmodifier: the functions are different because normally the first means 'stars whose magnitude is great enough to make them visible,' while the second means 'stars that can be seen because conditions (the weather, for example) are favorable.'

Identical tagmemes can be arranged in different syntagmemes. The result then "means the same" but the "style" is different: *I didn't see John* and *John I didn't see* contain the same noun-as-direct-object, but it occurs at the end of the first sentence and at the beginning of the second. *The gate is strait* and *Strait is the gate* are different syntagmemes with identical tagmemes in reverse order.

Phrasing and embedding

The most remarkable thing about syntax is its power to use the resources of tagmemes and syntagmemes to expand the syntactical classes and make each one reflect all the others in a potentially infinite regression, like a hall of mirrors. With this power—termed *recursive power*—the class of "noun" is freed from the list of nouns that a dictionary can enumerate more or less exhaustively and is expanded to include syntagmemes of various kinds—for example:

> *Noun phrase:* **Your early arrival** would be no surprise to me.
>
> *Infinitive phrase:* **For you to arrive early** would be no surprise to me.
>
> *Gerund phrase:* **Your arriving early** would be no surprise to me.
>
> *Clause:* **That you should arrive early** would be no surprise to me.

Similarly, the class "adjective" can be expanded to include *-ing* phrases, infinitive phrases, prepositional phrases, and clauses:

> The only river *navigable* is to the north.
>
> The only river *permitting navigation* is to the north.
>
> The only river *to be trusted for navigation* is to the north.
>
> The only river *for navigating* is to the north.
>
> The only river *that is navigable* is to the north.

This expansion of classes into strings can be called *phrasing.*

Phrasing throws the doors of language open to utterances of indefinite length by the process of *embedding.* Embedding follows automatically from phrasing in that, if a string can replace a class, the classes in that string can be replaced by other strings, their classes by still other strings, and so on:

> I went {yesterday}
>
> I went {after [somebody] telephoned me}
>
> I went {after [somebody (special)] telephoned me}
>
> I went {after [somebody (that I really wanted to see)] telephoned me}
>
> I went {after [somebody (that I really wanted to see/right then/)] telephoned me}
>
> I went {after [somebody (that I really wanted to see/as soon as I could/)] telephoned me}

There is no linguistic limit to the process, though there may be a psychological one. Most readers are annoyed at having to thread their way through embeddings as complicated as the following:

> For literary works may not vent ideas of importance if punishment of suppression be the author's or publisher's reward from juries of average

men instructed to cast a ballot of indictment upon their judgment as to whether a particular work is patently offensive to, and appeals to the prurient interests of, other average men.[12]

The study of syntax has been developing so fast in the past decade that no faithful picture of it can be drawn; the outlines change as the words are written. This section has afforded only a glimpse, from one point of view. More will be said later, when the time comes to speak of other linguistic theories (Chapter 11).

---

[12] Forty-third Annual Report, American Civil Liberties Union, June 30, 1963.

ADDITIONAL REMARKS
AND APPLICATIONS

1. When a word is used as a sentence, what elements must be added? Compare *absolutely* and *Yes I do, sir,* when spoken as follows:

$$\text{Ab}\,_{\text{so}}^{\text{lute}}\,_{\text{ly.}} \qquad \text{Yes}\,_{\text{I}}^{\text{do,}}\,_{\text{sir.}}$$

What do they have in common?

2. Test the following for the possibility of inserting hesitation sounds: *We told him to put out the lights but he didn't want to.* (It is better to repeat the whole sentence and insert only one pause at a time; otherwise the impression is distorted.) Besides *put out* is there another pair of words that is difficult, if not impossible, to break up?

3. Would you regard *mother-in-law* as a single word? What is its plural? What does this tell you about elements that can be inserted in such compound words? Is it significant that many speakers resist this and say *mother-in-laws*? Comment on the following, which is from a letter by one college professor to another: *Three potent bourbon and sodas are worth more than these few words.* Comment also on this, from a magazine: *seven Assistant Attorney Generals.*[13]

4. Cite some examples of acronyms or other words that appear to have been made up directly from sounds.

5. Comment on the scholarly outrage that greeted the proposal of a well-known linguist to call the unit of grammar a *grammeme.* (To find what was objected to, look up the primary meanings of *gram* and *graph* and compare *telegram, diagram, monogram, gramophone.*) Is this kind of purism justified?

6. Derivation has many uses, but the two commonest ones are to make

---

[13] *Harper's Magazine*, August, 1963, p. 73.

words in one category do service in another and to add various adverb-like meanings. Suffixes are generally used in English for the first, prefixes for the second. By putting suffixes on the noun *ghost,* the adjectives *ghostly* and *ghostlike* were made. By putting prefixes on *do,* the semantically modified verbs *undo* and *redo* were made. Give examples of suffixes used to make nouns from adjectives and verbs from nouns. Identify some words using the prefixes *dis-, pre-,* and *counter-.*

Compounds are bits of condensed syntax. *Roadblock* is 'something to block a road'; *carfare* is 'fare for a car.' Define *fishface, stumblebum, crowbait.*

7. Discuss the following as examples of the additiveness or non-additiveness of morphemes (you may need to look up the etymologies): *atone, whisker, rubber, sweater, selvage, lusty, lustful.* Note the realignment of syllables in *a-tone* and the shift of stress and change of suffix in *mischievous* as pronounced *mischiévious* by many people. What do morphological changes like these suggest about the submerged nature of many morphemes?

8. In some colleges and universities a regularly scheduled examination lasting an hour is called an *hourly exam* (calling it an *hour exam* or a *one-hour exam* would fail to suggest 'regular schedule'). Does this conform to the usual meaning of *-ly* as applied to *day, month, year,* and so on? Is the notion of 'schedule' present in the latter? Compare the twisting of *-ly* in *hourly* with the twisting of *-ee* in *escapee.*

9. The unlimited use of *the* with almost any common noun in English is an example of the freedom we have within the rules of syntax. How does this compare with the freedom within the rules for making words? English makes adjectives meaning 'having the quality of' by adding *-ly* to nouns. Pick out the ones from the following list that seem normal to you and comment on the discrepancies: *princely, kingly, presidently, husbandly, wifely, manly, childly, womanly, soldierly, sailorly, Christianly, Mohammedanly, sonly, unclely, fatherly, brotherly, auntly, daughterly.*

10. For each example below, give another using the same inflection.
    a. Possession in nouns: *mother-in-law's*
    b. Number in nouns: *churches*
    c. Pastness in verbs: *lived*
    d. Perfectivity in verbs: *stolen, kidnapped*

    e. Third-singular present in verbs: *browses*

    f. Imperfectivity in verbs: *selling*

    g. Comparison in adjectives: *finer, finest.*

11. Is there a difference between elements that may be attached in front (for example, a function word such as *the* or a source-morpheme prefix such as *pre-*) and elements that are attached in back (any suffix, including of course the inflections) in the readiness with which they may be contrastively accented? See if you can make up sentences in which the prefixes *un-, in-, anti-, pro-, dis-, counter-,* and *ex-* are contrastively accented. Try it with the suffixes *-ful* and *-less.*

12. How do dictionaries usually treat source morphemes and system morphemes? Would you expect to find separate entries for *work, works,* and *worked?* For *break, fast,* and *breakfast?*

13. List the allomorphs of the plural morpheme in the following words (remember that what counts is sound, not spelling): *trail, ditch, mouse, man, workman, face, desk, alga, analysis.* Do some words have different plurals depending on the sense? What are the usual plurals of (radio) *antenna* and *antenna* (of an insect)?

14. Make a rule for the allomorphs of the possessive morpheme in English, as in *Pat's, the man's, Sis's, Butch's, Madge's.* Express your rule in terms of which allomorph is preceded by which phoneme, and group the phonemes (for example, /m/ and /r/ are both voiced).

15. Assuming it to be worthwhile to describe the allomorphs of a borrowed form, state those of the negative prefix inherited from Latin in *inability, incredible, insensitive, impossible, impersonal, illiberal, illegal, irregular,* and *irresponsible.* How does the native English prefix *un-* compare with this?

16. Comment on the allomorph of the negative *not* in *mustn't, shouldn't, needn't.* What happens with *shall not?* Name other instances of the "contraction" of *not.*

17. If instead of *Why is he on trial? Because he killed a man* we had *Why is he on trial? Because he killed an orphan,* would it be possible to de-accent *orphan?* Try *guy, child, fellow, person,* and *sailor* in the same slot.

18. Are we as a rule mentally aware of the separate meanings of the components in *shortcoming, plaything, upper-case* (letter), *motor-*

cycle, nevertheless, sleight-of-hand, and *man-of-war?* Find other similar examples.

19. Make a rule for the formation of noun compounds like *man-eater, housebreaker, storyteller, bookmaker, letter carrier.* Does the way we write these compounds sometimes suggest how far the downgrading of the component words has gone?

20. Does English syntax have a rule that permits prepositional phrases to modify nouns by standing in front of them? Compare *the money on the table* and *the on the table money.* Does English morphology have a rule that makes compounds out of some prepositional phrases, which can then come before the noun? Consider forms like *an out-of-the-way place, an under-the-counter sale, an off-the-record remark, an after-the-fact requisition, a no-account (of-no-account) person.* Find other examples.

21. Do we find partial downgrading in *Leave me alone* 'Don't bother me' and *Never fear* 'Don't worry'? Find other examples of such idioms—complete sentences with a meaning that deviates from the sum of the meanings of the parts.

22. Identify the operators that distinguish the following: *Italian red wine* versus *red Italian wine; You either work or pay* versus *You both work and pay; Did he ask for me or John?* answered *Yes* versus *Did he ask for me or John?* answered *John; If he likes it he eats it* versus *Because he likes it he eats it.*

23. Write a passage of about thirty words. Omit the function words and give it to someone else to fill in the blanks. Rewrite it, this time omitting the content words, and give it to someone else to fill in words that make sense. Which task is more difficult? *Dah!*

24. What do *He did it easy, We showed him up good, They talk pretty* suggest about the classes of adjective and adverb for the speakers who regularly use such forms? How would you describe the resulting class?

25. Would the sentence *If he were a frequent visitor I'd understand, but I'm afraid he's only a seldom* be intelligible? What is wrong with it?

26. Is the sentence *The collision wounded the cargo* grammatical? If not, what is wrong with it in terms of word classes?

27. Are there words that overlap even the major parts of speech? Con-

sider *fast* in *He ran fast* and *a fast trip.* How many different things does the word *more* appear to be in the following?

> *He's more than winning.*
> *They ran more than fast.*
> *I'll give you more than trouble.*
> *He's more than just ugly.*

(Look for the parts of speech of the words with which *more* is compared.) Would it be easy to decide when *each* changes from noun to adverb in the following?

> *Each had five.*
> *John and I each had five.*
> *John and I had five each (= John and I had five apiece).*

28. Assuming that one of the following is rejected because it is ungrammatical and the other because it is an instance of semantic incompatibility, which is which?

> **Cows molt in the summertime.*
> **I convinced the bookshelf.*

29. Name two semantic and two grammatical features of the word *woman.* Does it differ from *lady* in terms of grammatical or semantic features?

30. If English verbs show a tendency to make the last syllable prominent, do English nouns show the opposite tendency? How do you pronounce the following when they are used as compound nouns: *hole in the head, free for all, pain in the neck, go-getter, down payment, meat loaf, apple pie?* (Not all speakers agree on these; compare *castor oil* and *olive oil.*)

31. Is the dreamed word sequence *a three-slip onion spout* grammatical? Give a semantically compatible sequence that has the same grammatical pattern.

32. Compare *Happily the play ended, The play ended happily,* and *The play ended, happily.* Do two of them contain the same tagmemes?

33. What do *He hurt himself crossing the street, He hurt himself when he was crossing the street, He hurt himself on crossing the street,* and *He hurt himself then* illustrate?

THE EVOLUTION OF 6
LANGUAGE: COURSES, FORCES, SOUNDS, AND SPELLINGS

A FEW HOURS in the life of any speaker of English will turn up curiosities like the following:

He himself is on the point of saying *No talking aloud* and changes it to *No talking out loud.* Even though he ordinarily favors *aloud,* he realizes after the words are out that he was afraid of its being misunderstood for *allowed.*

He hears a six-year-old say *Why do I have my hand be-back of me?* and puzzles over it until he realizes that somehow or other the child has managed to combine and rearrange the expressions *behind* and *in back of.*

He reads in the newspaper that thirty adult bicyclists "showed up last Sunday in the sunshine and sailed off on an 8.3-mile *sojourn* with only one tandem in the group." Momentary perplexity gives way to the realization that the writer thought that a sojourn was some kind of journey, a slow one most likely, right for a bicycle.

He sees in a magazine the phrase that he had always visualized as *still and all* but had never seen written, only now it is spelled *still in all.* He realizes that for the meaning 'nevertheless' this spelling makes more sense, and wonders how he could have been so unobservant.

These little events and millions like them are language in the process of change. Whether or not they add up to anything depends on how many people they affect. If enough of us are bothered by the confusion between *aloud* and *allowed,* a word may be lost. If enough are unwary, *sojourn* may actually adopt its illegitimate sense. It is not likely that anyone will imitate *be-back of,* but *still and all* is typical of countless phrases that become stereotyped in meaning and lose the significance of their individual parts, thus creating new words.

CUMULATIVE CHANGES

There is no question that language changes. But does it *evolve?* Evolution implies more than innumerable heterogeneous collisions, most of them canceling one another out. It implies a drift, a direction, almost a purpose. But our lives are too short for us to see this going on before us. Only rarely do we glimpse in a series of changes the tokens of some larger shift. One example is what continues to happen to the adjective forms based on the names of our states. We no longer call peanuts grown in Virginia *Virginian peanuts,* though we unhesitatingly call pineapple grown in Hawaii *Hawaiian pineapple.* An earthquake in California is never a *Californian earthquake,* though one in Alaska might be called an *Alaskan earthquake.* The *Iowan landscape* is impossible, but the *New Mexican landscape* seems natural. What we are witnessing is a gradual restriction of these adjectives to the status of names of the state's inhabitants: an Iowan, a Californian, a Virginian. With the newest states this has not yet been fully accomplished. A few generations ago we spoke of *Californian gold* just as we speak of *African gold* today.

But if it is hard to see what linguistic change is doing now, it is easy to see what it has done in the past. Reading a speech delivered fifty or sixty years ago, we are aware that a lot of windiness has gone out of public addresses. Reading the King James version of the Bible, and experiencing difficulties with some of its passages, we appreciate the changes in words and structure that have taken place in a little over three centuries. Most of all, when we are told that our own ancestors and those of the Germans spoke the same language, we can see the great cleavage that results when two streams of evolution are set in different directions.

The job of the comparative linguist is to measure and codify change. This he does by comparing a language with its earlier stages and with other languages or dialects. The first is now possible only where there are written records, though future linguists will have at their disposal the recordings that we are able to make of live speech. Where the record shows, as we read it backwards, that English, say, comes to resemble German more and more, and the German record in reverse shows an increasing resemblance to English, the conclusion has to be that the two languages were once the same. This tracing of languages into genealogical trees is the branch of scientific linguistics that developed first and has gone farthest. Much that could not be read in the record can nevertheless be inferred theoretically, with the result that a good deal is known about many prehistoric or "proto" languages of which there is no record at all.

The existence of systematic kinships among words in widely scattered languages suggests how this sort of projection backward in time is made possible. Two such word families, proving that Greek, Latin, Sanskrit, Germanic, and Slavic are all descendants of a single original language or group of dialects, are those with the meanings 'brother' and 'eat'; note their similarities in the following table.[1]

Greek	phrå̄tēr	édomai
Latin	fräter	edō
Sanskrit	bhrå̄tā	ád-mi
Old English (representing Germanic)	brōðor	etan
Old Church Slavonic	bratŭ	jadętŭ ('they eat')

Using such correspondences, comparative grammarians have reconstructed the parent language, Proto-Indo-European, and certain intermediate languages of which there was also no written record, such as Proto-Germanic. Now and then an archaeological find brings to light some written record that confirms and corrects the theoretical constructs. Greek scholars were until recently confined to the texts of Classical Greek and to inscriptions in theorizing about what the language was like in the centuries before Homer. In 1952, many of their suppositions were confirmed with the decipherment of tablets from Knossus and Mycenae inscribed in a form of writing that had been called Linear B and that no one before had seriously taken to be Greek. These tablets extended the written record of Greek to 1450 B.C., four hundred years before the earliest date attributed to Homer.[2]

---

[1] This outline and the one on page 86 are adapted from Winfred P. Lehmann, *Historical Linguistics* (New York: Holt, Rinehart and Winston, Inc., 1963), pp. 89 and 84.

[2] See Chapter 10, pp. 172–76.

The *comparative method,* as the tracing of kinships is called, can be illustrated by one instance on the large scale of Proto-Indo-European and by another on the smaller scale of Proto-Romance (Vulgar Latin). In both cases, the first step consists in setting side by side the obviously related forms of two or more sister languages. Suppose we want to reconstruct the verb *to be* in Proto-Indo-European. We proceed to match the forms of this verb in widely separated branches of the Indo-European family.

	Sanskrit	Lithuanian	Greek	Gothic
'I am'	ásmi	ēsmi	eimí	im
'he is'	ásti	ēsti	ésti	ist
'we are'	smás	ēsme	esmén	sijum

(The Latin student will recognize *sum, est,* and *sumus* as exponents of this same set.) It seems obvious that forms so closely related must stem from a common ancestor, and the problem is to devise hypothetical forms that will yield each of these descendants in accordance with what is known about the historical changes in each language. If Proto-Indo-European had had the forms *ésmi, ésti,* and *smés,* these would have developed into the forms given in the table. Each change from the original is confirmed by what is known about other words—for example, all instances of assumed *e* in Proto-Indo-European have *a* in Sanskrit. There is no way to confirm the deductions positively, since Proto-Indo-European has left no records. But it is safe to say that a great deal is known about the phonemic structure of the language, if not about how the phonemes were pronounced. With Proto-Romance we are in a better position because of the abundant literature of Classical Latin. The ancestor language of the present Romance tongues of the southern half of Europe was not Classical Latin, but it resembled Classical Latin so closely that when a form reconstructed—projected backward in time—on the basis of known Romance forms is found to agree with a Classical Latin form or differ from it in ways that can be accounted for, it is substantially confirmed. An example is the word for the human *chest* in the Romance languages: Sardinian *pettus,* Rumanian *piépt,* Italian *pétto,* Rhaeto-Romance (Northeast Italy and Switzerland) *péč,* Old North French *píc,* Old Provençal *piéits,* Catalan *pít,* Old Spanish *pečos.* Positing a Proto-

Romance *péktus* will account for all these in terms of the regular sound changes in each language, and *péktus* also coincides with the Classical Latin *pektus*.[3]

One way of viewing the history of languages is deceptively simple: to take genealogy literally and diagram the developments as a genealogical tree. One diagram that has been offered for the parent stock that underlies our present Germanic languages looks like this:

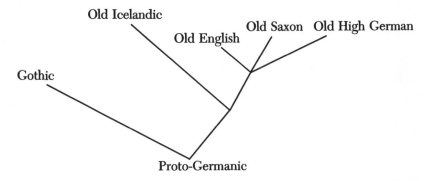

ADAPTED FROM Charles Hockett, *A Course in Modern Linguistics* (New York: Macmillan Co., 1958), p. 519. Other diagrams, p. 520, reinterpret the same data as wavelike changes.

The tree is misleading because it suggests an abrupt separation. Our knowledge of the dialects that make up every living language tells us that the seeds of change are present even while speakers are still in active communication with one another. The striking differences between Northern and Southern dialects in our own country are sometimes inconvenient, but they do not, as a rule, seriously interfere with understanding. But let a break occur in the channel—a political separation, a migration, an incursion of a hostile people that bisects the territory and cuts off one area from another—and the resulting isolation removes the checks on independent development. What were once dialects become mutually unintelligible languages.

The tree is misleading in another sense. It suggests that until a separation occurs the language remains uniform. Change, however, is unceasing. There is about as much difference between Modern English and Old English as between Modern English and Modern Dutch, despite a distance of more than a thousand years. Languages do not always diverge

---

[3] Adapted from Robert A. Hall, Jr., *Introductory Linguistics* (Philadelphia: Chilton Books, 1964), p. 306.

from one another any faster than they change internally. Often they develop along more or less parallel lines; two languages may tend in the course of their history to lose a complicated set of inflections and so come to resemble each other more, at least in that respect, than either resembles an earlier period of itself. Moreover, always in the past and increasingly in the present, commercial and other contacts have been maintained, and the network of international communication bends all branches inward.

FORCES OF CHANGE

Never a word spoken but language becomes a bit different from what it was, however microscopically. What we say displaces what we might have said and strengthens those words at the expense of others. Not even the same sounds in the same setting are ever quite the same twice; each minute difference erodes a phonetic atom here or there. We ourselves are creatures in flux. We have marvelous memories, keen hearing, and agile tongues—virtues that make language possible. But each of these has its fault. At times our memories are short, our hearing is bad, and our speech organs are clumsy. The resulting damage is always repaired somehow, but things are not quite the same afterward.

Not all the forces of change are within us. Some are imposed from without. A convicted man is thrown into a prison which has strict rules forbidding conversation at certain periods. He soon acquires the habit of speaking out of the side of his mouth and suppressing the movement of his lips. This distorts the sounds of his vowels and his labial consonants, /p b m f v/. There is little danger that prison life will affect the language of those on the outside, but similar drastic changes in the life of a society do have their effects. When the Norman invasion brought to English many words containing the phoneme /v/—*vile, very, vale, vain, venial, venom*— English altered its phonetic system just enough to turn the sound of [v], which it already had as an allophone of /f/, into a new phoneme. The same thing happened with /z/.[4] Over the past two centuries we have seen more and more professionalization of writing and speaking. Instead of standing up ourselves in town meeting and putting our views in vocal prose that has to be coherent to be convincing, we now delegate our

---

[4] Josef Vachek, "On the Internal and External Determination of Sound-laws," *Biuletynu PTJ* 23.53–54.

fluency to our elected representatives. Instead of remembering stories to retell to our children, we read to them from books, an activity that calls for the mental and linguistic capacities of a phonograph needle. Or we quite literally delegate the task to the phonograph. Instead of composing his own speeches, the public man hires a ghostwriter. A verbal description of a scene is wearisome to many modern readers habituated to the cheap and easy visualizations of television. These substitutes for individual control of language may be less calamitous than they sound, but they must somehow leave their mark.

Other forces of change are neither within nor without, but in the language mechanism itself. When we speak, several things go on at the same time. We organize our sentences into patterns of sound that signal to the hearer how he is to decode them so as to represent the individual words and their connections in his mind. To this we add an intonation contour, with peaks of accent, to convey our feelings and our sense of the important. Around this we wrap a gestural envelope: a facial expression is often our only clue to the difference between a statement and a question. Sometimes these levels interfere with one another. As we saw in Chapter 2, the [p] of *yep* and *nope* is the result of shutting the mouth in self-satisfied finality at the end of an utterance. The gesture affects the word. Someone who says *Now wa-a-it a MIN-ute!* makes his sentence more spirited by putting an extra accent on *minute* even though there is no question of 'minute, not second'—the normal way of saying *Wait a minute* is with only one accent, on *wait.* Since most English words have a fixed or lexical stress, this example illustrates a certain amount of friction between the lexical level—the forms of words—and the intonational level—the orchestration of sentences to make them sound effective. The result is like what happens when someone tries to eat and speak at the same time; the same organs are involved in both activities and each must yield a bit. One characteristic of intonational rhythm in English is that of placing a major accent close to the end of a sentence. Sometimes this leads to alternating pronunciations of the same word or even—with words most often used at the end of a phrase—to a permanent change. Take the suffix *-able.* Though normally when added to a verb it does not shift the stress *(permít, permíssible; cúltivate, cúltivatable; mínimize, mínimizable),* a good many speakers tend to move the stress to the right in longer forms, especially those with *-ize* or *-fy: réalize, realízable; vérify, verifíable; idéntify, identifíable.*

It is impossible to enumerate, let alone treat, all the forces of inner and outer change. All that can be done, in this chapter and the two following ones, is to identify some of the major forces and explain their effects.

BORROWING

Languages are contagious. No two can come in contact without a swift interchange between them, though the direction of the traffic is controlled to some extent by rules of prestige. The speaker of a language regarded for any reason as socially or culturally superior does not feel under any compulsion to learn a contact language regarded as inferior, though he may condescend to pick up an occasional word that saves him the trouble of inventing one himself. That is often the fate of contact languages that have been brought low by conquest. English shows little trace of the dozens of Indian languages that were once—and in many cases still are—spoken between the Atlantic and Pacific, except for the numerous geographical names such as *Mississippi, Oklahoma, Topeka,* and *Shawnee,* and a few names for material objects like *tobacco, chocolate, hammock, potato, skunk, raccoon, lagniappe*—and even these were often taken from French or Spanish, which had borrowed them first. Nothing so deep within the structure of the language as a pronoun or a verb ending or a phoneme or a particular order of words was affected in any serious way. On the other hand, borrowings *from* English in the lands under British and American rule have been vast, if not devastating. Words have been taken up wholesale, and here and there the deeper levels have been affected. In Chamorro, the language spoken on Guam, the phoneme /r/ has been introduced from English, as have certain consonant clusters that were not previously permitted and shifts of accent to vowels that could not formerly carry it.[5] In the Sicilian spoken in the United States, similar changes have taken place in the phonemic system, and other changes have occurred as well; for example, borrowed nouns and verbs have been limited to a few grammatical classes whose size is thereby swollen, and word order has been influenced by the borrowing of many adjectives that invariably precede the noun.[6] (Of course, the English of these speakers is drastically affected too. Most often, such "corrupted" English is only a transition to a full command of the language by the next generation of speakers; but now and then—as in India—it may settle down to a life of its own. Everything depends on how much contact there is with speakers of standard dialects.)

These changes sound more sweeping than they are. As long as a language is spoken, its core remains largely impervious to the direct impact of borrowings from another language, which is just another way of saying

---

[5] Donald M. Topping, "Loanblends: a Tool for Linguists," *Language Learning* 12:4.281–287 (1962).

[6] Robert J. Di Pietro, "Borrowing: Its Effect as a Mechanism of Linguistic Change in American Sicilian," *General Linguistics* 5:30–36 (1961).

that the core *is* the language and that the new words that stud its outer layer have only incidentally been mined from some other language and could just as well have been taken from pure imagination, as long as they satisfied the need of the speaker to name new things and concepts. The core may eventually be eaten into, but usually that only occurs when the collision of two languages is a part of the collision of two cultures, one of the effects of which is to accelerate other forces of change.

The deepest penetration occurs when two languages coexist on an almost equal footing, in such intimate contact that large numbers of speakers on both sides find it convenient to become bilingual. The Norman conquerors of England ended by speaking the language of the conquered, considerably modified but still more Anglo-Saxon than Gallic. Unlike the colonists in America, who encountered a widely scattered Indian population and never tried seriously to assimilate it, the Norman French moved into a compact little island where they were considerably outnumbered and set about governing rather than annihilating. The language of the field, the kitchen, and—most significantly—the nursery was English. English had already received some influence from Latin and was not, to begin with, radically different from French in its structure. Bilingualism was relatively easy, and children grew up knowing English as well as French. In time the social stigma was lost, and English triumphed.

Dialect borrowing

Loan words from a foreign language usually ride in on a wave of cultural diffusion. The wave may be an inpouring of commercial goods with their inventories, assembling instructions, and service manuals packed with terms that have no equivalents in the native language but must be adopted if the goods are to be put to use. Or it may be a new religion or philosophical system employing concepts difficult to translate and accordingly taken over wholesale. Such borrowing is close to the top on the scale of consciousness. Most of it is premeditated. Farther down on the scale is a homelier variety: borrowing from one dialect into another. Often what the speaker borrows is a word that is already in his vocabulary but with a different pronunciation. He assumes that the unfamiliar-sounding form has a special meaning and in the process unconsciously creates a new word:

> "He's an igernut, durn fool," said the mountaineer when my sister mentioned a local character.
> "He certainly sounds ignorant," she agreed, thinking to correct his pronunciation diplomatically.

"Oh, he ain't ignorant," the man retorted. "Lotsa folks is ignorant and can't help it. But he's just plain igernut. He don't want to learn nothin'. Them's two different words, you know."[7]

Probably no American west of the Alleghenies speaks a variety of English that is not to some extent a patchwork of dialects. Mostly the result is an enrichment of vocabulary, "doublets"—variant forms of a single word—like *girl-gal, curse-cuss, burst-bust, parcel-passel, vermin-varmint, saucy-sassy, creature-critter, ordinary-ornery, hoist-heist, rearing-rarin', shaken up/shook up, greasy-greazy, slick-sleek, stamp-stomp*. But it is also not uncommon to find traces of different systems of pronunciation in the speech of a single person who has been exposed to different streams of dialect. Many children in the Midwest who learned a Midland dialect at home were taken in hand at school by teachers from New England. At home they learned to say /fæyšən/ for *fashion;* at school they learned to say /pæšən/ for *passion*—two words that, except for the initial consonant, would otherwise have been pronounced alike. Such dialect borrowing seldom cuts deep into grammar, though one finds an occasional reshuffling of class membership. Many speakers nowadays would find **Whip him well** a poor substitute for **Whip him good,** though some of them would refuse to accept the adjective *good* for the adverb *well* elsewhere.

THE CONFUSION OF SOUNDS

A noted philologist has said that ignorance builds a language. The majority of superficial changes are mistakes, born of someone's unawareness of an earlier practice or maladroitness with it and propagated by imitators who are also unaware or indifferent or who, as we saw with *ignorant* and *igernut,* unconsciously sense an advantage and are quick to exploit it.

The most commonplace of all mistakes are the losses, spurious additions, and shiftings caused by some difficulty in hearing or reproducing a string of sounds. What we need is not so much a classification of mistakes as more knowledge of the physiological and psychological conditions that lead to them, for then we could predict them. But, lacking that, we must be satisfied to list a few of the things that happen.

---

[7] *Reader's Digest,* April, 1947, p. 90.

[1] **Loss**   For most Americans *láboratory* is *lábratory*, while for most Britishers it is *labóratry* (compare what the Portuguese have done to the same word stem in *Labrador*). For practically all of us the addition of *-ing* to *tickle* does not give *tickle-ing* but *tickling*, the syllabic /l/ being reduced. When the environment of a sound makes it hard to hear, it is liable to be lost. It may be that a word is collapsed by losing an entire segment—a phoneme is dropped, as when *fully*, formerly with both *l*'s pronounced as *wholly* still is today by many people, gave up one of them; or the segment may stay but lose some feature of length or quality, as when a full vowel becomes a reduced one—/prográm/ comes to be pronounced /prográm/, *nonsense* /nánsɛns/ becomes /nánsəns/, and so on. The loss generally takes place between generations. An adult may go on thinking that he puts a certain amount of rounding of his lips on the word *sure*, and he may actually do it part of the time; but his failure to do it consistently and clearly convinces his children that no feature of rounding belongs there, and they end by dropping it. A child who says *sherf* for *sheriff* is imitating what he thinks he hears. Two powerful forces making for complete loss are vowel reduction and lack of stress. In *laboratory* we can be sure that the syllable *lab-* will survive. The unstressed syllable next to it is in peril, as the pronunciation *lábratory* attests; similarly, we often hear *cabnet* for *cabinet*. Young children are our best harbingers of the future; they habitually drop syllables with reduced vowels: *'pression* for *expression* or *'raff* for *giraffe*.[8] Most of our nicknames—*Fred* for *Frederick*, *Will* for *William*, *Angie* for *Angela*, *Chris* for *Christopher*—are the happy result of childhood's refusal to carry a burden of unnecessary syllables. We tolerate a great deal of such pruning, so long as it does not interfere too much with sense. The words *and*, *in*, *than*, and *an* are all reduced to /n/ in rapid speech: *The pen 'n' pencil 'n the drawer are better 'n a typewriter to copy 'n easy thing like that.* We guess them from context.

[2] **Assimilation**   Our phonetic habits often lead to making sounds resemble each other. In *grandpa* there was first a loss, giving *granpa.* When /n/ and /p/ were thus brought together, the /n/ molded itself on the /p/, giving an /m/: *grampa.* Two sounds made on the lips are easier to pronounce together than one made with the tongue and one with the lips. This kind of change is called assimilation.[9] The word *government*

---

[8] Examples from Roger Brown and Ursula Bellugi, "Three Processes in the Child's Acquisition of Syntax," *Harvard Educational Review* 34.139 (1964).

[9] See Chapter 4, p. 43.

shows a series of losses and assimilations in the pronunciation of many people: *government* → *govermment* → *goverment* → *guvment* → *gubment.* Many speakers say *hap-past eight* for *half-past eight.* These are "contact" assimilations. We also find "distance" assimilations, like *Counfound it!* for *Confound it!,* where the influence of one sound on another overleaps the sounds between them. The actor who muffs his line and says *I slaw Sloane* instead of *I saw Sloane* is guilty of a distance assimilation between /s/ and /sl/.

[3] Dissimilation   There is a tendency to avoid repeating certain sounds within a single word, which affects /r/ and /l/ especially. The word *grammar* has two /r/s, and for many speakers of Middle English this was unsatisfactory so they changed it to *glamor.* The word *purpre* also had two /r/s and was changed to *purple.* Often the dissimilation results simply in a loss; this happens for most speakers, at least part of the time, with the first /r/ of *February.*

[4] Metathesis   A sound changes its position, as when someone intending to say *snap-shots* comes out with *snop-shats.* Usually such deviations are killed on the spot, but a few manage to survive. This is most apt to happen with combinations of sounds that are a bit difficult to say, causing many speakers to make the same adjustments. The word *uncomfortable* is commonly pronounced *uncomfterble,* with the /r/ moved to the following syllable. The clusters /ks/ and /sk/ are typical shifters. Many speakers say *ax (aks)* for *ask.* The two words *tax* and *task* go back to the same source and still show a certain similarity in meaning: *They taxed him with his failures = They took him to task for his failures.*

[5] Addition   Another way of dealing with a difficult cluster is to put a vowel in the middle. Most speakers nowadays make the extra effort necessary to put an /l/ before an /m/ or a /k/ that was traditionally lost or reduced to a vowel in words like *calm* and *milk;* but there was a time when many said *ellum* for *elm,* preserving the /l/ by separating it from the /m/. Some speakers still say *athalete* for *athlete.* Other additions come about accidentally: the speech organs, in passing from one position to another, move through the home territory of an intermediate sound. Many English words ending in -*mble* acquired the /b/ in this way, the /m/ having originally been in direct contact with the /l/: *grumble, fumble, humble.* The /d/ of *thunder* and *tender* has a similar origin.

The ways of change are infinite. We could add more classes to the five

listed above but there would be little gain in doing so. Too often, even
with these few, it is impossible to decide. Was the speaker who said
That sounds rather silted when he meant to say *That sounds rather
stilted* dissimilating the first /t/ of *stilted* from the second, or assimilating
the /st/ to the /s/ of *sounds?* When we say *habmt, sebm, sebmty,* and
elebm for *haven't, seven, seventy,* and *eleven* are we making the /v/ like
the /n/ or the /n/ like the /v/? Undoubtedly we are doing both, pulling
them from their old positions to a new one somewhere between.

Most confusions of sounds wither before a second speaker has a chance
to pick them up. We simply reject them as foreign bodies in our language
system. To have a chance for survival, many of them must tend in a
common direction. The American who says *gof* for *golf* follows a pattern
of previous change *(sov* for *solve)* and makes *golf* resemble highly frequent words like *cough, soft,* and *off.* In all likelihood he will not be
aware of having done anything to the language.

SPELLING PRONUNCIATIONS

When someone pronounces *pulpit* to rime with *gulp it,* it is a fair inference that he did not acquire the word from hearing it. Learning words
from the oral tradition offers the opportunity, though not the guarantee,
of saying them as they are customarily said. Guessing at them from reading, in a language that uses an alphabetic system of writing, provides as
many chances of breaking with this tradition as there are unreasonable
spellings. Left to guesswork, *hypocrite* will come out sounding something
like *cryolite,* and *epitome* like *metronome.* This is the penalty for not
spelling them *hippocritt* and *epitomy,* for those are the more regular
spellings of the sounds in question and, left on our own, we inevitably
regularize.

Of course, if the writing system is not alphabetic—if it is as divorced
from the sound as it is in Chinese—false associations of precisely this
kind do not occur. English spelling might conceivably be so remote from
pronunciation that we would throw up our hands and look for no connection at all. As it is, it is just remote enough to insure a maximum of
interference between the two.

The influence of writing on the spoken language is a condition of
literate societies. Universal literacy is too recent a phenomenon to reveal
long-range effects, but it seems reasonable to suppose that one such effect
will be to stabilize language to a certain extent. Reading is more widely
shared over a longer period of time than any form of listening: we "hear"
an author of a hundred years ago as clearly as we hear one today, if we

read him, and the cultivation of classics insures that we will. Words, images, and turns of phrase that might otherwise pass from the scene acquire a firmer hold, and become the property of all who share the culture. The separation of societies into cultural rivulets, each going its own way, is more and more a thing of the past.

Within this broader tendency toward uniformity, spelling pronunciations are both a confirmation and a contradiction. When spellings serve as reminders of how things are pronounced today, pronunciation is less apt to change: when we see *policeman* we are not so inclined to say *pleeceman.* Here spelling is merely conservative. When spellings lead to the revival of a pronunciation long since given up, their force is not conservative but reactionary. In Southern Britain the word *often* is coming more and more to be pronounced with a [t] and with the *o* of *odd.* When a spelling leads to a pronunciation that never existed, its influence is neither conservative nor reactionary but subversive. Many words that had long been spelled and pronounced with simple *t* were respelled with *th* by writers who enjoyed showing off their etymological erudition. One by one such words have taken on a pronunciation that they never had, suggested by the *th: theater, Catholic, author, Theodore* (the nickname *Ted* persists uncorrupted). The latest addition for many speakers is *thyme.* Somehow *Thomas* managed to escape—no doubt because there were more Toms among the common speakers and fewer among the idle intelligentsia.[10]

A number of spelling pronunciations reach back to the beginnings of general literacy. The written diphthong *oi* is often cited. One still finds now and then, in dialectal writings, *jine* for *join, rile* for *roil,* and *pint* for *point.* These dialectal spellings represent a pronunciation that, except for the influence of the spelling *oi,* would probably be standard today.[11] Here are some more recent examples:

1. *gynecology* like *guy* rather than as in *misogynist*

2. *conjurer, constable, wont,* like *don* and *con* rather than like *son* and *honey; hover* like *rover* rather than like *cover*

3. *dour* to rime with *sour* rather than with *boor*

4. *diphtheria, naphtha, diphthong* misread as containing simple *p* instead of *ph* pronounced [f]

---

[10] See Otto Jespersen, *A Modern English Grammar,* Part I (New York: Barnes & Noble, Inc., 1909), §2.622.

[11] See Josef Vachek, "On the Interplay of External and Internal Factors in the Development of Language," *Lingua* 11.433–448 (1962).

5. *thence, thither* to agree with *thin* and *thick* rather than with *then* and *there*

6. *chiropodist* like *cheerio*

7. *chaise longue* as if the spelling were inverted to *lounge*[12]

8. *short-lived* as if it had to do with the verb *live* rather than the noun *life*

The spread of popular education in America insured that spelling pronunciations would assert themselves more vigorously than in other parts of the English-speaking world. Some traditional pronunciations persist in Britain that have died out in most or all of the United States; for example, *Ralph* pronounced /ref/ (we see the spelling *Rafe* sometimes, but we do not even think of it as the same word). But many traditional pronunciations are falling in Britain too, notably among the place names that Americans find so strange: *Leicester* as /lɛstə/, *Happisburgh* as /hezbrə/, *Wotton* as /wʊtn/, and so on. The British themselves, except those who live in or near the place in question, are tending to pronounce the words as they are spelled.[13]

Shortly before and after the turn of the century, England and the United States witnessed a vigorous movement toward reform of spelling that enlisted many notable figures, including Charles Darwin, Alfred Lord Tennyson, and, more recently, George Bernard Shaw. For a time it even enjoyed an organization, the Simplified Spelling Board, with a subsidy of $25,000 a year from Andrew Carnegie and the official support of Theodore Roosevelt, who ordered the Government Printing Office to adopt some three hundred revised spellings. But, as H. L. Mencken pointed out, the effort to hasten things "aroused widespread opposition, and in a little while the spelling reform movement was the sport of the national wits."[14] Today one hardly ever hears of it, and spelling reformers are regarded as cranks. Meanwhile, with a little change here and a little change there, instead of spelling accommodating itself to pronunciation, pronunciation accommodates itself to spelling.

---

[12] This is a folk etymology, too. See Chapter 7, pp. 104–06.

[13] For these examples and other discussions of change in contemporary British English, see Charles Barber, *Linguistic Change in Present-day English* (University, Ala.: University of Alabama Press, 1966).

[14] *The American Language*, 4th ed. (New York: Alfred A. Knopf, Inc., 1936), pp. 399–400.

ADDITIONAL REMARKS
AND APPLICATIONS

1. The following passages are from the Dryden translation (Clough revision) of Plutarch's *Lives*. Point out the words and expressions that would not be used today, and give their modern equivalents:

   > The ambassadors being departed, he withdrew his forces out of the Roman territory.

   > The cities sent an embassy to Thebes, to desire succours and a general.

   > Crassus durst not appear a candidate for the consulship before he had applied to Pompey.

2. The word *light* comes directly from an Old English word related to German *licht*. In English we have *lucid,* from Latin, and *leucous,* from Greek. Would the resemblance among the originals of these words be further proof of kinship among these languages? See if you can find other examples.

3. English words tend to cluster in certain sequences: we can say *I went away quickly* or *I went quickly away,* but we have no choice between *I went away early* and **I went early away.* English also tends to space words so that the important ones can be heard to advantage. If you were on the point of saying *I'm seldom able to go back to sleep* but corrected it to *I seldom am able to go back to sleep,* would you consider that the rearrangement responded to an adjustment between the two tendencies?

4. Instead of taking over a foreign word bodily, a language will sometimes translate the parts that make it up. Medieval Latin took the Greek word meaning 'good tidings' (from which we later got *evangelize*) and translated it as *bonus nuntius.* The missionaries brought this to England and translated it again as *gospel,* 'good spiel.' With the aid of a good dictionary, explain the word *gainsay* as such a "loan translation." Compare it with *contradict.*

5. Explain the following, which are fairly common, as instances of dialect borrowing: *I'm beat—I can't go another foot; Well I'll be blowed!; I like reading whodunits; Lord, it's cold outside—I'm plumb froze;*

What are you all het up about?; He just sort of snuck up on us. Give the standard forms of the verbs.

6. Many speakers who say *He ups and hits me* in the present tense say *He up and hit me* instead of *He upped and hit me* in the past tense. Account for this in terms of loss. What does it suggest about our willingness to accept without question a rather destructive change when the context overshadows the meanings of the individual words?

7. Identify the phonetic alterations in the following: *pram* for *perambulator;* the /š/ of *horse* in *horse show; glanders,* related ultimately to Latin *glandula; sprite,* a form of *spirit; bird,* from Old English *brid; number,* related to German *Nummer;* dialectal *fillum* for *film; tremble,* ultimately from Latin *tremulus.* The Latin word *pænitentia* gave us *penitence* with little change except in the ending. What additional change produced *(re)pentance? penance?* (For the latter, pretend that *penitence* and *penance* were spelled as they sounded, *penitents* and *penants.)*

8. The plurals of words like *basis, analysis,* and *crisis* are written *bases, analyses, crises,* with the last syllable pronounced like *ease.* One often hears a spelling pronunciation modeled on this used with the plurals of words like *premise* and *process.* Would a similar spelling pronunciation be likely to be heard with the plurals of words like *mattress* or *promise?* Why? During the Jack Ruby trial in 1964 a radio announcer mentioned a "change of venue," saying *venóo.* Does this spelling pronunciation reveal a tendency on the part of some Americans to make an unfamiliar word actually *sound* unfamiliar, as if putting on Latin airs were a token of being educated? Does this account for the Latinizing of words like *processes?*

THE EVOLUTION OF 7 LANGUAGE: MEANINGS, INTERPRETATIONS, AND ADJUSTMENTS

By ITSELF, the confusion of sounds is hardly more than a problem of transmission. A few sounds are crossed up or crossed off here and there, but the main signal remains the same. The speaker who says *golf* and the one who says *gof* are saying the same word.

Matters become more complicated when, in addition to these minor mechanical shifts, there are also realignments of meaning. The most complex stage of all is where the whole system of the language reacts to an accumulation of changes in form and sense.

In the first section of this chapter we shall see how meaning brings about changes in form. In the second section, we shall see how other changes result from differences in point of view between one speaker and another, from each of us having his own inner world of meaning and grammar. In the third section, we shall see how the language system adjusts itself and keeps working in spite of all the mischief we make with it.

CONFUSIONS OF SENSE

Confusions of sense come in two varieties: those due to knowledge and those due to ignorance. Knowing too much and knowing too little can both cause trouble with the shapes of our words.

The trouble with knowing too much is that it puts at our disposal a *choice* of words, and in deciding (as a rule unconsciously, of course) among the choices we often mix them up. Whereas in the previous chapter the only sounds that were confused were the ones actually occurring before or after one another in the chain of the sentence, we now discover confusions among those sounds and others that *might* have occurred in the sentence if we had selected one synonym rather than another.

Here enters a fundamental distinction in linguistics, between certain phenomena known as "syntagmatic" and others known as "paradigmatic." In the sentence **Boys eat doughnuts** there is a relationship between **boys** and *eat*—both occur in this sentence, and **boys** is a subject noun taking *eat* as its verb. This is a syntagmatic relationship, one that rests on the connections within this particular sentence, a matter of *syntax*. But there is also a relationship between *eat* and *eats*. *Eats* is not part of the sentence, but is part of the *paradigm* of the verb **to eat**. We say that it "could" occur in the sentence if conditions were right—if the subject were **boy** instead of **boys**.

Relatedness in meaning is a kind of semantic paradigm. It can be shown by a diagram with syntagmatic items along the horizontal axis and paradigmatic ones along the vertical axis. Let's suppose that someone is about to say **A spurious scarcity of goods led to high prices:**

A spurious (A) scarcity   of goods . . .
            (B) shortage
            (C) sparseness
            (D) lack
            (E) dearth
                ·
                ·
                ·

If he says *a curious spaircity of goods* we know that he has confused two things, both of which he intended to say: **spurious** and **scarcity.** This is little more than a metathesis (it is a *little* more because he has said **curious** and not **scurious**—an existing word is always favored, even if wrong in sense). But if he says *a spurious sparsity of goods* he is probably confusing two things, only one of which he would want to say in a single breath: **scarcity** and **sparseness.** Enough speakers have made this confusion over the years so that **sparsity** is recognized (**sparseness** appeared in the early part of the nineteenth century, **sparsity** in the latter half).

It is quite possible that these paradigmatic chains are necessary for the creation of sentences. How do we think of the words we want to say? Our mental scanners seem to sweep over vast networks of words and phrases with deep and invisible connections. Normally this is done with lightning speed, but sometimes we have to make an effort to remember and then we can observe the process in slow motion. Let's say you have forgotten a certain synonym of *heartless* and *indifferent,* which you simply must have in order to make the sentence you want. First you think of something that seems altogether irrelevant: *girl who wears her heart on her sleeve.* But that leads to *impressionable, impressionable* leads to *susceptible, susceptible* leads to its negative *insusceptible,* and finally you have it: *unfeeling.* The paradigms of the language brood over each choice we make. It is no wonder that confusions occur that do not arise within the thin line of the sounds of the sentence itself.

[1] **Blends**   The most typical result of the collision of choices is a hybrid choice, called a *blend* or *contamination. Sparsity* is a blend of *sparseness* and *scarcity.* When an editor writes about "Bernard Reder's *portentious* trifles at the Whitney,"[1] we know he has in mind both *pretentious* and *portentous.* When a member of the family says that a singer has a *sachrymose* voice, it is clear that *saccharine* has been crossed with *lachrymose.* When a motorist rails at a *blatted* bridge that is out and keeps him from crossing a stream, we dissect *blasted* and *dratted.* Where the forces that make for blending are strong enough—and they are strongest when there is already some resemblance in form in addition to the resemblance in meaning—the result is apt to be a permanent addition to the language. On reading a news dispatch one might be surprised to learn of "atrocities by *rampacious* Congolese soldiers"[2] and suspect a blend of *rampageous* and *rapacious,* only to discover that this blend was recorded by dictionaries half a century ago. One may even find three-way blends. The verb in "That racket has *milked* the public long enough" suggests the metaphor of draining something laid onto a blend of *mulct* and *bilk.* The verb *riffle* applied to cards combines a blend of *ripple* and *shuffle* with a previously existing *riffle* in another sense. The blends most likely to stick are the ones that bring whole phrases together, for the larger the segment the less we are apt to notice and correct a slight change in it. A popular magazine says "a psychiatrist *rarely ever* saw those patients," combining *rarely* and *hardly ever.* A commonplace nowadays is *oblivious to,* which blends *oblivious of* and, possibly, *impervious to.* Clauses with *if* are crossed in curious ways: *"If we all do* alike *it makes for* better relations" combines "Our all doing alike *makes for* better relations" with *"If we all do* alike relations will be better." Multiple blends

---

[1] *The Nation,* December 23, 1961, p. 500.

[2] *Boulder Camera* (Boulder, Colorado), March 14, 1961, p. 1.

can be found: *Neither candidate had any comments on the issue* combines *made any comment, had any comment to make,* and *had any opinion.* Often we catch a blend in the act of breaking and entering, and throttle it then and there. An actor who is supposed to say *in jig time* fumbles the line and starts it *in a ji-,* obviously thinking of *in a jiffy,* but corrects himself before he completes the phrase. The opposite extreme is the blend that is deliberately coined; now and then one hangs on—*smog* from *smoke* and *fog;* but most of them—*tantrumental* from *tantrum* and *temperamental, glumlin* from *glum* and *gremlin*—do not survive the laugh they were meant to provoke. Unconscious blending, according to one linguist, may be the source of many—if not most—of the words now listed in dictionaries with "source unknown."

To say that blends are a result of knowing too much is to be overgenerous. This is a knowing that is half-knowledge; the speaker has a sizable vocabulary but a weak hold on it. He has one vague impression of *rampageous* and another of *rapacious* and chops them together in a mixed salad. The remaining manifestations of ignorance expose it in a purer state. The things confused are no longer synonymous or even appropriate to each other in some indefinite way, but only tangled up, perhaps on the basis of a chance resemblance in form, in the minds of a few speakers.

[2] **Malapropisms**   Here, one word is mistaken for another. There is a storehouse of these attributed to Mayor Richard Daley of Chicago: "*harassing* the atom," "rising to higher *platitudes* of achievement" (in the latter perhaps we can detect a blend: *planes* + *altitudes*). A political writer says: "A man *aggregates* to himself the right," intending *arrogates.* A weather man predicts "Five below zero, *nominally* a safe temperature for driving," intending *normally.* A linguist *hypothecates* ('pawns') a hypothesis instead of *hypothesizing* it. The odds against widespread acceptance of any of these pieces of false coin are high, but now and then the inspectors are fooled. *Mitigate* in the sense of *militate* continues to crop up sporadically; during the Dominican intervention in 1965 it was reported that "time mitigated against President Johnson's consulting the ministers of the OAS." Where there is a hint of blending, chances of survival are better. *To comprise* means almost the same as *to be composed of,* and many say or write *to be comprised of. Most* for *almost* is widespread; the two words are akin in sound and in the fact that both are used in comparisons. *To careen* for *to career* meaning 'to rush headlong' is another example; a vehicle careering down a road is apt to careen —lurch from side to side; for most American speakers of English, *careen* has replaced *career.*

INTERPRETATIVE CHANGE

The users of a language are not always at the mercy of the weaknesses within their own natures and the powers that bear upon them from outside. Each has within him the ability to "see" his language, building his internal grammar and dictionary on the basis of what he hears or gets away with when he experiments. Our language is, for us, the way we interpret the data that come to us in all forms, finishes, and sizes throughout our lives. But since the interpretation we make guides our output, and our output in turn is the input that helps to determine how others will shape *their* language, any bit of interpretative creativity on our part must be reckoned as a force of change.

For speakers to influence one another their individual visions of the language must be slightly different. If all were exactly alike there would be nothing to change. They must be closely similar, or we would not be able to communicate; but if the message is crude enough for an approximation to suffice, we may be able to reach one another even when using different grammatical patterns. A child comes into a store on an errand for his mother, buys something, and asks, "Will I get any change back?" The storekeeper says yes and completes the transaction; he is unaware that the child understands *changeback* as a compound noun, like *turnaround, shakedown, mixup,* or *sendoff,* and that he is asking, essentially, "Will I get any *change?*" He is unaware of it, that is, until one day the child asks, "Will I get any changeback back?"[3] The differences between grammars may be quite complex, though any two of them will still be closely similar. If one listens patiently enough, at least six different ways can be discovered in which English speakers combine the object and subject pronouns with each other and with nouns: *I overheard she and Millie talking about it* (from a popular television program), *It's for you and me, It's for you and I,* and so on.[4]

Interpretative corrections: folk etymology

A person encounters an unfamiliar word or phrase and assumes that something else was meant by it, something with which he is familiar. He corrects it to what he thinks is right before he passes it on. Sometimes the false correction sticks. The first American hearing a French trapper

---

[3] Reported by Mr. Richard Siegel as heard in a store in Denver, May, 1963. Compare *itsy-bitsy, as is,* and similar examples, Chapter 5, p. 65.

[4] Pointed out by Fred W. Householder, Jr., in *Linguistic Speculations,* Chapter 1 (to be published in 1968 by Prentice-Hall, Inc.).

in Colorado refer to the **Purgatoire River** judged that what he heard was **Picket Wire** with a foreign accent. To many inhabitants of Miami Beach, Florida, the Fontainebleau Hotel is the **Fountain Blue Hotel.** Young children often make such substitutions. For one six-year-old discussing **chicken pox** with another, the name was **chicken pots;** for the other it was **chicken fox.** To many children, on first acquaintance an *ice cream cone* is an *ice cream comb;* here the substitution of the familiar for the unfamiliar is aided by the tendency to assimilate the two nasal sounds and make *cone* end like *cream.*

It is not necessary that substitutions make sense; it is only necessary that they be familiar. But if they make some kind of sense, all the better. This is what has given the name "folk etymology" to the phenomenon: to linguists it appeared as if the "folk" were giving themselves airs as etymologists in looking for associations of meaning, analyzing a word in a spurious way. Thus, many who heard the term *renegade* applied to some sort of outlaw and who lacked the verb *to renege* as part of their vocabularies established instead a connection with *run* and *gate* ('road, way'), for renegades were generally fugitives; *renegade* became *runagate.* Now and then a folk etymology makes such good sense that it crowds out its rivals. The adjective *secrétive* was originally stressed on its second syllable, but so many speakers have associated it with *sécret* that now *sécretive* is more general. The past tense form *shined* was once looked upon as substandard, but enough people have assumed that it ought to be related to the noun *shine* (as in 'to give a *shine* to') that now it is respectable to distinguish between **The sun shone** and **He shined his shoes.**

Evidence for folk etymology is sometimes roundabout. When someone calls for a *slam* or *belt* of liquor we can guess that he has thought of *slug of liquor* as if *slug* were the *slug* of boxing and not from the Irish *slog* 'swallow.'[5] There may be a change in form so slight that it passes unnoticed. So much confusion already exists between *wh-* and *w-* (most Southern Britishers, and many others, drop the /h/ in *where, which, while,* and so on) that when some speakers heard "He's a *wiz* (= wizard) at math" they thought it referred to intellectual quickness, to whizzing through a problem; *wiz* became *whiz.* The extreme case is found where there is no difference in form at all and we are unaware of any change until we see it written. There is no audible difference between "to give something *free rein*" and "to give it *free reign*," but the latter, rather common, spelling reveals what has happened in the writer's mind.

Folk etymologies are not quite the same as the "guesstymologies"

---

[5] Arthur E. Hutson in *American Speech,* February, 1947, p. 20.

sometimes invented by etymologists when they are not sure how to account for a word. *Catnip,* for example, means the same as *catmint,* and the phonetic differences could be explained by a combination of assimilation, metathesis, and dissimilation—the /t/ becomes /p/ by contact with the /m/, the /n/ dissimilates from the other nasal (/m/) by disappearing, the /p/ and /t/ change places, and the resulting /tm/ becomes /tn/ by assimilation: *catmint* → *capmint* → *capmit* → *catmip* → *catnip.* But not all that is plausible is true. *Catnip* really comes from *cat + nep, nep* being another name for the same plant.

Fusion

If malapropisms and folk etymologies prove that a little knowledge is a dangerous thing, fusions prove that pure ignorance is bliss. A word or phrase has a historical tie with the parts that make it up, but we reinterpret it as a unit. The single, set meaning that it now carries is enough for us; the source no longer counts.

Once again we see the shape of the future in the mistakes of children. When a boy of seven says *He shot his bow and arrow at me,* pronouncing *bow and arrow* as if it were *bow narrow,* we know that this phrase has for him become fused to the point where *bow* and *arrow* are no longer separately meaningful. When he later declares that he never wants to become a *juvenile,* we can infer that for him the word *juvenile* exists only in the phrase *juvenile delinquent,* which he feels free to clip just as he clips *Frederick* to *Fred.*

Fusion seems to be more important for some languages than for others, though curiously the evidence is often cited to suggest the opposite of fusion. In comparing German and English it is sometimes claimed that German is more "transparent" and English is more "opaque" because in German, for example, one can see behind the word for *thimble, Fingerhut,* the meaning 'hat for a finger,' whereas in English a thimble is a thimble, revealing nothing (unless you are an etymologist, in which case you would see a relationship to *thumb*). But the question is whether Germans really think about fingers and hats when they use the word *Fingerhut.* Most of the time, they probably don't.

The same thing happens with fusions in English. Once a meaning is set we forget the original associations. We may even be surprised when someone points them out to us. As one linguist observed, "It is common experience that the user undergoes a psychological shock when his attention is directed for the first time to the transparency of certain words which he has been *using* for years without ever wondering whether they were opaque or transparent."[6] It is not only the underlying sense of compounds that eludes us, in words like *barefaced, crackpot, telltale, stock-still,* but sometimes that of the most obvious phrases: *to be tied up* and unable to keep an appointment, *to have one's hands full* with an assignment, *to keep one's shirt on* when there is need for patience.

Fusion is not necessarily accompanied by a change in form, but it often is, and that is the best evidence of what has happened. When we say *Yes, truly* we make the comma break loud and clear; when we say *Yes, indeed* we drop it. Compounds give various signs of fusion. One is speed: the more fused it is the faster it goes; we say *borderline* more quickly than we say *border zone.* Another is vowel reduction: *mailman* is more fused for most speakers than *trashman,* with audible effects on *man.* Another is the regularizing of inflection: *baby-sitted* instead of *baby-sat, pinch-hitted* and *broadcasted* as the past of *pinch-hit* and *broadcast,* and plurals like *snow mans* and *sweet tooths.* Still another is our reluctance to break up the compound. If one goes to the counter in a library, hands a borrowed book to the librarian, and asks to have it renewed because one wants to "make a *book report* on it," we can be sure that *book report* is a unit, for otherwise it would have been more natural to say "make a *report* on it"—under the circumstances, *book* is obvious.

The most extreme case of fusion, reaching so deep in history that speakers are no longer able to dissociate the elements, is that in which one of the fused parts becomes a mere attachment on the other. This is the source of many inflections, especially those of verbs. The French *finirai* 'I'll finish' was originally *finir + ai,* from Latin *finire habeo,* 'I have to finish.' The Russian passive-reflexive suffix *-sja,* as in *obvinjat'sja* 'to be accused,' was originally the same as the reflexive pronoun *sebja* in *obvinjat' sebja* 'to accuse oneself.' The Uzbek (Turkic) *ëzaëtirman* 'I am writing' was originally *ëza-ëtirman* 'I writing lie.'[7]

It is fortunate that we can forget, that it is no longer necessary to think of *chilblains* as 'blains caused by chills,' of *How do you do?* as an inquiry about how one does, of *never mind* as an injunction not to notice something. New associations create new meanings, and old meanings are a clutter.

---

[6] Giulio P. Lepschy in *Linguistics* 15.48 (1965), commenting on Professor Stephen Ullmann's use of the *Fingerhut* example.

[7] Examples from V. M. Žirmunskij, "The Word and Its Boundaries," *Linguistics* 27.86–87 (1966), and Charles E. Bidwell, "The Reflexive Construction in Serbo-Croatian," *Studies in Linguistics* 18.45 (1965–66).

Change of meaning: synthesis

A first look at *ticket* and *etiquette* reveals no similarity in meaning, though the similarity in form is obvious, yet both go back to a common Germanic source that survives almost intact in the English verb *to stick.* French borrowed it to make a verb, *estiquer,* and out of that came a noun, *etiquet,* which was re-borrowed into English as *ticket*—a label or poster, something tacked up or stuck on a surface. Spanish also borrowed the French noun in the same sense to make *etiqueta,* and in the early part of the sixteenth century this was extended to posted rules of conduct at court and diplomatic functions, thus coming to mean 'the prescribed thing to do.' French borrowed back the new meaning, and it passed once more, as *etiquette,* to English. No one could have foreseen these wanderings, and the deflections of meaning would have been as hard to predict as the direction of a ricocheting bullet. To hold to this analogy for a moment, we might say that the bullet remains more or less intact, flattened a bit but in this case with the element *-tik-* still quite identifiable, while the meaning, the direction the bullet takes, reflects not only the direction it has on impact but also the surface it happens to hit. The person, the occasion, the need, the moment's fancy, all are factors that can deflect it toward the unknown. This is typical of meaning. It is far less stable than form.

A deflection in itself is not a change of meaning. It is only the raw material of change. Court ceremony called for doing things "according to the ticket," or posted rules. A ticket was still a ticket. But speakers kept hearing *You have to act according to the ticket.* Before long the "have to act" part, the notion of prescribed behavior, overshadowed the reference to written instructions, and *etiquette* took on a full-fledged new meaning. We are constantly weighing and measuring the semantic data in this way, to yield the best interpretation.

Of course, the circumstances themselves may change. Groups of speakers are exposed to altered data and forced to reinterpret accordingly. The social environment is in constant flux. Ordinarily we think of a *happening* as something accidental; but when in 1965 and 1966 these "accidents" came to be deliberately staged, *happening* began to take on somewhat the same secondary meaning as *incident.* The scientific environment is in flux too. Take the word *light.* Light was, by definition, that which made things visible. At one time such an idea as "invisible light" would have been an absurdity, like gay funeral marches or circular squares. But when the physical basis of light became known, it was natural to transfer the meaning to the *energy* that produces light, and from there to the "same" energy that lies beyond the range of the visible;

with the discovery of infrared and ultraviolet, *invisible light* was no longer a mystery.

More often, it is our personal experience with words that changes their meanings. We do not encounter, or perhaps we simply ignore, part of the data. Mr. Abbott's mental computer adds up the contexts of *segregate* and Mr. Maguire's does the same, but the sum is different: Mr. Abbott is used to contexts like *Segregate the stuff from those old files before 1929 and throw it away,* while Mr. Maguire has met only references to segregating the races, and for him *to segregate* means something like having inferior accommodations for Negroes. Mr. Abbott, afraid that Mr. Maguire and his friends will misunderstand him, begins to refrain from using *segregate* in a broader sense, which appears less and less and is finally lost. For obvious reasons—one does not want to use a word in a "good" sense if others think it "bad"—unfavorable meanings are prone to develop this way: *trust* for 'an unlawful business combine,' *anarchist* for 'bomb-thrower,' *Jesuit* for 'casuist'—add a bit of emotional discoloration and a word goes downhill fast. The unfavorable connotation picked up by *not about to* in only the past decade is instructive. It shows how something already isolated in form can acquire a restricted meaning that quickly monopolizes it. The affirmative *to be about to* is almost always buttressed with *just: I was just about to leave.* The negative does not require *just (I was not about to leave yet),* and originally served merely as an infrequent substitute for *not going to.* But *going to* was not hampered by *just,* and was too common an expression for any narrowing of context to occur: *I was going to help him* and *I was not going to help him* are the positive and negative sides of a single meaning. *Not about to,* however, was an easy victim for negative meanings that happened to be almost exclusively unfavorable; and now "He [the farmer] is not about to become one of the migrants to the city if he can help it"[8] signifies not just a contrary intention but a feeling that to suppose anything else would be presumptuous. Its meaning has passed from mere negative intention to defiance.

Many of the expressions that we call idioms have acquired their meanings in the same way. When leftovers are consigned as bird feed it does not take long for the association in our minds to pass from the purpose to the value; hence *It's for the birds,* 'It's worthless.'

The reinterpretation that our mental computers make is often simply bound up with the passage of time. Our great-grandfathers used *to spoon* in a generic sense, but to their descendants it came to mean 'the old-

---

[8] Joseph P. Lyford, *The Talk in Vandalia* (New York: Fund for the Republic, 1962), p. 27.

fashioned love-making of our elders.' Here time has restricted the meaning. It may also broaden it. During World War II a great deal was said
about *postwar* conditions. Since these conditions were pretty much
idealized during that period, *postwar* gradually took on the sense of
'ultra-modern,' and later, during the actual postwar period when these
hopes were not realized, *postwar* continued to be used for 'ultra-modern'
or 'futuristic.' In 1947 a soap company offered a *postwar kitchen* as a
contest prize. But the favorable sense soon faded. Nowadays, *postwar*
is associated not with the hopes but with the disappointments: *postwar
conditions* of political turmoil, *postwar housing* of shoddy construction,
and so on.

Our reinterpretations lead not only to the synthesizing of new meanings for old words but to the unintentional creation of new words. It is
tempting to think that new words are made by sitting down and coining
them. Occasionally they are, especially in the trades and sciences when
a new product or compound comes along and someone has to name it.
(Even this bit of linguistic novelty is not spun from air; no one can
invent words as if all past linguistic experience were a blank. But the
degree of originality will vary.) More generally a new word is borrowed
from another language, or appears by accident (by blending, for
example), or is born from a peculiar form of cellular division that we
call *bifurcation,* combining reinterpretation and change in form.

There comes a moment in every phonetic change when some speakers
are using the older form and some the newer. This is the potential source
of bifurcation. If I use *burned* as the past of the verb *to burn* and you
happen to prefer *burnt,* and our conversation turns on the subject of
something charred and you refer to it as burnt, I may suspect that you
are in possession of a formula that I lack, whereby a thing gets burned
and ends up burnt. It is as if I said to myself, "He is using a different
form; it must mean something different." Perhaps my impression is supported by the length of the words—*burned* takes longer to say, it sounds
like something going on, while *burnt* is short, like something finished.
No more than this may be needed to balance our calculations in favor of
a shift of meaning, if we start with the suspicion that any difference in
form must be intentional. Our mental calculators immediately go to work
to assess the slightest difference in context or association, to interpret
what the difference is.

At any moment there are probably dozens of latent distinctions in the
back of our minds, ready to crystallize into unmistakable bifurcations
once enough speakers develop similar leanings. Suppose you are in the
habit of saying *C'mere* as a familiar way of asking someone to approach.
This would be a normal phonetic reduction of *Come here* spoken on

home grounds, where everyone already half-knows what is going to be said and where there is no need for ceremony. Equally normal under the same circumstances would be a sentence like *Tell her to c'mere*. But one day your spouse mentions a relative in Maine or California who plans a trip but is undecided where to go, and you say *Tell her to c'mere*. Something sounds wrong, and you correct it to *Tell her to come here*. On reflection you realize that *c'mere* is not appropriate for a two-thousand-mile-trip. *Come here* in the altered form *c'mere* has been reinterpreted in your mind as the kind of coming that requires no more than a trip across the hall.

Not all reassortments of meaning pass quite so unnoticed as bifurcation. It would be simpler if we could speak of conscious changes and unconscious ones, but nobody knows where to draw the line; we seem to be half-awake to what is going on about as often as we are wide awake or dead asleep. Still, some of the things that we do to meanings are closer to daylight than others, and they, as much as the forces that work in the dark, lead to reinterpretations by the speakers who come after us. Among these are certain figures of speech and certain ways of avoiding misunderstanding:

[1] Metaphor   Coin an apt comparison and you invite imitation. A couple of hundred years ago some sailor likened long-winded storytellers to spinners of yarn; generations of patient listeners have loved his idea and repeated it. This is how a figurative *He likes to spin yarns* was reinterpreted as meaning literally *He likes to tell yarns* and *yarn* became a synonym of *story*. Countless present meanings are embalmed metaphors: *to lie low, to walk out on something, to raise the roof, to go ahead full steam*. Most of our abstractions are borrowed metaphors from Greek or Latin: *to insult* means 'to jump on,' *eccentric* is 'off center,' a *hyperbole* is 'a throwing beyond.'

[2] Euphemism   A name for something unpleasant produces the same qualms as the unpleasant thing itself, and tends to be avoided. But the time always comes, taboo or no taboo, when the thing has to be mentioned, and then we look for a milder substitute. If we hesitate to call someone a liar, *prevaricator* will do. The word *Jew* has been used unfavorably by so many of the world's big and little defamers that it is sometimes avoided even at the expense of grammar. A Sunday supplement discloses that "Refugees were aristocrats during the French Revolution and Jewish in Hitler's era"—matching the noun *aristocrats* with the adjective *Jewish*.[9] If such a word already has some other strike against it, the result is oblivion. To refer to a woman aviator as an *aviatrix* sounds quaint nowadays, and even *actress* is sometimes dropped in favor of *actor*—mention of sex seems inappropriate except for humor or insult. This has spelled the end for the words *Jewess* and *Negress;* they join *popinjay* and *Papist* as historical relics.

[3] **Hyperbole**   Offer someone his choice between a cannon and a pistol and he will choose the cannon. We strive for effect and like the word with the biggest bang. Of course, the bang is from the powerful associations that the word has had in the past, and once these are trivialized it fizzles out. Hence the ruination of many good words. *Elegant* is only now recovering from having once been inflated to a general synonym of *excellent.* Sports writers have so long used *crippled* as an exaggerated equivalent of *lame* that for some persons *lame* is now the stronger word. *Straw potatoes* was a term once used for potatoes of the best quality grown under straw on the surface of the ground; it was vitiated by dishonest dealers who applied it to any crop of potatoes, and in the course of time was dropped.

Hyperbole—when fresh—is effective because it shakes up the hearer. The best hyperbole is some real shocker, a *dysphemism* or highly unfavorable term used playfully. "Well, if it isn't Jack Connors, you old son of a gun!" is euphemistic in that *son of a gun* is used instead of *son of a bitch* (even *son of a bitch,* we remember from *The Virginian,* is all right if said with a smile), but dysphemistic in that an epithet has replaced a compliment such as *my dear friend.* The words *rogue, scalawag, scamp, devil, vixen, jerk,* and *mischievous* have all been scaled down in the same way. When a mother says to her infant, "You're a *naughty* little *rascal,*" she is being etymologically insulting.

A milder form of hyperbole consists in piling up modifiers unnecessarily. A word that is a rapier by itself is strapped to a club and the combined weapon neither cuts nor hits very well. A *deadly poison* says enough—it can do no more than kill; a *very deadly poison* turns *deadly* into a mere intensifier. A *disaster* is the ultimate in mishaps, but a *serious disaster,* by trying to say more, says less.

[4] **Conflict of homonyms**   Some reinterpretations are the result of interference. When two words once different in form come by phonetic change to sound the same, speakers may avoid one of them lest they seem to be

---

[9] *This Week Magazine,* December 20, 1953.

saying the other. Most of the time homonymy does not bother us—two identical-sounding words are tolerated because we are not really listening to the words by themselves but to the phrases that contain them, and these may be totally different; we no more avoid one because of the other than we avoid saying *Helen* because the first syllable is the same as *hell.* But sometimes the phrases too are similar, and then we are in trouble. About two centuries ago the words *queen* and *quean* coincided phonetically. *Quean* originally meant 'woman,' and as a result both words appeared in many identical phrases: *She is a queen (quean)*. But *quean* had also come to be used for 'harlot.' It would have been difficult for two such words to coexist for long, and *quean* was dropped.[10] Fundamentally, there is no difference between a collision like this and one between antagonistic senses of a single word. A century ago a *saloon* was 'a large hall,' especially one for receptions or exhibits. But the proprietors of grog shops in the United States began to call their establishments saloons to raise them in the public esteem. The effect on the word, of course, was the opposite—it was lowered. As a result, one sense of the word has been relegated to history (including television westerns) and the other has been replaced by the French cognate *salon.* The phrase *to wax and to wane* is common and causes no trouble since *wax* coupled with *wane* is clear. But while we readily say *It waned* or *It is on the wane,* we avoid *It waxed* and cannot say **It is on the wax* at all. Conflict of homonyms forces us to say *It is on the increase.*

[5] **Conflict of synonyms**   Though reinterpretation usually has the effect of diversifying meanings—this is bifurcation—sometimes it deflects them toward each other. In the resulting competition a word may go down. The Old English word for the left-hand side of a ship looking forward was *backboard,* but there was also another: *ladeborde,* possibly meaning 'lading or loading side.' In time the latter was reinterpreted to eliminate any reference to loading, and the two words became rivals. *Ladeborde* won, helped by being transformed into *larboard,* a perfect mate for *starboard.* The subsequent history of *larboard* and *starboard* shows how a feature that leads to victory in one moment—the attractive similarity between two companion terms—can lead to defeat in the next, through the conflict of partial homonyms. Complete homonymy was necessary to destroy *quean,* for though it crossed the path of *queen* all too often, the two words were not forced to keep constant company. *Larboard* and *starboard* were bound tightly together, and eventually their riming

---

[10] Edna Rees Williams, *The Conflict of Homonyms in English* (New Haven, Conn.: Yale University Press, 1944), pp. 83–89.

similarity proved to be a nuisance, not unlike the problem of a driver asking his companion, who is watching the signs, whether to turn left and getting the reply *Right,* meaning 'That's correct.' There must have been quite a few nautical accidents before a newly reinterpreted word, *port,* entered the competition and eliminated *larboard.*

Change of pattern: analogy and analysis

We have seen how speakers compose and revise and keep up to date their internal dictionaries by synthesizing countless bits of semantic data that come their way. They also build an internal grammar by comparing billions of individual arrangements and sorting them into likes and unlikes. After hearing innumerable combinations like *the man, the fence, the people, the bag, the lights,* a child learns that a definite noun phrase is formed by *the* plus a noun; give him a noun that he has never heard before and he will try *the* with it—this is a rule of his grammar.

Analogy, multiplied over and over, is the process by which a grammatical rule is formed. The same process appears in word formation, and there it can be studied in sharper outline because the result is often achieved in a single act of creation. A speaker familiar with *macadamize* from *Macadam, mesmerize* from *Mesmer,* and *Hooverize* from *Hoover* sets up a proportion in his mind: *Mesmer* is to *mesmerize* as *Hitler* is to X, giving *Hitlerize.* This is not a fully operative rule of grammar, for we do not attach *-ize* to proper names at will; there is no *Churchillize, de Gaulleize,* or *Kennedyize.* But the rule of grammar starts with the same kind of proportion and differs only in being enormously extended—not to a few items but to a whole class. *The* goes with the *class* of nouns. If after coining *Hitlerize* the coiner goes on to say *Hitlerized* and *Hitlerizing* he is extending an analogy that already embraces every member of the class of verbs: their participles are formed by adding *-ed* and *-ing.* Of course, it is part of the process to reveal the classes too: items that behave similarly in these analogical proportions are members of the same class.

Grammatical rules call for digesting such enormous amounts of widely available data that there is not much room for differences between one person and another. It is inconceivable that any two native speakers of English would not have as part of their internal grammar the same rule for forming noun phrases with *the.* Still, deviations are possible on a small scale. Speakers may agree by and large on the rules and classes, but disagree here and there on what words or expressions belong to what classes. For example, we have in English grammar the opposing classes "human" and "nonhuman," revealed in numerous ways, among them by the interrogative pronouns: *"Who* was it, John or Mary?"; *"What* was it, the clock or the radio?"[11] The two classes impose subtle restrictions on the way verbs and nouns may combine, even when meanings seem to be the same: *He grew his corn* but *He raised his children.* Reinterpretation takes place when a speaker is not exposed to enough examples to make the standard generalization. An adolescent speaker was heard to say *It's up to how much time I have. To be up to* and *to depend on* are close synonyms: *Whether I can accept the job is up to my mother; Whether I can accept the job depends on my mother.* But *to be up to* refers to a decision and is normally restricted to human objects: *It's up to you, It's up to the President,* not **It's up to the weather* or **It's up to how soon they get married.* If enough speakers do this with enough different items, the categories of human and nonhuman will be blurred.

Here and there one can find a growing minority of speakers disagreeing with the majority on the class membership of certain items. This may foreshadow the extinction of a class. If two classes already overlap extensively, there may come a time when it seems more logical just to throw them together, making a few minor adjustments in the individual items to bring everything into line. We have in English a class of verbs that take the infinitive with *to* as their complement: *Help me to do it, Force him to pay, Lead him to believe, Urge them to accept, He agrees to wait, He wants to work, He expects to win.* Opposite this class stands another that takes complements in *-ing: Restrain him from attacking, Prevent him from leaving, Desist from complaining, Refrain from smoking.* Looking at these examples, we are tempted to make exactly the generalization that many speakers do make: that *to* and *from* mean the same here as everywhere else—*to* refers to promoting something, to moving toward it, and *from* refers to avoiding something, to moving away from it. To these speakers it comes naturally to say *Forbid him from doing it, Forbear from speaking,* and to be uncertain with a verb like *hesitate (A traffic violator would hesitate running from a traffic officer)*[12] even though *Forbid him to do it, Forbear to speak,* and *Don't hesitate to complain* are the traditional expressions. Other verbs will probably fall in line; it is not hard to imagine *He declined from doing it* on the analogy of *He begged off from doing it.* In the end the rule for *to* with infinitive may be forced to agree with the rule for *to* as preposition, and we will no longer say *He is reluctant to agree, He refuses to cooperate,* or *He neglects to submit his reports.*

Sometimes a shift of membership and the subsequent adjustments call

---

[11] Compare the animate-inanimate classes, Chapter 5, p. 70.

[12] *Boulder Camera* (Boulder, Colorado), December 13, 1962, p. 18.

for a stairway of analogical steps. It is impossible to reconstruct with any certainty, for no log is kept as words travel through conversational space and by the time the effects find their way into print the original events are beyond observing. As a fair guess, take the expression *He's a wrong guy.* The first step may have involved the expression *all right,* which, along with *awake, asleep, amiss, akin, apart, alive,* and so on, belongs to a class of adjectives that obey a rule of position: they are used in the predicate but not directly before a noun—we say *Two things were amiss* or *Two boys were asleep* but not *two amiss things nor **two asleep boys.* But analogy is undermining the class:

> The guy is good : He's a good guy : :
> The guy is all right : He's an all right guy

shows how analogy with the synonym *good* is able to bring *all right* in front of the noun. The second step could have been like this:

> The guys are alike : Like guys flock together : :
> The guys are alive : Live guys flock together : :
> The guys are all right : Right guys flock together

whereby *all right* loses *all.* Meanwhile, other speakers may have accomplished the same result in the predicate simply by dropping the *all:*

> The guys are all (completely) bad : The guys are bad : :
> The guys are all right : The guys are right

This use of *right* in the sense of 'trustworthy' has been known in underworld usage since the early 1920's. With these two possible sources of *right* in a new sense now leading in the same direction, the stage is set for giving *wrong,* its antonym, the contrary new meaning, 'untrustworthy':

> He's the right guy : He's the wrong guy : :
> He's a right guy : He's a wrong guy

from one direction, and

> The guy is right (not mistaken) : The guy is wrong (mistaken) : :
> The guy is right (trustworthy) : The guy is wrong (untrustworthy)

from the other.

It is evident from these examples that our mental computers are constantly at work storing the expressions that we use according to certain internally elaborated regulations, endeavoring to bring order into an otherwise chaotic un-system of individual words and phrases, putting each where it can be found when needed. The linguist ferrets out the formulas and states them as grammatical rules, but ordinary speakers create them. Variations in amounts of data and sharpness of contrast explain why at the core of its grammar a language is almost immovably regular, but at the edges it defies rigid formulation and mocks all rules with hosts of exceptions—and also why, if a language could be subjected to an overall system such as Esperanto or Basic English, it would still go spiraling off sooner or later like a disobedient cloud of gas from a central sun.

COMPENSATORY CHANGE

We have examined a variety of small and medium-sized forces of change. Do these scattered gains and losses and minor realignments add up to something? Is there a flow that gathers up the eddies and carries them in some determined direction? Clearly, if changes do not cancel out one another, over the years a movement in a set direction ought to become visible, a slow but engulfing transformation that alters the physiognomy of the language, setting it off from others: "German differs from English in the freedom with which it forms compounds"; "Czech differs from English in the ease with which it shifts the position of words to gain emphasis"; "French differs from English in its comparative reluctance to put a major accent anywhere but at the end of a phrase." These are statistical differences, not absolute ones; every language is such a melange that one can find examples of practically anything in it; but the relative amounts fluctuate, creating a distinctive flavor for each language, an impression that our ear catches and that tells us when a particular language is being spoken even when we cannot understand it.

The linguist Edward Sapir referred to the gradual process by which these different proportions were achieved in each language as "drift." As an example of drift, let us consider the "slope," as Sapir would have called it, that is manifested by word order in English.

As any high-school Latin student will tell you, the arrangement of words in Latin is comparatively "free." As far as the most vital part of the message is concerned, the bare facts of who does what to whom and when, it makes little difference whether one uses *Pater puellam amat,* *Pater amat puellam,* or *Puellam amat pater.* The form of the words— declension of the nouns and conjugation of the verbs—puts them in their proper relationship. No such freedom exists in Modern English. *Father loves daughter* and *Daughter loves father* do not mean the same, and **Father daughter loves* is nonsense.

Old English was different. It had a system of case endings and verbal inflections much like that of Latin, providing the hearer with the clues he needed to make the right word-to-word connections and leaving the order of words comparatively free. But between the tenth and the four-teenth centuries most of the inflections were lost. In part, at least, this was the result of the Scandinavian invasion and settlement of parts of England, which brought speakers of two Germanic languages in close contact with one another. For a foreigner, the morphology of a language is, next to the brute memorization of vocabulary itself, the hardest thing to learn. One can guess at syntax—*People many candy ate* is not English, but if you heard it you would probably take it to mean 'Many people ate candy'—and the sounds can be mastered in a few days, but inflectional endings are infuriatingly arbitrary even when there are no "irregular verbs," which there invariably are (and always the ones you have to use the most). We can imagine a Dane communicating with a speaker of Old English and trying to make himself understood with the bare stems of words shared by their two languages. One thing that no doubt helped was a particular sentence order—probably that of subject-verb-object—already so highly favored that both could comfortably use the first noun as subject even if it lacked the proper ending.

The second event that limited the freedom of English word order was the Norman Conquest. The Norman French spoke a language much less closely related to English than that of the Danes. They contributed hosts of new words not easily fitted with English sounds or English inflections.

To compensate, English reorganized itself both phonetically and gram-matically. On the phonetic side, one major problem was that of stress. English words were typically stressed on the first syllable, French words on the last. The result of the blending was a new stress system in which the old rule of stressing the first syllable was partly relaxed. English now has a fairly stable pattern of nouns like *mascot, creole, format, topaz,* and *furlong,* where the typical stress on the first syllable has asserted itself but the former stress has left its mark in the full vowel ("secondary stress") on the second syllable. A more important result is that the breakup of the old rigidity has made possible the growing distinction between nouns, with stress on the first syllable, and verbs, with stress on the last. Most people now say *cómbat* for the noun, *combát* for the verb. Other examples are *áddress, addréss; súrvey, survéy; álly, allý.*[13]

The reorganization of grammar was equally sweeping. When the Old English inflectional endings gave way, their functions were largely taken over by prepositions and word order.[14] Instead of determining the nomi-

---

[13] See Chapter 5, p. 73.
[14] Tauno F. Mustanoja, *A Middle English Syntax* (Helsinki, 1960), Part I, Parts of Speech, p. 68.

native case by an ending, we now determine it by its relative position—
it is the noun or pronoun immediately preceding the verb, the *John* of
the utterances *John can see Mary, Mary John can see* ('As for Mary,
John can see her'), *What John can see.* Instead of marking the indirect
object by an ending, we now mark it by its position relative to the direct
object: *John gave the dog the fish, Show me it.* There are drawbacks:
when word order is laden as heavily as it is in English, sometimes it must
lay part of the burden down and simply hope that some other means of
distinction will pick it up—perhaps "what makes sense" as against "what
makes nonsense" in the general situation. This happens with *Joe I'll give
mine* and *Mine I'll give Joe,* where people get things, not things people.
But the system works, and if it breaks down one can always fall back on
a paraphrase.

The real trouble that English brought upon itself with this "gramma-
ticizing" of word order is difficult to appreciate if we continue to think
of the order of Latin and Old English as "free." It was not really free, but
it expressed a part of the message that was secondary to who does what
to whom and when, though still important. *Pater filiam amat* and *Pater
amat filiam* do not "mean the same." The first answers the question "What
is the father's attitude toward his daughter?" (It is one of *love*—the climax
word, *amat*, comes last.) The second answers the question "Toward
whom does the father manifest love?" (Toward his *daughter*—again the
climax word comes last.)

If this seems too subtle a distinction to bother with, the answer is that
English still does bother with it on a sizable scale, in spite of its arthritic
order of words. We are still eager to put the climax in the end position,
if we can. One place where it is possible, in fact quite easy, is in the
positioning of clauses: *After he ate he left the house* answers the question, "What did he do after he ate?"; *He left the house after he ate*
answers the question "When did he leave the house?" The climax expression comes last. A nicer example is the "introduction," where we are
presenting something for the first time on the mental scene: *Around the
corner ran two dogs* brings the dogs into view more effectively than does
Two dogs ran around the corner. So with *Into my face blew a gust of
wind, Over the radio came an alarm, Out of the night sounded a scream.*

A group of Czech linguists refers to this tendency of many languages to
put the known first and the unknown or unexpected last as "sentence
perspective."[15] They point out that, in order to communicate the sentence
dynamism that has been partially lost by the stiffening of word order,

---

[15] See Jan Firbas, "From Comparative Word-order Studies," *Brno Studies in English*
4.111–22 (1964).

English must resort to other stratagems, and these are among the things that give the language its distinctive syntactic appearance. What are some of them?

First, English makes a heavier investment in the passive voice.[16] Suppose we have a sentence like *Goethals built the Canal.* This serves very well in response to "Tell us about Goethals," but less efficiently for "Tell us about the Canal"—for the latter, we are apt to say, "Well, *it was built* by Goethals, it took ten years to build," and so on. Had it not been for the loss of inflections, we might today be saying something like *Built it Goethals.*

Second, we find an increase in the number of sentences with indefinite subjects. To answer "What's a haberdashery?" one might say, "In the United States, it is a place where *they sell* (or *you buy*) men's clothes," with indefinite *they* or *you.* English sentence structure forces us to express a subject, but we have no reason to mention any particular one. The passive voice, which might otherwise enable us to eliminate the doer of the action altogether *(clothes are sold*—we don't have to say by whom), will not work, because it prevents us from putting *clothes* where we want it, at the end—we can't say **where are sold clothes.*

Third, speakers of English lean more heavily on intonation. In place of *It was built by Goethals,* we could say, putting the kind of accent on *Goethals* that calls for raising it to the highest pitch,

$$\text{We}^{ll,}\ \text{G}^{o\ e}\text{thals}\ ^{built}\ _{i}{}^{t}\ldots$$

And with the *clothes* example we could do the same, now using the passive voice for the sake of its actor-eliminating function:

$$\text{It's a }^{place}\text{ where }^{men's}{}^{clothes}\text{ are sold.}$$

Written English, of course, lacks this last resource. One result is that the climax word of a sentence cannot be highlighted by a freely-placed intonational peak. To make up for this, writers tend to do the next best thing and put it as close to the end of the sentence as possible, which is where speakers put the peak anyway when they have no special plans for it. Readers come to expect it there and are miscued if it is placed anywhere else. In answer to *Couldn't you tell Jane by her green dress?*

---

16 See Ljiljana Mihailovic, "Some Observations on the Use of the Passive Voice," *English Language Teaching* 17.77–81 (1963).

if we wrote *Mary wore the green dress* we would probably be misunderstood, though in speech

$$M^a$$
$$ry \quad wore \quad the \quad green$$
$$dres^{s.}$$

would be perfectly intelligible. In writing we must put *The green dress
was worn by Mary* (or use another syntactic trick to show where the
highest pitch comes: *It was Mary who wore the green dress*—one more
feature of English that a frozen sentence order makes necessary).

ADDITIONAL REMARKS AND APPLICATIONS

1. Recall from your own experience some sound-and-sense connection that led you to a word or name you wanted. For example, you have forgotten the name of a neighbor you had two years ago. Suddenly you think you have it: **Olds.** Then you realize that the Olds family lived next door to you *ten* years ago, and the name you had been searching for was **Newman.**

2. Identify the ingredients of the following blends: *Give them the tone with your pitchfork; They made up after their little spiff; The test will include both speaking as well as reading; It will go down in posterity; I've gone through a lot of expense to do this; She isn't far from wrong.*

3. Identify the correct forms to replace the following malapropisms: *The issue would be more quickly enjoined; I made them a sincere offer but they flaunted it; He lives in Pepsi Cola, Florida; She couldn't get into that college because they refused to waver the requirement.*

4. If a child said to you *The sky was pitch black,* you would understand. Suppose the same child says later *The sky was pitch red.* Did your earlier understanding of *pitch black* imply that you both had the same conception of *pitch?* Does this indicate that we can get along with slight differences in our internal dictionaries?

5. Explain what association (folk etymology) the speakers who used the following forms had at the back of their minds: *hybrid* pronounced with the second syllable like *bred; tommytoe,* a small tomato; *typewriter* pronounced *tapladder; vagary* pronounced *vágary* and meaning 'point that someone is confused about'; *We don't want to do things in a half-hazzard way* (from a letter).

6. Is fusion an essential part of building up larger and more complex units in language? (Review Chapter 5, pages 53–55.) You have probably had the experience of having used some expression all your life

and then suddenly realizing what it "really means," for example, *The coast is clear,* alluding to invasion by sea. Can you recall an instance?

7. Consider whether speeding up for fusion is a manifestation of a more commonplace phenomenon, *familiarity.* If you live on the other side of a lake, and say *I've got to row home,* would you normally say it as fast as *I've got to go home?* If you are at a college with some students from Thailand and say *We have several Thais,* would it be as fast as *We have several ties?* How does the degree of expectedness of what we say affect the speed with which we say it?

8. Would you be surprised to read or hear the statement *Those students need more tuition* in the sense 'need more instruction'? If so, give your idea of the meaning of *tuition* and account for it as a reinterpretation on the basis of contexts like *The tuition* (instruction) *is too high, They paid my tuition* (like *They paid my trip*), *How much is tuition at that school?* and so on.

   Can you identify the changing circumstances that led to the phrase *horse cavalry,* despite the fact that the *cavalry* (from *caballus* 'horse') were always traditionally mounted on horseback?

9. Traditionally, a person's house or place of business was indicated by the simple possessive: *I'm going over to Mary's; I bought it at the grocer's; Right now he's at the doctor's.* How has this been reinterpreted by people who write *They took him to the cleaners?*

10. Would *beau* be used nowadays for *boyfriend?* (And does a boy who has a friend who is a boy refer to his *boyfriend?*) Think of some other words that have become old-fashioned.

11. Following are some variant forms of the "same" word or phrase; do they mean the same for you?

till, until	*broke, broken*
further, farther	*pent up, penned up*
lighted, lit	*struck, stricken*

12. Mixed metaphors (*The idea was no sooner born than it faded; The dark corners of their ignorance fell before his eloquence; As you go down the path of life, drink it to the full*) are condemned as bad style. If a folk etymology is a reinterpretation that "gives depth" to an expression, what effect do these reinterpretations have on the depth of the expressions?

13. An article refers to Army terminology that is not *"exclusive to* a particular department." Can you explain the probable reason why *peculiar to* was not used here?

14. Look up the etymologies of the words *rogue, scamp, jerk, mischievous, naughty,* and *rascal.*

15. Agent nouns made from verbs regularly use the simple suffix *-er: brew, brewer; view, viewer; do, doer.* Can you think of a reason why *suer* from *sue* is now obsolete and *suitor* is used instead? Why is the word *succour* no longer used? A radio program used the expression *There's a fording place there.* Traditionally this would have been *There's a ford there.* Why the change?

16. In the United States the word *shivaree* has gradually crowded out its rival synonyms *(serenade, belling, bull band, horning, callathump, tin-panning, skimmerton).* Does its sound in any way favor it? Compare words for other lively celebrations: *spree, corroboree, jubilee, husking bee, jamboree.*

17. A certain legume popular as an article of food was formerly spelled *pease* and belonged to the grammatical class of mass nouns, like *wheat, corn, barley.* Explain the analogy that shifted it to the class of count nouns like *beans, peanuts, lentils.*

18. In general, adverbs of time are freely placed in a sentence:

   Immediately the people left.
   The people left immediately.
   The people immediately left.

What happens with adverbs of place? Consider

   Outside the people were shouting.
   The people were shouting outside.
   The people outside were shouting.

Does the last sentence differ from the first two in meaning? In order to have phrases like *the people outside,* has English been forced to compensate by restricting the free movement of certain adverbs that modify the verb or the sentence as a whole?

THE EVOLUTION
OF LANGUAGE: VIEWS
AND MEASUREMENTS

T o speak of "the forces of change," as the preceding chapters have done, is to picture them as beyond human control—speakers are buffeted by winds of fusion and metathesis and by waves of invading terms from other languages and are forced to bow to them. But man can be viewed as master of his circumstance as well as its victim. Everything in language is manmade. It is not before some irresistible force of nature that we bow, but before the might of millions of other speakers like ourselves whose individual acts of creation or error pour over us like a flood. The waters build up because each of us adds to them. The way we add is determined by the form of the language as it came down to us, but *what* we add is induced by a dimly conceived intent or in the full light of deliberation as often as through surrender or indifference.

Viewing change as creation rather than as the operation of impersonal forces requires us to think not of causes but of resources. What does our language offer in the way of means to do with it as we will, to give it a future that is molded and not merely blundered into?

To answer this question would call for recasting in a different perspective everything that has been said. Even if there were room to do so, the tools are lacking: too little is known about language as an instrument. One meager sample was the emphasis on source morphemes in Chapter 5. The area where creativity is most obvious is that of the invention of new words. We know a little about composition as a source—

the combining of words to make a word, such as *wave* + *length* to give *wavelength*—and about derivation—the addition of affixes to stems such as *auto-* + *intoxication* to give *autointoxication.* But about other kinds of change that might be effected intentionally, such as what resources are available for making a new grammatical contrast should the need arise or for constituting a new phoneme or salvaging an old one, we shall continue to be wise after the fact for some time to come.

In Chapters 13 and 14 we shall meet again, in a different guise, the problem of whether men control language or language controls men. For the present, we shall ask two very general questions: Is change for the good (which it ought to be, if human beings are to guide it and guide it sensibly)? Can change be measured?

PROGRESS

We like to think of ourselves as moving onward and upward. Is there evidence that the broad shifts in form that language undergoes over long periods of time betoken progress toward a "better" state?

To become better later implies that something must have been worse before, and this suggests that we ought to be able to look over our language and find flaws in it. We say, "Of course—look at English spelling. What a mess!" And, as was noted in Chapter 6, determined—though unsuccessful—efforts have been made to reform our delinquent orthography. But spelling is comparatively exterior to language as a system of spoken communication, and faults of a different sort make better examples.

Pronunciation is hard to judge, because speakers sail over difficult combinations of sounds without noticing them. Yet some combinations are undeniably more difficult to pronounce than others: *mulcts* and *bursts,* for example.

At the level of words, most of us feel frustrated at one time or another because we are unable to get a convenient term for our meaning. Usually this is just because we forget, but sometimes the lack is real and the fault is not ours. We even make jokes about some deficiencies, such as the favorite of old-time vaudevillians: *Take one pill three times a day.* There is no single satisfactory word for 'one's given name'; we have to use a phrase. Usually the circumstances and the context conceal the bad coin so that we are unaware of it until some caviler insists on his due, like the jaywalker who told the judge that the sign said *Don't walk* and that he had a perfect right to run; there is no one term in English that means 'to locomote with the feet.' At other times we are boxed in with no escape except to change our expression completely. *It's bad weather* is normal English, but adding *too* gets us into trouble: *It's too bad weather, too bad a weather, a too bad weather, a weather too bad*—all are somehow unsatisfactory. Or suppose we want to intensify *fewer*. We have no trouble with *more* and *less* when we say *much more money, much less money*, in which despite the apparent contradiction of *much less, much* has lost all but its intensifying function. Not so with *many: many more* does not displease us, but *many fewer* is next to impossible.

Sometimes a lack is partially made up. The verb *to err* was lost from everyday speech many years ago, possibly for phonetic reasons (it doesn't *sound* like a word), and was even killed off as a learned word when teachers refused to accept the solution of pronouncing it the same as *air*. We had to resort to *muff it, make a mistake*, and other phrases. Then between 1950 and 1960 the verb *to goof* caught on, and has satisfied at least that part of the semantic area of *err* that has to do with *blundering* error.

But lack of particular words is hardly more than a blemish on the surface of something with strata as deep as those of language. A bit farther down we encounter a defect that caused us no end of struggle when we were children (and would infuriate us now if we were learning English as a foreign language)—the lack of consistency in the forms of various classes of words. There would be advantages if all verbs, for example, were regular, on the model of *like-liked-liked, hate-hated-hated*, rather than *do-did-done, see-saw-seen, sell-sold-sold;* and many verbs have in fact regularized themselves, for example *work*, which has discarded *wrought* in favor of *worked*. But quite a few have gone in the other direction, *digged* turning into *dug, sticked* into *stuck*, and, for many speakers, *dived* into *dove*. The difficulty with "progress" in these morphological caverns is that rival standards are set up: while one speaker is busy trying to level *sped* into *speeded*, another is trying to level *speeded* into *sped*, and a third, wondering what the argument is about and offered a choice between them, blithely uses them both with a difference in meaning, thereby destroying any chance of eliminating the inconsistency (*He sped down the road* 'went fast'; *He speeded down the road* 'drove his car fast'). The would-be regularizers unconsciously defeat each other.

A language, then, has a hard time achieving consistency. To the extent that it succeeds, it makes progress of a sort, but by an outside, objective standard it is rather sterile progress, like repairing an old organism instead of evolving a new one. Nevertheless, this kind of progress is fascinating to watch, for it gives us our best understanding of language as a system—an integral whole in which nothing can happen in one chamber without echoing in another. An example often quoted is the phenomenon known as the Great English Vowel Shift. Somewhere in the Middle English period, speakers began to alter the sounds of the long vowels, pronouncing them with a higher position of the tongue. Since every event has to have a beginning somewhere, the chances are that only one of the vowels was affected at first. If it was the first vowel in *name*, the effect was to raise it away from its original *ah* sound toward the sound it has today. But this was a threat to the vowel that already had that sound, for example in *sheen* (sounding like *shane*), which for self-protection moved up toward the pronunciation it has today, and in turn collided with the vowel in *wife;* and this vowel, with no place to go—the [i] is the highest position—turned into a diphthong, probably by accentuating a tendency that some already had in their speech. A similar chain reaction took place in the back vowels:

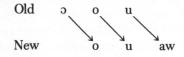

Languages are super-systems in which each sub-system is in barely stable equilibrium. Every time some accident unbalances the equilibrium at one point, the entire sub-system reacts to it. This is a way of saying that, when something happens to blur the audible distinctions between the parts of our message so that one comes to sound too much like another, we usually do something about it if the means are within sufficiently easy reach. For example, when the [g] sound was lost at the end of *sung, king,* and *fang,* speakers could no longer rely on it to distinguish these words from *sun, kin,* and *fan.* But the sound of the allophone of /n/ before /g/ was still there and sufficed to maintain the distinction. What formerly was just an automatic variant of /n/ before /g/ or /k/ (try saying *sun-kissed* fast and see if the /n/ is not apt to turn into /ŋ/) became a new phoneme. Needless to say, speakers do not decide that they need a new phoneme and consciously select one. The process is unconscious.

But while most of the changes are a part of history and hence irreversible, a few of them survive as choices among which we select automatically. The word for *one* which evolved into our indefinite article lost all but its vowel when used before a word starting with a consonant *(a man);* but before a word starting with another vowel the /n/ was retained *(an ape).* One can interpret this as blind evolution, the /n/ being lost where it was hardest to hear, or as having a trace of purpose in it, the /n/ being kept where it was most needed to preserve the identity of *a, an* as a word.

We see that a language in making "progress" toward internal consistency does little more than catch up with itself, and this is hardly progress in a real sense. Can we, recognizing that our language is not all that we would like it to be, apply some other standard that would enable us to say that some languages are better than others, hence have "progressed more," and therefore hold out the hope of progress to their lesser brethren?

This is a judgment that most linguists are reluctant to make. With memories of the cultural snobbery that has colored opinions about superiority in the past ("French is the most logical language, Italian the most musical, German the most scientific"), and with their discoveries of the beautiful intricacies of supposedly "primitive" languages fresh in mind, they have rejected the idea that any language is intrinsically better than any other, from which it follows that fifteenth-century English was just as good as twentieth-century English, and there has been no progress. Linguists are willing to admit that there is a constant, though slow, evolution toward greater fitness of the tool to the needs of its time, but point out that this again is just an instance of catching up—the needs are evolving about as fast as the language is, and the gap between them remains the same.

But what if the needs themselves grow more complex, so that language in catching up with a progressive culture seems itself to be progressing? One linguist frankly advocates using culture as the standard: "The assumption that all languages are more or less equally efficient in their respective cultures may be retained, but at the same time the differences in these cultures may be used as an external yardstick to assess the amount and the complexity of the work which languages are called upon and are able to perform."[1]

The probable fate of all theories of progress in language can be shown by what befell the theory of one of the great linguists of a generation ago, Otto Jespersen. Jespersen felt that one sign of progress—particularly marked in languages like English and Chinese—is the discarding of "reminders." When we say *Mary is the sweetest, dearest, loveliest girl I know,* we express the one superlative idea three times, in the suffix *-est,* as can be seen by factoring it out and saying instead *Mary is the most sweet, dear, lovely girl I know.* In the latter construction, supposedly typical of a later stage of language growth, we do not require an explicit superlative each time, but get the same results through the larger organization of the sentence. Jespersen was really reversing the older argument that Latin was a superior language because it was highly inflected.

This idea of nonrepetitiousness as a sign of superiority has been demolished by another trend of thought stimulated by information theory, the discipline that deals with codes and message-sending and serves, among other things, to measure the efficiency of our telephones. It turns out that if language actually did express a particular bit of information only once, it would not be intelligible unless all the channels of communication were functioning perfectly, free of noise and with undistracted attention on the part of the listener. If the idea of 'most' in

[1] L. F. Brosnahan, "Language and Evolution," *Lingua* 9.232 (1960).

the example above is given just once and that once happens to be obscured by noise, the message is lost.

Redundancy goes much deeper than out-and-out repetition of words or suffixes. Take the simplest case, the way languages squander their phonemes. Why, for instance, do we keep *superfluous* instead of reducing it to *sperfl?* The fleshing out of a word with more than the minimum it needs makes things easier for the listener. He has more cues. If he correctly hears either *superf-* or *-erfluous* he can get by. Or a word may be so obvious in a given position that almost any audible part of it is enough. In a sentence like *I'd just as soon Jerry stayed away; he's super-fluous around here anyway,* so few words other than *superfluous* would make sense in that spot that hearing just the first syllable betrays it. We catch our signals from sounds, contexts, situations, facial expressions, and our knowledge of what to expect—each repeating the other to some extent. Languages have to be redundant, and while particular redundancies might be done away with to some advantage, their loss in general would not spell progress.

So it seems that languages get better only in a relative sense, in spurts, as the culture veers off and the language moves to close the gap. Models of mathematical or logical efficiency are irrelevant and progress is only in terms of the progress of the culture as a whole. To claim that a language is getting better is to claim that its culture is getting better, and that is a bold claim.

THE MEASUREMENT OF CHANGE

Measurement requires homogeneity. It makes little sense to speak of the "average wealth" in a community made up of one millionaire and ten paupers, for the figure would suggest that all are comfortably well off. Does language evolve at a rate constant enough to be expressed mathematically?

Viewed close up, language changes by fits and starts. A linguistic regularity does not suddenly dissolve and reorganize itself into some new and different regularity, but fights on from the outposts even after it has lost the citadel. The seascape of our language is dotted with islands of little idioms that once upon a time embraced whole kingdoms of usage, but have shrunk to the point where all we can do is catalog them as quaint exceptions. The present passive participle vanished long ago from an expression such as *The oats are threshing.* It disappeared only yesterday from *The houses are building,* and is still part of the tricky style in *Time* magazine. It remains with us in *The coffee is making,* thanks in part to automatic percolators that have assimilated this construction to other kinds of activity that do not require the uninterrupted attention of the cook: *The water is boiling, The eggs are frying, The cereal is cooking.* The reinterpreted regularity is 'self-propelled activity,' but it was not achieved overnight.

At other times there are competing regularities that end by dividing their spheres of influence and declaring a truce. The use of nouns to modify nouns follows two main patterns, the French *oil of sesame* type and the Germanic *sesame oil* type. Pharmaceutical, poetic, and other elevated influences are wielded in favor of the former, congealing particular phrases that forbid the inroads of noun-plus-noun: *spirits of ammonia, tincture of iodine, heart of gold, day of wrath, letter of credit, house of cards*—while the opposite pattern takes a homelier turn and produces *business letter, cottonseed oil, molasses candy,* and so on. The two patterns have now become so interwoven with other constructions—*cup of tea* versus *teacup, time of life* versus *lifetime, collection of coins* versus *coin collection*—that it is practically inconceivable that either should ever efface the other.

Along the front of individual word meanings, retreat is even more disorganized. Words, or particular usages of words, that were once general are driven to take refuge in out-of-the-way phrases whose protective coloration they assume and where they are scarcely recognized for themselves. In current speech *babe,* generally 'good-looking girl,' is distinguished from *baby,* but it survives in its older sense in the phrase *babe in arms.* The word *thus* as an adjunct modifier, as in *thus many, thus much,* is never heard nowadays, having been replaced by *this* or *that,* except in one phrase: *thus far.* The two-word verb *come by* in the sense 'to obtain,' which appears in the preface to the King James Bible, "Translation it is . . . that removeth the cover of the well, that we may come by the water," is rarely found now except in the phrase *hard to come by.* Nowadays a *tempest* is usually found in a teapot and a *brow* serves little purpose except to be wrinkled, furrowed, or mopped.

The fault, of course, is that we stand too close. To see anything like a series of changes, or rather *kinds* of changes, that would allow of measuring the time span from one to another, in a field as vexed by contradictory impulses as syntax or semantics, would require a sweep of history beyond the reach of any record. An uninflected language can build inflections through agglutination—merely adding elements together; there is not much difference after all between *amo, amas, amat* and *Ilove, youlove, heloves,* if we want to think of the pronoun and its verb as a unit. An inflected language can lose its inflections. But whether inflection and lack of inflection are in some sort of historic alternation is beyond our ken. We can discover a nominal style gaining favor in Western languages—*to be in receipt of* for *to receive, to be in contravention of* for *to contravene, to reach the conclusion that* for *to conclude that,* and so on—

but we cannot measure the steps in the process. Even less can we grasp its alternation with other processes that cover ages of time.

Yet measurement, if we could manage it, would be immensely useful. Finding something that changes at a constant rate would give us a calendar for the strata of linguistics like the calendar of geologic time provided by carbon dating.

A decade or so ago it was thought that the key to such a "glotto-chronology" had been found. Working with American Indian languages, where written records were nonexistent and there was no way to esti-mate how many years or centuries had elapsed since two languages from the same stock had begun to diverge—for example, two related languages like Zoque and Totonac—some linguists theorized that any two languages sharing words or word stems of a certain basic type would be related to the extent of how many such words they shared. It was necessary to assume that not all words are equally reliable for this kind of measure-ment. A glance at the everyday terms shared by related languages reveals that some are so close to universal traits, needs, and experiences of the human race that they ought to resist the inroads of rival terms more vigorously than others do: *mother, fire, love, eat, hand, foot, three, sand,* and so on. If the number of such shared terms expressed the degree of kinship, the next step was to put the comparison into a historical perspective and imagine that each earlier epoch would reveal a closer tie, until, if we traced the lines of development back far enough, the two would converge—all the terms would be the same and the two languages would be one. The next question was crucial: were these terms basic items of vocabulary that, given enough time, would supposedly drop out one by one from each language, being lost at a constant rate? If so, we ought to be able to take cases where we do have historical documents to date the changes, as in the Romance languages, find out what the rate is, and then apply it to languages for which no documentation exists.

After much laborious testing and comparison with results from applying other yardsticks, most linguists have concluded that glottochronology will not work.[2] We cannot be sure that the social and historical forces of change have not been stronger in one epoch than in another, or that many items of supposedly basic vocabulary have not actually been bor-rowed rather than inherited (like *mountain* replacing *mount,* or *person* replacing *body*), or even that something as deep-seated as *mother* may not (as has happened with Spanish *madre* in some dialects) give way to another term. The history of *knave-boy, quean-woman, deer-animal,* and many other presumably basic words that have fluctuated is a warning

---

[2] See Eugenio Coseriu, "Critique de la Glottochronologie Appliquée aux Langues Romanes," *Actes du X⁰ Congrès International de Linguistique et Philologie Romanes* (Paris, 1965), pp. 87–96.

against setting too much store by counting vocabulary. As one linguist observes, the perfect list of words would have no words in it at all, because "the closer we get to universal validity, the fewer the items we have."[3]

The other possible candidate for measurement through time is change in the sound system. Whether this will fare any better remains to be seen, although one recent study suggests that it will not. A survey of the speech of the year-round inhabitants of Martha's Vineyard found that their desire to be different from the detested mainlanders is leading them to speed up certain changes in the pronunciation of their vowels.[4] Social pressures create variable rates of change in phonetics as well as in vocabulary.

Nevertheless, glottochronology has paid off in other ways. One interesting byproduct is the evidence it provides of what earlier societies must have been like. If several related languages have a certain body of terms in common, it is fairly safe to assume that the customs and artifacts tied to the terms must also have been shared. Using this kind of evidence from three languages spoken in the south of Mexico, it is possible to reconstruct the way of life of the speakers of the common parent language perhaps as long as three thousand years ago, even though no written records exist. They must have been farmers who cultivated maize, maguey, and probably also squash and chili peppers. They seem to have lived in permanent or near-permanent villages. They prepared maize as a food by soaking the grains in a leach of wood ashes and probably pounded it to produce the same *masa* that is used nowadays throughout Mexico for making tortillas. Corn was probably eaten as roasting ears, and other foods were probably steamed over heated stones in earth ovens. There may have been pottery, and in any case there were almost certainly bags and baskets for carrying and storage. Most likely their beds were palm-leaf mats spread on the ground, with woven blankets as bedclothing. Pine torches were used for light. Sandals were probably made and clothing woven from the fiber of the maguey plant, with maguey thorns used as needles. And the world was populated with gods of sun, moon, rain, and other natural phenomena.[5]

Though as a dating procedure glottochronology has been largely abandoned, it is still valued as a measure of closeness between languages and cultures; and for this, the term *lexicostatistics* is preferred.

---

[3] Professor Karl Teeter in *Language* 39.642 (1963).

[4] William Labov, "The Social Motivation of a Sound Change," *Word* 19.273–309 (1963).

[5] Robert E. Longacre and René Millon, "Proto-Mixtecan and Proto-Amuzgo-Mixtecan Vocabularies," *Anthropological Linguistics*, April, 1961, pp. 1–44, especially pp. 31–32.

ADDITIONAL REMARKS
AND APPLICATIONS

1. Is English efficient in handling comparatives when it builds one on top of another? We have no trouble with *He feels well enough to go out,* but suppose he has to be better by a measurable degree: can we say *He feels better enough to go out?*

2. At some time in the Middle English period, the velar spirant (the final sound in Scottish *loch* or German *ach*) was lost in certain words, for example *right, brought, daughter, through, plough.* In others it was kept but changed: *laughter, enough, trough, rough.* What sound was substituted? Was this sound similar to the velar spirant in terms of distinctive features?

3. The usual test for progress is efficiency. What is the yardstick used by purists when they complain of the deterioration of language? How would you go about judging expressions like *It is I* and *It's me* in terms of efficiency?

4. Point out the redundancies in the following:

    a. He walked slowly, carefully, and deliberately.

    b. Mary bought herself a new hat.

    c. He never says nothing to nobody.

    In c. is the redundancy really removed if *any-* replaces *no-?* Would *He never says a thing to a person* be intelligible?

5. One critic[6] argues that carbon dating is the wrong analogy for glotto-chronology, that instead the comparison should be with a biological model in which population size is a factor in the rate of change. What hints have been given in these chapters—and what others can you add—that larger populations are less exposed to rapid change?

---

[6] Robert D. Stevick, "The Biological Model and Historical Linguistics," *Language* 39.159–69 (1963).

DIALECT 9

DIALECT AND LANGUAGE

LINGUISTIC HISTORY records sweeping changes that affect vast bodies of speakers over long periods—some abrupt, even cataclysmic, so that everyone is conscious of what is happening, others so gradual that speakers may be unaware of them during their lifetimes. Dialectology looks upon the differences that set one community apart from another, that characterize the individual speaker even when they do not necessarily interfere with communication, that give society its flavor and no small amount of its mirth. Linguistic history is dialectology writ large, and dialectology is the idiosyncrasies of particular speakers writ medium. There is no clear separation of what one speaker does that others of his community do not do; nor is there any between what communities do that makes them different from one another or what it is that distinguishes one language from another. Techniques of discovery may differ—historical linguistics has elaborate strategies to hypothesize what cannot be observed because the evidence has long since vanished, whereas dialectology may be contemporary, capturing many of its facts almost as they happen. The facts in both fields are the same; the size of the bite is what distinguishes them.

But size makes a difference in our appreciation, for dialect differences are cut to the measure of our comprehension, while differences between languages may overwhelm us. Comparatively few individuals are bilingual. Every speaker is multilingual in the sense of understanding more than one dialect. And most speakers command different styles of speech which, if they are not to be called different dialects, are denied the name only because we want to reserve it for contrasts that are more pronounced. Whenever we speak in a more "reserved" or "decorous" manner, whenever we strive to avoid "grammatical mistakes," we pass from one dialect to another.

KINDS OF DIALECT

Every speaker speaks as many dialects as there are groups among which he moves that have different modes of speech. Some groups are biologically determined. Others are formed by more or less voluntary association. Here are some important ones:

[1] **Profession**   The speech of the minister differs from the speech of the merchant. Each occupation has its own things to talk about. But the difference goes beyond merely having different words for different things. It often embodies a variety of names for the same thing: the soothsayer has his *augury,* the weather man his *forecast,* the doctor his *prognosis,* and the scientist his *prediction.*

[2] **Sex**   Men's talk differs from women's talk. This line is somewhat blurred in our society, but it remains legible. Adjectives like *dreadful, precious, darling* are more apt to be encountered in women's speech than in men's—in fact, women are more liberal with adjectives in general. In some levels of society men are less inhibited in their choice of words than women. Women are less inhibited in their intonational range.

[3] **Age**   The infant differs from the child, the child from the adolescent, the adolescent from the adult. The most extreme case is baby talk, which, in the sense that its speakers are physically unable to speak otherwise, is not really a dialect, but it becomes one when its forms are imitated—and sometimes fabricated—by adults and used by them with young children. As with all dialects, forms from this one may be picked up and broadcast; a recent instance is *bye-bye,* which is heard more and more as an ordinary friendly farewell, not necessarily an intimate one. At the other extreme is the dialect that time imposes on us all: older speakers do not always adopt newer ways of speaking, and the older they grow the more

quaint their speech becomes. Nor is the process always purely automatic—a transition between age levels may be made consciously. Among
the Ainu of Japan, "there is a kind of speech that is characteristic of
older people which persists in its own right and is adopted by younger
people as they gradually mature"—an "old speech" which does not itself
grow old and die out.[1]

[4] Occasion   Even the most careful speakers permit themselves a style
of speech at home that is different from the one they use in public. Many
societies set up—not by legislation but by tacit consent—a standard dialect
that is used on formal occasions and that serves as a kind of inter-lingua,
available to any speaker when he wants to identify himself with speakers
at large rather than with speakers at home. The standard dialect takes on
the local color of the speaker but is nevertheless different from the
relaxed style used with friends, family, and neighbors. It is more neutral
and as a rule is more generally understood, but intelligibility is not
essential to its authority.[2] In some countries, any relaxation of the formal
standard in occasions that call for it is resented even if, as happens sometimes, speakers have difficulty understanding it (this may be likened to
the reactions of some people in our own culture to attempts to make the
Bible more intelligible by modernizing the English).[3] In India, formal
Hindi is stiffened by generous doses of Sanskrit.[4] In Chinese, a formal
lecture and a conversation may even differ syntactically: the idea that one
group of officials (A) is more numerous than another group (B) is
expressed in the lecture as

A	dwō	yú	B
A	numerous	than	B

and in the conversation as

A	bǐ	B	dwō
A	compared to	B	numerous[5]

[1] Shiro Hattori, "A Special Language of the Older Generations Among the Ainu,"
General Linguistics 6.43–58 (1964).

[2] Experiments have shown that "speakers of high status are more comprehensible for
speakers of all statuses." See L. S. Harms, "Status Cues in Speech: Extra-race and
Extra-region Identification," *Lingua* 12.300–06 (1963).

[3] Charles A. Ferguson, "Diglossia," *Word* 15.330 (1959).

[4] Paul W. Friedrich, *Language* 37.168 (1961).

[5] John de Francis in *Georgetown University Monograph Series on Languages and
Linguistics,* September, 1951, p. 50.

The standard in English is not clear-cut (it is never entirely so anywhere), but certain tendencies mark it off. The obvious ones are in the choice of words. Where a university press, announcing a competition, reserves to itself the *"first refusal* of manuscripts," the intent is not to be candidly pessimistic but to avoid the more accurate but too colloquial *first chance at.*[6] At a graduation one hears *All seniors will please rise* (or possibly *stand*); a relaxed occasion would call for *get up* or *stand up.* Certain contractions are avoided on formal occasions: the easygoing *show* harmonizes with *'em* in *Let's show 'em* but would hardly be used with the stiff verb *reveal: Let's reveal them.* In the supremely formal atmosphere of the church, even *let's* may be avoided: *Let's pray* would sound secular, if not sporting. And there are syntactic differences here and there. Take the use of adverbs. There is a variety of English, regarded as substandard, in which most adverbs are distinguished from adjectives not by the suffix *-ly* but by position after the verb or verb phrase: in *He wrote the letter real careful, careful* is an adverb; in *He wrote a careful letter* it is an adjective. (All dialects of English do this part of the time: *He made the trip fast, He made a fast trip.*) Standard English adds the *-ly* and uses the resulting adverbs rather freely as to position: *They left rapidly, They rapidly left.* But very informal—not necessarily substandard—English does not favor *-ly* adverbs before the verb or verb phrase. It prefers the other position or some adverb not ending in *-ly*: instead of *He grew steadily worse, I promptly told him,* and *She's constantly complaining* it will say *He grew worse and worse, I told him right there,* and *She's all the time complaining.*

There is practically no limit to the number of social affinities revealed in differences of language. To age, sex, occupation, and occasion it would be necessary to add religion, politics, lodge affiliation, preference as to sports or amusements, and any other circumstances under which people meet and speak. But overshadowing them all are two coordinates laid on every society that determine far wider differences than any thus far mentioned. One is horizontal, as on a map: Bostonese, for example, differs from the speech of the rest of New England, and the speech of New England differs from that of the Coastal South; geographical dialects are inevitable, because people do more talking to their neighbors than to those who are farther away, and where more is shared, differences are fewer. The other is vertical, as with layers: in stratified societies people are born to a social class; nothing stigmatizes a class more indelibly than its language, and differences in speech are often cultivated for this very purpose.

---

[6] MLA-Oxford Award, 1952–53: "Under the terms of the competition, Oxford will have first refusal of all manuscripts submitted," *Hispania* 36.116 (1953).

Probably because they touch us in a tender spot, the vertical and horizontal differences are the ones that come first to mind when dialects are mentioned. Geographical differences have ties with our loyalties to home, town, and state. Social differences are nourished on feelings of superiority and inferiority, and to some extent color all other differences. In a society where women and farmers are regarded as inferior, sex differences and occupational differences become class differences. As for differences due to occasion, inability to handle the standard dialect when the occasion calls for it is especially likely to be taken as a class difference, for the dominant social class is the one whose traits of speech are most fully embodied in the standard.

The linguist and the sociologist are selective in different ways in their attitudes toward dialect. The linguist focuses mainly on the horizontal coordinate. Differences from region to region are the specimens that attract him most, probably because they are the same, though on a smaller scale, as the ones already familiar to him from language to language. When he speaks of dialectology it is almost always in this sense, more specifically referred to as "linguistic geography," "areal linguistics," or "dialect geography." The sociologist focuses mainly on the vertical coordinate. He is interested in how social groups interact within a single speech community, in how language influences our opportunities and our behavior. He views language as a series of codes by which the individual acts out his roles in society.

LINGUISTIC CODES

The language of a profession, say that of law, is social distinction in its crudest form. It is part of an economic order in which everyone's way of earning a living somehow influences his speech because of the need to manipulate a certain set of objects and concepts that are the tools of the profession. But ordinarily it goes no deeper than the choice of terms to match the objects. What really counts for the sociologist is how the lawyer interacts with his banker and his grocer, and how the banker's son and the grocer's son are able, through having certain models to emulate in their parents, teachers, and others, to define themselves and by so doing to open or close the doors to growth and change of status.

The sociologist Basil Bernstein distinguishes two types of code that are socially significant: restricted and elaborated.[7] A restricted code allows one to interact with one's fellows in a highly predictable way. It is

---

[7] "A Socio-linguistic Approach to Social Learning," in *Survey of the Social Sciences, 1965*, ed. Julius Gould (Baltimore, Md.: Penguin Books, Inc., 1965), pp. 144–68.

associated with a certain social set or activity where only a limited number of things can be done. They are not necessarily prescribed in a particular order, as they would be in a game, but the choices are few. An example is the cocktail party, where the nature of the language used and the nature of the things talked about is known in advance and what one learns about new-made acquaintances is transmitted not so much by language as by look and gesture. The conventionality of the language enables speakers to relax in one another's company and communicate in other ways, much as the set movements of a dance remove the necessity of deciding what to do next. In a restricted code, individuality is submerged. The speaker and listener are in a well-defined relationship with each other, with verbal routines laid out in advance. There is not much choice of what to say simply because there is no need to say much, and the little that is said carries a heavy load of implicit meaning. The speaker is acting a role with speeches perhaps not fully written for him as they would be on the stage, but well supplied with stock items by the small department within the social structure where he happens to be moving at the moment. There is room for a bit of ad-libbing but little more.

In an elaborated code, the speaker and listener are acting parts in which they must improvise. Their standing with each other is such that neither can take much for granted about the other. Intentions and purposes have to be brought into the open and defined. What the speaker will say is hard to predict, because it is not about commonplaces but about something more or less unique, related less to some foreseeable role and more to him as an individual. He is wearing not a comic nor a tragic mask but his own face, and that is harder to put into words. An example would be that of a man told to do something by his boss and having to explain why it is impossible for him to comply.

All speakers communicate with both restricted and elaborated codes, but not all are able to switch codes with the ease that is needed to interact to their advantage with other members of their society. Some speakers have little practice except with restricted codes, and unfortunately some of the roles in the social structure that are carried by those codes—implanted in the child by his exposure to them—are looked down upon. A speaker who is forced to operate with a certain code because he has never had any other models to imitate will find that his only communication will be with other speakers who use the same code—it becomes self-enforcing and self-perpetuating. One of the tasks of education is to lead to an awareness of the limitations of one's code and to a large amount of practice with elaborated codes, where the speaker is forced to become conscious of his language, to "orient towards the verbal channel."[8] This

[8] Bernstein, *op. cit.*, p. 161.

is the individual's road of escape from the confinement of his every act by restricted codes laid on him by the social structure without regard for his individuality, capacities, or intelligence.

LINGUISTIC GEOGRAPHY

Serious investigation of geographical dialects began in the latter part of the nineteenth century. The first comprehensive study was made in North and Central Germany by Georg Wenker. A smaller study followed in Denmark, and between 1902 and 1908 Jules Gilliéron published his *Atlas Linguistique de la France*, the most influential work of its kind. Since the turn of the century materials have been collected for similar atlases all over the world. In the United States the model has been the *Linguistic Atlas of New England*, directed by Hans Kurath and published between 1939 and 1943. Other regional atlases covering most of the country have been drawn up as part of a comprehensive *Linguistic Atlas of the United States and Canada*, still in preparation.

As the name implies, a linguistic atlas is a collection of maps showing the prevalence of particular speech forms in particular areas. What the dialect geographer most often selects to mark off a dialect area is simply its preference for certain words. Differences in pronunciation or syntax yield a more reliable measure, but words are easier to work with; information can even be gathered by mail through a questionnaire that asks what words a speaker uses for particular meanings: is a field enclosure made of stone called a *stone wall*, a *stone fence*, a *rock wall*, or a *rock fence?* Are drains that take rainwater off a roof called *eaves troughs, water spouting, gutters,* or *rain spouts?* For greater accuracy, detailed phonetic information is needed. Trained interviewers must be sent to the scene and may spend hours with a single informant. Does he pronounce *soot* to rime with *boot* or with *put?* Is his final consonant in *with* like that of *bath* or that of *bathe?* Does his pronunciation of *tomato* end with the same vowel sound as *panda* or is it like *grotto?* The Swiss German atlas, published in 1962, was based on a questionnaire containing 2,600 items, which took from four to eight days to administer. Its phonetic discriminations were exquisite—as many as twenty-one different tongue heights, for example, in front unrounded vowels.[9] The items chosen for a questionnaire to test differences in vocabulary, pronunciation, and syntax

---

[9] William Moulton, review in *Journal of English and German Philology* 62.831 (1963).

are the ones most likely to reveal the peculiarities of everyday speech: names of household objects, foods, parts of the body, weather phenomena, numbers, and so on.

American dialect geography

Unless he is combining his interest as a linguist with an extracurricular one as a folklorist or sociologist, the dialect geographer is less concerned with the items in a questionnaire for their own sake than as indicators of where to draw the boundary lines and how to trace the routes of speakers as they migrated from one area to another. The latter—the fanning out of dialects from their original centers and their crisscrossing and blending as the wave moves outward—is of special significance in a country like the United States, with its extraordinarily mobile population.

Boundaries are set by mapping the farthest points to which a given form has penetrated. When a line—termed an *isogloss* if it has to do with words, an *isophone* if with sounds—is drawn connecting these points, it is usually found to lie close to the lines drawn for other forms—for instance, the same speakers who say **snake feeder** for 'dragonfly' are also apt to pronounce the word **greasy** as **greazy.** The interlocking lines form a bundle of isoglosses (or isophones) and represent the frontier of the dialect in question.

American English divides rather clearly into three grand dialect areas in the eastern part of the country. They reflect the settlement of these areas by early migrants from England who brought their dialects with them. One such dialectal transplant from England is the vowel in words like **half, bath, aunt, glass,** and **laugh.** We easily recognize one way of pronouncing these words as a feature of cultivated speech in the East and of over-cultivated speech elsewhere. It is by no means uniform (in Eastern Virginia, for example, it will be heard in **master** and **aunt** but not in many other words), and represents one side of a split that took place in the eastern counties of England before the American Revolution. The /a/ was transplanted from those counties as folk speech by immigrants to New England, but it also took root in London and so became established as fashionable speech in the parts of the country that maintained the closest ties with England.[10] The map on page 143 shows the three areas (plus subdialectal sections) known, from their geographical position, as Northern, Midland, and Southern.

---

[10] Hans Kurath, "Some Aspects of Atlantic Seaboard English Considered in Their Connections with British English," in *Communications et Rapports du Premier Congrès International de Dialectologie Générale* (Louvain, Belgium, 1965), pp. 239–40.

MAP 1   WORD GEOGRAPHY OF THE EASTERN STATES

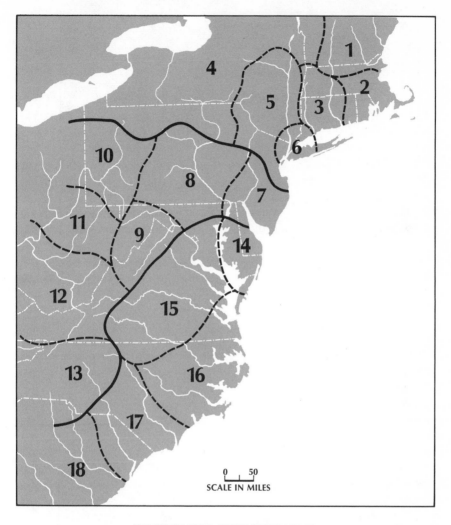

THE SPEECH AREAS OF THE EASTERN STATES

The North	The Midland	The South
1. N.E. New England	7. Delaware Valley	14. Delamarvia (E. shore of
2. S.E. New England	8. Susquehanna Valley	Maryland and Virginia,
3. S.W. New England	9. Upper Potomac and	and S. Delaware)
4. Upstate New York	Shenandoah Valleys	15. Virginia Piedmont
and W. Vermont	10. Upper Ohio Valley	16. N.E. No. Carolina (Albemarle
5. Hudson Valley	11. N. West Virginia	Sound and Neuse Valley)
6. Metropolitan	12. S. West Virginia	17. Cape Fear and Peedee Valleys
New York	13. W. No. and W. So. Carolina	18. So. Carolina

ADAPTED FROM Hans Kurath, *A Word Geography of the Eastern United States* (Ann Arbor, Michigan: University of Michigan Press, 1949).

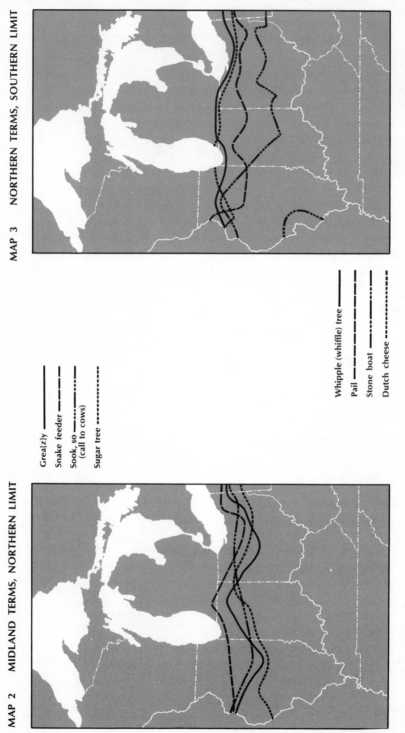

MAP 2   MIDLAND TERMS, NORTHERN LIMIT

MAP 3   NORTHERN TERMS, SOUTHERN LIMIT

Grea[z]y ─────────
Snake feeder ── ── ──
Sook, so ── · ── (call to cows)
Sugar tree ▬▬▬▬▬▬

Whipple (whiffle) tree ─────────
Pail ── ── ──
Stone boat ── · ──
Dutch cheese ▬▬▬▬▬▬

ADAPTED FROM Albert H. Marckwardt, "Principal and Subsidiary Dialect Areas in the North Central States," *Publications of the American Dialect Society* 27.10–11 (1957).

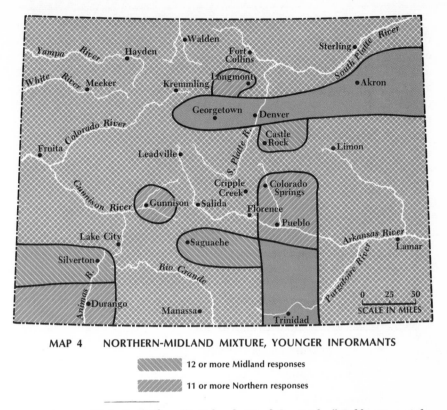

MAP 4   NORTHERN-MIDLAND MIXTURE, YOUNGER INFORMANTS

12 or more Midland responses

11 or more Northern responses

ADAPTED FROM Clyde T. Hankey, "A Colorado Word Geography," *Publications of the American Dialect Society* 34.24 (1960).

As the population spread westward the boundaries became more and more blurred. The earlier, more gradual movement extended them fairly evenly as far as the Mississippi. Maps 2 and 3 show the northern limit of certain Midland terms and the southern limit of certain Northern terms, as this rather complex bundle of isoglosses traversed the states of Ohio, Indiana, and Illinois. By the time the migrants had flowed up against the Rocky Mountains, the three tides had broken into a series of rivulets and eddies. Where a given area was settled mainly by speakers of a given dialect, that dialect of course prevailed. The area around Hayden, Colorado, was turned into a kind of Northern island by a group of women schoolteachers who came out from Ann Arbor, Michigan, and married ranchers there. Later, as younger speakers grew up and inter-married, Northern and Midland traits were blended. The shaded areas of Map 4 show this for Colorado.

Dialect blending is not confined to the West but goes on wherever the streams of communication, which seem to grow swifter every day, overflow the earlier lines. In northern Illinois, for example, which Maps 2 and 3 divide between a Northern and a Midland dialect area, the lines again are growing dim. The following list—of interest also as a sample of the kind of vocabulary used—enumerates words that are receding in the predominantly Midland area of Illinois, even though half of them were Midland to begin with:

1. window blind 'shade for a window, on a spring roller' (Midland)

2. woodshed

3. pigpen

4. pulley bone 'breastbone of a chicken, wishbone' (Southern, South Midland)

5. light bread 'bread made with yeast' (Southern, South Midland)

6. hay doodle 'small pile of hay' (Midland)

7. trestle 'saw horse with an X-frame'

8. poo-wee!, a call to hogs

9. poison vine 'poison ivy'

10. cement road 'concrete road'

11. to favor 'to resemble,' as in *John favors his father*

12. baby cab 'baby carriage' (Midland)

13. belling 'shivaree' (Midland)

14. belly buster 'dive in coasting prone on a sled, belly flop' (Midland)[11]

Two metaphors describe the extremes of diffusion. One is the relay race, the other the cross-country. In the first, a speaker picks up something from his neighbor to the east and runs with it as far as his neighbor to the west, always staying between them. In the second, a speaker breaks loose from the paternal neighborhood and travels to all points of the compass, picking up pieces at each stop and dropping them all along the way. The latter is the kind of diffusion that makes dialectology a haz-

---

[11] Roger W. Shuy, "The Northern-Midland Dialect Boundary in Illinois," *Publications of the American Dialect Society* No. 38, November, 1962, p. 59. Professor Shuy was kind enough to provide definitions.

ardous business. As Robert Louis Stevenson wrote in *The Amateur Emigrant,*

> I knew I liked Mr. Jones from the moment I saw him. I thought him by his face to be Scottish; nor could his accent undeceive me. For as there is a *lingua franca* of many tongues on the moles and in the feluccas of the Mediterranean, so there is a free or common accent among English-speaking men who follow the sea. They catch a twang of a New England port, from a cockney skipper, even a Scotsman sometimes learns to drop an *h*; a word of a dialect is picked up from another hand in the forecastle; until often the result is undecipherable, and you have to ask for a man's place of birth.[12]

The compilers of the new *Dictionary of American Regional English* are at present engaged in one of the largest word-gathering projects in history—a five-year (1965–70) survey of the dialects of the United States from Florida to Alaska in an effort "to collect the greater part . . . of the words and phrases, pronunciations, spellings, and meanings used . . . up to the present time."[13] Besides bringing to light the quantities of unregistered written forms in obscure places, this project will rescue uncounted expressions that would otherwise be lost as their users died away because the forms existed only in the spoken language. The estimated five million entries will be processed by computers. (The compilers of the vast *Oxford Dictionary* assembled three and a half million entries by hand.)

But geography is not all. The fading of differences is accelerated by social pressures. Where a normalized, cultivated speech gains in favor—and this, we should remember, was until recently the largest single result of formal schooling—everything with a pronounced local or, especially, rustic flavor tends to be rooted out. Thus, in the area of northern Illinois already discussed, the cultivated forms *I ran home yesterday, He did it, I'm going to lie down* are replacing the uncultivated—whether Northern or Midland—*I run home yesterday, He done it, I'm going to lay down.*[14]

Dialect geography in Europe

In Europe, dialect geography lacks much of the here-and-now flavor that it has in the United States. With a more stable population and with more

---

[12] South Seas Edition (New York: Charles Scribner's Sons, Inc., 1925), p. 9.

[13] Frederic G. Cassidy, "American Regionalism and the Harmless Drudge," *Publications of the Modern Language Association* 82:3.14 (1967).

[14] Shuy, *op. cit.*, p. 64.

radical linguistic as well as geographical and political barriers to surmount, European dialects are bound more tightly to their localities and have more to tell us about events long ago than about recent ones.

The most thoroughly investigated dialects anywhere in the world are those of the Romance languages, which are themselves, of course, just dialects of Latin that drifted apart in the early years of the Christian era. Since more is known about Latin—thanks partly to the very dialectal facts that it helps to illuminate—than about any other ancient language, dialectology in the Romance area has closer ties to historical linguistics than it has anywhere else.

As an illustration of these ties, take the conflict of homonyms, which was one of the main interests of those who worked on the French atlas. A perennial linguistic question is why words disappear. The most famous example is the French word for *cock.* In southern France, the normal development of the expected Latin word, *gallus,* would have been *gat.* But in the same area the word *cattus* had an equal right to give *gat,* and it actually did produce that form. Had *gallus* been retained, the result would have been two meanings, 'cat' and 'cock,' both carried by the same form; and, unlike *so* and *sew* or *be* and *bee,* these two were the same part of speech and were apt to occur in similar contexts where they would have caused confusion. As with English *queen* and *quean* (Chapter 7, page 113), one of them had to go, so speakers substituted other words for *gallus:* one meaning 'chicken,' one meaning 'pheasant,' and a third meaning, literally, 'priest.' In this case, knowing the dialectal facts helped to interpret the historical ones.

The dialectologist who looked most consistently to geography as a key to the history of dialects was the Italian Matteo Bàrtoli. It should be possible, he thought, to correlate the past evolution of dialects with their positions relative to one another, and he expressed the correlation in a set of four "areal norms":

1. Norm of the isolated area. An area that is cut off and shielded from communication tends to retain older forms.

2. Norm of the lateral area. Where a central area is wedged into the middle of a zone that presumably was once homogeneous, the edges tend to retain older forms.

3. Norm of the principal area. If the zone is split into two segments, the larger one tends to have the older forms. (This is in partial conflict with 1 and 2.)

4. Norm of the later area. An area that has been overrun—as by conquest—at a more recent date tends to have older forms.

Spain	France	Italy	Rumania
hermoso	beau	bello	frumos
mesa	table	tavola	masa
hervir	bouillir	bollire	a fierbe
entonces	alors	allora	atunci
día	jour	giorno	zi
más	plus	più	mai

FROM Eugenio Coseriu, *La Geografía Lingüística* (Montevideo: Instituto de Filología, 1956), p. 38.

The norm of the lateral area is the most picturesque, with its suggestion of an adventurous dialect driving across the territory of a sedentary one and overspreading it everywhere except at the edges. Using the Romance languages in their present state as evidence of what probably happened while the speakers of Vulgar Latin were still more or less in touch with Rome, we can see in the table above the effect of continued contact in France and Italy as against interrupted contact, and hence the retention of older forms, in Spain and Rumania.

The norm of the lateral area explains how it can happen that countries as far apart as Rumania and Spain share forms and meanings that are missing in the areas that lie between.

THE HORIZONTAL IMPOSED ON THE VERTICAL

When a rubber manufacturer in Akron, Ohio, imports low-wage laborers from West Virginia, he unwittingly turns a geographical dialect into a social one. The newcomers are readily identified by their strange forms of speech, and they are poor and uneducated. No matter how carefully they dress and conduct themselves, they cannot change their dialect quickly enough to merge with the rest of the community, and the result is that the one trait that marks them most distinctly is taken as a badge of their "class."

Or, to complicate things further, the imported laborers may speak a dialect that was socially non-standard even in the place of origin and is still further out of line with the standard speech of the new area. The most radically deviant form of English likely to be encountered in this country echoes the trade language that was used in the early part of the eighteenth century on the West African coast and was probably carried to the plantations of the South and used by speakers who had no other means of communication.[15]

This transplanting, as American dialectologist Raven McDavid points out, has happened and continues to happen all over the United States, and constitutes a grave social problem. For the fact is that nothing more thoroughly excludes a person from a social group than a manner of speech that has come to be identified as uncultivated. And, given the fact that the most extensive recent migrations have been from the poorest rural areas, especially those of the South, to the most tightly structured urban societies, those of our large cities, one understands how much language has contributed to the creation or deepening of class lines.

The best solution seems to be an enlightened "bi-dialectalism," fostered by the schools, where the basic job of integration has to be done. The form of speech approved by the local community is taught not as something that must be acquired and used under all circumstances but as something useful for general communication, while the imported speech is respected in its place on the playground, in the home, and in relaxed conversation.[16] "The first principle of any language program is that, whatever the target, it must respect the language that the students bring with them to the classroom."[17] The schools will need to be more sophisticated in their teaching of English. This calls for helping teachers to see that when students come to them limited to restricted codes in a nonstandard dialect what they need is not to be corrected in supposed mistakes but to be introduced to a new and in many ways different but related system, no better and no worse than the old one but more useful in their new contacts.[18] It may even be useful to teach some of the nonstandard dialect to the speakers of the standard. Acceptance, not just toleration, implies both knowledge and use.

SELF-CONSCIOUS DIALECT

All the dialects so far discussed have one thing in common: they come naturally. They are not adopted by their speakers for the sake of having a distinctive way of speaking. A child picks up the speech of his parents

---

[15] William A. Stewart, "Sociolinguistic Factors in the History of American Negro Dialects," *The Florida FL Reporter*, Spring, 1967, pp. 1–4.

[16] Raven I. McDavid, Jr., "American Social Dialects," *College English*, January, 1965, pp. 254–60.

[17] Raven I. McDavid, Jr., "Sense and Nonsense about American Dialects," *Publications of the Modern Language Association* 81:2.7–17 (1966), p. 9.

[18] This is being attempted in Washington, D. C., by the Urban Language Study. See J. L. Dillard in *The Linguistic Reporter*, October, 1966, pp. 1–2.

and playmates unconsciously. The social climber in the course of "passing over" from one group to another adopts a manner of speaking as part of a manner of acting. Individual words may be adopted more or less consciously and deliberately, but speakers do not ordinarily set out to acquire a whole new way of talking.

The most striking exception is the language of concealment, which exists in various forms in all cultures and interlocks in curious ways with the normal speech of its users. Among the Hanunóo of the Philippines there is an approved way of talking during courtship that calls for a high degree of skill in keeping messages from being understood by others, particularly by rivals and older adults. It may involve only certain mechanics—for instance, barely audible whispering, an extremely rapid rate of speaking, falsetto, or activation of sounds by inhaling rather than by exhaling. It may also involve a complicated rearrangement of the sounds, or the partial substitution of other sounds, in a word. For example, the word *rignuk* 'tame' may appear as *nugrik, rignuŋ, qayrig,* or *rinsiŋ,* or it may be spelled out according to the Hanunóo syllabary. The secret language is part of a pattern of concealment that includes clandestine trysts and disguises.[19]

Our culture's closest parallel to this secret language is of course pig Latin, which is the play money of English—it enjoys no status at all. But English does have a low-status parallel in the argot of the underworld. Unlike pig Latin, this relies less on mechanical distortions than on its specialized vocabulary, as is to be expected of any professional jargon. But argot differs from journalese, for example, in that it is not *meant* to be understood by anyone except another professional. Here are some examples of the argot of the pickpocket, as described by D. W. Maurer:

> When the tool locates the victim's bankroll or wallet he may name that location to the stalls in argot. That is, he may say in an undertone **Left bridge** or **Right bridge,** or **Kiss the dog,** or whatever instructions may be necessary to inform the stalls, so that they can put the victim into position for the tool to work. The tool may likewise communicate with the stalls during the theft, giving them instructions such as **Raust** or **Come through,** or **Stick,** or **Stick and split me out** or **Turn him for a pit,** etc. All tools give the stalls an *office* or signal when they take the wallet. . . . It seems incredible that the victim does not register this dialogue centered so personally upon him, but I do not know of any court case where the victim either caught the pickpockets in the act or became suspicious as they rifled his pockets, in which the victim reported hearing any of this interchange. . . .[20]

---

[19] Harold C. Conklin, "Linguistic Play in Its Cultural Context," *Language* 35.631–6 (1959).

[20] "Whiz Mob," *Publications of the American Dialect Society* No. 24, November, 1955, pp. 53–4.

ADDITIONAL REMARKS AND APPLICATIONS

1. Countless words in German, Dutch, English, Danish, and Swedish resemble one another as closely as similar sets in French, Spanish, Italian, and Rumanian. Yet there exists no written record, like Latin, which can be assumed as a source and to which the forms can be traced. How does what we know about dialectology justify the assumption that there was a primitive Germanic language that split into dialects that became the parents of these languages?

2. Note some differences that you have observed between your own speech and that of other social groups in your community. Do you use the adjective *cool* or *groovy* to mean 'good, excellent'? Or refer to clothing as *threads* or to a leather-jacketed slob as a *chook*? Or say of someone who is nutty that he is *out to lunch* or of something attractive that it is *chaud*? Relate these or other peculiarities to the group of speakers they characterize—perhaps "young adult" as against "adult." Consider whether groups that are more distinctive in other respects (hippies, for example) are also more distinctive in their language—to what degree does their language distinguish them?

3. Is there a relationship between formal speech and the speech of older generations? If so, how do you account for it? How would you account for the presence of older forms in relaxed speech than in formal speech? Relate your answers to two kinds of authority: the authority of age and the authority of a prestige dialect. *OK* began to give strong competition to *all right* in spoken English in the 1920's. Is it good formal English? Is it represented equally among older and younger speakers? Someone brought up in the Ozark backwoods might say *Hit don't make no difference*. Why do we reject this, in spite of the fact that *hit* is older than *it* and multiple negation goes back to Old English?

4. If you are a native speaker of American English, see if you can classify your own dialect by the following lists of words:

Northern	Midland	Southern
cherry pit	piece 'distance'	corn shucks
pail	green beans	you-all
comforter	wait on 'wait for'	snap beans
stoop 'porch'	quarter till	pallet
clapboards 'siding'	want off 'want to	chitlins 'hogs'
angleworm	get off'	intestines'
swill 'slop'	blinds 'shades'	light bread 'white
brook 'creek'	poke 'sack'	bread raised
hadn't ought	all the better	with yeast'
teeter-totter	(That's all the	tote 'carry'
eaves troughs	better he can	jackleg 'untrained
fried cake 'dough-	do it.)	person'
nut'	you-uns	clabber cheese 'cot-
johnnycake 'corn-	spouts 'gutters'	tage cheese'
bread'	snake feeder	mouth harp
spider 'skillet'	'dragonfly'	'harmonica'
darning needle		croker sack 'burlap
'dragonfly'		bag'
Dutch cheese 'cot-		carry (someone
tage cheese'		home) 'escort'
		branch 'small
		stream'
		pulley bone
		'wishbone'
		hants 'ghosts'

ADAPTED FROM Mima Babington and E. Bagby Atwood, "Lexical Usage in Southern Louisiana," *Publications of the American Dialect Society* No. 36, November, 1961, pp. 1–24.

If you are like many other speakers of American English, you may find that you use words from all three lists. Try to relate them to different contacts during your life—residence in particular areas or close association with certain speakers.

5. In a state such as California, populated by persons from all areas to the east, what competing forms are likely to be the most successful, those widely and generally used elsewhere or those restricted in their distribution? Take the expression *hot cake.* As a folk term, in

the East this expression is centered in Eastern Pennsylvania. But somehow it has found its way into formal English: "In parts of the Middle West ... one is likely to make *pancakes* at home, but to order *hot cakes* in a restaurant."[21] In California, *hot cake* is more general than *pancake.* Is it more likely taken from the Pennsylvania or from the formal usage?

6. In Chapter 6, pages 91–92, it was noted that dialect borrowing enriches vocabulary. Of the following pairs of competing dialectal terms, it may be that you use only one from each pair or that you use neither, but if you use both, consider whether they mean exactly the same or have come in your speech to represent different shades of meaning: *pancake, flapjack; roasting ears, corn on the cob; angleworm, earthworm; window blinds, window shades.*

7. Test your reactions toward some other dialect of English. If you are a Northern (or Southern) speaker do you find a Southern (or Northern) accent irritating? How do you react toward a speaker of British Standard (Southern British, or "Received Pronunciation")? Does it make a difference whether the other speaker is of the same sex as you, or the opposite sex?

8. If conflict of homonyms can result in a loss, can it also be a factor in preserving something? If you distinguish the vowels /a/ and /ɔ/ in words like *sot-sought, tot-taught, stock-stalk, sod-sawed,* but have only /ɔ/ in *ma-maw, rah-raw,* and in all one-syllable words ending in -/g/ such as *log, frog, dog,* consider whether this may be partly because disregarding the distinction in the latter words creates fewer conflicts.

9. Dialect atlas materials have various applications in linguistics. One, suggested by William G. Moulton, is as a test of the hypothesis of "phonological space," which is that phonemes tend to be distributed more or less evenly relative to one another. For example, if we imagine the tongue positions in the mouth to represent a sort of continuum (see Chapter 3, page 25), each vowel will tend to be about as far from its neighbor in one direction as from its neighbor in another. As a corollary to this, the more tightly packed the continuum is (that is, the more vowels there are), the less free any

---

[21] David W. Reed, "Eastern Dialect Words in California," *Publications of the American Dialect Society* No. 21, April, 1954, p. 8.

vowel will be to have a wide range of allophones—speakers will have to be more precise in their pronunciation. Moulton finds this hypothesis largely confirmed in the dialect atlas of Swiss German.[22] Assume that there is a phonemic system in which, for one reason or another, this even distribution does not obtain, and two vowels are very close together. If not too many words depend on the distinction, what is apt to happen? Apply this to the pronunciation of the examples in the preceding question (*sot-sought, tot-taught,* etc.).

10. Are there dialect problems among minority groups in your public school system? If so, see if you can identify some of the forms used. They may be phonological (*house* pronounced [həus], *pen* pronounced like *pin*), morphological (verb forms like *dove* or *might could,* or switching of preterit and participle forms like *He done it, He seen them, They had went, Somebody had stole it*), or syntactic (adjectives used as adverbs, as in *He did it easy;* non-standard clauses, as in *This is a recipe that if you don't do it right you won't like it;* interchange of cases, as in *Him and me don't like it,* or its opposite, by overcompensation, *It's for he and I*). Where are the speakers from? Are the forms they use standard in those areas? Do you use similar forms sometimes (for example, *Whom shall I say is calling,* an overcompensation)?

---

[22] "Dialect Geography and the Concept of Phonological Space," *Word* 18.23–32 (1962).

WRITING $\boxed{10}$

IF THE AZTECS before the time of Columbus had had schools with classes divided according to subject matter, a child taking instruction in language would have been taught the correct way to recite the texts of an oral tradition and might have been lectured on avoiding the Aztec slang of his day, but he would never have had to hand in a written composition and would never have been scolded for a misspelling. Writing, such as it was, would have been taught in his art class, and misspellings would have been impossible because there were no spellings. Pictures, then as now, could tell a story, but they did so in their own way, not as marks that represented particular words or sounds. A picture of a man or of a man's head, or a stylized figure of a man, meant a man, a male being, an old boy, an adult person of the male sex, or a man by any other name one might choose. The symbol pictured the meaning directly, with no particular sounds as intermediary, unlike the written drawings in our modern culture, where the letter signs *m* + *a* + *n* stand for a particular construct of sound that means one thing in the word *man* and something else in the word *mansion.*

Our own experience in school is so different that we are prone to think that writing *is* language and that speech is only a sort of replay of what is written, like a tape recording that is language in solid form but can be turned into sound if fed into a machine. We learned to speak so long ago that all the details have been forgotten, even if we could have been self-

156

conscious enough at that age to observe what we were doing. Our "language" class, therefore, did not teach us the sound or structure of English but concentrated on teaching us how to write; this is our most vivid recollection of language instruction, and it colors our notions of what constitutes language.

Yet the convergence of speech and writing—the use of writing to mediate language rather than to mediate ideas directly—was a process that took thousands of years and that even now many of the world's cultures have not undergone. Advanced as the Aztec culture was when Cortez invaded Mexico in 1519, it was centuries behind that of Europe in the development of writing and only a little more advanced than that of the nomadic tribes of Indians inhabiting what is now the United States and Canada. The Aztecs and Mayas were great artists, but they were cut off from the written art of other lands where the flow and counterflow of communication implanted the little innovations that led the cultures of the Old World to make great forward leaps in symbolization.[1]

To understand the past of writing we must begin with the present, which we know best.

CORRESPONDENCES BETWEEN WRITING AND SPEECH

Letters and phonemes

Almost all modern writing is *alphabetic.* It uses symbols that with more or less refinement correspond to individual sounds, and the degree of refinement is measured by how close the correspondence comes to being one-to-one. A perfect correspondence, with each letter symbol standing for one and only one distinctive sound, would of course be a form of phonemic writing. Some modern writing systems come very close to this ideal—Spanish, Czech, Finnish. Others, of which English is a dismal example, are so erratic that for a long time educators advocated giving up altogether the teaching of reading by letter sounds, using instead a global or whole-word method in which the child is expected to recognize word shapes but not break them into their phonetic parts. There has

---

[1] The idea that Mayan writing, though undeciphered, represents a more advanced form than this does have some defenders. Benjamin Lee Whorf, whose ideas on language and thought we shall meet in Chapter 13, pages 253–55, theorized about a phonetic value in certain Mayan characters, and he is supported by C. F. Voegelin in *Anthropological Linguistics* 3.77 (1961).

recently been a reaction against this approach,[2] which is fortunate because, imperfect as English writing admittedly is, it still is basically phonemic. Unless a reader is taught or develops on his own an ability to interpret the spelling of unfamiliar words, he will be cruelly handicapped. Most such spellings can be interpreted with confidence: we are safe in inferring that *sline,* if there were such a word, would be pronounced to rime with *fine,* not with *fin,* and that *wip* would rime with *rip,* not with *ripe.*

The nearness of alphabetic writing to phonemic writing gives linguists the chastening realization of how culture-bound their science is, and could serve as a lesson on how difficult it is for any science to step outside the culture of its time. It is hardly a coincidence that one of the greatest successes of linguistics in this century has been what could be characterized as simply a clean-up job on alphabetic writing. If the major languages of the world were written as most of them were two thousand years ago and as Japanese is today (see page 168), with symbols for syllables rather than symbols for distinctive sounds, it is safe to guess that syllables today would not be what we heard them called in an earlier chapter (Chapter 4, page 46), the "stepchild of linguistics."

An alphabetic system has the capacity to become completely phonemic, and if it has failed to do so the reason is that writers are not linguists and have other needs and interests than that of making their writing a perfect image of their speech. The needs are practical and the interests are both practical and esthetic. Among the needs are the functions that writing has fulfilled since its beginnings: communication across time (which until the invention of sound-recording devices was impossible for speech), communication across great distance (which likewise was impossible for speech until the appearance of the telephone), and communication to great numbers of people (which was closed to speech until the invention of radio). In modern times, the vastly greater size of the readership— for many publications, embracing readers of English from Tacoma to Calcutta—has made it necessary for writing to transcend local dialects and adhere to a standard that can be widely understood. A Southerner's *The poor roof bulged* would (in some areas) be transcribed /ðə poə ruf buljd/, and a Northerner's /ðə pʊr ruf bʌljd/; with both of them agreed on standard spellings, trouble is avoided.

Even a linguist can find some fault with a purely phonemic writing. Its worst feature is that it does not represent morphemes consistently. In

---

[2] See Charles C. Fries, *Linguistics and Reading* (New York: Holt, Rinehart and Winston, Inc., 1962).

English the spelling of the past morpheme *-ed* is phonemically bad but morphemically good for it is always the same: the identical spelling in **kissed, plagued,** and **faded** has to be transcribed phonemically in three different ways, -/t/, -/d/, and -/əd/. The possessive morpheme is consistently *-'s* or *-'*, where phonemically it has four different shapes: -/s/ in **Pat's,** -/z/ in **Ted's,** -/əz/ in **George's,** and zero in **the boys'.** The word *news* is spelled the same in **The news is good** and **I read the newspapers** even though for many speakers the latter has /nus/ rather than /nuz/. So in some ways a combined phonemic and morphemic or "morphophonemic" spelling is preferable to a purely phonemic one. It is possible that writers sense this, and that some spellings are preserved or changed accordingly, though many spellings are kept that are not good either phonemically or morphemically. The suffixes *-ible* and *-able* in **credible** and **believable** mean the same and sound the same but are spelled differently. How all of us as writers might affect the language for good or ill if we were allowed to go our own way nobody can know, for English spelling is not in our hands; it is controlled by schools and copyeditors.

Other, more trivial, advantages can be extracted from the disadvantages of our spelling. Though **Frances** and **Francis** sound the same, we can tell by looking that the first applies to a woman and the second to a man. A *troop* is identified as belonging to the military, a *troupe* as belonging to show business; similarly with **review** and **revue.** What might be ambiguities in speech are thereby sometimes avoided in writing. Of course, writing has other devices more systematic than random distinctions with letters: *my sister's friend's investments, my sisters' friends' investments, my sisters' friend's investments,* and *my sister's friends' investments* all sound the same but are different in writing; we can distinguish visually between **P-Score** and **Peace Corps** or between **youth rehabilitation** and **U-3 habilitation.**[3] A combination of special signs such as hyphens, diacritical marks, punctuation, and odd spellings can clarify a tangle of homophones, as shown by the last lines of the Carolyn Wells limerick:

> But I'd hate to relate
> What that fellow named Tate
> And his tête-a-tête ate at 8:08.

Esthetic considerations, too, prevent a writing system from becoming fully phonemic. There is hardly a town in the United States that does not

---

[3] Example from Professor Lee Hultzén, personal letter to the author, February 15, 1963.

boast at least one establishment with the sign *Ye Olde Tea* (or *Pottery* or *Antique* or *Curiosity*) *Shoppe.* Common English names are sometimes regarded as too common, and ambitious parents dress them up with exotic spellings: *Alyce* for *Alice, Bettye* for *Betty, Edythe* for *Edith*—a tendency that awaits the iconoclast who will dare to spell her name *Barrel* instead of *Beryl.* Some spellings are almost systematically prestigious—for example, the agentive suffix spelled *-or* rather than *-er: advisor,* not *adviser; expeditor,* not *expediter.* One esthetic attitude in particular has deflected writing away from speech and even created a counter-evolutionary trend: the deference that is felt in all societies, including our own, to the authority of the written word. For the Hindus, the Sanskrit writings embody "the language of the gods," and knowledge of Sanskrit and use of Sanskrit words has long been a prestige symbol in India.[4] In our society a respect for standard spellings is a requirement for social and economic advancement; the person who writes words with bad spellings in a letter of application will find it almost as hard to get a job as the man who has been caught writing bad checks. As a result, all spellings are locked in place and shielded from reform. Long after pronunciations have changed and speakers all over the English-speaking world have agreed on new ones, the old spellings live on: *-tion* for /šən/, *gh* for /f/, the *b* of *plumb, climb, limb,* and so on. This is the esthetic of tradition, magnified now and then by a pseudo-scholarship that creates fancied correct spellings that were previously nonexistent in the language: the *h* of *rhyme,* the *c* of *indict,* the *g* of *feign.* We have seen this actually affecting the pronunciation of certain English words in the added *h* of *theater, author, Catholic,* and so on. (See Chapter 6, page 96.) Writing was for centuries the property of a priestly or scribal caste in a domain of occult powers, spells, and incantations. Modern writing has shaken off its ties with magic but has never fully lost its pretensions to erudition. We are no longer in fear of it, but we treat spellings as if they were the living bodies of words.

Unwritten parts of language

While the lack of a full correspondence between writing and speech is occasionally to the advantage of writing—as in distinguishing *its* from *it's* or *indict* from *indite*—more often the advantage is on the side of speech, where writing has simply failed to incorporate some element of spoken

---

[4] Andrée F. Sjoberg, "Coexistent Phonemic Systems in Telugu," *Word* 18.276–77 (1962).

language. It is good to have homonyms spelled differently sometimes; but homographs—identical spellings of words that do not sound or mean the same—are a nuisance. A writer about to put down a sentence like **Some stamps will be acceptable in lieu of coins** needs to be careful lest the word (really *words*) *some* be misunderstood: if he intends /sʌm/ and not /sm/, he had better use *certain* instead.

But the worst deficiency of writing is that it never got around to providing a regular way of marking accent (writers can use italics, but good style allows them to use this device only very sparingly), and it has virtually disregarded rhythm and intonation. There is evidence that in certain medieval manuscripts spaces may have been left where pauses occur within compounds or between words, wider for longer pauses, narrower for shorter, as we might write today *wish ful* and *dish   ful,* or *If you see him   when you get home   call me.*[5] This tradition, if it existed, was lost. Punctuation serves as a rough guide to some of the rhythmic and intonational contrasts in speech, but it leaves too much out and what it puts in suffers from a confusion of two aims: the representations of the breaks that we *hear* and the divisions that logical-minded persons sometimes insist that we *write*—the two usually agree, but not always. Consider the following sentence: *It is common knowledge that, if we are to learn to speak another language well, we must spend a great deal of time practicing it.* There is no comma after *knowledge,* where a pause would normally come, but there is one after *that,* where most speakers would not pause at all.[6]

In all this we can detect the hand of an ancient tradition: that writing never fully symbolizes speech but serves as a *prompter* to what we want to say. The result is that writers have to make many choices that are not forced on them as speakers. An anecdote from the *Reader's Digest* shows the kind of compromise one must make because of the lack of markers for accent:

> We met frequently at the laundromat. "And where do you live?" I asked one evening while we were waiting out the cycles. "I *live* here," sighed the man. "But I have my meals and sleep in a bungalow a couple of blocks up the street with my wife and children."[7]

---

[5] Robert D. Stevick, "Scribal Notation of Prosodic Features in *The Parker Chronicle*, Anno 894 [893]," *Journal of English Linguistics* 1.57–66 (1967).

[6] Charles T. Scott, "The Linguistic Basis for the Development of Reading Skill," *Modern Language Journal* 50.540 (1966).

[7] September, 1960, p. 97.

Italicizing *live* was the best decision even though *here* has a stronger accent, because it is the word on which a prominent accent is less expected:

$$
\begin{array}{cccc}
 & & \text{h e} & \\
 & \text{l i} & & \text{r} \\
\text{I} & \quad \text{v e} & & \\
 & & & \text{e.}
\end{array}
$$

The lack of markers for intonation is seen in the faux pas of the person who felt so warmly toward an invited speaker that in his later thank-you letter he wrote *You would have been welcome if you had said nothing at all,* neglecting to note that what he intended as

You would have been   welcome   if you had said   nothing   at
                                                              all.

could be taken as

                                          wel
You would have been
                          come if you had said nothing at   all.

In writing we must put *even if* in the first of these, to signal the intention.

The jockeying necessary to overcome the lack of accent and intonation markings calls for a high degree of skill, which is part of the equipment of every good writer. Sometimes nothing can remedy the defect. Lord Acton's phrase *Compromise is the soul if not the whole of politics* remains ambiguous—we shall never know whether he meant 'is the soul, nay, more, possibly the whole,' or 'if not the whole, at least the soul.' Sometimes a simple repetition—unnecessary in speech—will clear things up. So with the phrase *more or less:* in the question *Are you more or less satisfied with the way things went?* one of the meanings can be pinned down by writing *Are you more satisfied or less satisfied . . . ?* The accommodation most often called for is a change in word order, with or without a change in construction. A speaker wishing to reprove someone for shouting can say *Is shóuting necessary?* and be clearly understood if he puts the main accent on *shouting* and de-accents *necessary;* but if the sentence is written, the regularity with which main accents fall at the end will lead the reader to interpret it as *Is shouting nécessary?* A good writer will change the wording to get *shout* at the end: *Is it necessary to shout?*

In one respect, writing, though visual, lacks a visual support enjoyed by speech. This is gesture. We have seen how paralinguistic gestures help us tell the difference between statements and questions (Chapter 2, page 14). Other gestures, too, cooperate with speech, as when one says *When I was about yea high,* accompanying the demonstrative *yea* with the hand held at a definite height. Writing is compelled to find substitutes.

Now and then we can make capital of a deficiency. Just as a piece of writing can—to advantage—span two or more dialects and so gain in universality, so by its very ambiguity it can at one and the same time embrace two or more actual utterances that we do not care to distinguish, and thereby gain in generality. At check-out counters in stores one often finds containers of free samples with a sign reading *Take one.* Ordinarily this represents the utterance *Táke one.* But if a customer were to help himself to several, the storekeeper might point out that the sign reads *Take óne.*

So we see both primary and secondary divergences between speech and writing: primary ones that are simply the lack on one side of some device that is present in the other—a graphic sign such as the apostrophe in writing, or a distinctive sound such as an accent in speech; and secondary ones that are the result of having to make alternative choices or arrangements in order to remedy a primary lack. There are vested interests in both.

Style

One of the earliest uses of writing was as a jog to memory. A series of visual symbols or written notes to serve as consecutive reminders in telling a story or making a speech have their simple modern counterpart in the string tied around the finger. We have seen this as one of the reasons why writing has never completely symbolized speech. Yet by freeing speech from its helpless dependence on memory visual symbols have conferred on language a completeness and elaboration that were not possible before.

The more elaborate the speech or story and the more it is to escape from raw improvisation, the more exact, and hence elaborate, the notes must be. So in time the elaboration becomes the hallmark of the notes themselves. The speaker edits them at his pleasure, and if he has a fully developed writing system at his command they are no longer mere reminders but are the substance of what he plans to say: he can turn off his mind completely as he reads them aloud, doing the whole performance as if by reflex, and still be understood. Or he can give them to someone else to read. And if the purpose is silent reading he can make his sentences more complex, knowing that if the reader misses them the first time he will go back. Writing is language in edited form, differing not just in the mechanics imposed by spelling and punctuation but in its polish and deliberation. "Developed prose" depends on our ability to write.[8]

So writing enhances the possibilities of style. It is no longer something that issues from the mouth and vanishes with the air but is an object of art to be contemplated and worked upon at leisure. With less dependence on brute memory, the devices that an orator or a storyteller might have had to use to help him remember and to help his hearer follow become less necessary—such things as rimes, alliterations, and summations. Elaborate language becomes less the province of a few; more intricate ideas can be grasped and more elegant expression attempted by every user of the language. The gap between writing and speech is widened. Writing creates a new environment with internal differences responsive to it. Some of them result from the display of words in space rather than in time: page references, words such as *former* and *latter* or *above* and *below*. Others reflect the conservatism and formality of writing. In conversation we would be apt to say that someone had *followed us around;* in formal prose this would probably be changed to *followed us about.* Above all, writing is characterized by amplification. One rarely finds parenthetical clauses in speech, but they are frequent in writing: *The President, who as we know has been under great pressure to reduce three of his budgetary requests (the latest having to do with public housing, but excepting the military), finally submitted a revised report, prepared by a specially appointed staff, to the joint meeting of the two committees last night.* There is no mistaking the lucubration of sentences like this.

Writing and speech are like two railroads with overlapping boards of directors that share, over part of the route, a single right of way. At times they seem to be the same, but there has never been a formal merger and their managements have too many ingrained rivalries now to approve one.

THE GROWTH OF WRITING[9]

The forerunners of our written signs were nearly all pictorial or diagrammatic. That is to say, they were *analog*, in the sense explained in Chapter 2, pages 16–17. Primitive pictures conveyed messages in the same

---

[8] Punya Sloka Ray, "The Formation of Prose," *Word* 18.318 (1962).

[9] This section for the most part follows I. J. Gelb, *A Study of Writing*, rev. ed. (Chicago: University of Chicago Press, 1963).

way as modern cartoons—the drawing of a man's figure might look more or less like an actual man, but its meaning depended on there being at least some resemblance. A diagram to point a direction really pointed in the direction intended, relative to the ground or to other points on a map. Notches on a stick to record the number of sheep sheared or soldiers recruited or vessels of oil delivered corresponded to the actual count. What men inscribed on wood or clay or graved on stone was intended to speak to the mind through the eye alone, not through the eye as a stimulus to the ear.

This is not to deny all connection with speech, nor to say that long strides were not taken toward an arbitrary digital system in representational drawing. Drawings could be digital: if notches could represent recruits, clearly circles or dots would do just as well; nothing compelled the artist to include more detail than he was interested in. But always the potential of depicting an actual characteristic was there: a stick figure might be enough to represent a man, but a man with an arm missing would be shown by a stick with a missing arm. And connections with speech were often close: some designs were drawn to be translated aloud, either as reminders for those who drew them or as messages calling for an interpreter. But they differed from writing in having no fixed correspondence between the design and the language; the interpreter was free to ad-lib. A three-part drawing in which a king was shown first assembling his hosts, then laying waste to an enemy land, then pausing to rest, might be read aloud as *After assembling his hosts and before pausing to rest, he laid waste the enemy land* or *In order to lay waste the enemy land he assembled his hosts, and afterward he rested* or *Before he rested he laid waste the enemy land with the hosts he had assembled* or in any number of other ways. The words could vary, and the actions did not need to be reported in the same sequence. Language, with its enormously greater resources, could run circles around the drawing, and this explains why each step toward a symbolization of language rather than a direct symbolization of things and events was bound to mark a gain in communicative power.

The main steps were three: the writing of words, the writing of syllables, and the writing of distinctive sounds. Each stage overlapped the following one. Even modern English writing has a few remnants of word signs and syllable signs: ¶ means 'paragraph' and § means 'section' (we even use the primitive device of pluralizing these by doubling them: ¶¶, §§); *bar-b-q* uses *b* and *q* to stand for the syllables /bɨ/ and /kyu/, as **OK** stands for the syllables /o/ and /ke/.

Archaeology enables us to estimate the dates of the three steps and credit their first appearance to particular societies, though we cannot be sure, even when a given piece of writing is assigned definitely to a given people, that some later archaeological find will not reveal that the style was borrowed from a near neighbor who invented it a century or two earlier. Thus, while the Phoenicians seem entitled to credit for the second step, it could have been taken first by some other group in their general area. What is fairly certain, in view of a number of finds clustering near one another, is that it did occur in that area.

Word writing

While the interpreter of a pictorial message was usually free to ad-lib, a few of the signs must always have referred to individual persons or things that could be mentioned in speech by just one name. A drawing of a small bear could have been verbalized as *small bear, little bear,* or *bear cub,* but if it designated a person known as *Little Bear* only that reading would have been admissible. A semantic annotation might or might not be added to help the interpreter—say, a figure of a man to which the figure of the cub is attached; the result was necessarily that a particular sign called for a particular word or phrase.

Something similar must have happened with pictorial messages where the interpreter was theoretically free to ad-lib. If the message was to himself—a series of reminders, perhaps, for recounting a story—a timid person no doubt did as he would do today and memorized the text. In that case, when he came to deliver it, using his notes for added confidence, each symbol for a particular meaning would also have stood for a particular word or phrase. It is not difficult to imagine almost from the first a tendency to link a written sign to its meaning, not directly, but via a particular word or words. Any such tendency must have taken hold quickly, for it put all the resources of language at the command of the writer and reader. For the first time writing was *phonetized:* a given sign represented a given complex of sounds.

When this step was first taken is impossible to determine. One cannot tell by looking at the earliest pictorial messages whether they were interpreted idea by idea, with the words ad-libbed, or word by word. The signs might have been direct representations of concrete objects, or figurative representations of one notion through another (sun for 'bright, brilliant, blinding'), or diagrams (an empty circle for 'empty, vacant, hollow')—nothing would prove that a word rather than a meaning was intended. Even an additional semantic indicator like the man beside the bear cub would not assure us that the sample was one of word writing, for the idea might be one that could be expressed by only one word anyway, such as the proper name *Little Bear,* and some semantic indicators would still leave room for ad-libbing: man plus mountain could stand for 'man from the mountain,' hence 'slave,' 'servant,' 'person of low birth.'

But somewhere in the word-writing stage an event took place that proved the word-by-word interpretation beyond a doubt. The pictorial stage would have found it very difficult to express abstract notions like tense and mood in the verb; so if we find *would be* symbolized by a drawing of a piece of wood and a drawing of a bee, we can be certain that the figures no longer stand for ideas. This is the *rebus;* something that we now associate with children's games was proof of the innovation of word writing.

Now nothing stood in the way of applying the same phonetic principle not just to whole words but to parts of words. Most languages contain words of more than one syllable, and often the syllables are the same in sound as certain one-syllable words. A slight extension of the rebus game enabled writers to use double characters for two-syllable words. In a modern rebus, *fancy* can be depicted by a fan and a sea, or *mumble* by a chrysanthemum and a bull. At first the sign-to-syllable relationship would not have been pure—a three-syllable word like *loggerhead* could have been represented by two signs, one for logger and one for head; but the basis for syllabic writing was laid, and the whole period of word writing was a mixture of word writing and syllable writing.[10]

The earliest developed form of word-syllabic writing was that of the Sumerians in Mesopotamia at the end of the fourth millennium B.C. The Egyptians had their own system within a century or so of this, but were probably influenced by the Sumerians.

Syllable writing

Even after the knack of writing by syllables had been acquired, pure syllable writing was rather long in coming. The older word signs were kept through tradition and inertia, and often a given word could be represented either by its own sign or by signs for its syllables. The second historical step—the discarding of all the word signs and the adoption of a straightforward system of syllable writing—had to be taken by disrespectful foreigners who had no romantic attachments to the old signs and merely borrowed what was practical.[11] These were the Phoenicians. Other borrowers of other systems did the same, but the Phoenicians are most important to us because they stand in direct line with the later development of the alphabet.

---

[10] Gelb, *op. cit.*, pp. 99–105.

[11] *Ibid.*, p. 196.

a	ka	sa	ta	na	ha	ma	ya	ra	wa	ga	za	da	ba	pa
i	ki	si	ti(tsi)	ni	hi	mi		ri	wi(i)	gi	zi	di	bi	pi
u	ku	su	tu(tsu)	nu	hu	mu	yu	ru		gu	zu	du	bu	pu
e	ke	se	te	ne	he	me	ye	re	we(e)	ge	ze	de	be	pe
o	ko	so	to	no	ho	mo	yo	ro	wo	go	zo	do	bo	po

(n)

FROM Fossey, *Notices sur les Caractères Étrangers,* p. 314; reproduced in I. J. Gelb, *A Study of Writing,* rev. ed. (Chicago: University of Chicago Press, 1963).

THE CHEROKEE SYLLABARY

This syllabary was invented between 1809 and 1821 by Sequoya (George Guess) and used by the Cherokee people and missionaries working among them. It is partly an adaptation of roman letters.

a	e	i	o	u	ʌ
ga	ge	gi	go	gu	gʌ
ha	he	hi	ho	hu	hʌ
la	le	li	lo	lu	lʌ
ma	me	mi	mo	mu	
na	ne	ni	no	nu	nʌ
gwa	gwe	gwi	gwo	gwu	gwʌ
sa	se	si	so	su	sʌ
da	de	di	do	du	dʌ
dla	dle	dli	dlo	dlu	dlʌ
dza	dze	dzi	dzo	dzu	dzʌ
wa	we	wi	wo	wu	wʌ
ya	ye	yi	yo	yu	yʌ

| ka |
| hna |
| nah |
| s |
| ta |
| ti |
| tla |
| te |

FROM H. A. Gleason, *An Introduction to Descriptive Linguistics,* rev. ed. (New York: Holt, Rinehart and Winston, Inc., 1961), p. 414.

The Egyptian table of syllable signs, or syllabary, contained two sets of figures, each representing a different kind of value. The figures of the first set represented particular consonants plus any vowel or no vowel at all; a single sign stood for *ma, me, mi, mu,* or *m,* or for *ta, te, ti, tu,* or *t.* The members of the second set were the same except that two consonants were involved; one sign, for example, stood for *tama, tame, tem, tma,* and so on.[12] The consistent omission of vowels was in line with the nature of the Semitic languages, where inflections are shown by internal changes instead of by affixes (like English *man-men* rather than *man-*mans* or *rise-rose* rather than *rise-*rised*); it was possible to sacrifice the vowels without losing the identity of the word, and thus make a saving in the number of different symbols written.

The Phoenicians entered the picture around the middle of the second millennium B.C. They imitated the one-consonant syllabary of the Egyptians, throwing out the rest. By about 1000 B.C. they had developed a completely syllabic form of writing with no word signs and no signs for more than one syllable. The vowels were still omitted, though where needed to avoid ambiguity they were often added in the form of consonants whose features resembled those of the desired vowel. For example, Semitic writing—including Phoenician—had syllabic signs for the semiconsonants /w/ and /y/ (plus a vowel), and used them as makeshifts for the simple vowels /u/ and /i/. There were other such makeshifts. The glimmerings of alphabetic writing were already visible.

Sound writing: the alphabet

It is a bit presumptuous of modern phonology to appropriate the term "distinctive sound" for its phonemes, as if the users of language would never have supposed at each new and successive refinement of the relationship between sound and symbol that they had at last hit upon the phonetic atom. This is dramatized for us now with the theory of distinctive features—what we had thought was the atom, the phoneme, turns out to be a rather complex molecule. Words and syllables must have been felt to be just as distinctively irreducible in their time. So if phonemes continue to be called distinctive sounds—and the phrase is too firmly entrenched to be got rid of easily—we should remember that the term refers to a set of phonetic features, at a certain level of refinement, which actually came into consciousness within the growth of alphabetic writing. For that we can thank mainly the Greeks of some three thousand years ago.

---

[12] Gelb, *op. cit.,* pp. 75–8.

The Phoenicians were the seafaring traders of the ancient world and carried their writing wherever they went as one of the tools of their trade. It was probably in the ninth century B.C. that the form of Phoenician writing that was to become the Greek alphabet was planted along the western shores of the Aegean.[13]

The Greek innovation—and it was gradual, like all the others—was to do consistently what the Phoenicians had done sporadically: to add the interpretative vowel signs to all their syllables. What they themselves must have regarded still as a syllabary thus became an alphabet by accident. A sign signifying /mu/ (as well as /mi me ma/) would not have needed any /u/ after it if the context made it clear that /mu/ was intended. An English sentence written *Y mst b crfl wth sch ppl* would give us no trouble—*mst* here can only mean *must*. But when the symbol for any *m*-plus-vowel syllable was consistently accompanied by a sign for a particular vowel, it was natural for the next generation of scribes to forget that it stood for the syllable and take it for the consonant alone. Now it was possible to go on to a full specification of all the phonemes. This was the form of writing that took hold in all the major languages of the world, including—with modifications—the Semitic itself, from which it was derived. We can never guess how far the progress and power of the Western world may have been due to the speedup of communication and the accumulation of recorded experience that was made possible when a quasi-phonemic writing that could be quickly learned took literacy away from a select priesthood and put it within reach of the general public.

Yet we need not be overly prideful of our Western accomplishment, for from the standpoint of sheer creativeness it was outdone by the Koreans some five hundred years ago. In 1446 King Sejong promulgated an alphabet—the date is still celebrated as a national holiday in Korea—in which certain strokes of the characters represented phonetic characteristics such as tongue position or force of articulation. The Koreans had had a good deal of practice with word and syllable writing using Chinese characters, and of course the whole evolution of alphabetic writing lay behind them, so they knew pretty much what they were doing in designing new forms; but their "visible speech," to borrow the name given to his own similar system four hundred years later by Alexander Melville Bell, was still a remarkable achievement. Unfortunately, it was slow in having the effect on education and general culture that the alphabet produced in the West, because the older system of writing continued to be used until after World War II; South Korea has still not gone over

---

[13] *Ibid.*, pp. 178–81.

STAGES OF THE DEVELOPMENT OF WRITING

NO WRITING: *Pictures*

FORERUNNERS OF WRITING: *Semasiography*

1. Descriptive-Representational Device
2. Identifying-Mnemonic Device

FULL WRITING: *Phonography*

1. *Word-Syllabic:* Sumerian (Akkadian)	Egyptian	Hittite (Aegean)	Chinese
2. *Syllabic:* Elamite Hurrian etc.	West Semitic (Phoenician) (Hebrew) (Aramaic) etc.	Cypro-Minoan Cypriote Phaistos? Byblos?	Japanese
3. *Alphabetic:*	Greek Aramaic (vocalized) Hebrew (vocalized) Latin Indic etc.		

FROM Gelb, *op. cit.*, p. 191.

completely to the simplified alphabet.[14] A similar attempt around 1650, by Francis Lodwick in England, received some attention in its time but had no practical effect. Honorat Rambaud of Marseilles had also "invented an elaborate notation on comparable principles" a century earlier.[15]

---

[14] Fritz Vos, in *Papers of the CIC Far Eastern Language Institute*, Joseph K. Yamagiwa, ed. (Ann Arbor: University of Michigan Press, 1964); reviewed by James D. McCawley, *Language* 42.171 (1966).

[15] David Abercrombie, *Studies in Phonetics and Linguistics* (New York: Oxford University Press, 1965), pp. 49–50.

DECIPHERMENT

One of the most fascinating chapters in the recovery of the past is the interpretation of ancient writings on scattered, fragmentary, and often fragile artifacts that have come down to us. Much of our ability to read them is due to the continuity of certain cultures that developed a writing system at an early date and have kept their tradition sufficiently alive to our own day to give us a basis of comparison with earlier systems related to them. Foremost among these traditions are the Chinese, Hebrew, Sanskrit, Greco-Roman, and Persian, the last having been carried on in India by the Parsees who fled there during the Mohammedan invasion of Persia in the eighth century. Now and then some precious bit of bilingual or multilingual evidence comes to light—a document, such as the Rosetta stone, on which identical messages appear in two or more languages, at least one of which could already be read. The Rosetta stone contained inscriptions in two varieties of Egyptian writing, plus Greek. The most impressive multilingual record of all was the Persian inscriptions done at Bisutun by order of King Darius, with parallel texts in Persian, Elamite, and Assyrian (Babylonian).[16] The Persian empire embraced peoples speaking these three principal languages, and other Persian inscriptions likewise are written in all three.

No two instances of decipherment are the same, but a close look at one will suggest some of the problems. The most recent—and among the most spectacular—is that of the Linear B tablets unearthed in Crete and on the Greek mainland in the southern peninsula of Peloponnesus. The man chiefly responsible for the discovery was the British architect and amateur cryptographer Michael Ventris, and the language, as it turned out, was a form of Greek about six hundred years older than any for which records had previously been known. The following is based on the account by John Chadwick, Ventris's closest co-worker.[17]

In one respect the Cretan and mainland finds were exceptional. Both had been stored at the site of ancient palaces that had subsequently been burned, with the result that large quantities of clay tablets containing the writing had been fired, just as brick and pottery are intentionally fired to harden them; had this not happened, the clay would long since have turned to mud. Ventris thus had several hundred tablets with which to work—the number of published texts is now about five thousand. This enabled him to ignore for the moment the question of what language he was dealing with and to concentrate instead on calculating the frequencies

---

[16] Holger Pedersen, *The Discovery of Language,* tr. John Webster Spargo (Bloomington, Ind.: Indiana University Press, 1962), p. 155.

[17] *The Decipherment of Linear B* (London: Cambridge University Press, 1960).

of the written symbols, making certain assumptions about what they were used for.

The first clue lay in the resemblance between Linear B and a much later form of writing from Cyprus that had already been deciphered. It was obvious that the two did not represent the same language, since when Linear B was given the Cypriote values the result made no sense, but it seemed likely that Linear B at least had the minimum similarity of being a related syllabary and not an alphabet. The assumption that it was similar led Ventris to look for certain signs nearly always found at the beginning of words and not in the middle. The reason for this was that in Cypriote the typical symbol stood for a consonant plus a vowel, as we have seen to be true of Semitic writing, and a word such as *sensible* would have had signs corresponding to *se-ne-si-bi-le*. But if a word *began* with a vowel, a different kind of symbol would have had to be used. Such symbols were found.

A second successful guess involved a sign that was commonly used at the end of particular groups of signs that were found repeated elsewhere without that ending. It appeared that this might be some sort of conjunction like the Latin *-que* for 'and,' attached to the ends of words.

A third deduction followed from mistakes that the scribes had made. In many places there were clear erasures, and what had first been inscribed and the correction written over it could both be read. In addition there were words that almost invariably appeared in a certain form, but perhaps once or twice, in a context so similar that it almost had to be intended as the same form, a writing differing by one sign appeared. It seemed a safe guess that these infrequent changes were uncorrected mistakes. Since mistakes are generally made between forms that resemble one another, this made it possible to tabulate lists of forms assumed to be similar but not the same, like English *p* and *b* or *t* and *d*.

A fourth deduction followed from the assumption that the language was an inflected one. If it resembled Latin, one would expect forms like *domin-a, puell-a, bon-a,* and *serv-a,* in which the inflection is in the form of a characteristic vowel that alternates with some other ending such as *-us.* But if Linear B was syllabic it could not show these endings directly. It would have had to use one sign for *-na,* another for *-la,* another for *-va,* and so on. A study of the tablets showed that there were words that stayed the same at the beginning, like the *domi-* of *domina,* and that had variable endings. It also revealed a small number of words that remained the same when followed by words having these unstable endings and that might well be prepositions. On the hypothesis that a given preposition would usually govern the same case, the variable endings were assumed to stand for syllables all ending in the same vowel—this being the marker for case—but with different consonants.

The inflectional theory also made it possible to match the consonantal part of each sign with that of other signs. Given a form such as *domi-na* and *domi-nus,* we would recognize variants of the same word, identified by the *domi-* part, and would assign the *n* to the stem: *domin-.* Therefore, the syllabic sign for *-na* and the syllabic sign for *-nus* must contain the same consonant, *n.*

Finally, there was a hint of gender distinctions in the pictograms that accompanied the writing. If a tablet whose form indicated that it was a catalog of some kind also contained the figure of a woman, the chances were that lists of women were involved; therefore, the names were feminine and all had the same set of vowel endings.

Taking these assumptions together, Ventris set up a grid in which signs were lined up from left to right in terms of having the same supposed vowel and up and down in terms of having the same consonant. A sample provided by Chadwick from the later work notes is given on page 175.[18]

Now began the task of trying to conjecture words. The tablets were clearly of a commercial nature, so it was likely that place names would figure, and Ventris plausibly reasoned that in the tablets unearthed at Knossus in Crete it was likely that both Knossus and the seaport town of Amnisos would be mentioned. The name of Amnisos was known from Homer and was a good candidate to work with because, for one thing, it had an initial vowel, and the vowel symbols had already been isolated. For another thing, the Cyprus writing had a peculiar way of handling consonant clusters, which was to write both consonants with the same vowel. So, assuming this peculiarity for Linear B, *Amnisos* would be written with the symbol for *-mi-* because the following syllable actually contained the vowel *i* and was of course written with the symbol for *-ni-: Am(i)nisos.* Ventris had already guessed correctly, from frequency counts, that a particular sign stood for *a-.* So now he looked for a word in which that sign came first and in which the second and third signs were already on his grid as containing the same vowel but different consonants. There was only one word on the tablets that gave this combination. Assuming that it was actually *Amnisos,* Ventris now had another sign that he could test, that of the last syllable, presumably *-so* or *-sos.* If this vowel was actually *o,* then all the other signs in the same column of the grid also contained *o,* and the next step was to look for a word containing three such signs and hope that it would be the name of the main city itself, which would have been written with the signs for *K(o)-no-so.*

It was not necessary to assume any particular language for names like *Amnisos* and *Knossus,* for place names are freely borrowed. But now

---

[18] Chadwick, *op. cit.*, p. 59.

VENTRIS'S GRID

Diagrammatic Representation of Linear B Tablets; a Diagnosis of Consonant and Vowel Equations in the Inflectional Material from Pylos

THESE 51 SIGNS MAKE UP 90% OF ALL SIGN-OCCURRENCES IN THE PYLOS SIGNGROUP INDEX. APPENDED FIGURES GIVE EACH SIGN'S OVERALL FREQUENCY PER MILLE IN THE PYLOS INDEX.

	"Impure" ending, typical syllables before -ȝ and -ȁ in Case 2c and 3	"Pure" ending, typical nominatives of forms in Column 1	Includes possible "accusatives"	Also, but less frequently, the nominatives of forms in Column 1	
	These signs don't occur before -ȝ-	These signs occur less commonly or not at all before -ȁ-			
	More often feminine than masculine?	More often masculine than feminine?			More often feminine than masculine?
	Normally form the genitive singular by adding -ȝ	Normally form the genitive singular by adding -ȁ			
	Vowel 1	Vowel 2	Vowel 3	Vowel 4	Vowel 5
Pure vowels?	⟨sign⟩ 30.3			⟨sign⟩ 37.2	
A semi-vowel?			⟨sign⟩ 34.0	⟨sign⟩ 29.4	
Consonant 1	⟨sign⟩ 14.8	⟨sign⟩ 32.5	⟨sign⟩ 21.2	⟨sign⟩ 28.1	⟨sign⟩ 18.8
2	⟨sign⟩ 19.6	⟨sign⟩ 17.5			⟨sign⟩ 13.7
3		⟨sign⟩ 9.2		⟨sign⟩ 3.3	⟨sign⟩ 10.0
4	⟨sign⟩ 17.0	⟨sign⟩ 28.6			⟨sign⟩ 0.4
5	⟨sign⟩ 17.7	⟨sign⟩ 10.3		⟨sign⟩ 4.1	⟨sign⟩ 10.2
6	⟨sign⟩ 7.4	⟨sign⟩ 20.5		⟨sign⟩ 14.8	⟨sign⟩ 14.4
7	⟨sign⟩ 4.1	⟨sign⟩ 44.0			
8	⟨sign⟩ 6.1	⟨sign⟩ 6.1		⟨sign⟩ 13.5	⟨sign⟩ 15.2
9		⟨sign⟩ 33.1		⟨sign⟩ 32.3	⟨sign⟩ 2.4
10	⟨sign⟩ 22.2		⟨sign⟩ 38.2	⟨sign⟩ 3.5	⟨sign⟩ 2.2
11	⟨sign⟩ 31.2	⟨sign⟩ 33.8	⟨sign⟩ 34.4	⟨sign⟩ 8.3	⟨sign⟩ 0.7
12	⟨sign⟩ 17.0			⟨sign⟩ 37.7	⟨sign⟩ 24.0
13		⟨sign⟩ 9.4	⟨sign⟩ 14.2		
14	⟨sign⟩ 5.0				
15	⟨sign⟩ 12.6				

AFTER Michael Ventris, September 28, 1951.

Ventris did assume that it might be Greek and examined some of the inflected forms of the names in the light of that assumption. He also assumed that the syllabary might not have been perfectly adapted to Greek and that certain of the sounds, particularly certain syllable-final consonants, might have been omitted. This was his boldest guess and the luckiest one, for it developed that if one were free to add final consonants—and these turned out to be phonetically related consonants—the result would spell Greek words. Pictograms were again a help—a tablet on which a chariot appeared contained the word which Ventris had reconstructed as the Greek name for 'chariot.'

A year after Ventris announced his discovery in 1952, new excavations at the site of the ancient city of Pylos brought to light a number of tablets on which his experimental syllabary could be tried out. Pictograms of vessels, identified by Greek names exactly as Ventris predicted they would be written, confirmed his solution beyond a doubt.

LINGUISTS AND WRITING

Attitudes

Linguists have changed their views toward writing several times in the past century or so, a fact which the average reader may find confusing if he encounters certain recent textbooks on English or on learning a foreign language, in which linguists are pictured as agreed on where to place writing in their scale of values. The usual pronouncement is that "writing is only a reflection of speech," and the corollary is that "writing is secondary to speech," hence not to be confused with speech, not to be studied before speech, and not to be studied out of relationship with speech. The linguist Leonard Bloomfield stated it this way: "Writing is merely a device for recording speech. A person is much the same and looks the same, whether he has ever had his picture taken or not. Only a vain beauty who sits for many photographs and carefully studies them may end by slightly changing her pose and expressions. It is much the same with languages and their written recording."[19]

There were good reasons for Bloomfield's concern, as we saw at the beginning of this chapter. Our schooling is so heavily literary that many

---

[19] Leonard Bloomfield and Clarence L. Barnhart, *Let's Read; A Linguistic Approach* (Detroit: Wayne State University Press, 1961). Quoted by Yakov Malkiel in review of same, *Romance Philology* 16.89 (1962).

people, including many teachers, have come to regard speech as a way of pronouncing what is written. This attitude is a handicap to learners. A person trying to master a foreign language must first master a new sound system, and if he is immediately given the written form in unlimited doses he will unconsciously read in the English values for the letters. A child learning to read will be slowed down if he puts written signs first and sounds last.

Bloomfield's convictions were also shared by many if not most of the group known as structuralists (see Chapter 11, pages 193–99), whose aims included the top-priority one of analyzing languages that had never been written. But it was not the view of linguists before that time—in fact, the whole of historical linguistics was based on written documents from which speech could only be inferred—and it is of secondary concern to the influential school of generative grammarians at the present time, for whom a language comprehends so much more than its representation in sound that whether or not spellings and sounds correspond seems rather trivial. A more temperate view is that "Bloomfield's linguistics has its distinct merit for the classification of field flowers"[20]—languages in the wild state, with no tradition of writing and lacking the good and bad effects that writing brings, including spelling pronunciations and perhaps the slowing down of some linguistic change.

Contributions

What influence Bloomfield and the structuralists may have had has been good for the teaching of reading in spite of their dogmatic tone. When a child who is already almost fully equipped with a language comes to the task of reading, anything that will help him transfer what he already knows to what he is expected to write and read is priceless. Exploiting the phonemic correspondences of English, clumsy as they are, is probably the greatest support for this at the stage of *learning* to read and, later, in identifying new words. Whether it is equally valuable for the *practice* of reading by children who already know how to read is not so clear. It may be just as important to break away from letter identifications in order to read efficiently as it is important to have those identifications at the beginning—quite possibly we need a phonemic approach first and later the whole-word method. It is curious that from the standpoint of speed of reading, and especially of writing, the history of writing as we traced it, with first pictures, then word signs, then symbols for syllables and

---

[20] Malkiel, *op. cit.*, p. 90.

finally letters, is not progress but the reverse. A picture tells a story at a glance, but the words of a story must be picked out one by one or at most in comparatively small groups. Word symbols, in their turn, have an advantage over symbols for smaller units: many more can be packed on a page, and the scribe, if he knows the system well enough, can go faster than if he must write syllable by syllable, and faster still than if he must go letter by letter. This presupposes, of course, a good, highly consistent word-writing or syllable-writing system—not all the historically attested systems could qualify, by any means. In our zeal to make it easier for people to learn to read and write we may have made it harder for them after they learn. With reading this is probably not serious, because mature readers in effect identify words—even spelled-out words—by their shapes as wholes, and are not slowed down excessively. But writing is another matter. One can read phrase by phrase; one must spell letter by letter. To remedy this we have shorthand, which is a turning back to the past, for shorthand cuts time by increasing the number of symbols—it is a kind of syllabary. And here we presumably enlightened moderns are in the position of the ignorant medieval soldier who paid a scrivener to write his correspondence for him; training in shorthand is reserved for specialists. Getting our thoughts on paper is laborious. We may never know how much our ineptitude has cost us through the centuries. With the advent of cheaper and cheaper recording machines, it is doubtful now whether any effort to teach wider writing skills could succeed, with or without the help of linguists.

What about distinctive features? If writing has progressed toward an ever narrower interpretation of the sounds that it symbolizes, should we not expect this latest refinement to be the next step in line? If so, linguists could be credited with a completely original contribution, untouched by any popular hand. Following is how *dog* might be written, with each column spelling out one of the phonemes /d ɔ g/:[21]

−vocalic	+vocalic	−vocalic
+consonantal	−consonantal	+consonantal
−strident	+compact	−strident
−grave	+tense	+compact
−continuant	+flat	−tense
−nasal		
−tense		

---

[21] From Fred W. Householder, Jr., "On Some Recent Claims in Phonological Theory," *Journal of Linguistics* 1.26 (1965).

If the distinctive-feature matrix were ever put to such a practical use it would not look as clumsy as this, for obviously the features would be represented by single symbols and not by spelled-out words. The gain, as pointed out in Chapter 3, pages 28–30, is in cutting down the number of different symbols, but, as with the alphabet in comparison with a syllabary, the number of running symbols that must be written for any given word is much larger. This does not bother a computer, but it is more work for people. If it is possible to doubt the value of an alphabet over a good syllabary or over some form of morphemic writing, it hardly seems promising to look in the direction of distinctive features for a practical writing system.

The greatest contribution of linguists to the writing of languages has been and will probably continue to be the analysis and phonemicization of languages as yet unwritten, conferring on their peoples the precious gift of an alphabet far simpler than ours, one that does not, to quote Bloomfield again, "waste years of every child's time" in trying to learn it. Will English-speaking peoples ever benefit in the same way? Perhaps they will, in lands that compromise on English to evade the rivalries of local languages and dialects—for example in India, where English is not only widespread as a trade language but is the native language of a hundred thousand Anglo-Indians.[22] A linguist at the University of Malaya, complaining of the two thousand different letters and letter combinations for the approximately forty phonemes of English, and of the plight of English-speaking children who require "up to two years more than children of other nations to acquire the simple art of reading," an expense that other people who want to use English cannot afford, argues that the standardization of English writing and other aspects of the language "should not only be the concern of the English or American people, but of all the nations."[23] It would be strange if spelling reform, shipwrecked so many times on the Isles of Apathy, should arrive at last in a diplomatic pouch.

---

[22] John Spencer, "The Anglo-Indians and Their Speech: A Socio-linguistic Essay," *Lingua* 16.70 (1966).

[23] S. Takdir Alisjahbana, "New National Languages: A Problem Modern Linguistics Has Failed to Solve," *Lingua* 15.530 (1965).

ADDITIONAL REMARKS
AND APPLICATIONS

1. Interpret the following figure, pretending first that you are reading it as a pictogram, then as a word symbol or logogram, then as a syllable symbol or syllabogram. What words might correspond to it as a pictogram? Of what words might it form part if it were a syllabogram?

2. List four letters which are fairly consistent in their phonemic values in English and four which are highly inconsistent. By and large, is it the vowel letters or the consonant letters that are more consistent?

3. List four words which have variant pronunciations in different parts of the United States but have a standard spelling. Writers of stories in dialect sometimes adapt their spellings to local pronunciations; give some examples.

4. Which would be more surprising, for someone to misspell *illegal* as *inlegal* (compare the same prefix in *indirect*) or to misspell *not bad at all* as *not bad a tall?* What does this suggest about our inclination to be swayed by morphemes rather than by sounds when we write?

5. In Chapter 7, pages 110–11, we noted that bifurcations in pronunciation enrich the language with new words. Are there also sometimes bifurcations in spelling, in which a word with more than one meaning comes to be spelled in different ways, though remaining the same in pronunciation? Look up the etymologies of the following pairs: *errant-arrant, crumby-crummy, coin-coign, born-borne.*

6. What has been the net effect of attempts at spelling reform in English? Consider the acceptability of variants like *color-colour, labor-labour, practice-practise, chastize-chastise, catalog-catalogue.*

7. The following sentences are from written sources. Each can be interpreted in two radically different ways. Read them aloud, adding the

unwritten elements (accents or intonations) that will make the meanings clear:

a. *Several cities have imported taxicabs propelled by light diesel engines.*
   Meanings: 'possess imported taxicabs'; 'have performed the action of importing cabs.'

b. *Physics and biology surely provide basic stuff for the critical mind of the humanist. Only science, to its own misfortune, is presently out of bounds for him.* (Just the second sentence.)
   Meanings: 'but science'; 'science alone.'

c. *Teixidor seems to feel that Ramírez himself would never have consented.*
   Meanings: 'Ramírez, as far as he himself was concerned'; 'not even as important a person as Ramírez.'

8. The following is from a scholarly essay by someone whose native language was not English. What betrays this?

   By the way, between 1927 and "the sixties" Alejo Carpentier became one of the world's distinguished novelists.

9. Are there differences among the parts of speech in the readiness with which the meanings of the words in each of them can be shown by representational drawing? If so, see if you can scale them for adjectives, verbs, and nouns. Between these three parts of speech on the one hand and prepositions and conjunctions on the other, which could be shown best by diagrams?

10. What is the significance of doubling in the signs *ff*. (after a page number) and *et seqq.?* Identify some other signs that are doubled for the same purpose and some that are not.

11. Contrast the stage at which a given sign could be given the interpretation 'peak, apex, vertex, top, cap, summit' with the stage at which it could be given the interpretation 'peak, peek, pique, Peke.'

12. Might the ultimate unintelligibility of pictograms have contributed to their being interpreted arbitrarily, that is, being taken to stand for sounds rather than for what they originally pictured? Consider the development of the Sumerian word for 'hand' from the easily recog-

nizable symbol on the left below to the cuneiform symbol on the right.[24]

Could the opposite also have happened, a loss of the original meaning leading to a carelessness with the form?

13. The units of writing, unlike those of speech, are often the creation of individuals. Consult any good encyclopedia, under *Cherokee* or *Sequoya,* for an account of the Cherokee syllabary (see page 168).

14. Do languages differ in the efficiency with which they can be written in syllables by contrast with distinctive sounds? Consider the variety of syllable types in English. Assume that each syllable *(ta, tab, tack, tam,* and so on) requires a separate and distinct symbol.

15. The more precise and fine-grained our writing system becomes, the more arbitrary it grows. In a pictogram it does not much matter whether a figure is made standing, recumbent, facing backwards, bent over, or upside down; it remains recognizable as the same figure. In a syllabary the syllables must be written in a certain order, and in an alphabet both the syllables and the letters must be arranged in a predetermined manner. Furthermore, in either a syllabary or an alphabet it is necessary to make other things significant than just the shape of the symbols—the letters p, b, q, and d all have exactly the same shape, differing only in their stance. So we have a scheme in which arbitrary signs occupy arbitrary positions in arbitrary groupings that proceed arbitrarily from left to right (in Western languages) and arbitrarily from top line to bottom line. Is this apt to cause psychological problems in some people? Look up the term *strephosymbolia.*

16. Long before it was suspected that Linear B might be related to Greek, historical linguistics had made certain hypotheses about what an earlier form of Greek might be like. How would such hypotheses be of help in the decipherment? How would a successful decipherment help the hypotheses? (One hypothesis was that, although Classical Greek lacked them, an earlier form of the language must have had

---

[24] E. H. Sturtevant, *An Introduction to Linguistic Science* (New Haven, Conn.: Yale University Press, 1947), p. 21.

labiovelar sounds like the /kw gw/ of Latin *quis, pinguis.* These were found in Linear B.)

17. Young children must be taught to read, and they must also be taught words that they do not already know in their speech. Should these two things be combined in the initial steps of learning to read? Explain.

18. If writing does help to slow down linguistic change (and it is hard to do more than guess here), do you suppose it is by virtue of being writing and hence more stable, or is it partly also due to the fact that more people with widely different backgrounds have a stake in it? If so, is it likely that other means of enlarging the speech community—radio and television, for example—are having the same effect?

19. How does your school system teach reading, by the whole-word method, by phonics, or in some other way? Are slow readers a problem? Does your school or high school have a program for teaching rapid reading? What devices are used?

20. If you know a system of shorthand, explain and demonstrate what kind of writing it is.

THE EVOLVING
APPROACHES TO
LANGUAGE

HERE IS A LESSON in the tardiness with which science has come to the disciplines of man. It is easiest to be objective about what touches us least intimately. The first part of nature to yield to scientific formulation was the movements of the sun, moon, and planets—put a heaven between us and the object of our study and we can be impartial. One of the newest sciences is psychology; in this field the job is far from finished, because the main concern is man himself, and preconceptions by the carload have had to be disposed of before the scientist could even get to work. Linguistics as a science is barely out of rompers, and one reason is surely that language is closest of all to what each human being feels is part of him.

And this part of him is not only his to use, but his to theorize about. The linguist Leonard Bloomfield was interested in collecting what he called "tertiary responses" to language. These come after "secondary responses," which are the viewpoints that any person—from layman to linguist—expresses about language. The tertiary response is the reaction that flares at any attempt to question the rightness of a secondary response. Bloomfield tells of visiting the house of a doctor who propounded the theory that a language such as Chippewa could contain only a few hundred words, citing as authority a Chippewa Indian guide. When Bloomfield tried to explain that the situation was not quite that simple, the doctor turned his back.[1] The record does not show that

---

[1] "Secondary and Tertiary Responses to Language," *Language* 20.45–55 (1944).

Bloomfield retaliated by offering the medical man a good prescription for scarlet fever.

The growth of linguistics as a science can be traced in five stages, each overlapping the preceding one but at some point breaking rather sharply with it and constituting itself an embattled school of thought. The five stages are traditional grammar, historical linguistics, descriptive linguistics, structural linguistics, and formal linguistics. Though born of conflict, they represent different emphases rather than irreconcilable rivalries; so each lives on. The new is a reassortment of the old to which are added deeper insights plus—for the troops who change sides—the spice of fashion.

TRADITIONAL GRAMMAR

To anyone who has gone through a language course since the early 1950's, "traditional grammar" doubtless has a bad sound. Textbooks and teachers using supposedly up-to-date methods in teaching foreign languages or English mention traditional grammar either unfavorably or not at all; it embodies, for them, all the outmoded practices of reciting grammatical paradigms, translating to English instead of learning to speak, and worrying about what language ought to do rather than what it does.

But at the moment there is a renewed interest in traditional grammar, largely inspired by a contemporary group of linguists who find in the traditional grammarians their spiritual predecessors. The *Grammatica Speculativa* of Thomas of Erfurt, written in the early part of the fourteenth century, offers numerous parallels to recent grammatical theory.[2] But one treatise is particularly close: the *Minerva* of the Spanish humanist Francisco Sánchez de las Brozas, published in 1585 and imitated about a century later by a grammar that became much more widely known, the *Grammaire Générale et Raisonné* of Claude Lancelot, usually referred to as the Port Royal Grammar.[3]

Sánchez and Lancelot held that particular languages are individual forms taken by an underlying oneness common to the race. This notion of universality can be traced to the ancients, but it was encouraged by the linguistic situation prevailing in Western Europe throughout the Middle Ages: Latin was the vehicle of learning, the vernacular was the

---

[2] Robert C. Godfrey, "Late Medieval Linguistic Meta-theory and Chomsky's Syntactic Structures," *Word* 21.251–56 (1965).

[3] Robin T. Lakoff, "Pre-Cartesian Linguistics," abstract of a talk at the meeting of the Linguistic Society of America, December, 1966, in *Meeting Handbook*, published by the Center for Applied Linguistics, pp. 43–44.

vehicle of commerce and daily living. Even after full dignity was accorded to each of the common languages and Latin was no longer regarded as superior—well into modern times—the sense of community among European scholars persisted. Their languages, especially the dominant Romance tongues of France, Italy, and Spain, were obviously related through Latin; underneath the superficial differences lay an immutable sameness. Whether universal grammar would have been so generally accepted if Europe had been sharply divided, say, between two languages as unlike as French and Hungarian, no one can say. But what was then perhaps an ill-founded idea comes to us now with a new suggestive power as we compare widely diverse languages and continue to find in them more similarities than differences.

Traditional grammar was at its best in describing the inflections, idioms, and sentence forms of particular languages, especially the differences from language to language in Europe; this had a practical purpose too, for it put the emphasis on what had to be learned if one already knew French and wanted to study Italian—the same principles are expounded in "contrast grammars" today. But there were weaknesses: "Traditional grammar neglects whole parts of language, such as word formation; it is normative and assumes the role of prescribing rules, not of recording facts; it lacks overall perspective; often it is unable to separate the written from the spoken word. . . ."[4] Not every contemporary grammarian would regard all these traits as faults—prescribing rules enjoys renewed popularity in current theories of language as "rule-governed behavior." But, such as they were, the weaknesses stemmed from the fact that traditional grammar was neither empirical nor experimental. It assumed that language was a system embodied in the writings of the best authors, something to be sheltered from change. From one standpoint this was useful: the view of individual languages as self-contained systems is essentially correct. From another standpoint it was harmful, because it blinded its advocates to the potential of language to renew itself from generation to generation. The potential for renewal was the all-absorbing interest of the up-and-coming younger generation of linguists at the beginning of the nineteenth century, who were so fascinated with the historical development of languages that they turned away from systematic descriptions. What descriptions had been made were thus cut off from criticism and became self-contained in every sense of the word. They fell into the hands of schoolmen who perpetuated them as stylebooks—not as records of what speakers did but as models of what speakers, especially schoolboys, ought to do. Where

---

[4] Ferdinand de Saussure, *Course in General Linguistics*, trans. Wade Baskin (New York: McGraw-Hill, Inc., 1959), p. 82.

usage differed from the books, usage was corrupt. So traditional grammar drew farther and farther away from language as it was, and more and more it became a policeman of correctness. Listen to a noted grammarian of less than a century ago fulminating against a construction that was being taken up by everyone, ***The bridge was being built,*** replacing ***The bridge was building*** (see Chapter 8, pages 130–31):

> As to the notion of introducing a new and more complex passive form of conjugation, as, "The bridge *is being built,*" ... it is one of the most absurd and monstrous innovations ever thought of. . . . This is certainly no better English than, "The work *was being published, has been being published, had been being published, shall or will be being published, shall or will have been being published;*" and so on, through all the moods and tenses. What a language shall we have when our verbs are thus conjugated![5]

It is easy for us to laugh at this, and of course normative grammarians *have* given a bad name to traditional grammar, which did not deserve it. But it would be wrong to censure ·authority in language simply because it is authoritarian. Every culture recognizes some styles of speech or writing as better than others, at least under certain circumstances. In our culture there is a standard, or prestige, dialect that more or less coincides with the formal modes of expression used among persons who are not acquaintances and who do not belong to the same social class—who are, in short, "not relaxed" with one another when they speak. In writing, it more or less coincides with the style that must be used in a letter to a stranger. As this is not a dialect that is ordinarily learned in the home, it has to be learned later, and its rules of usage are what we generally think of when someone mentions correct speech. Normative grammar is unassailable when it identifies itself with a prestige dialect and honestly recognizes its practical and esthetic aims. It goes wrong when it is taken over by quacks who peddle self-improvement in the form of lessons—in school or out—on how to avoid a few dozen "mistakes." (These will be looked at more closely in the last chapter.) It also goes wrong—at least according to one conception of democracy—when it polishes correctness as a badge of superiority. Thus, slang might be appropriate under some conditions and a form of literary expression under others, but the appropriateness of slang is never viewed as a sign of quality, while that of literary expression frequently is. This, of course, is the linguistic side of social stratification: the speech of superior people is regarded as superior speech.

---

[5] Goold Brown, *The Grammar of English Grammars* (New York: William Wood and Co., 1884), p. 379.

The nineteenth century was, of course, not completely barren of workers on individual languages besides the traditional grammarians. One remarkable figure at the beginning of the century was the German statesman and philologist Wilhelm von Humboldt, whose insights were sharpened in the same way as those of modern descriptivists, by studying what would now be termed "exotic" languages—in his case, Basque and the Kawi language of Java. Von Humboldt's ideas have been revived in our own day, but in his time they did not attract enough scientific co-workers to counteract the influence of the historical linguists.

HISTORICAL LINGUISTICS

If the intimacy of language is what makes it a late arrival to 'science,' it is also true that the least intimate part, the history of language, is what first took shape as an empirical science. The genealogy and family relationships of languages became a recognized discipline early in the nineteenth century and developed so vigorously and successfully that it took something like a revolution a century later to prove that linguistic science could be anything but historical.

This first great empirical theory—that languages now widely different can be traced to a common origin—was born of the intense interest of the 1800's in evolution, plus something that resulted accidentally from the English conquest of India: the discovery of Sanskrit. The effect of the latter has been described as follows:

> The knowledge of Sanskrit was found to have revolutionary consequences. The mere fact that scholars were unexpectedly confronted with a third classical language in addition to Greek and Latin was sufficient to shake their reliance on the easy-going ways of thinking that had satisfied previous centuries. Latin had been regarded as a sort of corrupted Greek, and the resemblances between Latin and the other European languages had been explained, in the same superficial way, as due to the preponderating cultural influence of Latin in Europe. But a similar offhand explanation of the resemblances between the ancient languages and this new-found Sanskrit was not possible: its home was too distant, and its remote cultural world was entirely independent of both Greco-Roman and modern civilization.[6]

---

[6] Holger Pedersen, *The Discovery of Language*, trans. John Webster Spargo (Bloomington: Indiana University Press, 1962), p. 21.

The evolutionary kinship was unmistakable. For the next two or three generations the chief preoccupation of linguists was with formulating it. We have seen how this formulation made it possible to reconstruct languages that are no longer spoken—it is known almost to a certainty what Vulgar Latin was like, for though records are lacking it was captured between Classical Latin and the modern Romance tongues, with records of both. A fair estimate can be made of the language that preceded modern German, Swedish, English, and other Germanic tongues, though there is no record of any close preceding stage. And, as we saw earlier (Chapter 6, pages 85–86), something is known about the hypothetical ancestor of all our Western tongues, Proto-Indo-European.

As each step in reconstruction had to be based on correspondences among languages that provided a clue to the reconstructed form, and correspondences, while potentially obvious, are seldom perfect, it became necessary to explain the differences. Out of these explanations—of why, for instance, Sanskrit had *śatá-m* for 'hundred' but the related word in Latin, **kentum,** showed differences along with its similarities—there developed theories about sound change that eventually grew dependable enough for comparative grammarians to make a sweeping claim: that all change is amenable to law. Exceptions there were, of course, but none because some law of sound had changed its method of operation—rather because many words were late borrowings that had no ancestry within the language or because of accidents such as folk etymologies or blends. This insight—the universality of law and the possibility of arriving at it by scientific methods—was the most pregnant discovery in the study of language during the nineteenth century. But it had to be rediscovered when linguists turned from the evolution of language to its involution, from changes in surface form to analysis of inner form. Once again the history of science repeated itself: what was most intimate resisted formulation.

DESCRIPTIVE LINGUISTICS

The person who did most to turn his colleagues away from their absorption with history and toward the investigation of the languages of their own time was the Swiss scholar Ferdinand de Saussure, himself a historical linguist. He envisioned languages as systems in unstable equilibrium, but with emphasis on the equilibrium—the integral, self-contained, and (to speakers, with their limited perspective) temporally arrested state that any language exhibits at a given period in its history. For

Saussure, there were two axes of linguistic study which had to be distinguished: that of the temporally arrested state just mentioned, termed *synchronic* (with or through a given time), and that of the history of a language, termed *diachronic* (across time). "Ever since modern linguistics came into existence," he complained, "it has been completely absorbed in diachrony." This was his manifesto: "Linguistics, having accorded too large a place to history, will turn back to the static viewpoint of traditional grammar but in a new spirit and with other procedures...."[7]

Traditional grammar had been static in a dual sense—not only in dealing with the state of a language and nothing more, but in its unawareness of the forces that work to overthrow the state. How speakers react to the little potential subversions that surround them is part of their linguistic behavior. Their moments of hesitancy, which reflect the language in flux, are as real and as much a part of the language *now* as their moments of certainty, which reflect the language in repose. "We can never truly know what a construction is like today unless we know what it was like yesterday: the direction of its development is a part of its identity."[8]

The old approach and the new were not really in conflict, though the shift of emphasis made them appear to be. How necessary the two are to each other was pointed out in 1927 by the man whom most linguists today regard as the dean of their guild, Roman Jakobson. Jakobson called for a historical linguistics in which the static viewpoint would play a key role: it was not the successive development of individual sounds that should be investigated but the succession of whole stages, for unless we knew the relationship of a sound to its fellow sounds at a given moment in history, we could never understand why sounds changed the way they did.

But events decreed that in the United States, at least, Saussure would be taken literally, and linguistic science in this century would develop along lines clearly synchronic. Where European scholarship carried on the older tradition that had seen first the attachment of philological study to the study of literature and then its convergence with the study of history, in America a new affinity grew up between linguistics and the aggressive young science of anthropology.

There were two stages in this development. In the earlier one the leading figure was the German-born anthropologist Franz Boas, who spent most of his life studying American Indian cultures and who early realized that the language of a culture was its most distinctive creation. Boas had the luck to acquire a student who was later recognized as "one of those

---

[7] *Op. cit.*, pp. 82–83.

[8] Anna Granville Hatcher, "Theme and Underlying Question," *Word* Monograph No. 3.43 (1956).

rare men among scientists and scholars who are spoken of by their colleagues in terms of genius,"[9] Edward Sapir, poet, critic, and amateur
musician as well as trained Germanist. To the inspiration of these two
men was added the desperation of anthropologists to record American
Indian data before it was too late—to find "enough scholars and enough
time to accomplish all that needed to be done in a field where the
extinction of languages is almost a yearly occurrence."[10] (Sometimes one
can even fix the day when a living language dies; for example, the death
of the Yahi dialect of the Yana language of California came with that of
its last speaker on March 25, 1916.)[11]

It was no easy task that the anthropological linguists cut out for themselves:

> The New World is unique in the number and diversity of its native
> idioms. There are probably well over one thousand mutually unintelligible
> American Indian languages, which are customarily grouped into more
> than one hundred and fifty different families. In California alone, accord-
> ing to Sapir, "there are greater and more numerous linguistic extremes
> than can be illustrated in all the length and breadth of Europe. Such a
> group as German, French, Irish, Polish, Lithuanian, Albanian, Greek,
> Basque, Turkish, Hungarian, Finnish, and Circassian—to list European
> forms of speech with maximum distinctness—exhibits a lesser gamut of
> linguistic differences, as regards both phonetic elements and peculiarities
> of structure, than an equal number of languages that might be selected
> from among those spoken in California."
>
> Nor is California unique in this. A similar diversity may be observed
> along the Pacific coast from Oregon to Alaska, where languages belonging
> to twelve different stocks are spoken; on the Gulf coast from Texas to
> Florida, with seven families of languages; and among the Pueblo Indians
> of New Mexico and Arizona, where peoples with remarkably similar non-
> linguistic cultures speak languages belonging to four distinct and widely
> divergent stocks.[12]

It is little wonder that linguists in America were so caught up with
the urgency of recording and analyzing native American languages that
they had little time or patience for anything else. The anthropological

---

[9] David G. Mandelbaum, ed., *Selected Writings of Edward Sapir* (Berkeley: University of California Press, 1951), p. v.

[10] Harry Hoijer *et al., Papers from the Symposium on American Indian Linguistics*
(Berkeley: University of California Press, 1954), p. 1.

[11] The moving story of that last speaker, Ishi, is told by Theodora Kroeber, *Ishi in
Two Worlds* (Berkeley: University of California Press, 1964).

[12] Hoijer, *op. cit.*, p. 3.

approach to language attained a similar prominence in England, at the School of Oriental and African Studies at the University of London.

The second stage in the development of anthropological linguistics in the United States came in the early 1930's from religious missionaries. A number of Protestant denominations with extensive missions abroad established the Summer Institute of Linguistics, with two principal aims: the linguistic training of missionaries (originally in summer classes at the University of Oklahoma, hence the name) and the translation of the Bible. Since practically all the languages in question were without an alphabet, one of the first tasks the Institute faced was to "reduce the language to writing." (This is the common phrase, but it should not be interpreted to mean that writing takes precedence over speech.) The Summer Institute has carried on a veritable linguistic conquest, for it has moved from small outposts among a few American Indian tribes to an operation that extends from Colombia to New Guinea and enlists the cooperation of government bureaus in more than a dozen countries. By 1966 it was conducting work in almost four hundred languages, with a staff of around 1,400 permanent members and about 500 new trainees a year.[13] The leading figure of the Institute is Kenneth L. Pike, whose view of linguistic structure is the tagmemic theory outlined in Chapters 4 and 5 (pages 39–40, 74–75).

Other religious organizations have been active in linguistics, though in recent years none with such far-flung interests as the Summer Institute. One is the Kennedy School of Missions of the Hartford Seminary Foundation in Connecticut. But the linguistic endeavors of missionaries go back many centuries. After the Spanish conquest of the Americas, the religious orders were charged with educating the Indians, and numerous grammars of Indian languages were written. In South America, the Jesuits even made two of the more generalized Indian languages—Guaraní and Quechua—their medium of instruction.

Linguistics under the influence of anthropology lived in a constant state of emergency. The anthropological linguists based in the universities were driven by the need to record the languages of cultures *in extremis.* The missionary linguists were driven by their calling to spread the Word. Urgency was stepped up to a frenzy when during World War II the American armed forces found themselves in the fearful situation of having to govern scores of Pacific enclaves with no one able to speak to the inhabitants, and they turned to the anthropological linguists to get a language program moving. Haste was the order of the day, and the

---

[13] Bibliography of the Summer Institute of Linguistics, Santa Ana, California, 1964, with figures updated.

climate of the 1930's and 1940's was wrong for profound reflection and all-encompassing theory. But the storehouse of observations was now so full that it cried for a stock-taking.

STRUCTURAL LINGUISTICS

American structuralism

The anthropological bias created a turn of mind in the United States that has confined linguistic theory to a rather narrow channel. A glance at how this came about will not only illuminate the nature of the theory but will show its ties to its times and to the work that went before.

Consider the first order of business for a missionary who wants to teach an aboriginal tribe to read and write its own language. He does not need to teach the language—the natives already know it; all they have to learn is a representation. As soon as the missionary-linguist has managed to isolate the phonemes, he is in a position to set up an alphabet and his main work is done. What is left after the associations between the written symbols and the distinctive sounds have been established is less imperative, because the previously illiterate native knows the syntax of his language and can unscramble a sentence like *NobodyknowsthetroubleIsee* about as readily as we can, even if the linguist knows so little beyond the phonemes that he omits the spaces.

This is an exaggeration—more than phonemes must be taken into account to determine the phonemes themselves, and translating the Bible calls for a delicate analysis—but it illustrates where the emphasis in anthropological linguistics was bound to lie. Until the phoneme was attended to, nothing systematic could be done with morphology or syntax. Thus forced to start at the bottom, the anthropological linguist had his priorities laid out for him: he had to analyze first the sounds, then the morphemes, and last of all the syntax.

There was very little in the recent tradition of linguistics to make him question this scheme. The great triumphs in historical linguistics had been in the laws of sound. In the schools it was the same: the learner of a foreign language must—like the anthropologist visiting a new tribe— master first the sound system and then the morphology, and then he can largely guess at the syntax; language teaching had the same priorities in the same order.

What had started as a combination of practical necessity and historical accident was thus elevated to a theoretical precept: "Do not attempt to deal with syntax before morphology, nor with morphology before pho-

nology; to do so is to *mix levels*." Since the units of each lower level were
the components of the units at the next higher one, it was impossible to
move up until the proper foundation had been laid.

Now a great "-eme" hunt was on. The categories of classical grammar
were gone—they were good for Latin but not, so it was thought, for
Hokan or Chinook. And linguists would have nothing to do with mentalistic notions imposed on language from philosophy and logic—in this
they were influenced by the behavioristic psychology in vogue during the
1920's and 1930's. Nothing was left but to find the needed entities within
the substance of language itself. The result was a concentration on what
has come to be called "discovery procedures." It was assumed that, since
human beings could react intelligently to speech, it must be on the
basis of sets of signaling units. One such set—the phonemes—had been
brilliantly demonstrated. It remained to ferret out the audible units that
enabled speakers and hearers to tell how the phonemes were assembled
into morphemes—were there phonemes of pause, or stress, that did this?
In a language where stress occupied a fixed position in a word, for
example, it would be possible to locate the word boundaries by counting
syllables to the right or left of the stress. And, at the highest level, were
there phonemes of rhythm or pitch that marked the beginning and the
end of clauses and sentences? Just enough evidence of this sort of thing
did turn up to encourage the hope that the whole pattern would one day
become clear, and we could speak as securely of the "sound" of a sentence
or of a word as we can now relate sounds to phonemes.

This was American structuralism, and one of its effects was the con-
tinual postponement of syntax. But an orphan can be neglected only so
long, and syntax was not to be denied. Structuralists brought to it their
morpheme-before-syntax philosophy and created a syntax that had the
same characteristics of fixed smaller units organized into fixed larger ones
that they were accustomed to in their building of phonemes into morphemes.

As before, the starting point had to be samples of utterances as they
were observed—the principles of organization were in the text, in the
spoken segments, not from outside nor from underneath. What is the first
thing that a linguist observes about the organization of a sentence if he
approaches it without preconceptions about subjects, predicates, sub-
ordinations, and the like? It is that elements that stand side by side tend
to belong together. This seems to hold in most human organization. In a
filing drawer, the items in a folder have more in common with one
another, and especially each with its nearest neighbor, than any item has
with those in the next folder, and the folders behind a single guide card are
more like one another than like those behind the next guide card, and so
on up to drawer-versus-drawer and cabinet-versus-cabinet. One of the

main uses of the phonology of the sentence that the structuralists thought they had discovered was this insertion of guide cards to separate a togetherness on one side from a togetherness on the other.

Two kinds of examples illustrate how pervasive the principle of togetherness is in language. One is our resistance to putting something between two things that are more closely related to each other than they are to what is inserted. Teachers find it hard to enforce the rule of interior plurals in forms like *mothers-in-law* and *postmasters general*—speakers want to put the *-s* at the end. They are even more reluctant to say *hardest-working person,* inserting the *-est* between the members of the compound *hard-working;* and though some might manage it there, probably no one would say **farthest-fetched story* for *most far-fetched story.*

The second kind of example shows up when two things that formerly did not belong together come to be viewed as if they did, because they are side by side. The attraction of nearness may even override an intervening pause. For example, the word *frankly,* which was common in half-apologetic statements like *I am, frankly, bored,* has become virtually an intensive modifier of what follows: *I am frankly bored.* Something similar has happened to certain prepositions which at an earlier stage were felt (as is customary) to be most closely bound to the following noun, but which have come to acquire a closer attachment to what precedes, as our manner of spelling sometimes indicates: *lotsa* for *lots of, kinda* for *kind of, sorta* for *sort of*—and the last two have taken the further step of being used as unit adverbs: *kinda nice.* The pull from two directions—from what precedes and from what follows—can be detected in mistakes that we sometimes make, like **an idea of which he was very fond of,* where the preposition is torn between *which* and *fond.*

Applied to linguistic analysis, this togetherness-by-levels was refined into a technique of identifying "immediate constituents." Given a set of morphemes or words, one can show their interrelationships in this fashion. Take the punning cartoon reported in the *Reader's Digest:* "At a greeting card counter: 'Well, I like this card, but it says "A Belated Wedding Wish," and they got married in time.' "[14] The use of a hyphen would have destroyed the pun: *a belated wedding-wish* versus *a belated-wedding wish.* The two words *ungraceful* and *disgraceful* have different constituent analyses:

---

[14] February, 1965, p. 144.

In the first, *-ful* is an immediate constituent of *-grace-* (the two are on the same level and belong together), while *un-* is an immediate constituent of the combination *-graceful;* in the second, *-ful* is not on the same level as *-grace-*, but rather on the same level as *disgrace-:* 'full of disgrace.'

Analysis by immediate constituents is the most effective way of showing how a complex sentence is layered; for example, *He said he wanted to marry her* is analyzed as follows:

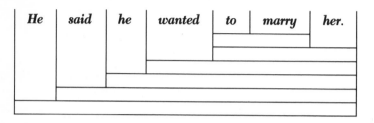

The same relationships are shown by a tree diagram such as the one below.

By itself, immediate-constituent analysis tells us how a stretch of speech is layered, but it tells us nothing about the nature of the elements nor the

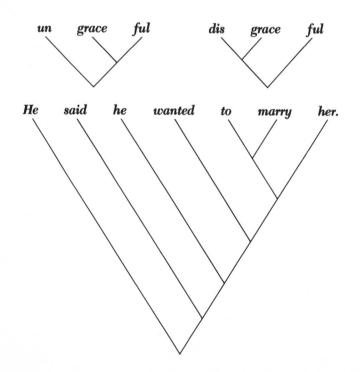

manner in which they are related. For example, *behind the house* and *only a few* have the same constituent diagram,

but the first is actually more closely related to *in back of the old stone house on the hill,* with a diagram that looks at first glance to be quite different:

in	*back*	*of*	*the*	*old*	*stone*	*house*	*on*	*the*	*hill*

There is an obvious similarity between diagrams of this type and those once used for teaching grammar in the schools, and it suggests what is needed to complete the analysis: something about parts of speech, or word classes, and about subjects, predicates, modifiers, and so on, or functions of the classes. The diagram begins to look more familiar when we label the spaces (see below).

The labeled diagram reveals both the layering and the unlimited possi-

It	*grows*	*in*	*back*	*of*	*the*	*old*	*stone*	*house*	*on*	*the*	*hill.*
							Compound noun				
						Noun modified by adjective			Inner noun phrase		
					Inner noun phrase				Prepositional phrase		
		Compound preposition			Outer noun phrase, object of preposition						
	Main verb	Prepositional phrase, complement of main verb									
Subject	Predicate										
Sentence											

bilities of embedding constructions within constructions: *in back of the old stone house on the hill* is a prepositional phrase that contains a prepositional phrase, *on the hill*. And *on the hill* could be lengthened to contain two more prepositional phrases, *on the hill up the river from here*, in which *up the river from here* modifies *hill* and *from here* modifies *up the river* as a unit, explaining how *up the river* is to be oriented.

on	the	hill	up	the	river	from	here

Immediate-constituent analysis, plus some form of labeling for classes and functions (tagmemes and syntagmemes—see Chapter 5, pages 74–75), is the syntactic style of American structural linguistics. It carries to a higher plane the buildup of smaller units into larger ones that appeared to work reasonably well at lower levels. It can be carried still farther: In the view of Kenneth L. Pike, human behavior as a whole is structured in the same way, and on top of morphemes and grammatical tagmemes there are "behavioremes," such as the organized activity of a game, a church service, or a meal.[15] The philosophy of most American structuralists—Leonard Bloomfield, Charles Fries, Charles Hockett, Z. S. Harris in his earlier writings, and others—is not so all-encompassing, but reflects the same tradition.

European structuralism: the Prague School

If one can discern tendencies at various times and places that are clear enough to be given the name of an "-ism" or a "school," it is more often than not the result of a fortunate meeting of minds under the inspiration of some strong and attractive personality. The "Yale group" in America was drawn together largely by the magnetism of Leonard Bloomfield. In England, the man whose ideas gained the strongest hold was J. R. Firth of the University of London; the London group is now carrying forward a vast survey of contemporary English usage under the direction of Randolph Quirk, and valuable theoretical work is being done by M. A. K. Halliday and other "neo-Firthians," whose collaborators and critics extend

---

[15] *Language in Relation to a Unified Theory of the Structure of Human Behavior,* Part I (Glendale, Calif.: Summer Institute of Linguistics, 1954).

to other British universities, as for instance William Haas at Manchester. On the continent, the Linguistic Circle of Copenhagen became known through the works of Louis Hjelmslev, who was ahead of his time in conceiving a comprehensive and abstract theory of language.[16] A number of scholars at the University of Edinburgh—Angus McIntosh, David Abercrombie, Elizabeth Uldall, and others—have been active especially in phonology. In Holland, the distinguished group associated with the journal *Lingua*—A. W. de Groot, Anton Reichling, E. M. Uhlenbeck, and colleagues—has ranged over problems of Eastern languages, phonetics, and semantics. No amount of space could do justice to all the centers from Rome to Stockholm where linguistic research is in progress. But of all the groups in Europe, the most influential has unquestionably been the Prague School, perhaps partly because no one figure dominated it and its contributions were enriched by numerous scholars of various casts of thought without the little dogmatisms that crop up when followers feel called upon to defend the views of the master.

Vilém Mathesius founded the Linguistic Circle of Prague in 1926. Several linguists of world renown have been identified with it, including Roman Jakobson, whose theory of distinctive features took shape during its early years. Essentially the same contemporary spirit infused Mathesius, Jakobson, and their co-workers that we have found in the American group, but it drew less on anthropology and behavioral psychology and more on traditional European humanism. Prague linguists were about as much involved with the phoneme as American linguists in the years before World War II, but instead of pushing this interest to a relentless conclusion as the Americans did, they applied it to historical change and balanced it with theories of syntax, meaning, and the child's acquisition of language. Though severely hurt by the War, the Prague group is now as active as ever, especially in syntax, where its studies on meaningful word order and other dynamic aspects of the sentence are a sort of counterweight to American generative grammar, which is touched on in the next section.[17]

Progress in linguistics is not confined to Western Europe and the United States. The most significant work in lexicography is being done by the Russians. Japan is the scene of notable investigations in phonetics. And the best studies of each individual language come from its native speakers, as they are trained to make them. Such training is coming fast, all over the world.

---

[16] See especially Sydney M. Lamb, "Epilegomena to a Theory of Language," *Romance Philology* 19.531–73 (1966).

[17] Notes on the Prague group are based mainly on Josef Vachek, *The Linguistic School of Prague* (Bloomington: Indiana University Press, 1966), especially pp. 3–39.

FORMAL LINGUISTICS

In the early 1950's, signs of restiveness began to disturb the calm of structuralism and by the end of the decade were blown into a storm. The revolt was abetted from other countries—there were European schools with traditions of their own whose influence was spread by visiting scholars—and from within by increasing contacts between linguists and specialists in allied fields such as psychology, mathematics, logic, and communications engineering. Linguists became conscious of some of the flaws in the structuralist edifice and began to ask themselves questions like the following:

1. Why should the sequence of phoneme-to-sentence, which might be useful for an anthropological linguist or for a missionary facing a tribe of hostile Indians, necessarily have any relevance to linguistic theory? Why not assume an interrelated system that is simply "there" and no part of which can be fully understood without a grasp of the whole? In diagramming it or writing a description of it one might want for the sake of convenience to scan up or scan down (most formal representations look as if they proceeded from more inclusive to less inclusive), but no priority would be implied. Some structuralists were quite willing to go along with this criticism.[18]

2. Why should it be necessary to dig up—or even expect to be able to dig up—an audible structural signal for every linguistic class? Why not accept the intuition of native speakers, in whose speech linguistic classes are seen to agree in subtle ways even though there is no apparent physical basis for the agreement, and carry on from there? That is what traditional grammar had always done, and it seemed to work, perhaps because it was close to the inwardness of language.

3. Why should the basis of linguistic theory be so narrowly defined that it could draw only upon those things that emerged from the field work carried on by linguists, avoiding universals as if they did not exist, and fearing abstract concepts just because they had once been used—and abused—by old-fashioned Latinizing

---

[18] "Tagmemic theory does not allow theory of grammar to start with sentence—or with any other one unit. The total system, including discourse, must be part of the setting within which any one unit is discovered, or adequately presented." Kenneth L. Pike, "Discourse Analysis and Tagmemic Matrices," *Oceanic Linguistics* 3.11 (1964).

grammar?[19] Other sciences would have been paralyzed without abstract theory.

4. How could a frame so confined as that of immediate constituents be expected to fit comfortably around the whole of syntax, when there are many important relationships that escape it? The classic example is the relationship between the active and the passive voice: *George sees Mary, Mary is seen by George.* An immediate-constituent analysis of these two sentences tells nothing about their underlying kinship.

5. Why should all the energies of linguists be spent in gathering more and more examples? The younger linguists had harsh words for specimen-grubbers. It seemed to them that we already had a superabundance of scattered facts and now it was time to fit the facts into a system.

The upshot of these doubts and queries was a cry for an all-encompassing theory of language that would, as theories must, see first the whole and then the parts; that would hypothesize and look for confirmation rather than gather specimens in the hope that broader principles would emerge magically from them; that would—if it were to be a theory of language and not of particular languages—boldly assume that there were universals in language; and that would have a more flexible apparatus than the mere labeling and chopping that went on in immediate-constituent analysis.

According to such a theory, each language must be viewed as a coherent system, with the possibility of writing a grammar for it that will embrace the whole. Two characteristics of such a grammar are that it is *self-confirmatory* and that it is *automatic.* We need to dwell on these for a moment to grasp what such a grammar is like and to see its relationship to theoretical models in general.

When a scientist makes a "model" or theoretical description of a body of facts, he does so on the assumption that there is an underlying unity in the facts, that they are so intimately related that if something happens to disturb one part of the system there will be an echo somewhere else. Where the facts are as complex as they are in language, the assumption of underlying system becomes a way of testing the theory. Suppose in our grammar of English we hypothesize that adjectives in front of their nouns have an underlying relationship to predicate adjectives—that is, that *the red book* and *the book that is red* both "come" from some archetypal

---

[19] Karl V. Teeter, "Descriptive Linguistics in America: Triviality vs. Irrelevance," *Word* 20.197–206 (1964).

structure that is very close in form to *the book that is red,* so that we can, crudely, set up the "derivation" *the book that is red → the red book.* Most native speakers would feel intuitively that this is correct, and that is enough for a hypothetical start. But to get from one of these two structures to the other, more than one step is needed. The adjective has to be moved in front of the noun, but before that the *that is* must be dropped. Dropping it gives *the book red,* with which we are not very happy because our hypothesis has predicted the possibility of something that we do not find in English. But we ask ourselves whether the language contains any other closely related structures that *would* fit at this point, and if so, whether they ought to be derived in the same way; perhaps there is some restriction in English that prevents the particular manifestation *the book red* but permits the same manifestation in another form. We find just such a manifestation in prepositional phrases. There is the same relationship between *the book on the shelf* and *the book that is on the shelf* as between *the red book* and *the book that is red.* And this time *the book on the shelf* is as far as we can go—there is no *the on-the-shelf book;* the predicted structure is just what we were looking for. As an extra dividend, we find that we have an explanation for some of the "exceptions" that crop up here and there—adjectives that remain behind their nouns, like *books galore,* and prepositional phrases that jump over to the left, like *under-the-counter sale.* It was not necessary for us to have had in our collection any such examples as these last ones. We have deduced their possibility from the hypothesis. The advantage of a theoretical model is that just such deductions can be made and confirmations sought.

The second characteristic, that the grammar is *automatic,* is just another way of saying that its rules must be explicit enough for a machine to apply them (assuming that a machine could be built that is vastly beyond our capabilities now). This is the sense in which the word *formal* is used: a formal grammar is one that does not need any intervention from outside to make it work. The best rules in any traditional grammar are the formal ones, the ones that have no exceptions that call for a standby intelligence to decide whether they apply or not. Take a traditional rule like the one stating that when a personal pronoun is preceded by a preposition it will be in the objective case: *from him, from her,* not *from he, *from she.* A computer can make this selection as efficiently as a human being. Formal linguistics goes beyond traditional grammar in assuming that everything is potentially automatic. True exceptions will be listed in the dictionary (the entry for *galore* will show that it follows the noun); apparent exceptions—resulting from imperfect rules—will call for revising the rules. A proper grammar will account for "all and only" those sentences that a native speaker regards as "well formed." In addition, it will specify how grammatical or ungrammatical a sentence is that does not quite make the grade.

A formal system needs a formal presentation. The disciplines that had already worked out a scheme for handling similar problems were symbolic logic and mathematics, and to them the formal grammarian turned. Take a simple example from mathematics, two number series like the following:

1, 7, 5, 11, 9, 15, 13, 19, 17, 23, 21 . . .

2, 8, 6, 12, 10, 16, 14, 20, 18, 24, 22 . . .

Inspection shows that in each series there are pairs *(1, 7; 5, 11)* that have a difference of 6 between their members, and that each such pair is larger than the preceding pair by a factor of 4. One way of describing the series would be to list them, but this could only be partial because they run to infinity. Another way is to pretend that you are *making* the series and to state the rule of operation. Probably the simplest rule here would be "Alternately add 6 and subtract 2." Such descriptive rules in mathematics are termed "generative," and the term has been borrowed for grammar. (The companion term, "transformational grammar," refers to a particular kind of operation that will be discussed in a moment. Popularly, "generative grammar," "transformational grammar," and "transformational-generative grammar" are generally substituted for the more inclusive "formal linguistics.")

An example of a generative rule in English grammar is the one that introduces relative clauses and accounts for the potentially infinite layering noted on pages 197–98. We know that a noun can be modified by a type of sentence,[20] which we term a clause, containing *that, which,* or *who* and occasionally certain other forms. Wherever one encounters a noun phrase, that phrase potentially subtends such a clause. We can write the formula

NP → N + WhS

"A noun phrase may be manifested by noun plus *which-* (or *who-*, etc.) sentence." But we also know that sentences often contain other noun phrases; for example, *who cuts the X* contains the noun phrase *X:*

WhS → Wh + V + NP

"WhS is manifested by *who* plus verb plus noun phrase." Now we can reapply the first formula for the included NP, giving

WhS → Wh + V + N + WhS

---

[20] For the generativist, a "sentence" is any construction manifested as a noun-phrase subject with its verb-phrase predicate. This includes not only the usual declarative *He eats the candy,* interrogative *Does he eat the candy?,* negative *He doesn't eat the candy,* and passive *The candy is eaten by him,* but also other transformations: *For him to eat the candy, His eating the candy, The candy having been eaten by him,* and so on.

"The included noun phrase is manifested by a noun plus its own WhS," so that the whole complex turns out to be something like *the man who cuts the meat that comes from the shop.* The process can be carried as far as native speakers will tolerate the addition of more and more clauses; a classic example is "The House that Jack Built." Rules that can be reapplied in this manner are called "recursive."

Intuition is so important to generative grammarians that one could almost call them the psychologists of language. They affirm an underlying psychological reality, that of the human being's native ability to grasp linguistic form whatever its specific content (from this standpoint differences between languages are trivial), and to infer the rules that will enable him to make his own sentences. There is an "innate mechanism responsible for a child's acquisition of a language." Without such a psychological premise it is difficult to explain "why there should be a certain structure and content found in every language."[21] The structuralists were confirmed anti-mentalists; their psychology, when they admitted any, was behavioristic. The formalists unblushingly admit their mentalism, and find in their theory one way of "seeing" the psychological reality that underlies the human power to communicate.

In its algebra, generative grammar is reminiscent of immediate-constituent analysis, and this kind of analysis does in fact make up a sizable part of generative description—the part that embodies the "phrase-structure rules," which describe the way sentences are broken into parts. The tree diagram is regularly used, but turned upside down, since the progression is from the sentence to the parts. See the diagram below of *That man lost a dollar,* which can be verbalized as follows:

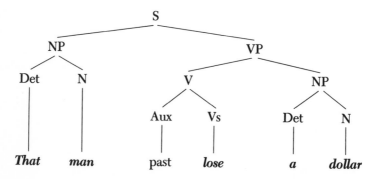

S(entence) is made up of a N(oun) P(hrase) plus a V(erb) P(hrase). NP is made up of a Det(erminer) plus a N(oun). The Det in this sentence

---

[21] Jerrold J. Katz, "Mentalism in Linguistics," *Language* 40.134 (1964).

is manifested by *that* (other members of the same determiner class which might have been chosen are *the, this, a,* and *my*). The N in this NP is manifested by *man.* The VP in this sentence contains a V plus an NP, which specifies the verb as transitive, that is, as object-taking (had the sentence been *The man died,* there would be no following NP). V contains an Aux(iliary element) plus a Vs (verb stem). The Aux in this sentence is manifested by just the past tense; it could be the present tense, or it could involve a modal verb like *can, may,* or *must* in addition to the tense. The Vs is manifested by the verb *lose.* The NP is made up in the same way as the earlier NP.

"That man past *lose a dollar"* of course is not an English sentence. It is a representation of morphemes, most of which happen to be representable as words. To get from the syntax to the actual sentence, more steps are necessary. The first step converts "past *lose*" into *lost.* (If we had shown grammatical number separately from *man* and *dollar,* as would have been necessary in a less schematic diagram, this step would also be responsible for turning out the form *man* rather than *men* and *dollar* rather than *dollars.)* The next step decrees that the indefinite article shall have the form *a* and not *an,* and in general it specifies the phonemes, or, if carried further still, the distinctive features that make up the morphemes. A more interesting example of this last kind of step is the attempt to give rules of word formation—a higher-level form such as /opæk/ giving /opæs/ if specified as noun and /opek/ if specified as adjective, for the words *opacity* and *opaque* respectively.

The illustration shows the pretensions to completeness—what one disgruntled critic[22] regards as a kind of linguistic totalitarianism—that generative grammar lays claim to, embracing the whole of description, from the full sentence to its minutest fragment. Yet why not? If language is a system, and most linguists agree that it is, nothing should be omitted. The only valid criticism is that giving names to barely explored subdivisions may create the illusion of controlling them, which we are far from being able to do as yet.

The area that generativists have worked hardest to bring under control is one that does not reveal itself through a phrase-structure diagram. It is the area mentioned earlier as neglected by immediate-constituent analysis through its inability to give form to the relationships that native speakers feel intuitively between such things as statements and questions, active voice and passive voice, emphatic utterances *(I did tell them)* and unemphatic ones *(I told them),* and so on. This calls for a separate component

---

[22] Gustav Herdan, "Quantitative Linguistics or Generative Grammar?" *Linguistics* 4.56 (1964).

in the grammar, a *transformational component*. It is the conspicuousness and originality of the transformational concept that has led to referring to the entire formal approach as "transformational grammar." The name most closely associated with it is that of Noam Chomsky, whose brief synthesis *Syntactic Structures* was published in 1957 and is regarded even by many erstwhile structuralists as representing the most significant recent "breakthrough" in linguistics.[23]

A transformation is a way of specifying, by rule, the relationship between the structures underlying sentences like *John saw Mary* and *Mary was seen by John.* It can be shown roughly by matching the two:

> *John saw Mary → Mary was seen by John*

But since the relationship applies to the syntactic elements, not just to these particular words, it is expressed algebraically:

$$NP_1 + Aux + Vs + NP_2 \rightarrow NP_2 + Aux + \textbf{\textit{be}} + \textbf{\textit{en}} + V + \textbf{\textit{by}} + NP_1$$

Or, to verbalize: The two noun phrases exchange places, with *by* placed before the one that now comes last. The tense (Aux) remains the same (past *saw* matches past *was*), but a form of *be* is inserted and the verb takes its past participle *(en)* form: *was seen.*

In similar ways it is possible to take a sentence like *John saw Mary* (remembering that the sentence is only the surface manifestation of the underlying structure NP + VP with all its subtended symbols) and relate it to *Did John see Mary?, John didn't see Mary, for John to see Mary, John's seeing Mary (was no accident),* and any other construction in which *John, see,* and *Mary* keep the same relationship to one another.

This confers a cohesiveness on grammar that it lacked before. Cohesiveness is essential if a language is to be described as a self-contained system. Transformations seem to account for the complex buildup of simpler constructions into more and more intricate ones better than any other scheme of analysis. The buildup is accomplished by embedding one construction in another, as we saw done with adjective clauses in the earlier example.[24] As another example, the NP object of the verb *to prefer* can be a noun, as in *They prefer pork chops,* or it can be a construction, as in *They prefer that nothing more be done for the present* or *They prefer a*

---

[23] The term is used by Charles F. Hockett, "Sound Change," *Language* 41.196–98 (1965).

[24] See also Chapter 5, p. 76.

specialist to examine John.[25] If we use X as a dummy symbol for the embedded sentence, the latter can be expressed as a composite:

$$\left.\begin{array}{l}\text{They prefer X} \\ \text{A specialist will} \\ \text{examine John}\end{array}\right\} \rightarrow \begin{array}{l}\text{They prefer a specialist} \\ \text{to examine John}\end{array}$$

The transformational rule here converts the verb to its infinitive form. It does the same when the embedded sentence has already been made passive:

$$\left.\begin{array}{l}\text{They prefer X} \\ \text{John will be examined} \\ \text{by a specialist}\end{array}\right\} \rightarrow \begin{array}{l}\text{They prefer John to be examined} \\ \text{by a specialist}\end{array}$$

This notion of embedding, of viewing certain parts of complex sentences as disguised sub-sentences (sentences that were "understood," as traditional grammar phrased it), goes back at least as far as the grammarians of the sixteenth and seventeenth centuries. Recent writings in generative grammar express it by writing S(entence) an unlimited number of times in a phrase-structure diagram (see below). For instance, *They saw John* and *They saw that it was John* have the same structure, differing only in that NP$_2$ is a proper noun in the first and a sub-sentence in the second.

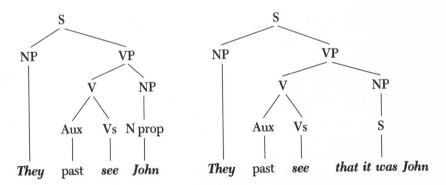

By thus combining active descriptions, or transformations, with static ones, or phrase structures and lexical items, generative grammar aims, in theory at least, to fulfill its claim of accounting for "any and all of the well-formed sentences in a language."

---

[25] Example adapted from Noam Chomsky, *Aspects of the Theory of Syntax* (Cambridge, Mass.: M.I.T. Press, 1965), p. 23.

WHAT NEXT?

Formal linguistics brings us up to date, and there is no radically different new movement in sight to mount an offensive against it. But this is no reason to suppose that the days of revolution are over and that our present views of language will go unchallenged for long. Their very success insures that they will not—in fact, that the cycle will probably be speeded up. Too many vigorous minds have been drawn to the study of language. A decade ago, not many young scholars in or freshly out of graduate school would have been proud to confess interest in a question like "What is the nature of manner adverbials?" or "Should modal auxiliaries be analyzed as ordinary verbs?" Now it is no more unusual than a similar absorption in steroid hydrocarbons or bacteriolytic viruses. Any weakness in the edifice is bound to be exposed by the probing of avid intellects that are never happier than when they can find something to unsettle and reorganize.

One change in viewpoint that appears to be taking place both inside and outside the ranks of American generativists involves the idea that instead of starting with structure, syntactic analysis ought to start with function and meaning. In the sample of generative syntax given in the last few pages, the first step is a description of the "surface structure" of a sentence in terms of its underlying structure or "deep grammar," and the last step is a semantic interpretation that reads off the meanings of the deep structures and the words that enter into them. Perhaps this is the wrong order of business. "What is the matter with making semantics generative?" ask two of the younger generativists.[26] A fairly elaborate effort in this direction has been made by the British linguist M. A. K. Halliday, who describes sentences in terms of networks of functional features. A given "surface" type of sentence represents the intersection of the features that characterize it. Halliday, like his American counterparts, distinguishes between surface grammar and deep grammar, but for him the structures are the surface and the features are the depths. Take for example the feature "extensive," which refers to the type of clause in which there is a process of X doing something to Y—a directed action with a doer and a goal. Obviously such a clause can have more than one surface manifestation—both *John lost the money* and *The money was lost (by John)* represent such a process—so more features are needed for a full characterization. One such feature is "operative," referring to the type of clause in which the subject is the doer—this eliminates *The money was lost,* where the subject is what was lost, that is, the subject is the goal or

---

[26] George Lakoff and John R. Ross, "Is Deep Structure Necessary?" (unpublished memorandum, March 27, 1967).

victim, rather than the doer. But there are also sentences of the type *John lost,* where he must have lost something though it is not named. To characterize these, the features "goal-transitive" and "goal-intransitive" are added, the first applying to sentences like *John lost the money,* the second to sentences like *John lost.* In this way every sentence can be specified in terms of the features that it contains. We start with features, or syntactic meanings, and interpret a structure out of them, rather than the other way around.[27]

But this is still within the intellectual framework of formal linguistics as we now conceive it. The American formalists themselves have gone a long way toward the adoption of a feature-type analysis, though they do it partly in terms of structure (thus the feature "transitive" applied to verbs would be represented by $+[\underline{\quad}NP]$, which means 'the kind of verb that occurs in a structure with a noun phrase after it'). What about something *really* different?

Only a fool would pretend to see beyond the interplay of theory that makes the present scene so fascinating, not to say confusing to the uninitiated, and imagine that he could foretell what weaknesses will some-day point the way to new strengths. But there are no laws against trying, and guessing can be fun.

Traditional grammar lost favor because, with all its fondness for universality, it refused to see the universality of change. Historical linguistics was pushed to one side because it traced individual *lines* of development and failed to grasp the succession of *systems.* Structuralism fell from grace because it was hypnotized with data and unwilling to make a place for conceptual frames and theories. It seems that the seeds of revolution are apt to lie in that part of the field to which the attitudes in vogue deny importance. The neglected evidence is shut out on one excuse or another (the structuralists often simply defined it off the premises: meaning, for example, was "not a linguistic question"); but it keeps accumulating, and all of a sudden its freshness and brightness outshines the turned and polished but too-familiar face of the ruling idea.

Does formal linguistics have an isolation ward in which maladjusted facts are confined to keep them from disturbing the theoretical calm of good citizens? We know that it criticizes a preoccupation with data, and we have seen the fundamental distinction it makes between "surface grammar" and "deep grammar." The surface grammar is the description of sentences as they come to us, with parts tangled and ambiguities galore, like the radio advertisement for an airline, *We have flown over a million satisfied passengers.* The sounds are classified, the morphemes

---

[27] See Halliday, "Notes on Transitivity and Theme in English, Part I," *Journal of Linguistics* 3.37–81 (1967).

identified, and the immediate constituents carved out, but no substructure is postulated. The deep grammar describes the surface by describing the structures that underlie it and the ways they are related; into this it reads the meanings of the constituent morphemes and thus interprets the whole. In the example just given, it would distinguish two sentences—each to be analyzed further—in one of which *fly* is transitive *(to fly passengers)* and in the other intransitive *(to fly under the bridge, into the sunset, over the city)*. Without the deep grammar we would be incapable of understanding the sentences that skim along the surface; but there is no cause to worry, because the ability to discover the deep grammar of the language is inborn.

What is unimportant for the formalist then is the surface, the realm of data, the ebb and flow of phenomena. We have already collected more of it than we can use, and anyway it is only the product of the successions of rules that are the real appurtenances of a grammar: "The critical problem ... is not a paucity of evidence but rather the inadequacy of present theories of language to account for masses of evidence that are hardly open to serious question.[28]

So we should be satisfied with the evidence we have and concentrate on the inner workings. The hopper is full. What needs our attention is the fineness of the grind. But the danger in putting a low price on observation is that analyses may be made too hastily. The analyst is overconfident of his ability to call to mind all the critical data—the surface facts—that he needs. If questioned, he is apt to reply "But I am a native speaker; I know my language." Unlike those linguists whose main business is to survey usage, who amass evidence and then attempt to set it in order inductively and formulate theories about it, the formalists take an early leap to their hypotheses and then test them deductively against the data.

To think of the surface as superficial is a self-deceiving metaphor. Nobody can predict the impact of a piece of evidence. After a million pieces that are worthless, the million-and-first may crack the ground underfoot. Suppose we list one or two bits of surface data that do not fit comfortably into the formalist scheme, just to show that such pieces can be found.

1. Formalists assume that "words" exist in deep grammar. No matter how a sentence may look on the surface—say, *They saw him, He was seen, His being seen, For him to have been seen, Their seeing him*—the lexical items contained in it, and their meanings, are supposed to be constant. The verb *see* occurs throughout, with the

---

[28] Chomsky, *op. cit.*, pp. 19–20.

same meaning. But as the examples *saw, was seen, being seen, to have been seen,* and *seeing* show, the surface form of a verb undergoes many changes, depending on the surface form of the sentence. The *existence* of the verb and its meaning is a deep fact; the *form* is only a surface fact and is irrelevant to the deep meaning. From the formalist's point of view, speakers apprehend the surface forms of a verb merely as manifestations of that verb colored by changes in tense and mode but without any more fundamental difference. Yet this is not always true. As we saw in our examples of reinterpretation (Chapter 7, pages 110–11), there is a rule of contrast whereby any difference in form can be infused with any meaning that its surface associations build up. If we are not surprised when *burned* and *burnt* come to mean something different, it should not surprise us if other verb forms also come to mean something different. Take the verb *to go: He probably went* refers to a goal, that is, 'went there'; *He must have gone* generally refers to a departure, that is, 'from here.' There is no such change in the verb *to leave: He probably left = He must have gone (left).* With the verb *to go,* surface form and deep meaning seem to be connected directly.

2. The deeper the grammatical rule, the more upsetting should be any violation of it—accidents hitting the surface are to be expected; for them to penetrate the interior is serious. So using the wrong category, for example a noun in place of a verb, ought to be worse than just using the wrong verb. This may be true most of the time. Yet if forced at gunpoint to choose between *Unhappiness may inaugurate the boy,* where one verb *(inaugurate)* is used in place of another *(discourage),* and *Unhappiness may heartache the boy,* where a noun is used for a verb, many speakers would prefer the latter.[29] Formalists have to make their cuts clean; English nouns and verbs are not that sharply distinguished.[30]

---

[29] See Chomsky, *op. cit.,* p. 152.

[30] Generative grammarians are not agreed on the imperviousness of the line between two grammatical categories. Some maintain that adjectives and verbs, for example, are the same in deep grammar, that is, *hungry* and *hunger (to hunger)* are only superficially different. (See George Lakoff, "Stative Adjectives and Verbs in English," Computation Laboratory, Harvard University, *Report* No. NSF-17, August, 1966, I–1 to I–16.) But generative grammar does not yet capture the extreme readiness with which English nouns, especially one-syllable ones, are converted to verbs. The example in the text would have been better in the form *Unhappiness may gloom the boy,* using the one-syllable noun *gloom.* Speakers who have never heard *gloom* used as a transitive verb (it is so recorded in dictionaries, and that is why it was not used in the example) would nevertheless not regard it as too unnatural in this context. The permeability of categories seems to be a surface fact.

It seems that the depths are where things are stored and the surface is where things happen. A better image than "surface" and "deep" is perhaps "firing line" and "rear." The activity is up front, on the firing line. There is where the speaker is a free agent. Until he learns better, a child treats the depths as if they were surface. They become depths when he is no longer free. The surface is the area of choice and of change, of monitorings and corrections and puns. It is the arena for the ambiguities and emergencies that will be described in the next chapter (pages 228–30), where a speaker is not only free to bend the rigid categories of formal grammar but forced to do so by the very nature of communication. The surface is where *life* is in language.

One can always warp the frame a bit to accommodate exceptions. Maybe the examples we have given and others like them can be accommodated without warping it out of shape. Formal grammar has shown a good deal of elasticity in the decade and a half of its existence; it shelters views that have diverged a long way from its simple beginnings. But if it is stretched too far—and if events at the surface should turn out to have an unexpected relevance to a related field (psychology, perhaps) that suddenly looms more important to linguistics than intuitions and mathematical models—we may well witness a reversal of our present weightings for importance. Nothing of what formal grammar has accomplished would necessarily go to waste. One proof of the success of a theory is how digestible it is as raw material for succeeding theories.

ADDITIONAL REMARKS
AND APPLICATIONS

1. Given an innate capacity for language, the rudiments of language organization, and a situation in which there is an intense need for particular forms and amounts of communication, speakers build up the communicative power of their language to the point where it almost exactly balances the need. What does this suggest about the frequently heard tertiary response that "primitive" languages (that is, those of unindustrialized societies) are inferior?

2. It is sometimes claimed that normative prescriptions have no real and lasting effects. Test this in your own speech by asking yourself which one of the following sentences sounds best to you:
    a. He has more than I.
    b. He has more than they.
    c. He has more than she.
    d. He has more than he.
    e. He has more than you.
    f. He has more than we.

   Normative grammarians have urged these as the correct forms rather than *He has more than her, He has more than us,* and so on. Many speakers avoid the dilemma by adding *do* or *does.* Do you feel less need to add this to any particular one of the above? If your choice is e., how do you account for it?

3. Loan-words were mentioned among the exceptions to sound laws. Actually, however, the moment a word is borrowed it is exposed to whatever laws are operating at the time, and hence will probably be modified, though not as much as a word that was borrowed earlier. One pervasive law in English affects borrowed nouns in which some other syllable than the first carries the stress: it tends to be shifted to the first syllable. (See Chapter 7, page 118.) Thus Italian *trombóne* has become *trómbone* for many speakers, and French *parlánce* has become *párlance.* Some words go through this process quickly: French *mascótte* was borrowed between 1880 and 1884, but soon

213

became *máscot.* Others resist. Note how you pronounce the following words and see if others pronounce them differently: *intrigue* (dated 1647 by the *Oxford English Dictionary*), *prestige* (1656), *crusade* (1706), *perfume* (1533), *parakeet* (1581). Now and then one resists indefinitely. How do you pronounce *garage?* (About 1915, *gárage*, riming with *carriage*, competed with the pronunciation that is general in the United States today.) How might another sound law change *garage* so that a shift of stress to the first syllable will be out of the question? Apply the analogy of *police-pleece.*

4. Descriptive linguists tended to be condescending, if not downright censorious, toward notions of correctness in language, and a certain amount of the "permissiveness" they inspired has seeped into the English classroom, arousing the ire of purists. Account for the linguists' attitudes in terms of their experience with linguistic change and widely divergent languages. How might their preoccupation with diversity also help to account for their neglect of universals?

5. Were the descriptivists who thought of words or morphemes as "made up of" phonemes deceiving themselves? A word is an element that has meaning, and when words are joined together to make a phrase or sentence, one can reasonably speak of the phrase or sentence as being "made up of" them. Phonemes are meaningless. Does a particular combination of phonemes such as what constitutes a word have any function in the language if that word does not already exist, and does rearranging them mean anything? (Take the phoneme combinations *slart* and *starl*, for example.) What about similar combinations and rearrangements of words? (For example, *feathered horses* and *horsefeathers.*) Distinguish between meaninglessness *(slart)* and nonsense *(horsefeathers).*

6. One of the audible signals that structuralists took to mean something was the slowing down or lengthening that we have already encountered (Chapter 3, page 26), where a syllable containing a full vowel is followed by another syllable also containing a full vowel. The structuralists noted how often this succession occurred with compounds like *guidebook, passport, tinsmith, turnkey,* and *telltale,* and with derivatives like *deactivate, discord,* and *unfit* (the element *tin-* in *tinsmith* is slower, for example, than it is in *tinny*), and took the phonetic fact to be a signal of the division into separate morphemes. In these examples the separate morphemes are obvious—*un-*, for instance, is a negative prefix with a definite meaning, attached to *fit.*

But there are other words with the same slowing down that cannot be divided: *trombone* (exactly like the divisible *hambone*), *Nimrod* (like the divisible *ramrod*), *wombat* (like *combat*). Find additional examples.

7. The regrouping in *lotsa, kinda,* and so on is an example of reinterpretation (see Chapter 7 and page 195). Something similar has happened in the expression *I'm sorry for you (him, John,* etc.), which formerly meant 'For you, because of you, I am full of regret.' The *for* belonged with *you.* But nowadays we link *for* with *sorry,* giving a phrasal verb meaning 'to pity.' Given the sentence *It is impossible for him/to do it,* equivalent to *For him it is impossible to do it,* see if you can explain the shift that took place with the *for* phrase and gave rise to our use of *for* as an empty word introducing infinitive phrases like those in *For him to do that would be unbelievable* and *The only alternative would be for you to resign.*

   The following sentence appeared in a magazine: *They do not have to, as the American Indian does, think of themselves as outcasts.* Does the position of the comma point to any particular affinity of the word *to?*

8. Use immediate-constituent analysis to show different senses of the following: *more competent workers; clean water intake; one horse show.* Analyze the sentence *His asking why makes no difference.*

9. Is the analogy between linguistic behavior and other behavior close enough to justify Pike's "behavioreme"? Compare the consequences of defying the conventions of breakfast-eating (for example, by dividing the meal into two snacks, the first at seven and the second at nine) and defying those of language (for example, by dividing a sentence so that another sentence comes between its first half and its second half). How does the fact that language is a system that points beyond itself, that has a *reference,* affect the consequences? Would it be appropriate to say that *ritualistic* behavior (eating a meal, playing a game) differs fundamentally from *symbolic* behavior?

10. Review Samuel Martin's list of universals (Chapter 2, page 18). Consider whether the following traits would be likely to be represented in all languages:

   a. Some way of distinguishing between what is real (or, more specifically, what is going on now) and what is unreal (what went on in the past). How is this represented in English?

b. Different ways of addressing superiors and inferiors.

c. Comparison—that is, devices for showing "more" and "less."

Following are some traits of languages you may know. Consider whether they are universal:

a. In German, a system of cases (some school grammars used to list *of the table, to the table, O Table!,* and so on, as noun cases in English).

b. In French, a gender system.

c. In Italian, a progressive construction, *Essi stavano dormendo* 'They were sleeping.'

d. In Greek, Latin, English, and others, a decimal system of numerals.

11. The class of nouns known as mass nouns does not have an easily recognized set of formal characteristics like the ones that distinguish nouns as a whole (for example, any noun is replaceable by a pronoun; any noun can serve as the subject of a verb). Yet the fact that certain nouns in English, even though singular, behave like plurals compels us to theorize that such a class exists; for example, *lots of money* is like *lots of boys* and unlike **lots of boy; some (sm) furniture* is like *some (sm) chairs* and unlike **some (sm) chair.* If we hypothesize that this resemblance to plurals will be carried through in other parts of the structure, is our hypothesis confirmed by the way nouns behave when *the* is omitted in sentences like *The money is valuable, The coins are valuable, The dollar is valuable?*

12. Take the sentence *Where can they go?* symbolized as Wh + Modal + NP + VP (which also applies to sentences with other interrogative words, like *who* in *Who can it be?, how* in *How could you know?*) and explain what happens to such a sentence when it is embedded after an expression like *I don't know.* Compare this transformation with the one that occurs when the *why* of a sentence like *Why can't you fight back?* is replaced by *how come.*

13. In the sentence *Whatever he says is true,* S has replaced the subject NP of a sentence like *His words are true.* Make up a sentence in which S replaces *tomorrow* in *I'm going tomorrow* (you will need an adverbial conjunction like *when, while,* or *after*).

14. Anthropological linguists have worked mainly on languages with which they are at least partly unfamiliar. (During World War II, certain exotic languages were even "taught" by linguists who did not know them; working with the class, the linguist analyzed utterances elicited from a native speaker.) Formalists have worked mainly on languages with which they are completely familiar—they have "served as their own informants." Could this make a difference in how "deep" the analysis goes? How does it help to account for the sympathy that formalists feel toward a traditional grammarian such as Otto Jespersen? Look at Jespersen's five-volume *Modern English Grammar on Historical Principles*.

MEANING 12

T WHAT POINT does language break free? Distinctive features make phonemes, phonemes make morphemes, morphemes words, words sentences, sentences discourses, discourses monologs or dialogs or stories or whatever, and these are puffed or puffable into novels, trilogies, encyclopedias, or higher units as large as one may please. Looking up and down the stairway it seems as if there is no escape. Yet at some point—and it surely is not necessarily the last and highest—language must make contact with the outside world. This contact is what we call meaning.

The term *meaning* is used in many ways, not all of them equally relevant to language. Saying **I didn't mean to hurt him** is the same as saying **I didn't intend to. Another child means an extra mouth to feed** or **Smoke means fire** signifies an inference. **The German hund means 'dog'** is a translation. And so on. The meaning of "meaning" that, while not itself linguistic, is closest to language is that of the example **A red light means 'Stop.'** It is not quite the same as **Smoke means fire.** We do not make smoke in order to mean fire with it. Traffic lights, like words, are part of a communicative system with arbitrary values. We infer the meanings because we put them there ourselves; we only get back our investment. It is the same with language. The linguistic counterpart of **A red light means 'Stop'** is **X linguistic form has 'Y' meaning,** for it expresses the value of the code, the price tag that we have attached. (It may be that psychologically **A red light means 'Stop'** and **Smoke means fire** are iden-

218

tical, the code having been so thoroughly assimilated that we react to the warning of the color red as if it were a natural phenomenon. But this is not a question for linguists.)

Traffic signals are like linguistic signs the way counting on two fingers is like calculating with a computer. One is simple, the other complex. Traffic signals are ordinarily one for one: red for stop, orange for caution, green for go. Only rarely do two or more together have a special meaning, as in Massachusetts, where red plus orange means 'Walk.' Linguistic signs are built of units built of units. Not all levels are penetrated equally by meaning.

It is pointless to look for meaning in distinctive features, phonemes, and syllables, for these are members of the phonological hierarchy and are meaningless by definition (Chapter 4, page 48), though we did observe a curious relationship between vowels and the notion of size (Chapter 2, page 17). With morphemes we begin to find units to which meanings are attached, and this carries on through words and sentences. So the question comes down to which of these levels—from morpheme upward—is the real tie with the outside world.

The answer must depend on how we picture the outside world. If it is a kind of idealized collection of entities that keep their shapes no matter what kaleidoscopic patterns they take whenever they are shaken up, our choice will fall on morphemes or words. If it is the patterns themselves, it will fall on sentences. This is because a sentence—a particular sentence, not a sentence type—does not mean in the same way that a word means. The meaning of a sentence is something in the outside world at a given time and in relationship to given persons, qualities, and objects. The meaning of a word is potential, like that of a dollar bill before it is involved in a transaction. The statement *X word means 'Y'* carries a prediction of how a speaker will use *X* word. To make it refer to a real event we must turn it into a sentence—an exclamation like *John!* when we unexpectedly see a friend or *Run!* when danger threatens. The same is true of sentence forms, though not of sentences themselves: the sentences *Boy meets girl* and *Girl meets boy* involve the same forms, including that of *X*-as-subject, which suggests something about who takes the initiative. A speaker will use this or any other form in an actual sentence to match some real event, but the arrangement is only a linguistic potential, a bit of linguistic substance with a meaning that tends to remain constant.

The problem of meaning, then, is one of fitting together the partially (but never firmly) fixed semantic entities that we carry in our heads, tied to the words and forms of sentences, to approximate the way reality is fitted together as it comes to us from moment to moment. The entities are the world reduced to its parts and secured in our minds; they are a purse of coins in our pocket with values to match whatever combination of bargains, fines, and imposts is likely to come our way. The problem of meaning is how the linguistic potential is brought in line with non-linguistic reality whenever a speaker creates an utterance, or even—since we manipulate our environment almost as readily as our language—how the real is brought in line with the potential. (This has the ring of the philosophical dispute that shook the schoolmen of the Middle Ages: which is primary, the things in the world to which we merely give names, or the entities in our minds that we project outward? The answer seems to depend on whether we stand on the linguistic or the non-linguistic side of meaning.)

THE SEGMENTATION OF REALITY

The expression *outside world* does not mean what is "outside us" but what is "outside language." It may well be inside us. If I say I have a headache, or that I saw you with a red hat in my dream last night, I am relating something that no one else can observe, yet I put it into words as readily as I refer to the weather or to the day's major league baseball scores.

This is the sense in which we must take the term *reality*, for it includes what is viewable only from within as well as what can be seen by anyone. In fact, for mentalists the inner view is the more important one. They point to the absence, in most utterances, of any correspondence with external events going on at the moment. Utterances in which we comment on what is happening, like *Now I get up, now I walk to the window, now I look out,* are exceptional; more normal are *Last night I got up because I couldn't sleep* or *If you'll hand me the wire I'll attach this hook* or *Nobody's going to vote for him,* involving memory or prediction—language would be of little use if we did no more with it than report what anyone can see just by looking. Whatever it is that represents these past and future or imagined events to our minds is a main part, if not the whole, of reality as we grasp it. Defining it is for psychologists and philosophers. In language we must assume it and go on to its links with words and sentence forms.[1]

---

[1] This is the zone of conflict between mechanistic and mentalistic linguists. The mentalists suppose that in order to refer to a dream or to a person who is not present we must have an "image" in our minds. Modern psychology is a bit kindlier toward images than was the behaviorism that influenced most American linguists in the 1930's and 1940's, best exemplified by Leonard Bloomfield (see especially his chapter on "Meaning" in *Language* [New York: Holt, Rinehart and Winston, Inc., 1933]), for whom meaning was a set of conditioned responses. The philosophical side

What conditions need to be met for the signs of language, limited in number, to designate reality, which is infinite? The first condition is that reality must be *segmented.* Whenever we manipulate an object we separate it from its environment. Part of the act of separating it is the act of naming it: a cumulus cloud, a wall, a stick, a laugh. Language gives us a map of reality in which everything is covered but much detail is left out. The second condition, necessary for the first, is that the segments must be *repeatable* and that we must have some mechanism to recognize similarity between one appearance and the next so as to call the two by the same name. A wall in the dark must still be a wall in the daylight. The third condition is built-in *ambiguity;* absolute identity of segments cannot be required, for dealing with the continuum of experience would then be impossible—explicitly or implicitly we have to be able to say X *is* Y and mean 'X is a kind of Y,' 'X is like Y.' Otherwise we might learn to apply the name *dog* to Fido but could never extend it to other dogs (and might even fail to apply it to Fido when we saw him a second or third time). A fourth condition is simply *memory,* which is not specific to language; there must be provision for storing the linguistic units to make them available for future use.

How is the connection between unit and segment made, so that when the segment presents itself the speaker will respond with the unit, or, in the role of hearer or under some form of self-stimulation, so that when the unit is presented the segment will be invoked? The basis for this is the permeation noted earlier (Chapter 1, page 2). It may be that as we grow expert in the use of language, "outside world" is to be taken in a less and less material sense; but in the beginning it is concrete—the child learns his verbal responses to things in a way that makes those responses part

---

of mechanism is determinism: the speaker does not produce utterances, nor the hearer interpret them, as a matter of choice or will but as an organism responding to stimuli, hence automatically. What chiefly distinguishes recent mentalists is not so much their break with mechanism as their break with determinism; the favorite theme at the moment is creativity, manifested in our ability to make infinitely many and infinitely complex sentences, seemingly too much to expect of a set of automatic responses. Apart from the fact that this is a bit reminiscent of the arguments against evolution that point to the complexity of the human eye and ask how such a complex organ could have been developed by natural selection, there is another side on which the mechanist deserves to be heard: granted that there is creativity, is it a linguistic ability? To pretend that it is is to claim a sizable psychological beachhead for linguistics. It is just as reasonable to suppose that creativity goes on at an imaging level in psychology, and that sentences are coded automatically in response to what goes on at that higher psychological level. This of course tells us nothing, psychologically speaking—it merely shifts the burden of investigating creativity onto the shoulders of the psychologists, where many linguists would be happy to put it. Speakers do not create sentences, we might say, but sentences are the automatic response to a creativity that is psychologically "upstream."

of the complex manifestations of the things themselves. For a dog to become a recognizable and repeatable segment of reality, the child needs to make enveloping contacts with it—feel the hair, see the tail wag, watch the fawning behavior, hear the bark—and hear, whenever older children or adults are about, utterances replete with a certain pattern of sounds, /dɔg/. The attributes of a particular dog are not only a texture of hair and a certain size and shape and color of eyes; they include also the name *dog*. It is true that the color of eyes and texture of hair are "always there" and the name *dog* is intermittent, but the dog's bark is intermittent too and is nevertheless a characteristic. Continuity is not a requirement; we can identify a dog by his bark as readily as by his size and shape; all that is necessary is a predictable relationship, and just as under predictable conditions of excitement the dog will bark, so under predictable conditions of conversation he will be referred to as a dog.

Given permeation, we need one more psychological mechanism: an instinct for taking the part for the whole. This is characteristic of all human behavior. A mother is identified by a voice or the touch of a hand; a glimpse of a face is enough to identify the man behind it. If through permeation the name of a thing becomes part of the complex that to our minds is the thing, the name can then be abstracted to stand for it. Sentence patterns as well as words are names in this respect. There are only two differences between linguistic units and other identifying features: the linguistic units are put there in order to be abstracted later, and human beings vocalize them.

Kinds of segmentation

Our words come so naturally and unconsciously that they seem rather simple tokens of reality. This is partly because on the few occasions when we do think about the relationship between words and things we almost always pick the simplest category, that of nouns, and the simplest examples from the category: *dog, toy, sun, page, house.* Yet the truth is that literally any combination of things, traits, or ideas can be segmented. If we should ever need to talk regularly and frequently about independently operated sawmills from which striking workers are locked out on Thursday when the temperature is between 50° and 60°F., we would find a concise way to do it. Of course, it is no small accomplishment for our language to be able to perform that segmentation in the way just illustrated—by accumulating segments already named, which intersect at the desired point. Sometimes the accumulation—if it is not too long— becomes a set unit, and we forget or only dimly remember its former associations. We saw this with fusions (Chapter 7, pages 106–07), typically compounds.

But it is not necessary that a linguistic unit be morphologically complex—like a compound—in order to be semantically complex. Some of the simplest words harbor an amazingly explicit set of wayward traits, of which we are almost never aware until someone misuses them. Here are some examples:

1. The word *disease* is more formidable than its synonyms *illness* and *ailment* because it is viewed as existing apart from the person or other organism afflicted. Diseases are classified and labeled. Since it is an entity in its own right, a disease can be "caught"; we do not ordinarily say *catch an illness* or *catch an ailment.*

2. The verb *to return,* when it takes an object, refers to the source of something; its synonym *to take back* is noncommittal on this point. So *We took Junior back to the zoo* might refer to letting him visit the place again, but *We returned Junior to the zoo* calls him an inmate.

3. The verb *to know* is always applied in the light of all the information that the speaker has at his command at the moment of speaking. In this respect it differs from *to think, to be sure, to be absolutely certain, to believe,* and so on. So, referring to the present, one may choose between *I know the answer is correct* and *I am absolutely certain the answer is correct;* but, referring to the past, *I was absolutely certain the answer was correct but it turned out to be false* is normal while **I knew the answer was correct but it turned out to be false* is not. If *knew* is used it must be qualified verbally or by tone of voice: *I thought I knew,* or *I just <u>knew</u> it, but. . . .*

4. The verb *to read* includes not only the visual perception of the symbols but the ability to interpret them; it means 'to see and to understand.' There is no companion verb on the auditory side meaning both 'to hear' and 'to understand.' This forces us to an awkward parallel: *If you know Spanish you will find Portuguese easier to read but Italian easier to understand by hearing it.*

   Furthermore, the "interpreting" that we do when we read is not full understanding but signifies just the ability to react to the symbols as elements of language—it is normal to say *He read it but didn't understand it.* Again, there is no parallel on the auditory side, and we must say something like *I could make out what he was saying but I couldn't understand it,* using the word *what* to refer to the mere linguistic substance.

There seems to be no limit to the number or kind of ingredients that may form part of the semantic recipe of a word. Yet certain of the ingredients show up in enough words that are different in other respects to tempt one to look for sets of semantic features that will do for meaning what distinctive features do for sounds. For example:

1. A number of verbs contain[2] the ingredient 'success,' which their synonyms may lack. *He managed to do it* tells us that he tried and succeeded; *He was able to do it* is noncommittal. *He went home* tells us that he got there; *He headed home* leaves that question unanswered. Sometimes the 'success' ingredient is unstable. Thus, one is unlikely to say *I phoned him yesterday* unless the connection was completed; here 'success' is necessarily implied (with *I called him yesterday* it would make no difference). But while **I phoned him yesterday. He wasn't in,* expressed as two sentences, is unusual, it is possible to combine the two: *I phoned him yesterday but he wasn't in.* This would be impossible if the 'success' element were stable, as in **I went home but I never got there.*

2. Many words either contain a 'positive' ingredient or are 'neutral.' *Behave yourself* implies the 'positive' ingredient of 'well'; *He behaved badly* leaves it out. *He climbed the wall* implies 'up' but in *He climbed down the wall, climb* is 'neutral.' The most typical expressions are those of measurement. To the question *How deep is it?* we can answer either *It's quite deep* or *It's quite shallow—deep* in the question is 'neutral'; in the answer it is 'positive.' Similarly with *How tall is he?—He is quite tall (quite short), How long is it?—It's quite long (quite short),* and so on. The corresponding nouns are similar, but they vary in the extent to which they lean toward 'positive' or 'neutral.' Thus, *tallness* is almost invariably 'positive'—*He couldn't be hired because of his tallness* means that he was tall; but *height* is more likely to be 'neutral'—*He couldn't be hired because of his height* does not tell us whether he was tall or short. In general, the nouns with the *-th* suffix *(width, breadth, girth, length, depth)* are likely to be 'neutral' but can be 'positive,' while those with the *-ness* suffix are 'positive.' The nouns *size* and *draft* (of a vessel) are purely 'neutral.' The noun *age* is like the *-th* words when it refers to

---

[2] Saying that a word "contains" an ingredient is a metaphorical short cut for saying that it covers a particular segment of reality or covers it in a particular way. We should not view the word as a container.

people (so *He can't work because of his age* can mean either that he is too old or that he is too young, though *He has difficulty walking because of his age* would almost certainly be said only of an old person); but it is 'positive' when it refers to things. It is possible to say *Because of his old age he could not stand much stress,* since *age* can be 'neutral' and *old* clears up the ambiguity; but it is impossible to say **Because of its old age it can't stand much stress—old* must be omitted since *age* is 'positive' and **old age* is like **young youth.* (The contrast with persons is between *young age* and *old age;* with things, *newness* and *age—*the antonym *newness* has the 'positive' *-ness* suffix even though *age* lacks it.) In short, there are interesting lights and shadows in the play of 'positive' and 'neutral' on the picture of nouns and adjectives, but it shimmers too much to get it in clear focus.

3. There is a wag's definition of an optimist as one who says that his glass of beer is half full, while a pessimist is one who says it is half empty. A number of words and expressions contain this ingredient of looking up or down on a scale, contrasting with others that do not look in either direction. The same concrete situation can be stated as *There were about ten or eleven eggs in the carton, There were nearly (almost) a dozen,* or *There were not quite a dozen. About* looks in neither direction while *almost* looks up and *not quite* looks down, as we see in the frequent coupling of *almost but not quite (not quite* is a unit here—simple *quite* is not used in **There were quite a dozen). Close to* is unstable. It tends to look up: *There were close to a dozen;* but it may be noncommittal, like *in the neighborhood of: You said fifteen but I'd say it was close* (or *closer*) *to a dozen.* The words *minimum* and *minimal* are also unstable, but unlike *close to,* which combines looking up with not looking in either direction, these two words combine looking up with looking down. The result when speakers or writers get careless is an ambiguity that context often has difficulty clearing up: the sentence *The position of the members implies a minimum of subordination* reads as if it had the downward-looking sense 'the least possible' but was intended to have the upward-looking one of 'not less than a certain amount.'

There are other scales. One that, like *almost, nearly,* and so on, is also a measuring scale differs in that the view is not upward or downward to any particular point but only in a relative sense. The same absolute number of eggs or notions or books can be expressed by *few, several,* or *many;* the difference is in the standard one adopts, with *few* looking down, *many* looking up, and

several noncommittal. *Seldom-often* and *little-much* contain these
same ingredients.

Many words are on a scale of intensity. *To disillusion* is mani-
festly more intense than *to disappoint.* Sometimes the scale is
pretty elaborate. *Surprise, astonish,* and *flabbergast* stand in that
order of intensity, and the majority of speakers would probably
agree on where to place at least two more terms: *surprise, astonish, astound, amaze, flabbergast.*

4. Many expressions contain the ingredient 'principal' as opposed to
'subordinate.' In some it is explicit: a *satellite* is explicitly subordinate to a larger body; a *servant* is explicitly subordinate to a
master. In others it is implicit but provides the contrast between
words that would otherwise be synonymous. We say *The paper
adheres to the wall* but not **The wall adheres to the paper. John
left the army* implies no subordination but **John abandoned the
army* is ludicrous unless John is the commanding general. To
refine this ingredient still further, it might be looked upon as that
which is standard or fixed versus that which is relative to the
standard. Thus we say *My house is close to Cincinnati,* but we
are less likely to say *Cincinnati is close to my house; close to,*
like most prepositions, makes its object the standard or point of
reference: *The stone falls to the earth,* not, in spite of Einstein,
*The earth falls to the stone. But it is hard to say how far to go
in abstracting an ingredient, or when to stop looking for it if it
begins to phase out: is 'subordinate' an ingredient of *student*
relative to *teacher,* for example?

5. Probably the most pervasive ingredient of all is an attitude of
'approval' or 'disapproval.'[3] The adverbs *soundly* and *roundly* are
synonymous, but in *He soundly berated them* the speaker indicates his approval of the action, while *He roundly berated them*
is neutral. Some more obvious pairs, with the neutral term first
and the loaded one second, are *big-overgrown, sweet-cloying,
uninformed-ignorant, palatable-delicious, subordinate-understrap-
per, odor-fragrance.*

It might seem that we ought to be able to separate some ingredients
as secondary, say as not having to do with the meaning of a word but with
something like the "circumstances of its use," while others are primary,
covering the "real meaning." Thus, *at this time* and *right now* both refer
to the present moment, but *at this time* is aloof and formal while *right*

---

[3] See Chapter 13, pp. 257–65.

now is informal and friendly: ***The doctor can't see you at this time (right now).*** The degree of informality, from this point of view, would be the circumstance of use. But in a broader sense any aspect of reality that restricts the use of a word is a circumstance of its use: degree of formality in *at this time* and *right now* is as much a part of reality as the time of day, and while it may be less important for some words it is more important for others—for distinguishing among *sir, mister,* and *hey, Mac* as forms of address, for example. Primary and secondary are matters of degree.

Semantic features

Of course, it would be easy to limit ourselves to the ingredients that are obviously central to a given word, and that, in effect, is what most dictionaries do for lack of room to do more. If we adopt this restriction and on top of it consciously or unconsciously select examples of just certain types of words, say those designating manmade objects or manmade institutions, our collection of words will lend itself to a comparatively neat chemical analysis. Men make musical instruments, for example, putting various predetermined parts into them and using them in various predetermined ways, each having its name. Those names can then be listed as semantic ingredients of the words in question—we can call them, following some recent studies on meaning, "semantic markers" or "semantic distinctive features."

The universe of meaning could then be conceived as a vast and multidimensional field of crisscrossing features. At the point (or chunk) where 'keyboard instrument,' 'stringed instrument,' and 'percussion instrument' intersect we would find *piano.* Where 'keyboard instrument,' 'reed instrument,' 'wind instrument,' and 'hand-bellows instrument' intersect we would find *accordion,* while at the neighboring intersection of the first three of these with 'foot-bellows instrument' we would find *harmonium.*

Whether such a treatment could ever be extended very far beyond the sphere of manmade things is debatable. But on a reduced scale it is good for showing relationships in a limited semantic field. On page 228 is a grid of features that has been set up for the words *breakfast, lunch, tea, dinner,* and *supper* as they are used by speakers of four different dialects in Jamaica. The initials stand for these features: +H 'the heaviest meal of the day,' +L 'a light meal, usually including a hot drink but not hot food,' +P 'a meal between 4 P.M. and midnight,' +N 'a night or very early morning meal, between 10 P.M. and 7 A.M.,' and +E 'an evening meal, between 7 and 8:30 P.M.' The + and − signs have their usual values of 'feature is present' and 'feature is absent' respectively; −H −L would be a meal that is neither heavy nor light—that is, medium.

	Breakfast	*Lunch*	*Tea*	*Dinner*	*Supper*
Upper middle class	− P + N − L − H	− P − N − L − H	+ P − N − E + L	+ E + H	+ P + N + L
Lower middle class	− P + N − L − H			− P − N + H	{ + E + L + P − N − E − L − H
Estate laborer	− P − N − L − H		− P + N + L	+ E + H	
Peasant farmer	− P − N + H		− P + N + L	+ P − N − E − L − H	+ E + L

FROM review of Frederic G. Cassidy, *Jamaica Talk,* by David DeCamp, *Language* 39.544 (1963).

Reading this grid for the lower middle class, for example, we see that breakfast is a night or very early morning meal (+N) but not one eaten before midnight (−P); it is not the heaviest meal of the day (−H) but it does include more than a hot drink and cold food (−L). The terms *lunch* and *tea* are not used. Dinner is the heaviest meal (+H), taken at some time other than between 4 P.M. and 7 A.M. (−P−N). Supper may be a light meal (+L) taken between 7 and 8:30 P.M. (+E) or a heavier (−L) though not the heaviest (−H) meal taken between 4 and 7 P.M. (+P−E) or between 8:30 and 10 P.M. (+P−E−N).

Built-in ambiguity: the "something-like" principle

What makes a cut and dried treatment of meaning unsatisfactory in the long run is the fluidity of our segmentations. The inherited ones never keep their shapes, and we add to them on the spur of the moment. Reality presents itself in such a variety of faces, glimpses, perspectives, distortions, and perceptions sharp and dim that at no time can we be absolutely certain that what we see today is the same as what we saw yesterday. Unlike machines, we cannot ask to be fed clean choices between either-or alternatives; human beings must work always with one or two unknowns and several maybes in their equations. That is why it was necessary to assume a mechanism for recognizing similarities as part of a child's innate equipment. This was needed not only because of nature's condition of indefiniteness but also because of nature's size: there would not be enough words to go around if the universe required a semantic blanket with no holes in it.

It is often said that context determines the meaning of a word. This claim can be taken in either of two senses:

1. That the "larger context"—the whole discourse or the whole experience of the speaker or the whole language—cumulatively colors each word as it occurs against one background after another. This sense will be looked at later.

2. That the immediate context, by canceling out those *known* meanings of a word that are inappropriate, leaves the one meaning that fits. This may be the context of situation—a doctor referring to an *oral passage* means something different from what a teacher about to give a dictation would mean by it. Or it may be the verbal context—*evaporated water* is water vapor; *evaporated milk* is milk reduced in volume by evaporation. In this second sense, **context** "determines" meaning by a paring-down operation.

There is no question that this process does go on in the mind of the hearer every time he decodes a message. But what about the speaker encoding it? He must bend and expand his meanings so that they will meet and cross and thereby make it possible for the hearer to get a fix with his mental sextant. Also he has to fight against time—there is not always leisure for precision even when the language supplies the means for it. So a passing motorist may call out *You're smoking on the left rear there; I think your brake is dragging,* extending the reference of *you* to include the other car as well as its driver. *Smoke is issuing from the left rear part of your car* will not get the same attention and takes longer to say.[4] When a housewife remarks *I guess it's time to turn the cereal off,* she could have said *It's time to turn the heat off under the cereal* or, still more accurately, *It's time to turn the gas off at the burner under the cereal* (or *turn the valve off,* or *turn the handle of the valve to "off"*). In this context the semantic reach of *turn off* has been expanded through a fairly long causal chain to meet that of *cereal,* which is known from the situation to be 'cooking cereal.' This process is just as important as the one that enables the hearer to understand that *turn off,* in any of the ways of expressing this operation, is not the same as *turn off* in *turn off the*

---

[4] For this use of the pronouns see Jespersen, *op. cit.,* III, 11.5$_1$.

road. When a lawyer advises a debtor that he need not pay because *the statute of limitations has expired on that bill,* he does not mean that the statute of limitations is no longer in force but that the period of time during which according to the statute of limitations the bill was legally collectable has expired; *statute of limitations* is shorthand for *statute-of-limitations period,* which is shorthand for the still longer *time during which according to,* and so on. We can call what underlies this process the "something-like" principle. Take a sentence like *Look at all those flowers ready to bloom.* Since they are not flowers *until* they bloom, we know that a prior stage is referred to. So why not say *Look at all those buds ready to bloom* and be accurate about it? The answer is that we do not ordinarily say that buds bloom but that they open; the blooming is the coming into full flower. So our original sentence was designed to expand the meaning of *flower* to include the stage of the opened bud. The something-like principle is essential to the segmentation of a reality that does not come in fixed forms. Since the universe never repeats itself exactly, every time we speak we metaphorize, and each metaphor is what one linguist calls a new "instantial" meaning, a meaning associated with the *"actual* living manifestation of a form in its context."[5]

When conditions are right, the something-like principle gives us needed designations for new segments of reality. When straws were first used to imbibe drinks they were literally the dried stems of cereal grains. Later the same name was given to tubes made of paper or other material—attention was no longer on the material but on the function. One even hears *glass straw.* In the same way, we now drink from *glasses* made of plastic, bake waffles on *irons* made of aluminum, cool our foods in *ice boxes* that contain no ice, and so on. Many ultra-modern banks have replaced their tellers' cages with open counters, each teller having his assigned position; yet when a teller is absent his position carries a sign reading *Next window, please. Window* has come to mean 'teller's assigned post.'

Speakers not only share the same code but also share the ability to see the same resemblances between what their code already designates and what they would like it to designate, and so to make the old forms reach out to new meanings. This is how language breaks free of its rigidity. A word is like Antaeus, revitalized by each contact with the earth. "Every language provides ways to extricate itself from bondage to its own commitments in the formal registration of meanings."[6]

---

5 See Angus McIntosh, " 'Graphology' and Meaning," in McIntosh and M. A. K. Halliday, *Patterns of Language: Papers in General, Descriptive, and Applied Linguistics* (Don Mills, Ont.: Longmans Canada Ltd., 1966), p. 105 and note.

6 Punya Sloka Ray, "The Formation of Prose," *Word* 18.323 (1962).

Language as part of reality

Most of the time it works fairly well to speak of how a word segments reality without worrying about what kind of word it is. Yet we know that not all words deal with reality in the same way and that this is the basis of syntax, in which each category has its functions and imprints them on the words that it encompasses. In this sense the categories embody the semantic ingredients that are the most fundamental of all, for they are so important to the language that they brand its structure. There is a "nounness" among nouns—they take a static view of the segments that they designate, even when the segments are actions (in *Murder will out,* murder, an action, is dealt with as if it were something that we could make hold still long enough to treat like a thing). There is a "verbness" among verbs—they put things in motion and pass them through time. All the same, these ingredients are not essentially different from other kinds, and we find different languages elevating different ones to the status of categories of their grammar. In the Senufo languages of Africa, "size" becomes a subcategory of nouns—those designating large objects are formally distinct from those designating small ones.[7] In Chontal, a dialect of Mayan spoken in southern Mexico, there is an elaborate categorization of things that is required whenever things are counted: separate mor-phemes are used to classify the world of objects into people and most animals as distinct from other things, flat objects like leaves and sleeping mats, plants and standing trees, slender objects like snakes and sticks, unharvested fruits and nuts, drops of liquids, things rolled up, objects cut lengthwise, and so on.[8]

But some words—and these tend to fall outside the most populous cate-gories of noun, adjective, and verb—deal with what is a very special part of reality as far as language is concerned, that of language itself. We have met them already and given them the name of *function words* (Chapter 5, page 57). An example or two by way of reminder:

1. Woodrow Wilson was reported to have served notice on the Ger-man people that they "must choose between Hohenzollernism and Despotism on the one hand and liberty and world peace on the other."[9] The expressions *on the one hand* and *on the other hand* are

---

[7] William E. Welmers, "Notes on Two Languages in the Senufo Group," *Language* 26.131 (1950).

[8] Kathryn C. Keller, "The Chontal (Mayan) Numeral System," *International Journal of American Linguistics* 21.258–75 (1955).

[9] *Fellowship,* September, 1964, p. 10.

used by the speaker to clear up a problem of linguistic grouping caused by the ambiguity of *and:* 'The first two things that I have named belong together and so do the last two things, and the *and* that appears between the pairs goes with *between.*'

2. *Unless* and *if not* contrast in terms of point-of-view ingredients much like those already discussed. *Unless* implies 'This bit of linguistic reality is to be viewed affirmatively,' *if not* implies the opposite. So we get the difference between *I'll send the money if you don't want me to keep it, in which case you may expect to receive it in a few days,* where *in which case* shows what will happen if the addressee does not want the writer to keep the money, and *I'll send you the money unless you want me to keep it, in which case I'll deposit it in the bank here,* where *in which case* shows what will happen if the addressee does want the writer to keep the money.

As function words differ from other words only in the special kind of reality they segment, and the line separating that reality from the other kind is a hazy one anyway, we need stay with them no further.

Sharing of the range

If, instead of taking our stand on the word and focusing our camera on the segment and the way the word carves it out, we take our stand on the segment and focus inward on the word, the picture we get is one of words in fierce competition. The semantic field is divided, subdivided, excluded, consolidated, and otherwise traded back and forth in ways that try the lexicographical surveyor's spirit when he attempts to determine the ownership of each bit of semantic real estate. Speakers do not mind these interlocking interests at all, so long as some bit of a semantic ingredient, however small, distinguishes the combined property of one word from that of the next. The result is an extremely complicated state of affairs and a good deal of claim-jumping in the semantic interconnections of words.

Some words, such as *complex* and *complicated* or *complex* and *simple,* have ranges that are related and hence comparable. Others, such as *amorous* and *axiomatic,* have ranges that are not related. Relationships among ranges vary, but two are of special interest: overlap and opposition.

Synonyms are words with overlapping ranges. The term is not used, however, unless the overlap is so extensive as to make the ranges almost identical. We have no term for a slight overlap, and even words with extensive but not approximately complete overlap are not generally regarded as synonyms. Thus, **man** and **boy** overlap in all major respects except 'age,' but we do not think of them as synonyms. The reason is that it is precisely this difference that we want to emphasize; in a given conversation the fact that someone is 'human' and 'male' will probably be taken for granted, whereas the difference in age may well be the point at issue. There is also another reason. It is difficult to find two terms that do not overlap in some imaginable way: **toenail** and **typewriter** are both 'material objects.'

So the term *synonym* is not applied unless (1) the overlap is almost complete and/or (2) the area outside the overlap is, for a given purpose, unimportant. (Overlap applies, of course, to comparable ranges. **Flush** is a synonym of **blush** in the sense 'turn red,' where the overlap is almost but not quite complete. Other senses of **flush** have no bearing.) We would call the words **hitch** and **tether** synonyms in the sense 'make fast,' but not if the important thing happened to be a distinction between hitching to a wagon with the object of moving it and tethering to a post with the object of preventing motion. The verb **tie** in one of its senses could be added, and in fact its range embraces that of the two others; **moor** might also be added in a theoretical discussion of synonyms, since it differs only in the kind of thing that is tied up.

The kind of synonymy of which **sauce** (for meat, poultry, or fish), **gravy** (for bread or potatoes), **topping** (for ice cream), and **dressing** (for salad) are examples is of little more than theoretical interest. For synonyms to be of practical interest there must be some expectation of their being substituted for each other, and with 'edible liquescent coverings for foods' that is not likely to happen, despite the semantic overlap.

We find this substitutability under two sets of conditions. The first is simply a matter of precision. A writer or speaker is about to say **He delivered a lengthy apology** and realizes that he may be taken to mean an excuse and not a justification, which he intended; so he uses **justification** instead. The second is a matter of contrast, of finding something that sounds different. Sometimes a speaker needs this to avoid distracting attention from his ideas to his words. Our stock of phonemes is not unlimited and now and then plays us false by serving up two words that sound so much alike—they may even be identical—that if we use them together we are liable to be misunderstood or thought to be making a pun: **That was a fine fine you had to pay!; The painter succeeded in painting the pain on her face all too plainly; That weakness is one that he does not to my knowledge acknowledge.** If we replace the second **fine** with **penalty,** the **pain** with **anguish,** and the **acknowledge** with **admit to,** the problem is avoided. This is a milder form of the conflict of homonyms that we noted earlier (Chapter 7, pages 112–13); the difference is that instead of being driven out of the language the conflicting form is simply driven out of the immediate context. In a more subtle form, contrast is a matter of semantic shading, of avoiding the repetition of the same word with the same sound when it is supposed to have a slightly different meaning, both meanings being well within the normal range for the word. The first sentence of the second paragraph of this chapter was originally written "The word *meaning* is used in many ways...." When the line was edited it appeared that *word* might be taken in the sense that it had at the beginning of the preceding paragraph, namely words as a level in linguistics. To avoid this it was replaced with *term.* It was not so much that either *word* or *term* could not be used in either sense as that, by not repeating, the reader would be warned away from assuming a repetition of the same meaning. The need to do this is often erroneously treated in books of rhetoric and elsewhere as just a mechanical avoidance of repeating the same word,[10] and some unwary writers take this advice seriously and write sentences like *Shakespeare's* **The Tempest** *is his most enthralling work; in it the great dramatist pours an emotive force that is missing elsewhere—how well the genius of the English stage knew his public,* etc., etc., with the metamorphosis of Shakespeare continuing through *the prince of European letters, the creator of Hamlet, the Bard of Avon,* and so on. The truth is that the avoidance of repetition is keyed directly to the need in every context to define terms in such a way that if the least contrast is intended it will be physically manifest in the words we choose. This is the beauty of having synonyms and the "something-like" freedom to expand them beyond their normal limits: if we cannot find a prefabricated contrast among the synonyms at our disposal, we can make one to order.

Do any two words different in form ever have exactly the same range of meanings? If they are words in common use, probably not. Interpretative change will differentiate them (see Chapter 7, pages 104–17). Possibly a few technical terms with only slight differences in form may be close enough to be called the same: *coterminous* and *conterminous,* for example. Practically speaking, there is no such thing as an identical synonym. The language demands its money's worth from every word it permits to survive.

Antonyms are words with opposing ranges. It is as hard to pin down the "opposition" of antonyms as the "sameness" of synonyms, but one thing is always to be understood: the opposition is not absolute but is enclosed within a sameness. The overlap of synonyms can be shown by a diagram like the one at the left on page 235. That is, two synonyms may

---

[10] Maclay and Osgood refer to "the stylistic requirement of educated English to search for synonyms rather than to repeat previously used words," *Word* 15.43 (1959). Z. S. Harris refers to "the school admonition to use synonyms instead of repeating a word," *Language* 28.10 (1952).

have virtually complete overlap but fail to share some part of the range
(*hitch, tether*), or one may cover the other completely and extend beyond
it (*tie, tether*). Two antonyms would appear as separate circles within a
common larger range, as in the diagram at the right above. They share the
same semantic ingredients except for one, and that one difference is focused
on. We saw earlier that that was the quality that prevented *man* and *boy*
from being synonyms—despite the nearly complete overlap, 'age' was too
important. If the age factor were more clearly delimited, *man* and *boy*
could be regarded as antonyms.

A typical pair of antonyms is *large-small*. It fits into a box of shared
ingredients referring to 'size'. Antonyms such as *large-small* are "con-
traries"; something may fall within the box and still not be inside either

circle—it may be extra-large, extra-small, medium, and so on. It is hard
to find examples of "contradictory" antonyms, pairs that divide the range
between them and leave no middle ground. It can be managed logically
by prefixing a *not: large* and *not-large* are contradictories; but they are
not antonyms in the usual sense. Natural language is not the same as logic.
If we have to be free to expand and contract the range of meanings to
accommodate the multifarious facts of experience, generally a middle
ground can be squeezed in somehow: *Are you going to hold it or let go
of it? Neither one; I'm going to control it by a magnetic field; Are you
going to keep it or throw it away? Neither one; I'm going to give it to
John.* Still, here and there a pair of antonyms seem to be true contradictories.

keep	*dispose of*
HAVING CONTROL	OVER SOMETHING

Keep and *dispose of* divide the range between them; one would probably
not say **I'm neither going to keep it nor dispose of it. Never* and *sometimes* are contradictories, too.

Many antonyms leave a middle ground that itself carries a regular name or names. Between *large* and *small* is *medium*. Other examples are *right-center-left*, *good-fair-poor-bad*, and *open-ajar-shut*. A few have a middle ground that itself contains a pair of antonyms: with *always-often-seldom-never* we regard *often* and *seldom* as enclosed antonyms. A similar set is *hot-warm-cool-cold*. *Warm-cool* and *often-seldom* are themselves antonyms because they are the same distance away from the center line that already separates *hot-cold* and *always-never*.

There is no restriction on the other semantic ingredients nor on the grammatical features that can be shared by an antonymic set. *To hurry* and *to go at a leisurely pace* are antonyms differing in grammatical form, though of course both are verb phrases. *Always-often-seldom-never* and *hot-warm-cool-cold* resemble each other in having a pair of enclosed antonyms; but while the enclosed antonyms can take grammatical comparison—we can say *more often, more seldom, warmer,* and *cooler*—two of the enclosing ones can, *hotter* and *colder,* and two cannot, *more always, *more never*. But if we were to fit *tepid* between *warm* and *cool,* and *occasionally* between *often* and *seldom,* we would have terms in both sets that are not normally compared: *more tepid, *more occasionally*. Some pairs of antonyms are opposed in terms of more than one set of ingredients: *to work* and *to rest* are antonyms on the basis of 'presence or absence of productive activity'; *to work* and *to loaf* are opposed on the same basis plus the basis of 'concern versus indifference.' The basis of antonymy between *noise* and *silence* is not the same as that between *noise* and *music*. Words from virtually all categories can form pairs: nouns such as *good* and *evil;* adjectives such as *good* and *bad;* adverbs such as *fast* and *slow;* prepositions such as *out* and *in;* pronouns such as *mine* and *thine*.

But some pairs are more clearly antonymous than others. *Square* and *round* are antonyms in *square peg in a round hole,* but the rest of the time they are no more so than *oblong* and *rectangular*. *To rest* is more properly an antonym of *to be active* than of *to work,* since it differs equally from *to play,* itself an antonym of *to work* in terms of another ingredient. What makes the study of both synonyms and antonyms impressionistic rather than scientific—"merely taxonomic," to use a current expression of disfavor—is the fact that it consists in cataloguing words rather than analyzing semantic ingredients. If we could decompose the ingredients of two words assumed to be antonymous and identify the ones that are actually in opposition separately from the rest, we could define a pair of antonyms as two words which in a given context are opposed on the basis of those ingredients. The words *square* and *round* would then not be antonyms unless—as in *square peg in a round hole*— the ingredients of angularness versus curvedness were the essential opposition. This would dispel the false notion that words either are or are not antonyms. Degrees of antonymy would be recognized. High on the scale would be pairs of words regularly associated, such as *good-bad, high-low, full-empty.* Farther down would be pairs like *calm-upset* and *calm-frightened.* At the bottom would be pairs like *borrow-steal,* where the opposing semantic ingredients of (in this case 'legitimate versus illegitimate') acquisition would seldom be invoked. Some pairs would appear clearly as antonyms in regular use; others would be antonymous if we make them so for the purposes of our discourse, exercising the same right that we noted earlier in adjusting synonyms to pick some advantage out of a slight difference wedged into a complex of similarities.

Synonyms and antonyms are not the only sets of words that are joined through shared or opposed semantic ingredients. There is probably no limit to the groupings that would make sense for one purpose or another. Examples:

1. Reciprocals: *come-go, buy-sell, read-write, give-receive.*

2. Characteristic object: *eat-food, drink-beverage, hear-sound, spell-word, wrap-package, ask-question.*

3. Characteristic action: *heart-beat, mind-think, fire-burn, wind-blow, rain-fall.*

4. Characteristic subject-action-object: *employer-employ-employee; donor-donate-donation; inventor-invent-invention; thief-steal-loot; preacher-preach-sermon;* and with indirect object added, *payer-pay-payment-payee; giver-give-gift-receiver.* As is evident from these examples, the semantic sharing is often matched by a sharing of morphemes. In certain sets a member may be semantically defective; so, in the set *drunkard, go on,* and *binge,* the verb *go on* is less explicit than *pay,* for example, with reference to its co-members *payer* and *payee;* similarly with *commit* in *criminal-commit-crime.*

5. Characteristic quality: *water-wet, summer-warm, feather-light, prairie-flat.*

6. Symptom and state: *smile-happiness, smoke-fire, groan-pain.*

7. Included segments: *matter* includes *solid, liquid,* and *gas,* and specifically *H_2O* includes *ice, water, vapor; color* includes *red, yellow, orange,* and so on; *member* includes *arm, leg, head; organ* includes *stomach, heart, liver; school larnin'* includes *readin', writin', 'rithmetic.* Here belong all the groupings not only of nature but also of our occupations and daily associations: *curriculum* includes *mathematics, history, chemistry; baseball scores*

include **hits, runs, errors; church service** includes **prelude, offertory, sermon, doxology.**

To these more down-to-earth sets we could add something as abstract as 'incipience' in **gain-lose-learn-seek-find-acquire.** These imply a transition, through time, from having (or not having) to not having (or having). Having knowledge is the end result of learning, having possession is the end result of getting, and so on.

Ranges that a word can cover

If we take our stand once more with the word and look out to the spread of its meanings, we find every degree of system and unsystem, homogeneity and heterogeneity. As with the word **saloon** (Chapter 7, page 113), two antagonistic ranges may develop within the span of a single word, with the result that one has to go. Except for students of etymology, there is no difference between the conflict within the meanings of **saloon** and the conflict illustrated by **queen** and **quean**—we might as well speak of two words that both happen to be pronounced /səlun/ and spelled **saloon.**

But ordinarily things do not reach such a pass, and various meanings are able to coexist in the combined ranges of a single word. We have the right to call it a single word because, though the senses have split off to some extent, they still resemble one another closely enough to be classed together.

Multiple senses are typical. Few words have not gone off in two or more semantic directions. The reason is that individual words are only a step up from morphemes and, like morphemes, are valences in larger combinations rather than entities in their own right—we do not operate with individual words in one-word sentences as a rule, but with more or less fixed combinations. The difference between morphemes and words is one of degree;[11] the combinations of morphemes are simply tighter than those of words.

If more or less predictable combinations are the rule, then we do not depend on a word's formal individuality to identify it. The combination in which it occurs will take care of that. Take the word **cell.** In a sentence like **The cells of the human body have various forms and functions; some cells carry nutrients, oxygen, and hormones,** we know that the second **cell** is **cell of the human body** just as in **pre- and post-natal care** we know that **pre-** is **pre-natal.** It is customary to regard the first as a rebuilding from context and the second as a rebuilding from truncation, but there

---

[11] See Chapter 5, pp. 51–56.

is no real difference. Any word pulled out of one of its normal contexts is to some extent truncated.

With combinations to fall back on we can tolerate a word's branching out in several directions from a central core. *Cell* can refer to protoplasmic cell, dry cell, honeycomb cell, and communist cell, among others. It is even possible for a word to develop opposing senses. *The stars are out* means that they are shining. *The lights are out* means that they are not shining. *She dusted the furniture* means that dust was removed. *He dusted the tomato plants* means that dust was applied.

If it were not possible to use individual words in this way, a language would require a vastly larger stock. The situation is much the same as with phonemes: by reusing them in different combinations we keep their number down. With words there is the advantage that the central core of meaning is an aid to storage and a jog to memory. If we had to use different words for each variety of cell, for each separate sense of *time (time to go, time enough to eat, a good time, time of day)*, for each action subsumed under the verb *feel (feel pain, feel love toward someone, feel the wind, feel the surface with your hand)*, our powers of association might well break down.

This does not mean that the central core is never broken up with the result that the association is useless or perhaps even misleading. The latter happened with *saloon*. Elsewhere the breakup may be an inconvenience—the multifarious senses of *flush*, for example—but it is no worse than the fact that the syllable /say/ occurs in *sigh, silo, siphon, psyche*, and *sisal*. The larger configuration rescues it.

But in the normal situation a core of shared semantic ingredients is retained. *The airplane is a mile high* and *The mountain is a mile high* do not mean exactly the same kind of height, but both refer to a vertical measurement and the nature of the objects takes care of the rest. The word *laundry* covers a sizable range of different meanings but they all meet at the base.[12]

It appears that there are two ways in which a hearer may get a fix on the meaning intended by the speaker when terms or constructions are used that have more than one meaning. One is by the process just noted—stereotyped combinations that are recognized at sight. If *royal flush* is used, the hearer does not need to deduce anything; *royal flush* is a unit. But if the combination has no such obvious face value, the paring-down process may be called for (page 229). Hearing *That fellow's a bad actor* one might take it to mean someone's lack of skill on the stage; but if the speaker goes on to say *Watch out for your valuables if he is around,* one revises the choice to 'dangerous or untrustworthy person.' Presumably

---

[12] On *laundry* see B. Hunter Smeaton in *Word* 16.134 (1960).

our brains are equipped to handle both processes at the same time. It would be hard to decide which is uppermost in our understanding of a sentence like *They set the clocks and put out the lights before going to bed.* If our minds are already calculating by the time we hit the verb *set,* then the process is one of keeping two alternatives before us—*did set* or *do set?*—not committing ourselves until a decisive word comes along. But if we automatically jump to conclusions, then we will not wait until all the parts are arrayed in front of us but will simply take the verbs *set* and *put* one way or the other, past or present, and hope for the best. The paring-down process will not be invoked unless we strike a snag—we might, for instance, have taken the sentence to mean that they always do those things before going to bed, and then the speaker goes on to add *but forgot to lock the doors,* which forces us to reassess the verb and pick a different meaning. This would seem to be more efficient and is probably the way things happen, especially as ambiguity is rarely so complete as in the example just quoted and our guess is more likely to be right than wrong. It may well be based on the statistical probabilities that we learn to sense through long experience with the language. Someone hearing *Did you see that gull?* would guess the highly frequent meaning 'bird' rather than the infrequent 'gullible person,' and no mental switching would be called for unless he was wrong, which would not be too often.

THE ARBITRARINESS AND NON-ARBITRARINESS OF MEANING

If the history of writing gives hints about the history of language, the first forms of communication must have been imitative. The use of pictograms to convey messages long before the development of syllabaries and alphabets—not to mention the universality of imitative and expressive gesture—seems so natural that we can only suppose a primitive stage in which sounds were related to sense. The imitation need not have been perfect—in fact, the very difficulty of copying the sounds of nature with the human voice would have been an advantage because speakers would have had to ignore imperfections and accept substitutions that were less and less like the originals—but mimicry there must have been.

Those colorful beginnings have faded to a uniform gray. As we saw earlier (Chapter 2, page 15), even in our common onomatopoetic words the imitation must give way to the system of sounds that the language imposes. The result is almost always an imperfect copy. If we listen to the note of the whippoorwill we observe an appreciable pause between *whip* and *poor: whip-poorwill, whip-poorwill.* But English has the habit of reducing interior syllables and clicking them off at a faster rate; the result is that we say something like *whipperwill.*

But if through the centuries our art has declined, our apparent sophistication has grown. We are not bothered by imperfect copies. Until someone calls them to our attention we do not even notice them. Perhaps it is not sophistication so much as conditioned reflex. If a bell is as good as a taste to the salivary glands of Pavlov's dog, *ding-dong* can be as good as the ringing of a bell to us. This is the effect of permeation.

So it would seem that language should be set down as an almost purely conventional code, with a few exceptions listed as curiosities. Certainly there is no essential relationship between the sound of any phoneme, or the combined sounds within any word, and any event beyond language, barring the frayed remnants of an occasional onomatope.

But how is it then that language can express reality? Does not this rough denial of expressiveness do language an injustice? If we look at the stippling in a picture or the grain in a photograph, we note an equal lack of correspondence between dots or grains and the flesh of the human face, whose image is nevertheless clearly reproduced. What if words are only the grain of language and the non-arbitrary picture is filled out at a higher level?

The sense in which language is most expressive and least arbitrary, according to Roman Jakobson,[13] is in its status as an elaborate diagram. The lowest common denominator of a diagram is simple togetherness. If two things react upon each other in our experience and we want to talk about them, whatever device is normally used for one (say, x) or for the other (say, y), the result in what we say is going to be an xy or a yx. The words *cat, bite,* and *dog* may be arbitrary, but if a dog bites a cat we can reasonably expect that these words will keep close company in what we say about it. This of course is non-arbitrary, because the togetherness of the words reflects the togetherness of the things and events. Actually, the diagrams of a language are far more expressive than this, for its devices have little purpose except to talk about things and events. If when a particular event occurs we can predict with some certainty what is going to be said about it—and our daily experience proves that we can, even with events that have never occurred before—then we know that the correspondence of the points on our diagram to the externals that they stand for is anything but arbitrary. Language uses arbitrary units to sketch non-arbitrary pictures.

A better analogy might view language as a whole not so much like a map as like a collection of snatched tokens of old maps stored according to a certain filing system that we know as the grammatical and semantic paradigms of the language. The notion of the map would then be reserved

---

[13] "A la Recherche de l'Essence du Langage," *Diogène* 51.22–38 (July–September, 1965).

for the sentence or utterance. A sentence, we would say, is what really maps these old fragments—words and combinations—onto a fresh cut of reality in which each fragment acquires a slightly altered value by virtue of its relationship to the rest and to the part of reality that it is meant to cover. Then the meaning of a word would be what it brings to the sentence—what it enables but never quite forces the speaker to do with his sentence; and also, transformed to some slight degree, what it takes away when the sentence is broken up and its fragments are stored to be mapped afresh at some future time.

Phonesthemes

Even the units turn out to be somewhat less arbitrary than they appear at first sight if we look beyond just the primary association of word and thing. Given a particular word for a particular thing, if other words for similar things come to resemble that word in sound, then, no matter how arbitrary the relationship between sound and sense was to begin with, the sense is now obviously tied to the sound. The relationship between sound and sense is still arbitrary as far as the outside world is concerned (and would appear that way absolutely to a foreigner), but within the system it is no longer so.

So we find words clustering in groups with a vague resemblance in sound—too hazy to carve out as a definite morpheme—to which has been given the name *phonestheme*. Most of the words ending in *-ump* suggest heaviness and bluntness: *rump, dump, hump, mump, lump, stump, chump, thump, bump.* Children sense these associative possibilities and coin words with them: *If the house is as old as that it's raggy, shaggy, and daggy,* remarked one seven-year-old; and referring to the muck at the bottom of an excavation the same speaker said *It's all gushy—it's like mushy dushy.* The makers of multiple-choice tests find phonesthemes useful as distractors for their questions; if *twisted* is offered as an equivalent for *knurled,* as was done in one test, it is on the assumption that persons not fully acquainted with *knurl* will assume that it is related to *twirl, whirl, birl, tirl, furl,* and *spiral.* Shifts of meaning often go in the direction of a family of words having phonesthematic ties. The word *bolster* no longer suggests a padded and comparatively soft support but rather a stiff and rigid one, because of the attraction of *brace, bolt, buttress.* (Of seventeen persons tested on this point, thirteen voted for 'rigid.') Phonesthemes are often a principal ingredient of new words: *hassle* probably follows from *tussle, bustle, wrestle.*

If words become parts of things to our minds, as they must if language is to do its job efficiently (in spite of our trying, in philosophical moments, to break the bondage), at least a partial association of sound and sense can hardly be avoided. When other aspects of things hit our eyes we do not hesitate to infer a kinship in the things if we detect a similarity in the aspects, and it is only natural for us to do the same with words: no two girls ever toss their heads in the same way, but one's doing it should mean somewhat the same as another's; two words such as *flout* and *flaunt* are not identical, but they are similar enough so that they *ought* to be related in meaning. We feel a lurking sympathy for the seventeen-year-old who produced the following definitions:

Ossify: this means to astonish, to frighten to death.

Palpable: good to the taste, good to eat.

Pander: that means run fast, panting down the track, thundering down, you know, pander, pander, pander, that's the way it sounds.

Pariah: that's the black pariah, the wagon that takes away the drunks.

Platitude: that's how high aviators get into the air.

Aptitude: that is the feelings you have about something. Your father says, "I don't like your aptitude toward using the car."

Brandish: that is what you have in restaurants sometimes, brandish cherries. They burn with ice cream.

Henchmen: those are the guys that sit on the bench, I suppose, the ones the coach never uses.

Flagrant: that is the way flowers smell, or a field of daisies.[14]

Not all of us go so far in blurring the arbitrariness of language with this kind of poetic truth, but the outlines are never perfectly sharp for any of us. Who nowadays feels comfortable with *disinterested* as a synonym of *impartial?*

LINGUISTS AND MEANING

Linguists are sensitive to reputations. It has been so cozy inside the formal system, with everything ticketed and orderly, that they have been reluctant to allow any rowdy element on the premises. Meaning, as we have seen, is an exceedingly ill-assorted fellow. One can scarcely invite him into the house without admitting at the same time one or more of his drunken

---

[14] Mildred G. Downes and Rita S. Schuman, "Pathogenesis of Reading Disability," *New England Journal of Medicine* 252:6.218 (1955).

friends. The technique has been either to lock him out or to demand a password and slam the door shut the moment the legitimate guest is inside, which not infrequently has cost him part of an arm or leg.

Linguists have not been averse to keeping company with meaning when first making their way through the dark streets of a new language. He is the one familiar face in a crowd of strangers, a handy guide and a prompter of hunches. But once the preliminary acquaintances are made and the moment of high theory arrives, he must offer credentials or stay out.

In theory—though not always in practice—American linguists of the past thirty years have kept their investment in meaning as low as possible by dealing with it in one of two ways: admitting only a well-defined minimum of it or not admitting it at all and pretending it was already there—that is, carrying on with its ghost.

Differential meaning

The first approach is an outgrowth of field work and makes use of "differential meaning." This is the minimal sort of meaning that an informant relies upon when we ask him whether *uru* and *ulu* are the same in meaning or different. We have heard him say both and we want to know whether [l] and [r] in his language are distinct phonemes or allophones of one phoneme—unless we are the victims of an unlucky coincidence (as with English *vial* and *phial;* see Chapter 4, page 41), the response "same" or "different" ought to settle the question.

Even this much meaning seemed excessive to some American linguists, who proceeded to try to show how the phonemes of a language could be analyzed just in terms of their relation to one another. One would note, for example, that what appeared to be a [p] sound kept recurring in definite environments and that what appeared to be a [b] sound also occurred in certain environments. If there was no way to tell one set of environments from another, then the two were presumably variants of the same phoneme—either we were fooling ourselves in thinking that we heard two different sounds, or there were two but the difference was not distinctive, the way a speaker will produce one kind of /t/ in English *bitter* when he is speaking normally and another kind when he is speaking emphatically. But if both occurred in the same immediate environments but not in certain broader environments, then presumably they were distinct phonemes. For example, in English *booby* and *soupy* the immediate environment is the same for both [b] and [p]—[u] on one side and [ɨ] on the other; but then we note that whereas *booby* occurs *boopy* does not, and whereas *soupy* occurs *souby* does not—the larger phonetic environment allows one but not the other. Since this is the way sounds behave when they are in contrast, we assume that the two are distinct phonemes. The environmental theory involved many more refinements, of course, but even so it has few adherents nowadays. No actual analysis of a language was ever made using it alone, and there are several theoretical flaws.[15]

Differential meaning, on the other hand, has been of such great practical use that one can understand the feeling that if one could just frame one's questions properly it ought to be enough. But in practice the field worker always leaned on other aspects of meaning, sometimes less, sometimes more. Suppose two informants disagree on "same" or "different." The only way to settle the argument is to try to find exactly what the words do mean; and this is referential meaning, not just differential. Suppose the informant is not bilingual and fails to understand the question posed in our language, and we are unable to pose it in his—there is no way even to ask, "Is this the same or is it different?" We must then appeal to objects, pantomime, or whatever kind of dumb play two persons use when they have to communicate without language. But worst of all—and this is where the breakdown comes in theory—suppose we intend the question on one level of language and the informant infers it on another. We have assumed that one can sensibly ask "same or different?" as if these notions were a kind of absolute instead of being conditioned by the structure of the language, which is the very thing we are trying to find out. *Seal* and *seal* are the same, phonologically, but our informant may think we are talking about a seal on an envelope in the first instance and a seal in the ocean in the second, and so answer "different." *The boy walked to the school* and *The man plodded from the station* are the same syntactically, but if it is not understood that we are talking about syntax then an informant is going to call them different.[16] It is pretty generally admitted nowadays that more than differential meaning is needed to analyze a language, even at just the level of the phoneme.

Distributional meaning

Differential meaning was an attempt to set limits on how far one should go with meaning for certain purposes. It was not intended as a definition or description of meaning from a linguistic standpoint. That is the aim of the second approach, which undertakes to deal with meaning without going outside language. It is a refined version of the idea that "context determines meaning"—if we know the company that a word keeps within the society of words, then we know what it means.

---

[15] See W. Haas, "Relevance in Phonetic Analysis," *Word* 15.1–18 (1959).

[16] Paraphrased from Kenneth L. Pike, *Language in Relation to a Unified Theory of the Structure of Human Behavior* (Glendale, Calif.: Summer Institute of Linguistics, 1954), pp. 23–24.

But now context must be taken in a large sense. It is not enough to look to the immediate context. One could encounter the word *rhizome* over and over—*He pulled up the rhizome, The cow ate the rhizome, The rhizome crept under the ground, It was a tender rhizome*—and still not learn what it is. So one must reach far afield: "Let us assume that the total and potentially infinite set of utterances containing a given lexical item exactly specifies the meaning of that lexical item."[17] Meaning is to be expressed in terms of "collocations"[18] or "the intralingual relations contracted by linguistic units."[19]

The difficulty with theories of meaning that play only with associations within language and seal themselves off from the outside world is that they are ultimately circular. Take a simple instance like *He strummed the guitar.* If we do not know the meaning of *guitar*, the context tells us that it must be a musical instrument because only musical instruments are strummed. If we do not know the meaning of *strum*, the context tells us that it is most likely a form of playing because that is what one normally does with musical instruments. But what if we do not know either *strum* or *guitar*? A dependence on context has to assume that we know everything except the one item in question, but if we do not know that item, and context is a string of interdependencies, then we cannot be sure that we know the context either. At some point it is necessary to break out of the circle, to get a foothold outside language. A theory of meaning that will do this is obviously easier to ask for than to get, and one sympathizes with the linguist's nostalgia for the time when he could enter his monastery and let the rest of the world go by. Unfortunately, with meaning that is impossible.

Yet it seems to be in tune with the times. The linguists who lock themselves within language are matched by the cloistered practitioners of nonrepresentational art who make the interconnections within their idiom the substance of their pictures and poems, extracting in a poem, for example, the meanings of words that are suggested by their relationships of sound and grammar and sense to other words rather than to the external world—in such a line as that of Dylan Thomas, "What sixth of wind blew out the burning gentry?"[20]

---

[17] Murray S. Miron and William K. Archer, "Qualification in Natural Language," *Linguistics* 11.43 (1965).

[18] Martin Joos, "Semology: A Linguistic Theory of Meaning," *Studies in Linguistics* 13.53–70 (1958).

[19] William F. Wyatt, Jr., review of John Lyons, *Structural Semantics: An Analysis of Part of the Vocabulary of Plato*, in *Language* 41.505 (1965).

[20] See Winfred P. Lehmann, "The Stony Idiom of the Brain," in *Literary Symbolism* (Austin: University of Texas Press, 1965), pp. 11–30.

ADDITIONAL REMARKS
AND APPLICATIONS

1. Comment on the meaning of "meaning" in the following:

   Seven o'clock means breakfast in our household.

   Keep out. This means you.

   Do you mean to wait?

   Without love, life would have no meaning.

2. Do traffic and other such signs have, in addition to their one-to-one relationship to what they mean, a tendency to be suggestive or pictorial? Would green for 'Stop' and red for 'Go' be just as good as the reverse? What is the sign used in many communities that means 'Watch out, children playing'?

3. Explain the difference between a syllable and a morpheme.

4. Seeing similarities is sometimes linked to being able to abstract, supposedly a higher intellectual faculty. Consider a child who has had only cats as pets and on seeing a dog calls it a cat. Or a child who on seeing a strange man calls him Daddy. Is this a kind of abstraction, or is it a lack of ability to discriminate? How is it necessary for language?

5. The color of fire boxes is red, part of the complex of features that we recognize as a fire box. How is it analogous to the names that we give to segments of reality so as later to abstract the names to stand for the segments?

6. A speaker was about to say *I didn't be born to serve as somebody's slave,* but checked himself when he realized that the sentence would not be grammatical and substituted *I didn't come on this earth to serve as somebody's slave.* The grammatical passive *I wasn't born* would have failed to express his meaning. Explain why, in terms of how active and passive constructions relate to real events.

7. A passage in a magazine article reads "One of those hellish Southern California brush fires had destroyed the home where Aldous [Huxley]

lived with Laura.... He and Laura had scarcely escaped with their lives, but Aldous' manuscripts had been reduced to ashes."[21] Would you use *scarcely* here, or *barely?* Would *scarcely* sound better if *but* were changed to *and?* See if you can explain the difference in the semantic ingredients of the two words. Compare *I scarcely can tell the difference* with *I barely can tell the difference.*

8. Discuss the use of *minimally* in the following, from a study of graduate education: "Casual inspection reveals that most schools of education are overwhelmed with the magnitude of keeping the schools minimally staffed."

9. What is there about the meaning of prepositions that makes *the tree beside the lake* and *the money inside the box* more usual than *the lake beside the tree* and *the box around the money?*

10. Might it be said that the meanings of words like *unique, perfect, unparalleled, full, empty, complete,* and *unsaturated* contain an 'absolute' ingredient? What happens to them when intensifiers are added—*very unique, highly unsaturated, most perfect?* (See Chapter 7, page 112.)

11. Make a semantic grid for *clock, watch, sundial,* and *hourglass.* Make a grid for your own meal terms like the one on page 228.

12. A popular magazine carried a cartoon showing a junior official who has just discovered a microphone hidden in his office. He is exclaiming, "Somebody cares! I've been bugged!"[22] Compare this with the example *You're smoking on the left rear there* in the text, and comment on the meaning of the pronoun *I.*

13. Comment on the following sentences, keeping in mind the central meanings of the italicized words:

> A dictionary—you consult it but don't *read* it.
>
> I'm *cooking* four things: cereal, eggs, coffee, and *toast.*
>
> These apples are for cooking, *not eating.*
>
> Don't *eat with* your knife.
>
> Burn lamp *upside down.* (Directions on a lamp that is supposed to be mounted bulb-down.)

---

[21] *Harper's Magazine,* May, 1964, p. 55.

[22] *Saturday Evening Post,* October 24, 1964.

14. Explain how the noun *record* came to have 'phonograph record' as one of its meanings. Would the semantic ingredients that we now associate with *record* in this sense make it usable to refer to a tape recording? Has the word *modern* applied to art been stereotyped in a similar way? Comment on the meanings of *cooked cereal* and *pre-pared cereal.* Is the first unprepared and the second uncooked? Does *floor model* refer to a particular model of appliance?

15. Can a semantic ingredient which was secondary become primary as the result of an extension of meaning? Consider the contrast between *pen* and *pencil,* which probably hinges chiefly on the wetness of the first and the dryness of the second. Then someone advertises a "liquid pencil": "You can whisk off the writing with an ordinary eraser." What is primary now?

16. Linguists are usually averse to assigning meanings to the categories of grammar, preferring to look only at their interrelated functions (how nouns and verbs relate to each other in a sentence, for example). Yet categories do cluster about common meanings. For example, how do mass nouns view the substances to which they refer *(sugar, water, anger,* and so on)? How do count nouns *(sugarlump, raindrop, flareup)*?

17. After a long explanation of some point, a writer or speaker often begins a shorter portion of his discourse with the word *briefly.* Does this word mean just that he is going to be brief, or is it also an operator marking a certain relationship between what he has just said and what he is going to say? If so, does this suggest that some words divide themselves between linguistic reality and external reality?

18. Do we generally try to avoid rimes and alliterations in making phrases? Consider whether the following are normal and if not what is usually done about it: *mighty mild, mighty miffed, pretty prim, awful lawful, very various, very varied, really reedy, quite quiet.*

19. Improve on the following sentence: *This hammer strikes a spark every time I strike a nail with it.* Are the two senses of *strike* identical? Is *strike* a bit more essential in one of the two places than in the other? (Compare *strike a match.*) If so, choose a synonym for the other place, making the best contrast you can.

20. Does English have formal ways of building antonyms? Name the antonyms of the following words: *decent, likely, pro-French, trust* (verb), *clockwise*. Compare the use of *not* in the following pairs of sentences: *He is trustworthy, He is not trustworthy; He is American, He is not American.* See if you can replace the *not* with *un-*.

21. The word *sweet* is sometimes paired antonymously with *sour,* sometimes with *bitter.* Does this make *sour* and *bitter* synonyms? If not, why?

22. Words vary in the degree to which they adhere to particular contexts. Contrast the words *boy* and *spell: There was a boy, There was a spell.* Does one sentence seem less complete than the other? What might you add to complete the sense? Consider also the word *lull.* How would you react if someone said, without preamble and without adding anything, *I hope there will be a lull*?

23. The sentence *I got a good price for it* can be rephrased as *I got a high price for it,* and *I got it at a good price* can be rephrased as *I got it at a low price.* Does this mean that *good* has developed two opposing senses, 'high' and 'low'?

24. In a recent article criticizing certain dictionary definitions, it was asserted that to define *inspect* as 'to examine carefully' is inaccurate because *to inspect carelessly* is a normal English phrase. Is this a fair criticism, or does one of these phrases really have to do with different senses of *inspect*? Compare *A lawyer's job is to persuade, Jones is not persuasive, therefore Jones is not a lawyer.*

25. Contrast the words *capital* and *lawn* as examples of different degrees of cohesion and compactness of the central core. Consider senses of *capital* like those encountered in *Capital!* ('wonderful'), *capital crime, capital city, capital letter.* The Merriam-Webster *Third International Dictionary* defines *lawn* as 'grass kept closely mowed, as around a house or part of a garden or park.' In your speech would you refer to a lawn in a park? a garden? a cemetery?

26. Automatic recognition versus paring down depends partly on whether a semantic ingredient is carried forward or carried backward in a context. The ingredient 'past' in *set* and *put* (in the example *They set the clocks and put out the lights before going to bed but forgot to lock the doors*) had to be carried back from *forgot.* But if the sentence had been *They locked the doors, set the clocks, and put out the* *lights before going to bed,* 'past' would have carried forward and attached itself automatically to *set* and *put.* Is this analogous to the automatic carrying forward of the negative in *He has no time, patience, or desire to indulge himself?* Could this be taken to mean that he has no time but he does have patience, since the *no* is not repeated?

27. The word *zany* was originally a noun meaning 'clown' but has come to be used as an adjective. Is this based on a resemblance to other adjectives with the ending *-y?* What does this suggest about the difficulty of drawing a sharp line between imitations based on apparent morphemes (since *-y* is a morpheme: *grainy, sunny, grassy*) and imitations that are phonesthematic?

28. If you were asked which of the two words *coins* and *cash* more strongly suggested 'noisy bits and pieces' which would you pick? Can you relate your choice to a phonesthematic family? Do related sounds always suggest related senses? What about *pill, pile, pole, poll, pal, pool, pull, peel, pale, pall, pell?*

29. Use differential meaning to identify certain phonemes in the following pairs: *say-stay; sigh-die; fuss-fuzz.* Could one also use differential meaning to identify a morpheme in the phrases *two dogs, two cats, two churches, two bridges?*

30. Do words vary in the extent to which we learn their meanings from the company they keep in the language, as against their connections outside language? Compare the words for which dictionaries can supply pictures or diagrams with words like *divine, soul, bewitch.* How does "negative seeing" make use of the outside world to grasp the meaning of a word such as *soul?* (For example, we keep hearing someone referred to as soulful, as having a soul, as selling his soul, and so on, but we see nothing to correspond to it except a way of behaving; we conclude that a soul is immaterial but that it affects one's actions.) Consider the word *honor* in the same light, relating it to its contexts *(That man has no honor, His honor is at stake,* and so on).

MIND IN THE 13
GRIP OF LANGUAGE

CONTROL BY LANGUAGE

A LITTLE GIRL ASKS, "What does the wind do when it doesn't blow?" or "Where did I live before I was born?"—and we smile at her naiveté. But if she asks, "Where will I live after I die?" most people in our culture will take her seriously, though it will cost them to find an answer.

The idea embodied in those questions has weighed on linguists and on sociologists working at the borders of linguistics for a long time: "To what extent is our thinking influenced by the language we use?" The problem was first popularized in the 1930's by a school of philosophy, still active, known as *general semantics*, which saw in our use of *words* a kind of surrender of the flexibility and refinement of thought for the sake of traffic in verbal *things*. Much was made of the uncritical use of generalizations, of the difficulty of pinning a statement like the following down to a set of precise referents: "It is the ability of a community to achieve consensus on the great issues and compromise on the lesser issues which lies at the heart of the democratic process. . . ."[1] The critical reader must ask: Can communities as a whole have abilities? Can the difference between great and small issues be recognized? Is there ever consensus without compromise? Is democracy a process? And so on.[2]

---

[1] Speech by W. W. Rostow of the U.S. Department of State, January 26, 1964.

[2] For an up-to-date statement of the general semanticist's position see S. I. Hayakawa, *Language in Thought and Action,* 2nd ed. (New York: Harcourt, Brace & World, Inc., 1964).

The Whorf hypothesis

It remained for a linguist, Benjamin Lee Whorf, to turn the question away from individual words and toward the structure of language as a whole. He was not the first to take this step—the German philologist Wilhelm von Humboldt (see Chapter 11, page 188) preceded him by a century—but he was the one most successful in dramatizing it. Whorf's perception of language as a pair of glasses with more or less warped lenses through which we view our surroundings was sharpened by his work with a language about as different from English as any language can be—that of the Hopi, a tribe of Pueblo Indians living in Arizona. Whorf had what Archimedes demanded in order to move the world—a place to stand; and he maintained that French or German or Russian was no good as a platform, since in fundamental structure these languages—in common with others of Indo-European stock—are the same.

One of the chief things that English and its sister languages fasten upon the experience of all their speakers is a prior categorization of the reality outside us into nouns and verbs. The noun pictures things as detached from the processes that surround them, making it possible to say *The wind blows* or *The light flashes*, though wind cannot exist apart from blowing nor flashing apart from light. Not only does it *enable* us to say such things, it *forces* us to: by itself, *snowing*, as our English teacher said, "is not a sentence"; where no subject is handy, we must throw in a plug for one: *It is snowing*. Whorf writes:

> English terms, like *sky, hill, swamp*, persuade us to regard some elusive aspect of nature's endless variety as a distinct *thing*, almost like a table or chair. . . . The real question is: What do different languages do, not with . . . artificially isolated objects but with the flowing face of nature in its motion, color, and changing form; with clouds, beaches, and yonder flight of birds? For as goes our segmentation in the face of nature, so goes our physics of the cosmos.[3]

Two examples will suffice to show the arbitrariness of this segmentation, its dependence upon the local interests and transitory needs of the culture that attempts it. The word *vitamin*, coined in 1912 to designate a group of substances supposed at the time to be amines, covers such a strange agglomeration of chemicals that the Merriam-Webster *Third International Dictionary* requires fourteen lines to define it, in spite of the fact that it is given only one sense. Yet to the average user of the term it seems to name something as clear and definite as the house next door. 'A thing in nature' becomes 'a thing in commerce,' and the pill-

---

[3] "Languages and Logic," *Technology Review*, April, 1941.

taker is not concerned with what it "really is." Similarly, the term *complex* was applied around 1910 to a combination of psychological factors that, as the name implies, were difficult to separate and simplify; but the existence of the term, and the identification of some particular ailment as a "complex," gave all that was needed for a new entry among our realities.

Coupled with a categorization of "thingness" in nouns is a categorization of "substance" in the subgrouping known as mass nouns, and English and related languages have a special technique of combining these with certain formalized "counters" in order to carve out segments: *a piece of meat, a glass of water, a blade of grass, a grain (bushel) of corn, a stalk of celery.* The resulting picture is one of a universe filled with taffy-like aggregations that can be clipped into pieces by our scheme of numbers: *earth, air, stone, iron, light, shade, fire, disease,* even—and especially— abstractions like *love, honor, dismay, courage, dictatorship,* and *accuracy.*

Out of this substance-operated-on-by-numbers, this notion of *jewels* as "contained in" *jewelry* and *guns* as "contained in" *artillery,* our language has evolved an elaborate vocabulary having to do with an all-containing *space*—the term *space* itself is a mass noun that subsumes in an abstract way all other mass nouns. And here is where the world view of our language departs most radically from that of the Hopi: our concepts of space are so pervasive that we are able to transfer them almost totally to *time.* We treat time as a mass, and carve it into units and count them: *five hours.* We use the same prepositions: *before, after, in, at;* the same adjectives: *long, short, same, different, right, wrong, hard, nice, more, less;* and many of the same nouns: *stretch* of time, *segment* of time, *amount* of time. And, of course, we capture events in our space-like nouns—the word *event* itself, plus *rain, dance, movement, stir, riot, invasion, courtship,* and countless others. This, Whorf points out, is almost never done in Hopi:

> Our own "time" differs markedly from Hopi "duration." It is conceived as like a space of strictly limited dimensions, or sometimes as like a motion upon such a space. . . . Hopi "duration" seems to be inconceivable in terms of space or motion, being the mode in which life differs from form, and consciousness *in toto* from the spatial elements of consciousness. . . . Our "matter" is the physical sub-type of "substance" or "stuff," which is conceived as the formless extensional item that must be joined with form before there can be any real existence. In Hopi there seems to be nothing corresponding to it; there are no formless extensional items; existence may or may not have form, but what it also has, with or without form, is intensity and duration, these being non-extensional and at bottom the same.

Our custom of quantifying time is illustrated by the sentence *Ten days is greater than nine days,* which contrasts with the Hopi expression of

the same idea in terms of duration, *The tenth day is later than the ninth.*[4]
Events of brief duration cannot be captured as nouns in Hopi: "lightning,
wave, flame, meteor, puff of smoke, pulsation, are verbs."[5]

So where Western philosophers—from Plato and Aristotle with their
concepts of matter and form to Kant with his *a priori* space and time—
have imagined that they were intuiting general laws that applied to all
of nature or at least to all of mankind, what they actually were doing was
exteriorizing a way of looking at things that they inherited from their
language. Much that is difficult in recent physics as well as in philosophy
and logic has been the struggle to climb out of this rut, all the harder to
escape because we are in it, unconsciously, from the moment we begin
to speak. Whorf surmised that a world view such as that of the Hopi
might be more congenial to the concepts of modern physics than the
languages of Western Europe. In a similar vein, Y. R. Chao has argued
that Chinese is more congenial than English to certain approaches of
symbolic logic.[6] For example, the normal Chinese *Yeou de ren shuo jen
huah* 'There are men who tell the truth' is closer to the logical formula
than is the normal English *Some men tell the truth.*

Partial escape from the trap

Linguists now feel that Whorf's position was exaggerated. Western philosophers and physicists *did* evolve their analyses in spite of their language; Whorf *does* explain his position in English, implying that a reader
of English can grasp the concepts that English presumably fails to
embody in its structure; *There are men who tell the truth is* an English
sentence, almost as commonplace as *Some men tell the truth;* and in some
ways language answers to nature rather than the other way around.[7] It
must be, then, that languages are more pluralistic than a catalog of their
bulkier categories seems to suggest. English escapes from its hidebound
subject-predicate, noun-verb formulas in the construction *There's singing
at the church,* using an *-ing* form whose *raison d'être* is precisely that it

---

[4] "The Relation of Habitual Thought and Behavior to Language," in *Four Articles on
Metalinguistics* (Washington, D.C.: Foreign Service Institute, U.S. Department of
State, 1949), pp. 37 and 24.

[5] Whorf, "Science and Linguistics," in John B. Carroll, ed., *Language, Thought, and
Reality* (Cambridge, Mass.: The Technological Press of M.I.T., 1957), p. 215.

[6] Y. R. Chao, "Notes on Chinese Grammar and Logic," *Philosophy East and West,*
5.31–41 (1955). Chao draws no sweeping conclusions.

[7] W. E. Bull, in his *Time, Tense, and the Verb* (Berkeley: University of California
Press, 1960), argues that this is even true of time, all languages being constrained
by the nature of time (or man's view of it) to express certain relationships in similar
ways.

does blur the line between noun and verb, and omits the subject. Another example is inceptiveness, the "get-going" phase of a continuing action, which many languages categorize sharply (Latin, for example, with the suffix *-escere*); to the casual outsider it might appear that English lacks suitable means for expressing this. But the lack is handily made up by liberal use of the verb *start*—in *He came in and called me names* we have the sensation of something left out; generally we want *He came in and started calling me names.* Many languages have clearly formalized categories of animate things and inanimate things, distinguished in the form of the words, and it might seem that English speakers, lacking the form, must also lack the appreciation; but English does not allow **I hit the car in the engine,* a normal construction with animate beings; a man may be *sick in the head,* but a car is never **broken in the clutch.* These and other examples suggest that the difference is not so much in kind as in explicitness and degree. What one language builds into the broadest layers of its structure another expresses informally and sporadically; but both have it.

All the same, this does not mean that some very common category in our language will not magnify certain of our ways of seeing things and diminish others. Better examples than those in comparisons of structure can be found in comparisons of lexical equivalence; for we do unquestionably "structure" our universe when we apply words to it, sometimes—especially when the phenomena are continuous and do not exhibit seams and sutures—quite arbitrarily.

The example most frequently cited is that of colors. The visual spectrum is a continuum which English parcels out into six segments: *purple, blue, green, yellow, orange,* and *red.* Of course painters, interior decorators, and others concerned with finer shades and saturations employ a more elaborate vocabulary; but the additional words are generally defined with those six as reference points: *turquoise* is 'between blue and green'; *reseda* is 'between green and yellow'; *saffron* is 'between yellow and orange.' In Zuni, orange and yellow are combined into a single range named *łupzʔinna* (whose borders are not necessarily the red end of orange and the green end of yellow—all we can say is that *łupzʔinna* roughly coincides with our orange plus our yellow). In Navaho, the two colors *łičíiʔ* and *łico* divide somewhere between red and orange-yellow. How these different habits of naming can affect our "thinking"—symptomized by the efficiency with which we communicate—can be shown through recognition tests: the monolingual Zuni, presented with a small set of different colors and then asked after a brief period to pick out the ones he saw from a much larger collection, will have trouble recognizing the ones for which his language does not have convenient names.[8] Other

---

[8] See Herbert J. Landar, Susan M. Ervin, and Arnold E. Horowitz, "Nahavo Color Categories," *Language* 36.368–82 (1960).

continuums present the same problem across languages—temperature, for example, where the English *hot-warm-cool-cold* do not coincide lexically or grammatically with the corresponding terms in other languages.[9]

Continuums are the limiting case. Where the experience is discrete, languages are apt to have more easily translatable terms. It would be strange if *dog* or *tooth* did not have a corresponding term in every language of the world, exactly equivalent at least in the central area of its meaning. But in between the continuums and the fragments are all the other things we experience, which are carved up in different ways. In Khacci a single verb is used for 'eat, drink, smoke.' English represents 'eat, drink' with *ingest* and 'eat, drink, smoke,' and a great deal more with *take in,* but the borderlines do not coincide. We are faced everywhere with a semantic mismatch that simply reflects the areas of experience that our culture renders important for us or—and here the dead hand of the past is laid on our eyes—at one time *did* consider important and now passes on to us in its old images. There is no reason to expect, for example, that any other language than English will give itself the luxury of insisting that a chicken *molts* but a snake *sheds,* or that any other language than Malayan will focus on the same minute and specific area as *kĕloṅkah-loṅkah,* 'the sound of loose planking straining in a ship in heavy weather.'[10] Yet each speech community patrols such distinctions relentlessly. The child who would rather not have to distinguish between *jar* and *bottle* is quickly driven into line.[11]

CONTROL THROUGH LANGUAGE

Neutrality and the "semantic differential"

If the lenses of our language that stand between us and reality are slightly warped, they are also tinted. It is one thing to see a certain kind of fish narrowed down to *eel;* it is something slightly different to see eels as repulsive creatures. Yet our language—plus other associations that we *act out* in connection with eels under the tutelage of fellow members of our culture—decrees both things: the focus and the affect. Every term we use apparently has the power to sway us in one direction or another. Experiments on this semantic differential, as it is called by the psychol-

---

[9] See Clifford H. Prator, "Adjectives of Temperature," *English Language Teaching* 17.158–64 (1963).

[10] J. Gonda in *Lingua* 2.173 (1950).

[11] See W. F. Leopold, "Semantic Learning in Infant Language," *Word* 4.179 (1948).

ogist Charles E. Osgood and his co-workers, show that persons presented with pairs of antonyms such as *wise-foolish, good-bad, deep-shallow, light-heavy,* and the like will relate other terms in rather consistent ways to each of these extremes, even when there seems to be no logical connection. The technique is to draw a seven-point scale with the antonyms at either end, for example

light ____ ____ ____ ____ ____ ____ ____ *heavy*

and to give subjects a term such as *skittish* with instructions to locate it at one of the points. While it would not be surprising, in view of associations with other terms such as *light-headed,* if everyone agreed that *skittish* ought to go well over to the "light" end, what is surprising is that subjects will even agree on where to locate something as apparently outlandish as *wood* on a scale between *severe* and *lenient.*[12]

Does this mean that, in addition to making us see reality in certain shapes and sizes, our language is also one of the most powerful factors in forcing us to take sides? If all the speakers of a given language share a prejudice, language will transmit it. Take for example the associations of insanity. Most of them are "funny": *crazy, nutty, loony, daffy, half-witted, hare-brained, loopy,* and so on. They reflect a culture in which psychopathological states are not diseases to be treated but deviations to be laughed at. It has required a vigorous reorientation of our attitudes to put mental disease on a footing other than ridicule or shame so that it *could* be treated. We can excuse language by saying that the way we behave colors the words we use; but it is just as fair to say that the words, in their daily use and with their associations, color the way we behave.

Of course, a competitive society results in competing values, and some measure of neutrality is thereby achieved. As one noted linguistic theorist declares, "The grammatical rules of a language are independent of any scale of values, logical, esthetic, or ethical."[13] Language is used by all parties to every controversy—Republicans and Communists, atheists and religionists, militarists and pacifists; by being pulled in all directions, it is forced to remain more or less impartial.

A better term would be *potentially* impartial. If people use language to get the cooperation of their fellows, then little if anything that is ever said is entirely neutral; communication is more often to influence than

---

[12] See Charles E. Osgood, George J. Suci, and Percy H. Tannenbaum, *The Measurement of Meaning* (Urbana: University of Illinois Press, 1957), and Uriel Weinreich, "Travels Through Semantic Space," *Word* 14.346–66 (1958).

[13] Louis Hjelmslev, *Prolegomena to a Theory of Language,* trans. Francis J. Whitfield (Madison: University of Wisconsin Press, 1961), p. 110.

to inform. From the orator or advertising man who calculatingly chooses expressions that will sway his audience to the scientist who in his enthusiasm over his discovery calls it *proof* or *an important departure,* every speaker is guilty of decorating his information. And since everyone does it, the devices for doing it inhere in the language and are hard to avoid even when we try.

If accusing language of this form of seduction seems a strange idea, we can trace our surprise once more to the false importance that our culture gives to writing. Some degree of impartiality can be achieved in print. But in speech we must contend with intonation and its running emotional commentary, insinuating whether we like what we say, whether it is said to persuade or command or to abase ourselves or overawe another, and in which some elements are always more highly colored and stand out as more important than others. Leaving this out, as writing manages to do in part, creates the illusion of uncolored fact. The colors are still there, only paler.

What distinguishes the world-view distortion that we saw in English versus Hopi from the suasive coloring that we are considering now is that the first manifested an indeterminacy of *things* with respect to *language,* while the second manifests an indeterminacy of *language* with respect to *things.* In the first, the very form and substance with which reality is revealed to us was affected; in the second, within a single language a given bit of reality can be *presented* in more than one way. Both processes are normally unconscious, but the first is seldom otherwise while the second may be not only conscious but deliberately and often maliciously cultivated. The degree of consciousness corresponds fairly well with the grading of linguistic devices from crude to subtle, from straightforward lexical name-calling to the hidden bias of a syntactical construction.

Naming

As we inherit our nouns—and the categorizations of reality that they represent—we also inherit the right to *make* nouns, which is one of the few truly inventive privileges that our language affords us: anyone can make up a name for something and many people do, while inventing a new suffix or a new syntactic pattern is practically impossible.

The act of naming, with all we have seen it to imply in the way of solidifying and objectifying experience, becomes one of our most powerful suasive tools, enabling us to create entities practically out of nothing. The speaker who says *We want no undesirables around here* projects his inner dislikes onto the outer world. Turning *undesirable* into a noun makes it possible to avoid a clearly tautological *We don't want the people we don't want.* A noun tells us "It is there; it is something that can or ought to be dealt with": as long as people were left to their own resources to find things to do, 'being without work' was generally a matter of choice or ability; when large numbers became dependent upon industry, the condition was objectified as **unemployment.** We are used to having *things* about us; naming reassures us that the elusive threat has been cornered:

> I learned a useful trick from a certain noted doctor. I wondered how he got by without the criticism I encountered when I failed in an attempt to get fluid from the pleural cavity. Occasionally, following pneumonia or pleurisy, fluid will accumulate between the lung and the chest wall, giving such discomfort that it must be drawn off. Whenever I tapped a side and failed to find what I was looking for, the patient or relatives would question my skill, but the noted doctor seemed to be able to create increased confidence, even if he failed to find the fluid.
>
> I finally learned his secret, when I had an opportunity to call him in consultation on a case of suspected pus in the pleural cavity. He asked for a hollow needle, and pierced the chest wall several times without getting a drop. With an air of satisfaction, he turned to the patient and parents, and exclaimed, "Ah, great! I've got it!"
>
> "What is it, Doctor?" cried the interested ones.
>
> "A dry tap! A dry tap! Splendid! Better than I expected!" The patient and relatives said, "Isn't it wonderful? A dry tap." Everybody was happy, and the noted doctor remained noted.[14]

The importance of the name, rather than the real virtues, of a commercial product is proved by the long record of litigation over trade names like *aspirin* and *cola.*

Favorable and unfavorable naming: epithets

Over and above the mere fact of naming—which already to some extent prejudices the case—is the clearly prejudicial application of epithets, terms that are crudely and frankly favorable or unfavorable. We find them in all four of the "content" parts of speech—nouns, adjectives, verbs, and adverbs—and they operate at all levels of awareness; but in general the adjective and adverb are more aboveboard than the noun or the verb. If someone says *That wretched picture bored me to death,* the hearer can deal with the detachable adjective and, if he likes, replace it: *I didn't think it was wretched; I thought it was interesting.* Similarly with *He deliberately insulted me*—the hearer is free to substitute *But perhaps*

---

[14] J. A. Jerger, M. D., "City Doctor," *American Magazine,* February, 1939.

he did it unintentionally. The adjective and adverb are a kind of simile, an overt and explicit attachment of one idea to another. The noun and verb are metaphors: the comparison is smuggled in, the person or thing or act is not *like* something good or bad but *is* that something. It is no coincidence that many epithets actually are metaphors of fairly recent memory: *He is a bum, He is a prince, She is an angel, She is a tramp, She cackled, He brayed.* The hidden temptations that the lexicon offers the average user of the language are practically irresistible. Most of the areas of our experience are mapped out epithetically, and the person who wants to steer a middle course has to keep his eye constantly on the narrow and shifting channel between good and bad. The most insidious examples are not the ordinary antonyms like *clumsy-graceful, easy-difficult,* or *democratic-fascistic* but terms that are synonyms in that they name the same objective fact, antonyms in the attitude that they solicit toward the fact (see table below).

Favorable	Quasi-neutral	Unfavorable
convert		apostate
upright, righteous, virtuous		goody-goody, puritanical, prissy
conciliation		appeasement
patriotism		chauvinism, jingoism
defense		militarization
aide, right-hand man		lackey, bootlicker
far-sighted, man of vision		visionary, starry-eyed idealist
brilliant		show-off
liquidate		murder
smile		leer
indoctrination		brainwashing
progress	change	reaction
intercede	intervene	interfere, butt in
attorney	lawyer	shyster
bachelor girl	unmarried woman	old maid

A brief history of the term *hoarding* will illustrate how epithets fluctuate in popularity, how they are applied in different situations to influence action, and how the colorful import outweighs the literal one.

Hoarding is now used with the connotation of 'undesirable saving'—rather, we should say that this is the way the dictionary would condense the real and somewhat disparate connotations that the word has had from time to time. The primitive sense had to do with the laying by and keeping of goods. As happened with so many Old English words, this one eventually leaned toward the unfavorable. In the present century it has enjoyed two periods in the limelight, the first in 1932–33 and the second in 1942. The first grew out of the Depression, when persons owning money or securities were frightened into holding them and spending as little as possible. This created a tight-money situation that aggravated the causes that had produced it. Articles appeared with titles like "Insurance Policies as Hoarding" and "How to Bring Currency from Hoarding."

A year later the reference changed. In 1933 the United States abandoned the gold standard, gold coin was called in, and when it was announced that the government was going to pursue hoarders, everyone knew that gold hoarding was implied. From 1934 to 1937 the word all but dropped from view; but the 1937 recession brought out a brief flurry of examples in 1938, with the same meaning as in 1932. The year 1939 saw it wane again, but the war fright of 1940 battened savings down once more, and the cry of *hoarding* was used again in 1940 and 1941 to pry them loose.

The second upsurge occurred in 1942 with the entry of the United States into the war and the threat of rationing. *Hoarding* now meant 'the undesirable saving of trade goods for consumers, especially food.' Six articles on this type of hoarding appeared in national magazines in April alone.[15]

After the war, with plenty of money and no rationing, *hoarding* fell into disuse. The fallout shelter campaign of 1959–62 brought advice from the government to do—with food and other necessities—the very thing that two decades earlier would have been deemed unpatriotic. But now it was called *stocking up* or *stockpiling*.

Elevation and degradation

Since the epithet is language aimed at the heart of social action, it is bound to receive from the culture as well as give to it. While we are not

---

[15] I am indebted to Betty Collins for these data, gathered from indices to contemporary literature.

concerned here with semantic change—that is a question of the evolution of language—but rather with the existence at any one time of linguistic forms that influence us, it is pertinent to note how the stock of terms with favorable or unfavorable connotations is maintained against the social realities that undermine it. Two processes are at work, or rather two directions of a single process, which are generally called *elevation* and *degradation*. If for reasons that have little or nothing to do with language a thing that has carried an unfavorable name begins to move up in the world, the name moves up with it. In religion, many once-opprobrious names have faded. Probably the majority of religious eponyms—names imitating the personal name of the founder—were to begin with unfavorable; but many were in time adopted by the followers of the religion (**Christian, Lutheran, Calvinist**), others have become milder (**Campbellite**), and few but the most recent might still be resented (**Russellite, Buchmanite**).

The opposite effect is observed in the negative associations of a term attached to something that moves down. Where **captives** were put to menial tasks and forced to live wretchedly, **caitiff** took on the meaning of 'wretch, villain.' As we saw earlier (Chapter 7, page 109), where separation of the races came to be viewed as morally wrong **segregation** was debased. The most prolific source of negative connotation and of the constant replacement of terms that are downgraded is the phenomenon of social *taboo*. The taboo against strong language results in minced oaths: **darn** for **damn, gee** for **Jesus**. The taboo against referring to certain bodily functions results in a succession of replacements, each term being discarded as it too vividly and nontechnically comes to suggest its referent: H. L. Mencken listed two pages of synonyms for *latrine*,[16] itself borrowed as a polite word from French (it originally meant the same as one of its modern substitutes, 'washroom'). What was a denatured term for one generation ceases to be for the next one, as the direct association with the buried taboo reasserts itself.

This denaturing process we have identified as *euphemism* (see Chapter 7, pages 111–12). In political life, favorable reference to the enemy is taboo: in World War I **sauerkraut** became **liberty cabbage** and the **Katzenjammer Kids** were renamed the **Shenanigan Kids;** in 1940 the Nazis changed the name of **Wilson Station** in Prague to **Main Station**. Likewise in politics, it is taboo to admit the unpleasant; so we have **fair trade** for **price-fixing, training** for **conscription, depression** (and later **recession**) for **panic, casualties** for **dead and wounded**. As one writer points out, "If you hear someone say that it is time for a government to

---

[16] *The American Language, Supplement One* (New York: Alfred A. Knopf, Inc., 1945), pp. 640–41.

follow a realistic line, you can interpret this as meaning that it is time for principles to be abandoned."[17] The same taboo applies doubly to the business world. One could find material for an essay on how not to say *small:* in soap brands we find series like *giant, family,* and *regular; large, medium,* and *guest; giant, large,* and *medium.* The word *pint* has virtually disappeared from beverage sizes—it is now the *half quart. Imitation* becomes *costume* (jewelry) or *simulated* (pearls). Radio and television *advertisements* become *announcements.* Hair *dye* becomes *rinse.* A *salary cut* becomes an *adjustment.* And so on. Ordinary noncommercial and non-political euphemisms, which cover our nakedness and other shortcomings, tend to be humorous: the plea is not to elevation but to tolerance. *Belly* becomes, besides the elevated *abdomen,* the facetious *paunch, corporation, bay window,* and *embonpoint.* A *libertine* is a *wolf.* The synonyms of *drunk* have proliferated to the point where a nonsense word inserted in the blank of *He was just a little bit* ____ will suggest it.

Hints and associations

The ordinary epithet or euphemism is a bludgeon. True finesse is found among the less obvious loaded terms that hint rather than designate. Here the "semantic differential" comes into its own. The associated term is not obviously epithetical and therefore gets past our guard; but it is colored, darkly or brightly, and the color rubs off.

The lexicon abounds in loosely associated semantic sets having intimate ties with codes and practices in society, which for lack of a better name will be called *norm classes.* They comprise a catalog of "fors" and "againsts" to which we pay unthinking and often ritualistic respect. The norm classes—the associated word sets—are enough by themselves to invoke this respect. Merely mentioning one of the words will command it.[18]

Since human circumstances are always particular, never general, the problem with any particular act, in order to give it a place in a well-regulated society, is to fit it to the proper symbol. The extreme case is

[17] Mary McCarthy in *Harper's Magazine,* July, 1961, p. 46.

[18] C. Wright Mills dubbed the cruder manifestations of norm classes "vocabularies of motive" (*American Sociological Review,* December, 1940, pp. 904–13). The ideas that embody or are embodied in the complex of norm classes and the social norms themselves were called "idols" by Francis Bacon and more recently have been termed "symbols" by Franz Boas (*The Nation,* August 27, 1938, p. 203), Howe Martyn ("Symbolism in Advertising," *Frontier,* January, 1967, pp. 9–11), and others.

that of interpretative law: a homicide has been committed; the jurors must determine whether it was *self-defense* or *murder*. *Self-defense* belongs to the norm class of *preservation of life, a man's house is his castle, resistance to aggression,* and so on. *Murder* belongs to that of *destruction of life, taking the law into one's own hands, disobedience to the Commandments,* and so on.

A less dramatic example is the norm class of *clothed (covered, decent, modest)* versus that of *naked (exposed, immodest, exhibitionist).* As beach attire has grown scantier and scantier, bathers can be said to be approaching a state of nakedness; yet the emphasis is on the fact that they do have something on, and this has usually been enough to prevent legal interference. And we may be sure that if ever the last vestige is cast off, it will be in the name of *nature (Praxiteles, Michelangelo, the nobility of the human figure),* not of *nakedness.*

Very early in life the child is made aware that he is expected to justify himself; in the average home, by the time he is able to talk almost every youngster faces the inquisition of "Why did you do it?" after any willful act. Propriety is served almost as well, it would seem, by our picking the right norm class for what was done thoughtlessly as by thoughtfully choosing the right behavior in the first place; and in the course of time we become quite expert at it. If we admire Russian communism, we call it the Russian *experiment,* attaching it to the norm class of *scientific investigation, withholding judgment until results are in, condoning temporary mistakes,* and so on. If we disapprove of reparations payments to Cuba, we call them *ransom,* which suggests both *kidnaping* and *cowardice.* Where the American public might have condemned dispatching *troops* to Nicaragua in 1927, no excitement was aroused by the sending of *marines;* the word had romantic associations.[19] Hitting upon the right norm class gives the emotional release of discovery, and skill at doing it is esteemed: the person accused of running up a *white flag* wins the argument by saying that he ran up a *white banner.*

A frequently used shift of norm class involves substituting a *physical* context for a *social* one—an instance of the fallacy of reduction. A man interfering with police work by erasing the chalk marks left by a traffic officer might say that he was only *rubbing off white stuff;* one arrested for profanity might justify the offense as an act of *merely emitting sounds.* The classical example of the fallacy of reduction is "The table in front of you is only atoms."

---

[19] Frederick Alexander Kirkpatrick, *Latin America, a Brief History* (New York: Macmillan Co., 1939), p. 371.

Speech level

On the surface it appears that when a speaker shifts from one style of speech to another, he does so with the intention of influencing his hearer in other ways than directly through his message. It is not necessary for the style adopted to be one that was previously out of the speaker's normal range (as when an American imitates a Southern British accent), though that is the kind of shift whose latent purpose is most evident since he is apt to be clumsy at it. He may shift from one level to another within his average capabilities, to keep himself in tune with his audience—a labor official addressing members of his local in their union hall does not use the same modes of expression as when he addresses a ladies' discussion group.

Viewed this way, the very existence of a number of different speech levels within a single society appears to answer to suasion in some form or other. But viewed differently the observation is trivial; it is the same as saying that when I address my English-speaking friends in English rather than in German I do so with a concealed motive. The motive, if one can call it that, is simply to be understood; and if my speech level within English is consonant with that of my hearers, it is to be better understood, to have nothing in my speech that will distract. Even the phenomenon of speakers adopting a dialect other than their own in order to be accepted by the members of some other group can be likened to that of learning another language in order to be accepted by its community of speakers. The desire to belong can hardly be separated from the desire to communicate.

Nevertheless, there are shifts of level whose primary intent is to influence rather than to be understood. The test is simple: instead of aiding understanding they interfere with it, and are used anyway. The typical example in our society is *authoritative language*, adopted on suitable occasions by anyone who wants to impress his reader or hearer, but most characteristic of bureaucrats and writers of official reports. It is a conglomeration of abstract vocabulary and grammatical involutions that yields such things as *It is imperative that the present directive be effectuated expeditiously* where the meaning is *Do it now*. One famous example was the order concerning blackouts during World War II, submitted to President Roosevelt for his approval:

> Such preparations shall be made as will completely obscure all Federal buildings and non-Federal buildings occupied by the Federal Government during an air raid for any period of time from visibility by reason of internal or external illumination. Such obscuration may be obtained either by blackout construction or by termination of the illumination. This will,

of course, require that in building areas in which production must continue during the blackout, construction must be provided that internal illumination may continue. Other areas, whether or not occupied by personnel, may be obscured by terminating the illumination.

The President amended this to:

> Tell them that in buildings where they have to keep the work going, to put something across the window. In buildings where they can afford to let the work stop for a while, turn out the lights.[20]

Americans have perhaps been more severely bitten by aspirations of grandeur than other speakers of English. At least, its symptoms have been with us for a long time and its condemnation likewise. James Fenimore Cooper remarked that the man of true breeding "does not say, in speaking of a dance, that 'the attire of the ladies was exceedingly elegant and peculiarly becoming at the late assembly,' but 'the women were well dressed at the last ball'; nor is he apt to remark, that 'the Rev. Mr. G_____ gave us an elegant and searching discourse the past sabbath,' but, that 'the parson preached a good sermon last Sunday.' "[21] Cooper himself was no angel of clarity. In *The Last of the Mohicans* he wrote, "Without any aid from the science of cookery, he was immediately employed, in common with his fellows, in gorging himself with this digestible sustenance." Mark Twain chided him: "This was a mere statistic; just a mere cold, colorless statistic; yet you see Cooper has made a chromo out of it. . . . Cooper spent twenty-four words here on a thing not really worth more than eight. We will reduce the statistic to its proper proportions and state it this way: 'He and the others ate the meat raw.' "[22]

Authoritative language has its stereotypes, which are designed to impress. But its success is also due to another quirk of human nature, our willingness to accept complication for profundity. Where profound thoughts make for hard words, hard words pass for profound thoughts.

Constructional non-neutrality

Words are plentiful enough to supply all needs, suasive and other. It is possible, as we have seen, to have a class of epithets whose primary pur-

---

[20] Associated Press dispatch, March 11, 1942.

[21] Quoted by Mitford M. Mathews, *The Beginnings of American English* (Chicago: University of Chicago Press, 1931), p. 127. See also James Thurber, "The Psychosemanticist Will See You Now, Mr. Thurber," *New Yorker*, May 28, 1955, pp. 28–31, and Ethel Strainchamps, "Caveat Scriptor," *Harper's Magazine*, August, 1960, pp. 24–27.

[22] *Letters from the Earth* (New York: Harper & Row, Inc., 1962), p. 140.

pose is to influence, besides other words tinged in every imaginable degree.

Structures are too few to exhibit this variety. A prepositional phrase cannot *per se* be specialized for suasion, since it has too many other things to do. Nevertheless, certain structures are enabled to compete at least partly by lending themselves better than others do to suasive uses. In syntax, "competition" implies some sort of transformational relationship: is the passive voice, for example, better suited than the active to some form of suasion?

[1] **Intonation**   Intonation is the one part of linguistic structure whose chief function is suasion. An intonation contour is *intended* to influence the attitude of the hearer toward what is said. This is clearest in solicitations—questions and commands—where information content is generally low; and these types of utterance are the ones most sharply demarcated by intonation. But it is also true of statements, for which intonation wins acceptance by contours of commanding or wheedling, besides putting the hearer on notice about a number of other things. Examples were given in the earlier section on intonation (Chapter 3, pages 30–34).

[2] **Morphology**   Contributions at this level are actually to the lexicon of epithets. Certain bound morphemes are themselves very nearly epithetical, and are used mainly in coining words that are definitely so. A label of the 1964 presidential campaign was **Goldwaterism,** with the suffix *-ism,* nowadays found most frequently in epithets: **McCarthyism, reductionism, fascism.** The related suffix *-ite* is similarly used, as are the prefix *pro-* and the suffix *-phile* in **pro-German, pro-Hitler, Francophile, Russophile.** English is not as systematic in its pejorative and meliorative affixes as some other languages are, but their number is still large: *-phobe, -kin, -let, -ify, -itis, -ette, -ling, -ese,* and so on. There is no clear semantic borderline between deriving with affixes *(Negrophile)* and compounding with words *(nigger-lover),* and even the morphological line is not clear *(downgrade, degrade).*

An instance of a suffix that is not in itself suasive but is heavily used in epithets is -/ər/, spelled *-er* or *-or.* The epithetical use trades on a fraudulent association. Normally this suffix means a "professional, habitual agent";[23] a *singer* is one who sings, an *actor* one who acts, a *bookseller*

---

[23] Hans Marchand in *Language* 42.138 (1966).

one who sells books, and so on, all referring to *occupations*. The epithet adopts this for things that are not occupations, implying that the person stigmatized does them as consistently as if they were: *hymn-singer, boot-licker, trouble-maker, muckraker, Bible-banger, herring-choker, mud-slinger*. It may go even further, making the same allusion with an act that is performed just once: a person who tells a single lie is a *liar;* one who deserts just once is a *deserter* or *defector;* one who commits only one murder is a *murderer*. It is as if to say, 'These acts, like occupations, brand indelibly.' Though it is out of place here, we may note an identical use of the perfect tense, which is normally 'indefinite' as to time and whose indefiniteness is capitalized upon to suggest persistence of effects. Of a man who was in jail once, we say *He has been in jail,* no matter how long ago it was. We would not say *He is suing because he has been turned away from that hotel* if the situation is that he was turned away two years ago; but we might well say *He is suing because he has been accused of disloyalty,* when the accusation was two years in the past—this is something that puts its brand on a man.

[3] **Syntax**   The syntactic devices that lend themselves to suasion fall into three classes: animation, indeterminacy, and ambiguity.

Animation—the attributing of qualities of living beings to inert things—is a device for shifting responsibility, for making ourselves out to be the victims of circumstance rather than its masters. The syntactic fulcrum is the verb, typically reflexive, with inactive (usually impersonal) subject and often with personal object. In describing an automobile accident, a speaker may say *I was driving down the street when all of a sudden that other car presented itself broadside to me,* or *I was driving down the street when all of a sudden that other car aimed itself directly amidships at me;* either way, he wins—the responsibility is on the other car, which is pictured as capable of self-directed action.

The devices of animation, of course, are mixed—they are part syntactic and part lexical. Our syntax facilitates it because it permits us to fill the "actor" slot—suggesting, of course, capability of action—with anything we please. Our lexicon facilitates it by providing reflexive verbs, or by permitting a verb to be used both transitively and intransitively, or by offering semantic pairs like *fall-drop* and *escape-forget*. Examples of the first are the *presented itself* and *aimed itself* sentences just quoted. Examples of the second are *It broke (on me)* instead of *I broke it* and *It tripped me* instead of *I tripped over it*. The third is exemplified by *It escaped me (slipped my mind)* instead of *I forgot it* and *It fell (out of my hands)* instead of *I dropped it.* Here also belong the verbs *seem* and *appear,* which pair with *infer, see,* and so on, and with which the inactive subject is often personal: **Smith seems to offer only three explanations,** a common excuse given by reviewers of books that saves the trouble of re-reading and counting up to four. The forthright equivalent is **As far as I have taken the trouble to see, Smith offers only three explanations.**

Another syntactic device for evading responsibility is *modification in noun phrases,* and the freedom with which it is allowed to shift sometimes from one element to another. When we permit a modification like **red paint** we imply something close to a logical proposition: "There is paint that is red.' But now and then we throw in the modifier almost at random, trusting to luck that the hearer will attach it where it belongs: **She's lost her first tooth** for 'She's had her first loss of a tooth,' **Put on some warm clothing** for 'Put on some clothing that will keep you warm,' **There is a definite shortage** for 'There is definitely a shortage,' and so on. This makes it possible to refer to a **careless mistake** or an **uncertain origin** instead of 'a mistake made by a careless person' or 'an origin about which people are uncertain.' The heavy dependence of modifiers on context leaves a convenient loophole through which we can pass and shed our ineptitude on the way or deal politely with another's ineptitude.

Indeterminacy finds its place in those structures where some item of information is left out and the speaker is able to take advantage of its absence. In the active voice, the presence of a grammatical subject is obligatory; in the passive, the corresponding noun phrase with *by* may be omitted: **Joe Doakes accuses President of bad faith, President accused of bad faith (by Joe Doakes).** The ordinary speaker will use the passive with *got* to escape responsibility: **The dishes got broken;** or will use the passive with *be,* omitting the *by* phrase, to suggest that the agent transcends mere individual human beings: "As a white housewife in a Birmingham supermarket told Robert Baker of the *Washington Post* (September 19), it [the retaliation against Negroes] was 'terrible' but 'that's what they get for trying to force their way where **they're not wanted.'** "[24] (The passive here does much the same thing as the noun **undesirables** in the example on page 259.) One verb is stereotyped in this way: **to be supposed to.** Newspapers use the passive with *be*—but with *be* omitted in headlines—to cover up the insignificance of the actor. It seems safe to say that part of the survival value of the passive voice is that it enables the speaker to be noncommittal.

Ambiguity is the suasive device most apt to be consciously dishonest. Lexical ambiguity is fairly easy to detect. The word **brown,** for example,

---

[24] *I. F. Stone's Bi-Weekly,* September 30, 1963, p. 8.

signifies 'brown in color,' but also, in the compound *brown sugar,* signifies a certain process of manufacture in which cane sugar retains some of its color. A refiner of beet sugar has taken advantage of the ambiguity to market as *brown sugar* a mixture of refined beet sugar, molasses, and coloring.

Constructional ambiguity is more elusive, but certain types have been heavily used, especially in advertising. One is the unmodified subject: *Athletes have found chewing a natural aid to high-speed effort.* The subject in this construction may mean 'some athletes' or 'all athletes.' The advertiser protects himself legally with the first meaning and hopes that the reader will infer the second. We have already seen a similar perversion of the perfect tense: *John Jones has switched to X whiskey* is literally true but trades on the 'persistence of effects' implication of the perfect tense, which may or may not be true.

A study of the uses of ambiguity makes us realize that probably the most important ingredient of communication is the attitude of the communicators toward each other: an intention on the part of the speaker not to misinform, and good will on the part of the hearer in trying to interpret as the speaker intends. Literal truth is not enough, if for no other reason than because there is so much about language that is always present but only vaguely inferred and scarcely subject to definition. Take for example the simple matter of coordination in a sentence and the matter of sequence of the items coordinated, and what we infer from these two things. Coordination implies 'These items are on the same level': we do not say *°He is an embezzler and a lover of horses,* even though each part of the coordination taken separately may be true. As for sequence, if there is a possibility of inferring one item from another we normally place first the one on which the inference can be based: *The clock is accurate and dependable* is more likely than *The clock is dependable and accurate; The house is broken down and uninhabitable* is more likely than *The house is uninhabitable and broken down.* So when a certain brand of meal puts on its package the statement *Enriched and degerminated,* it is falsifying on both counts. Enrichment and degermination do not belong on the same level, and nothing about degermination can be inferred from enrichment. The reader is tricked into regarding degermination, which he only vaguely grasps anyway, as a virtue. A truthful statement would read, "We are ashamed to say that in order to keep the stuff from spoiling we had to remove the germ, but we *did* add some synthetic vitamins to compensate for the loss."

A language that would enable us to report things as they are and that would be used by speakers without the infusion of their own personalities and prejudices is the ideal of every science; and every science has to some extent developed a denatured language to make this possible. But whether our human condition will permit it to be realized generally is doubtful; if Whorf was right, we do not grasp things as they are but always to some extent as our language presents them to us—or, in broader terms, as our society incorporates them in terms of all its habits of acting and talking. And as for avoiding the body heat of our likes and dislikes, the irony is that scientific language itself takes on authoritative overtones. The moment it finds its way into general use, we are plagued as much by pseudo-scientific pretentiousness as by any other form of non-neutrality. It would seem that language is bound to be suasive as long as it is human, that the effort to be neutral cannot be carried out in the language as a whole but must represent a will and a purpose in each small act of speech.

ADDITIONAL REMARKS
AND APPLICATIONS

1. How might language be one basis for animistic religion? What would be the concluding sentence in the following proportion?

   The man moves : The man sleeps :: The sun moves :

2. A number of colleges and universities are abandoning the system of academic "credits" as a way of measuring the work done by students. What might some of their objections be to keeping *credit* as an entity among our realities?

3. Compare the following two statements and comment on the view of time and activity they imply:

   a. *He gave me more time to finish the work.*
   b. *He allowed me to consummate later.*

4. Even where a category thoroughly permeates a language structure, it may have little or no semantic value. In the Romance languages, for example, *gender* affects nouns and adjectives and has a certain semantic basis in words that actually discriminate according to sex (*mother,* feminine; *soldier,* masculine). For speakers of these languages would words like *table, house, vision,* which are feminine, or *foot, tree, danger,* which are masculine, carry a sexual connotation?

5. English compels us to distinguish *brothers* from *sisters* (if we want to be scientific we can refer to *siblings*), forbids us to distinguish *cousins* (we have to resort to compounds, *girl cousin* and *boy cousin*—but what about when they are grown, *man cousin* and *woman cousin*?), and gives us a choice with our immediate ancestors (*parents* or *mother* and *father*). What is the situation with such family terms in other languages you may know? Make a chart showing the terms in relation to gender and number.

   See if you can find other sets like *stand-sit-lie, walk-run, fog-mist-drizzle-sprinkle-rain-downpour-deluge,* where another language would be apt to carve up the continuum in a different way.

6. In large segments of Western society, sex is regarded as "dirty." Is this partly due to the associated vocabulary? Has it provoked a reaction in the opposite direction from neutrality, with favorable associations like "naturalness," "beauty of the human figure," and so on?

   Consider racial segregation as partially a problem of associated vocabulary.

7. Discuss the adjective *unwelcome* in *I rejected his unwelcome suggestion* as a disguised sub-sentence (see Chapter 11, page 207). Find other examples of how we exploit syntactic disguises for ulterior purposes.

8. List the favorable or unfavorable counterparts of the following words: *stingy, portly, innuendo, sawbones, prodigal, slim, conspiracy.*

9. *Mischievous* originally meant 'harmful.' What has happened to it? What kind of parental attitude has caused this change? What has happened to the once-neutral word *informer?*

10. Comment on the words *conscript-draftee-trainee-selectee* as an attempt to sweeten compulsory military service. What is each new term an instance of?

11. Comment on the following: "When a crime is committed by someone else, the average citizen wants to know all about it; he calls that Free Press. But when he himself is involved in a crime, the average citizen wants it kept out of the papers; he calls that Fair Trial."[25]

12. Terms like *adjustment, revision,* and *new scale* belong to an economic norm class that is often appealed to. Discuss their relationship to *lowering* wages and *raising* prices.

13. Translate the following sentences to ordinary English:

    a. The major limitation on the exchange programs of the Department of State appears to be their chronic fiscal starvation.

    b. The principal use of federal funds today is to accelerate the development of particular university resources when university priorities in on-going programs do not accord with national needs.[26]

---

25 *The Nation,* April 11, 1966, p. 421.

26 These two passages are from Harold Boeschenstein, *et al., The University and World Affairs* (New York: Ford Foundation, 1960).

c. The evolution of an optimum scientific payload will require a continuing dialogue among all potential investigators and the engineers responsible for implementing their scientific goals.[27] ("Scientific payload" refers to the cargo of instruments that a space craft would carry for an exploration of Mars.)

14. Is part of the suasive impact of -er words, especially compounds, due to humorous or contemptuous metaphor? Consider *head-shrinker* 'psychiatrist,' *pill-pusher* 'doctor,' *ambulance-chaser* 'lawyer.' Find others.

15. Comment on the use of *proudest* in the following: *The President has now signed the Bail Reform Act of 1966, affecting Federal bail practices. It is the proudest experiment that I have ever been connected with.*[28]

16. Comment on the following:

    a. *My memory played a trick on me.*

    b. *Smith gives the impression that he doesn't care.*

    c. *You have drawn a foolish conclusion.*

    d. *He is rumored to be in love with his neighbor's wife.*

    e. *Appetite improves 100% with Polyvims.*

    f. *He can't vote because he has been convicted of a felony.*

17. Consider what is implied by the order of the items in the following: *French bread consists of flour, water, salt, and yeast; I like bread and butter; Steel is iron and carbon; The shipment contained several books, pamphlets, and leaflets; The present she gave me was a shirt and tie.* (To test this, try reversing them.)

    Now comment on the following phrases appearing on the labels of canned goods: *Pork and beans; Mixed nuts, containing Brazil nuts, pecans, walnuts, cashews, and peanuts* (the can actually contains two each of the first four items, the rest consisting of peanuts).

18. Discuss the term *mind-expanding,* as applied to certain drugs, in the light of norm classes. Contrast it with *hallucinatory.*

---

[27] Quoted by Theodore M. Bernstein, *New York Times Magazine,* July 4, 1965, p. 13.

[28] Justice Bernard Botein, quoted in *New York Times Magazine,* January 15, 1967, p. 44.

SOME PRACTICAL MATTERS 14

AUTHORITY IN LANGUAGE

HELL IS FOR THOSE who are offered the light but spurn it. The heathen is blameless if he ignores a gospel that he has never heard, but damnation awaits our neighbor who has been shown the way and refuses to take it. Speakers of a foreign language are like the heathen; they are forgivable because their only fault has been the lack of opportunity to learn to talk as we do. The speaker of some unfamiliar dialect of our own language we resent because he has had the opportunity—he proves this by the fact that we can usually understand him—but has obviously misapplied it. The foreigner is so unlike us that we can make no invidious comparisons; he challenges our magnanimity. The native speaker betrays himself by being intelligible and nevertheless not getting things quite right—something about his intonation or the way he drawls his vowels or gestures a shade too slowly or a shade too fast fails to measure up to standard. And the standard, naturally, is the way we ourselves talk and the way we look and act when we talk.

The universal dislike of variation is a reflection of the conventional nature of language. The efficiency of a convention depends on its observance: the slightest deviation is the threat of a greater one and must be stamped out. A community can be educated to disregard this threat to a certain extent—it is the mark of a wider humanism to be able to overlook differences; but our primitive social desire for uniformity continuously asserts itself. The pressure to abolish differences in behavior—above all in linguistic behavior—is unrelenting.

276

Fortunately we are not single-minded in demanding recognition for our particular mode of speech but are willing to acquiesce in a larger standard. This comes from long practice. A language community is not a closed guild to which only journeymen are admitted. It is an open union numbering both masters and apprentices in all stages of in-service training. There are always learners—outsiders moving in, young generations moving up. As children we all accept authority; the habit of learning and willingness to take others as guides is implanted early and never lost.

So authority in language imposes itself by the need to keep variations at a minimum and by our willingness to make certain adjustments in our own speech to keep it in line with the speech of others. But uniformity is never achieved without some discomfort, and when it is laid on with a touch of arrogance the resentments boil over. In our time these have prompted attacks on purism and counterattacks on permissiveness, with embattled progressives on one side and conservatives on the other, and angry disputes over whether Johnny is being properly disciplined in his English class.

Two kinds of authority

A language or dialect can impose its authority formally or informally. Informal authority is the pressure exerted by the speakers with whom the individual identifies himself. It needs no formulated rules but serves as a model to follow and acts immmediately—through the surprise, incomprehension, or amusement of its users—to drive offenders back into line. The mistakes are not identified. Nobody takes the trouble to catalog them and give them names. They are fumbles, without status.

Informal authority is inseparable from the speech level or geographical or occupational dialect that enforces it. It may be oriented in any direction: a literary speaker may be ridiculed into being colloquial or a colloquial one into being literary. Until he learns the jargon every newcomer feels out of place, and whether it is high or low, nautical or rural, Northeastern or Midwestern, makes no difference.

Formal authority, on the other hand, is self-conscious. Rules of correctness are its stock in trade. It comes into existence where informal authority cannot be exercised in the normal way. Informal authority depends on the overpowering effect of the many on the few. One newcomer in a community does not need a school to teach him how to speak, nor does the youngest child in a family where everyone else is more versed in the language than he is require more than their presence to keep him straight. But where large groups of aspirants are isolated from their models, the latter must assume artificial forms—codified rules and schools to transmit them. The situation is much the same as that of one who tries to learn a foreign language while staying in his native land; ways must be devised to bring the norms and models before him. While formal authority has some role to play even in a homogeneous society—children, for example, have their ways of behaving at home and need a bit of help in learning how to behave in public—its chief problem in America is created by tight groups of migrants in new communities where the ticket to the larger society is the very familiarity with the new form of speech that their isolation prevents them from getting in the most natural way.

The job of formal authority is therefore a simple one: to give the aspirant a new set of skills. But, like so many other tasks that are shouldered onto the schools, this one is complicated by having to adapt itself to an established curriculum; there is no logical place to fit it except in the English class, which is already expected to provide for budding secretaries interested in business English, speakers of the local standard learning to write in elevated styles, and an occasional foreigner who knows no English at all. The usual temptation presents itself to try to find one diet for all digestions. For a class in English, this means setting up a universal standard usually based on the edited usage of good writers. For teachers secure in their knowledge of the literary standard it is not altogether amiss to strive for such a goal, but too few of them are secure, so the solution adopted is a negative one: if the teacher cannot serve his students as a model of what to do, he can at least memorize a list of things that they are not to do and crack the whip if they do them. In place of an affirmative day-to-day practice in what the community does or approves on various levels of usage from literary to colloquial, the student is triggered to react whenever he has an impulse to do some particular thing that the code of misdemeanors forbids. He neglects the many in his anxiety over the few, often ending by making worse mistakes than the ones he is trying to avoid:

> Grammar mattered even more to Miss Mape than to most teachers. She jumped Lloyd Furman so effectively for saying *He don't* and *It don't* that she drove him one day into a *They doesn't*.[1]

Or a way out is found through exaggerated efforts to discover a substitute that will avoid both the "mistake" and the studied "correction" with which one cannot feel comfortable. Speakers have been so browbeaten about the redundant *at* in *Where is he at?* that they tend to avoid any such final *at,*

---

[1] *New Yorker*, May 24, 1947, p. 61.

even in **Whose place does he room at?**, which parallels **Whose house does he live in?**, not avoided by anyone except sticklers for keeping prepositions away from the end of sentences. Speakers goaded into saying *were* for *was* in **If I were John** often replace every *was* after *if* with a *were*: **If John were here last night why didn't he call me?** Such artless dodges are numerous.

Concentration on errors is like the concentration on sin in an old-time religion. The list of thou-shalt-nots is somewhat longer than the Ten Commandments but still brief enough so that one can substitute learning them by heart for the more arduous task of acquiring a command of a second dialect of English. Lists vary, and many if not most of the items on them deserve to be condemned, but the faults of any such negative approach can best be illustrated by the insensitive and often ignorant condemnation of usages that are both widely accepted and practical. Following are a few culled from high school and college handbooks:

1. **Faze: "You could not faze her by your criticism. Say daunt."** *Faze*, 'to affect unfavorably, in whatever degree,' is one of the most recent popularizations in English. *Daunt* is too specific.

2. **Claim: "He claims that he was cheated. Use says, declares, maintains, etc."** *Claim* connotes disbelief. The other verbs cannot substitute for it.

3. **Plan on: "We planned on an early departure, We planned on leaving early. Say instead We planned an early departure, We planned to leave early."** But *to plan* is to schedule and arrange the thing itself, while *to plan on* is to arrange one's affairs with a view to the plan—one can plan on something that is not within one's power to plan directly, for example **He plans on my cooperation;** hence the contrast in "Don't *plan* a trip, just pick up and go— it's more fun that way"; "Don't plan on a trip this summer, with all this work to do."

4. **Blame on: "Don't blame the accident on me. Say Don't blame me for the accident."** The value of *blame on* is that it enables the speaker to maneuver *me* to the end of the sentence, a more effective position for emphasis.

5. **Lose out: "Omit out except in referring to sports."** This ignores a useful distinction between missing a particular opportunity and missing a general one: **We called him, but he wouldn't come along, so he lost out** (missed what everyone had a chance to get).

6. *Too:* "*I was too startled to speak.* Say *too much.*" Is this supposed to require also *I was too much tired to stand, I was too much crippled to walk, She was too much spoiled to make a good wife?* Any participle that has been accepted as an adjective has a right to *too* without *much.*

7. *Only:* "*Only* must go directly before the word it modifies." This ignores several things. First, phrasal stereotypes: *If I only could* and *If only I could* mean slightly different things; the first suggests a stronger will to have a try at it; *if only* has become a stereotype of hopelessness. Second, accent: if *only* modifies a single element and not an entire phrase or clause, the two words are similarly accented: *He ónly found thése* is unambiguous. Third, interference between different connotations: "Sir Isaac Newton . . . usually got the result before he could prove it; indeed one discovery of his . . . was only proved two hundred years later"[2]—the intended 'not until' would become 'not more than' if shifted. *Only* is the victim of an unfair attention that never falls on its companion terms *even* and *just,* which are allowed to go where they please: *It éven terrified mé* (for *It terrified even me*), *It will just take a minute* (for *It will take just a minute,* which is more precise about the time but lacks the overtone of reassurance).

8. *Because:* "Avoid *the reason is because;* say *the reason is that.*" It is odd that, of all adverb clauses, this one should be singled out for reprobation. No one objects to *the time is when, the place is where,* or *the question is why. Is* has the same linking function in all of them.

One could add rules about not splitting the infinitive *(I want to just sit),* avoiding the comparative or superlative with absolutes *(the most perfect specimen),* ending sentences with prepositions *(the man I was talking about),* restricting *they* and *their* to plural contexts *(Everybody has their preferences),* and a good many more. These are enough to show the futility of drawing up a grammatical Baedeker of places to avoid as a way of not having to teach when to visit them and when to stay away. We cannot be sure that any particular list is relevant to a particular group of students at a particular time and place. Besides, blanket prohibitions are clumsy interferences with the need for language to keep pace with experience by growing *into* the new meanings that experience breeds in such profusion.

---

[2] *Harper's Magazine,* July, 1951, p. 87.

For the schools to play their authoritarian role more effectively, they must have enough trained people to do the job. The teacher needs to be thoroughly familiar with the regional standard in addition to the universal written standard and to be aware of other dialects and their scales of acceptability, especially the ones that are native to his students. Beyond that, the chief requirement is an ability to make his students see their language objectively. This means overcoming the defensiveness of those who regard their way of talking as an extension of their personalities and any criticism of it as a criticism of themselves. It also means disarming the notions of superiority cherished by other students who already command the regional standard. It is ethically correct and linguistically sound to instill an equal respect for all dialects as forms of language that one puts on and takes off at the behest of the community. One device is the enlightened bi-dialectalism suggested in an earlier chapter.[3] Another is the capsule lecture that justifies a fault—on all grounds except those of convention—before proceeding to correct it, thus wiping out any stigma that it may carry. For example, if the teacher is working with a newly arrived group that habitually uses *workin'*, *sellin'*, and *playin'*, he might explain the situation like this:

"Of course everyone around here says *working, selling*, and *playing*, and that is the way we must do it except at home and on the playground, but if you slip up and someone smiles at you just remember—and keep it to yourself—that the joke is really on him, because *workin'* is historically correct. Some members of the upper classes in England still use it. What happened is that there were two rival forms of pronunciation, just one of which was favored by the schools and became the standard about two hundred years ago. But they never could drive out the other form and I'd bet that if you listened closely to the people here you'd notice that they use it sometimes. They would probably never say **Whatcha composin'?** to a composer, but it wouldn't surprise me at all to hear them say **Whatcha cookin'?** to a cook."

An example or two like this is enough to break the ice—the teacher does not need to be an expert in the history of English. Since false notions of logic are also intertwined with notions of correctness, it is not out of place to point out how much more sensible some of the supposedly incorrect forms are, "but there it is, there's nothing we can do about it." A constructive approach takes imagination, sympathy, and a little more knowledge than the ordinary, but it achieves its objective, which no fanatical hunting of grammatical scapegoats can do.

---

[3] Chapter 9, pp. 149–50.

Authority on the grand scale

Formal attempts to impose one dialect as standard on all the speakers of a language are usually superfluous, because the conditions that make it desirable—closer communication and greater economic and political inter-dependence—are already at work in informal ways to bring about a kind of standardization. As speakers of different dialects are thrown together, they absorb more and more from one another where doing so enriches their communication and discard more and more of their idiosyncrasies where doing the opposite would interfere with it.

Yet for various reasons and in numerous places people have felt that attaining a standard by unpremeditated accommodation would be too slow a process, and reformers and would-be reformers, official and unoffi-cial, have stepped in. The impulse may come from a burgeoning national-ism that seeks identity in a common language, or from a centralization of government with the rising need to communicate with all citizens quickly and efficiently, or from a technological or commercial interdependence that must no longer be hobbled by a division of tongues.

During the nineteenth and early part of the twentieth centuries the typical kind of interference was that which promoted the spread of literacy, a consequence of the democratization that followed the American and French revolutions. Its mechanical genius was the printing press, which demands standardization: a single dialect and a uniform spelling. Its scope was usually confined to the limits of a single language; the speakers all more or less understood one another already and reforms were relatively painless—making them so was one of the aims of the reformers.

Take the standardization undertaken in Norway by Ivar Aasen a cen-tury ago. Norway was emerging from domination by Denmark and the Norwegian peasantry had become a political force. Aasen sought an authentic Norwegian language with which to replace the Danish that was still used by the ruling classes, and he found it by synthesizing Nor-wegian dialects in a language that all patriotic Norwegians would feel was natural and right. The result was the New Norse, or *Landsmål*, which is still extensively used.[4]

Another example is the re-Latinization of Rumanian at about the same time.[5] Though Rumanian was originally a Latin language, over the centuries it absorbed a great deal from Turks, Greeks, and neighboring

---

[4] See Einar Haugen, "Construction and Reconstruction in Language Planning," *Word* 21.188–207 (1965).

[5] Pointed out by Professor Dumitru Chitoran of the University of Bucharest.

Slavs, especially by word-borrowing. As in Norway, the upsurge of nationalistic feeling brought with it a desire for an authentic Rumanian free of non-Latin elements. The other Latin languages, especially French, were imitated, and not only was much taken over in the way of vocabulary but even the syntax was modified to some extent—with such changes as the simplification of the verb system, the dropping of the neuter gender, and the strengthening of the infinitive at the expense of the subjunctive.

An example from this century is provided by Turkey, among the sweeping reforms carried out by the dictator Kemal Atatürk. In 1932, after he had abolished the traditional Persian script and replaced it with Roman, he created a Turkish Linguistic Society, to which he appointed party members and school teachers, and gave it the job of revamping Turkish.[6]

More typical of the problems faced by language planners now is the rise not of submerged classes but of submerged peoples. It is no longer dialect against dialect but language against language, and easy adjustments are impossible. Parts can be interchanged on the same make of automobile, but where the engineering design is different a composite would refuse to run. This is the situation that confronts most of the new nations that have emerged and consolidated themselves since World War II—about forty in Africa alone, besides Indonesia, Israel, Pakistan, Malaysia, the Philippines, and many more. It also confronts some political entities of long standing, such as India and China, whose loosely federated parts the new nationalism has pulled more closely together. In all these countries important segments of the population speak mutually unintelligible languages, so that it is difficult to make any one of them official. At the same time, nationalistic fervor demands that the language of the colonial power—which paradoxically had fed nationalism during the colonial period by supplying a unity that had not existed before—be thrown off.

The upshot is that these nations have had to decide what language to adopt and then seek ways to have it accepted by persons who do not speak it natively.[7] There is a parallel to the consolidation and mergers that one observes on the American business scene, where small enterprises, like languages with but a few speakers, cannot survive in a world of competitive giants.

---

[6] Einar Haugen, "Linguistics and Language Planning," in *Sociolinguistics, Proceedings of the UCLA Sociolinguistics Conference, 1964,* The Hague, Netherlands, 1966, pp. 50–71.

[7] See Maximo Ramos, *Language Policy in Certain Newly Independent States* (Manila: Philippine Center for Language Study, 1961).

While conditions around the world are so diverse that no one case is typical of the others,[8] the Philippines can serve at least as an example. More than three hundred years of Spanish rule and forty years of American rule failed to establish either Spanish or English as more than rather widely accepted trade languages. Just after independence was achieved in 1946, the census showed six languages spoken by at least half a million people each, the chief one being Tagalog with about seven million speakers. The question of which one should be adopted had been officially posed a decade earlier with the creation of an Institute of National Language, after several years of agitation that saw even the Philippine Medical Association appointing its own committee on a national language. With its preponderance in numbers and its strategic position in central Luzon, Tagalog was favored from the first and in 1937 was proclaimed the basis of the new National Language and appointed to be taught in all primary and secondary schools beginning in 1940.[9] The Philippines have thus set out to do by internal diplomacy what formerly was achieved by military conquest—impose a language that is foreign to almost two-thirds of the population, with education and propaganda as the weapons.

The linguistic engineering under way in Malaysia and Indonesia shows all degrees of persuasion and compulsion. In both countries the Malay language is official. In Malaysia it was legally established in 1967, but English continues to be recognized in the courts and in Parliament, not only because of the close ties with England but also because only fifteen per cent of the population is Malay, the rest being mostly Indians and Chinese who are happy to stay with English.[10] Indonesia, by being less fortunate in the European language originally planted there (it was Dutch, no longer of importance in world-wide communication), may be more fortunate in the long run. Without the crutch of English to rely upon, Malay is more readily accepted and much is being done to bring it into step with the modernization that is being carried forward in all aspects of life. One detects a new determination, a break from the fatalism that led linguists in the past to view linguistic change as if it were as inexorable as the drift of time, which no amount of tampering could prevent. The Indonesians are simply assuming that deliberate change is

[8] See Punya Sloka Ray, "Language Standardization," in Frank A. Rice, ed., *Study of the Role of Second Languages* (Washington, D.C.: Center for Applied Linguistics, 1962), pp. 91–104.

[9] See Ernest J. Frei, *The Historical Development of the Philippine National Language*, (Manila: Institute of National Language, 1959); also José Villa Panganiban, "The Family of Philippine Languages and Dialects" and "A Filipino National Language Is Not Impossible," *Unitas* 30.823–33 and 855–62 (1957).

[10] *New York Times*, April 16, 1967, p. 10.

possible and are taking steps to realize it, enriching their language with new words—and, incidentally, even new phonemes—as vehicles for technical and scientific reforms.[11]

How well this new variety of politico-linguistic authority will succeed against internal rivalries, old colonial attitudes, and simple inertia remains to be seen.

Academies

Until our own time it was rare for any government to intervene directly in matters of language, but in several countries of Western Europe official charters were granted to societies whose members were interested in letters generally but particularly in "purifying the language." Behind the first of these lay the spirit of the Renaissance: the vernacular had just come into its own, and now must be protected, as Latin had been, against the corrupting influence of uneducated people. Oldest of the societies still in existence is the Accademia della Crusca, founded in 1582 and incorporated with a still older academy, that of Florence, founded in 1540; both had the avowed purpose of perfecting the Tuscan dialect of Italian. In time, imitators appeared in other countries. The following are still active: the French Academy, founded in 1630 largely at the instance of Cardinal Richelieu; the Spanish Academy, founded in 1713; and the Swedish Academy, founded in 1786, whose original purpose was to purify the Swedish language but which is now more celebrated as the body that confers the Nobel Prize in Literature. On the whole, the academies have thrived in the Romance-speaking parts of Europe but not in the Germanic-speaking. The Germans attempted one in 1617, again to purify the mother tongue. Plans for an English Academy (circa 1712) and an American Academy (1821) fell through.[12]

For all the excessively prescriptive tone of pronouncements by official bodies, the academies, through the dictionaries and grammars they have published, have been useful in supporting a prestige dialect. The value of this is simply that it helps to maintain a common language, keeping open certain lines of communication that might otherwise pinch themselves off in the course of time. The Spanish Academy is the best example of this kind of influence because of the great scattering of the Spanish-

---

[11] S. Takdir Alisjahbana, "New National Languages: A Problem Modern Linguistics Has Failed to Solve," *Lingua* 15.515–30 (1965).

[12] See *Encyclopedia Britannica*, 11th ed., s.v. "Academies," and Allen Walker Read, *"That* Dictionary or *the* Dictionary?" *Consumer Reports*, October, 1963, p. 490.

speaking community over several continents and among sixteen countries, each with its nationalistic ambitions. Linguistic authority has partly succeeded where political authority failed.

THE DICTIONARY

The aim of a descriptive grammar is to be consistent and complete, not to serve as a guide to usage. It records what it finds and leaves to the school handbook the selection and elevation of one dialect or set of forms over another. The handbook aims to be authoritative but seldom is very comprehensive; since it is intended for native speakers, the bulk of the patterns in the language can be taken for granted; we do more things "right," without prompting, than we do "wrong."

It is not the same with dictionaries. Until the appearance of the Merriam-Webster *Third New International Dictionary* in 1961, the fondest hope of the commercial dictionary publisher was that his book would not only be comprehensive ("It contains over 600,000 entries") but would be considered—as the *New International* once dubbed itself—the "supreme authority." With the appearance of the *Third* a new criterion was adopted forthrightly for the first time in a large unabridged dictionary. But the controversy that raged for several years after the appearance of the *Third*—including what amounted to a vote of censure by the editorial board of one magazine—testified to the deep-seated attitudes of the public toward what a dictionary is supposed to represent. That traditional role deserves examination.

The authoritative dictionary

Lists of words are both easier to make and easier to understand than grammars. The first overt linguistic interest that the average person acquires is in words; he has learned the framework of his speech and forgotten how he did it, but all his life he is confronted with new terms. So he finds a dictionary not only more within his grasp but a prime necessity in trade, profession, and pastime (word games are almost the only point where linguistics and entertainment meet—crossword puzzles rival schools as promoters of dictionary sales). Few people need a grammar, but involve a man in a lawsuit over the meaning of a word in a contract and he craves authority fast. What importance the publishers of dictionaries have attached to this may be seen in a blurb for the

Merriam-Webster *Second* that appeared in 1940, citing testimonials from the supreme courts of six states.

But the real key to the authoritative position of the dictionary in American life lies in our history as a colony of England. Cut off from English-speaking cultural centers during the first decades of our national existence and insecure in our own ways of speech, we looked for written standards, like people who lack confidence in their social graces and turn to Emily Post and her sister columnists. "We gradually sloughed off our colonialisms ... in manufacturing, in producing an American literature, in directing foreign affairs," wrote Allen Walker Read, "but linguistic colonialism was the last to go. ... The old habit of running to the dictionary remained, whereas an Englishman simply followed the usage of the people around him." Read's study appeared in the publication of a consumers' organization that tests products destined for everyone's medicine cabinet, laundry, and garage[13]—eloquent proof of the importance of the dictionary as a commodity in American life.

With such a background, it is not surprising that word lists were compiled earlier and have attained wider circulation than any other books about language. The following concerns the influence wielded on pronunciation by the dictionary of John Walker published in 1791:

> Not only does Walker's pronunciation prevail today in many individual words (... his recommended pronunciations of *soot, wreath, slabber, coffer, gold, veneer, cognizance, boatswain, construe, lieutenant, nepotism*, although all admittedly not general usage in his time, are now standard American pronunciation); but also Walker's efforts to secure an exact pronunciation of unstressed vowels have had a tremendous effect on modern American pronunciation.[14]

The content of a dictionary is determined not only by what words and idioms are extant in the language (and of course the resources of the publishers) but also by the need the dictionary is intended to serve and the amount of information available to satisfy it. Dictionary makers rely heavily on other published studies of words; if no comprehensive dialect atlas exists, certain information about pronunciation or meaning may have to be left out even if it falls within the intended scope. But the real shapers are the people who use the book and the kinds of information they want. Here is where the craving for authority has left its mark.

---

[13] *Consumer Reports*, October, 1963, pp. 488–92; November, 1963, pp. 547–52; February, 1964, pp. 96–97; March, 1964, pp. 145–47.

[14] Esther K. Sheldon in *Publications of the Modern Language Association of America*, March, 1947, p. 145.

The standard dictionary gives five items of information: spelling, pronunciation, part of speech, derivation, and meaning, usually in that order. Leaving out the part of speech for the moment, we can say that the remaining four are where the average user looks for final pronouncements. If he needs to write a word but has forgotten how to spell it, or sees a word and is unsure of its pronunciation, the dictionary fills his wants. If he is curious about the word as a word, he will probably look for its origin; etymology is the branch of linguistics that has been with us long enough to arouse a bit of popular interest. And if the word is new to him, he will want it defined or illustrated.

The order in which the four items are given has had certain consequences. Putting the spelling first has abetted the tendency of the average person to take the written word as primary and basic and the spoken form as an unstable sort of nuance attached to it. A linguist might argue for a kind of normalized pronunciation first, using a phonetic respelling. This would have advantages for the child and for the nonscholarly foreign learner of English, who would not need to know whether a word begins with *sk, sch, sc,* or *squ* in order to find it. But to most users the gains would be doubtful, because too many words are encountered for the first time in writing and also because spelling has been standardized more than pronunciation. A second effect of the spelling-first order is that it fastens a left-right letter sequence on every word so that groupings are easy by beginnings but impossible by endings; if one wants to know all the words beginning with a particular prefix they can be spotted immediately, but suffixes are another matter, and English is a language in which suffixes are more important than prefixes.

The limitations that are reflected in the four-way order can be summarized in this way: they emphasize externals. Spelling is the written trace of a word. Pronunciation is its linguistic form, like the shape that a die puts on a coin, but has little or nothing to do with value. Derivation is a snatch of history, sometimes without relevance. The value system, or meaning, comes last, and in reality includes so much that what the dictionary offers is hardly more than a sample, a small reminder that generally suffices only because the average user already knows the language and can guess at what is left out.

The break with authority

The Merriam-Webster *Third* does not escape these shortcomings, but it does break with the authoritarian tradition and follow undeviatingly a trail dear to the heart of linguists that was blazed in 1947 by the *American College Dictionary*—still one of the best of the desk-size volumes—

with the announcement that "no dictionary founded on the methods of modern scholarship can prescribe as to usage; it can only inform on the basis of the facts of usage."[15] In pronunciations and definitions, and above all in the words it includes, the *Third* has abandoned the pretense of standing as a lexical canon, an exclusive club to which words may apply but are not admitted until they have been decontaminated in the charity hospitals run by the socially daring among The Good Writers. If a term is pronounced in a certain way by a substantial portion of the population, the *Third* records it, and it does the same with meaning. Of course, *any* up-to-date dictionary is bound to give this impression when it first appears—even of the *Second* it was said that it "went to the street" for its new words and meanings. But in the two areas of pronunciation and meaning the *Third* has discarded all the trappings of purism. One criticism that has been fairly leveled at it is that, having decided to cover the spectrum, it ought to have labeled the colors more carefully, as the *American College Dictionary* did; it is harder than before to tell when a term is regarded as respectable and when it is not, or what level of speech it belongs to: extreme vulgarity is marked, as for *piss* or *fart,* but most other degrees of formality and informality are not, as for *jerk* or *gripe.*

In one area, the *Third* is almost as authoritarian as ever: spelling. To be consistent, if everyone's pronunciation everywhere was to be used in striking statistical averages, everyone's spelling everywhere—in informal notes and personal correspondence as well as in things intended for print—ought to have been collected and digested before deciding what spellings were to be recorded. Many people "carelessly" write *principle* for *principal,* *lead* for *led,* and *kinda* for *kind of,* just as they "carelessly" say /pʌlpət/ for /pʊlpət/ or /kanstəbl̩/ for /kʌnstəbl̩/, but the careless pronunciations are recorded and the careless spellings are not. In spelling the dictionary is not a dictionary in the modern sense but a style manual, one of those authoritative guides put out by learned bodies, publishers, and the government to control the appearance of the printed page: type faces, spelling, punctuation and hyphenation, syllabication, and paragraphing. (See Chapter 10, page 159.)

And unfortunately, for all its reforms, the *Third* (as well as every other dictionary) is as far behind the times as any of its predecessors when they first appeared, for just as it was moving toward better rapport with linguistics, linguistics moved further ahead and widened the gap again. How would a dictionary look if it tried to satisfy the new demands of linguistic science? It would have to be what it is only in a half-hearted way now: a companion to a grammar. One general linguist advises lexi-

---

[15] *American College Dictionary*, p. ix.

cographers "to prepare a complete syntactical grammar of their language as a necessary preliminary to writing their dictionary."[16] A generative grammarian puts it more technically: "It appears that the sub-component of syntactic rules which enumerates underlying phrase markers is itself divided into two elements, one containing phrase structure rules and the other containing a *lexicon* or *dictionary* of highly structured morpheme entries which are inserted into the structures enumerated by the phrase-structure rules."[17] This is simply to say that words and other similar tightly-bound units enter into the structure of phrases in specific ways that are among the rules of a grammar, and that a complete dictionary would have to label its entries according to the rules that apply to them.

We can now look back at that fifth bit of information provided by the standard dictionary that we skipped before, the part of speech. This is the one label of the kind referred to that is actually there. The label "noun" indicates a certain function in the phrase, as do "adjective," "verb," "adverb," "preposition," and so on. The label "verb" attached to *eat* gives a crude sort of cross-reference to a grammar, which in turn will explain that *eats* and *eating* are correct forms and that *People eat* is a correct sequence while **The eat* is not. Correspondingly, the label "noun" on *food* tells us that *the food* is normal but **fooding* is not. In fact, we are given a trifle more than the undivided categories of verb and noun: with verbs, we are told when there may be an object and when not, by the labels *v.t.* and *v.i.*; and from the capital letters attached to nouns we can deduce sometimes (as with *Taranto* and *Bizet,* though not with *Moor* or *Savior)* that the noun is grammatically proper—that is, used without the article.

Labeling by part of speech is good as far as it goes, but it is an inheritance from Greco-Roman grammar that falls far short of the subtler classes and subclasses that modern grammar demands. One who looks up *whim* in the *Third* will find it marked as a noun and grouped with the synonyms *caprice* and *fancy,* and also, under *folly,* grouped with *indulgence, vanity,* and *foolery;* but there is nothing to tell him that *a little whim* refers to something small, while *a little indulgence* or *vanity* or *foolery* probably refers to an amount. In short, the dictionary fails to label the subcategories of mass noun and count noun. (This is essential information to any foreign learner of English, and at least one of the

---

[16] Fred W. Householder, Jr., "Lists in Grammars," *Logic, Methodology and Philosophy of Science, Proceedings of the 1960 International Congress* (Stanford, Calif.: Stanford University Press, 1962), p. 576.

[17] Paul M. Postal, "Underlying and Superficial Linguistic Structure," *Harvard Educational Review* 34.253 (1964).

smaller special dictionaries provides it—the *Advanced Learner's Dictionary of Current English.*[18]) The definition as often as not throws out some hint from which one may guess the category—for instance, *sugar* is defined as a "substance," and presumably one would know that a substance is a mass (though here the word *substance* itself is not a mass noun!). But this is hit-or-miss lexicography.

Mass nouns and count nouns are only a couple of the most obvious of the subcategories whose labels could be added. Here are some additional examples:

1. Under adjectives, the question of comparison. Most standard dictionaries show when an adjective can be compared with *-er* and *-est* but fail to show what is to be done with the others. Some, such as *initial, seismic,* and *annual,* do not admit of comparison with *more* and *most;* others do. One can only guess from the definitions.

2. Under adjectives, the order classes that determine *the old book, my good friend,* rather than **old the book, *good my friend;* or *first good news* rather than **good first news;* or *beautiful wintry day* rather than **wintry beautiful day.* If labels were adopted here, *all (of), half (of)* (and other fractions, like *one-third*), *some (part) of,* and one or two more, would carry the number "1"; *the, a, this, that, my (your,* and so on), *each,* and a few more, would carry the number "2," and so forth, to indicate the relative position in the noun phrase.

3. Under adverbs, each of the subcategories that depend on which of the various things the adverb can modify. In *well-bred, fast-disappearing* (not **well white, *fast new*) it modifies forms of verbs but not adjectives. In *very new, very white, very quickly* (not **very undertaken, *to speak very*) it modifies adjectives or adverbs but not verbs (*very excited* is a test for the conversion of *excited* to an adjective). In *Usually it does* it modifies a sentence; in **Precisely it does* it cannot. In *Leave out the details* it forms a two-word verb with *leave;* in **Leave quickly the city* it does not.

4. Under verbs, all those that, though intransitive or transitive with object expressed, require something further to complete them.

---

[18] 2nd ed., by A. S. Hornby, E. V. Gatenby, and H. Wakefield (New York: Oxford University Press, 1963).

They might be termed *unsaturated*. The sentence **He puts the money* is incomplete in spite of the fact that subject, verb, and complement are all present; a further complement—for example, *on the table*—is needed. Similarly with **He sets the money*, although in *He sets the clock*, *sets* is saturated—the label would have to be attached to different senses of many verbs: **I saddled him* (needs, for example, *with responsibilities*) versus *I saddled the horse*.

For a dictionary, this kind of meticulous analysis and classification obviously has a point of diminishing returns. There is probably something to be gained, even though the list is small, in labeling the adjectives that normally come after the noun rather than before it—the user of the *Third* cannot tell, if he looks up *afire*, that he is not permitted to say **an afire house*, and he will find a similar warning under *alive* for only one of the senses, when it should apply to all. But a little farther out we encounter classes that are more and more tenuous, that apply to fewer and fewer elements, until, theoretically, a given rule might apply to only two morphemes in the language. Should one, for example, recognize the opposing categories of animate-inanimate because one can say such things as *They beatified her* but not **They beatified it* and can describe a person as *philosophical* but not a classroom? Some interesting pairs of adjectives split across this border—for example, *skinny-narrow* (a person can be physically skinny but not physically narrow; a thing can be narrow but not skinny), *mindful-reminiscent*, *healthy-healthful*, *hostile-inimical*, *young-new*. On the strength of *gradual, slow, abrupt*, or *sudden* inspiration (something that *happens* in *time*), but only *gradual* or *abrupt* hill, or on the strength of *long, lengthy, short*, or *brief* visit, but only *long* or *short* pencil, would it be reasonable to recognize opposing categories of temporal-spatial? Or perhaps one could have a dim category of sex in the fact that a man can have *children* but only a woman can have *babies*, or a sub-subcategory of count nouns on the strength of *all that day, all my family* (entities having "homogeneous parts") but not **all that shoe, *all the typewriter* ("indivisible")?

We may never see a dictionary, even for specialists, that spins its definitions and labels out so fine. But even the book intended for everyday consultation needs to go somewhat further than any has up to now in articulating itself with a grammar of the language. The dictionary, like the grammar, should be "maximally generative."[19]

---

[19] Uriel Weinreich, *"Webster's Third: a Critique of Its Semantics,"* talk given before the Linguistic Society of America, Chicago, December 28, 1963.

LEARNING A SECOND LANGUAGE

Fifty years ago the native-born American who knew a second language well enough to utter more than a phrase or two for comic effect or to show his erudition was comparatively rare. Nowadays this sort of isolationism is on the decline. Most school systems require foreign languages at least as early as high school and some as early as the first or second grade of elementary school. Colleges make sure that students who enter without a foreign language will make up the deficiency. Graduate schools refuse degrees in most subjects unless the candidate can handle one or more languages besides English that contain writings pertinent to his field.

In the United States, more than in any other large country, learning a foreign language means learning it in school. Instead of being hemmed in by several more powerful neighbors whose languages we are more or less exposed to from birth, as are the Czechoslovakians, or numbering four disparate linguistic communities among our own nationals, as happens with the Swiss, we have only a fraction of our borders touching on lands where anything but English is spoken, and we have only a scattering of settlements that preserve a waning remnant of French, Portuguese, Armenian, or Greek. While America long claimed to be the melting pot of the world, it was never the melting pot of the world's languages; its philosophy has been "learn English or else," and second- and third-generation Americans have tended to conform and to forget the language of their ancestors if it was distinct from English. The schools will be the purveyors of whatever foreign languages most Americans learn for a long time to come. How well they teach them is everyone's concern.

Language learned through language

If the theory of a linguistic instinct is correct, the instinct apparently blooms and fades quickly. We lose our childhood capacity to absorb. Or perhaps we lose not the capacity but the inclination to apply it; our firmly entrenched native habits become such a universal grappling tool that we insist on using them even to grapple with a new language. In either case, control of new learning passes from instinct to the giving and taking of directions, and as this is done through language we may say that a second language is learned largely through the medium of a first one. Each new performance involves not an organization of previously unorganized activity but a reorganization of what has already been learned. Part of the things we have learned are themselves techniques of reorganization, and these are brought to bear in reshaping the old linguistic patterns to make them conform to a new standard—or, more accurately, in shaping new ones out of old ones without losing the old.

In more usual terms the learning of a second language by an adult is rational. Instead of arriving at a grammatical pattern by sorting out the details of a huge number of crude examples and testing them by trial and error, an adult can be shown a selected few examples and given a translation of the semantic field; this usually suffices to put him on his way to handling an endless number of further examples of the same pattern.

As an illustration, suppose that the adult learner is a native speaker of English who is learning Spanish and is expected to master the conversion of adjectives to nouns, which is general in Spanish but restricted in English: in place of *the big one*, with a nominalizing empty word *one*, he must use the equivalent of *the big*. Our hypothetical student is then reminded of what a noun is—this category is virtually the same in the two languages and so can be used as a starting point—and, after being shown selected examples of the type *el grande* 'the big one,' *los altos* 'the tall ones,' and *los que llegaron* 'the ones who arrived,' he is told simply to add them to his category of nouns—that is, to use them in any of the accustomed situations where nouns are used. As a finishing touch, he may be shown some of the scattered instances where English does the same thing: *the good, the true, and the beautiful; a word to the wise; Henry's the oldest (one)*, and so on.

This predigestion—made by linguists—of the patterns that the adult must learn presupposes a foothold in the learner's experience, something held in common between the native language and the target language, like the category of nouns just mentioned, from which he can make his start. It also presupposes translatability, which is to say that there is no area of meaning encompassed by one language that cannot be encompassed by another—more awkwardly sometimes, but never with such imperfections that the idea cannot be put across. Fortunately, both presuppositions are largely fulfilled. No matter how different any two languages may be (and how great the differences can be is scarcely appreciated by persons whose experience of a foreign language is limited to those closely allied to their own, like English to German or French to Italian), there are enough universal similarities to make the first step possible. And regardless of the great difference in techniques of encompassing an event that one may find between two languages, both can usually manage it.

Contrast grammars and textbooks

The linguist plays a role in second-language learning, though he has not done so—at least up to now—in first. His task in second-language learning, at least the one he may be said to have carried off reasonably well, is the making of contrast grammars. These are grammars whose coverage is generally limited to the points of difference between two languages, although a great deal that is similar may have to be included in order to present a given point in its proper setting—as with the category of noun in English and Spanish. The contrast grammar therefore differs from the descriptive grammar, whose coverage is supposed to be complete. While a contrast grammar theoretically ought to be based on a good descriptive grammar of each of the two languages compared, actually it seldom is. More often, it is compounded of the difficulties that native speakers of one particular language experience in learning another particular language, plus the linguist's identification of the source of trouble as he searches the two linguistic structures for clues. Actually, contrast grammars have probably given more to descriptive grammars than they have received in return. Our first awareness of some peculiarity of our own language frequently comes from trying unsuccessfully to transfer it to another.

Can linguistics contribute something besides contrast grammars? This is a subject of warm debate at the present time.[20] Eventually, in the guise of psycholinguistics, it may lead to more efficient teaching of languages, and in that of sociolinguistics it may help to define the goals. Until then, in an enterprise that is more an art than a science, it is rash to credit linguistics with having much more to offer than a careful but still somewhat impressionistic description of the objects of the art.

The linguist's job is not finished, however, unless the description is properly done. If it fails to describe the spoken language and omits the patterns that happen not to be revealed or to be revealed accurately in writing, students may think of language as something primarily written. If it neglects to treat differences of dialect, students will form an impression of language as a monolithic entity with immutable standards of right and wrong and will be hampered when they try to communicate with ordinary speakers. If the patterns are broken into unrelated pieces, leaving the underlying structure unrevealed, students may resist their apparent arbitrariness. Where linguists have intervened to clear up such misunderstandings, as happens pretty regularly now with the many programs for improving foreign-language teaching, it is to undo the harm of inadequate texts and uninformed teaching.

The contrast grammar, as the linguist turns it out, is like a machine tool. It is designed to produce other tools, which in turn manufacture the

---

[20] See Noam Chomsky, "Linguistic Theory," Northeast Conference *Reports of the Working Committees*, 1966, pp. 43–49. See also Braj B. Kachru, review of Robert Lado, *Language Teaching: a Scientific Approach* (New York: McGraw-Hill, Inc., 1964), in *Linguistics* 31.87–107 (1967).

consumer's product. These other tools are the textbook grammars that students use in or out of class. In the chain of instruction they rank alongside of the teacher, not just for what they do for the student but for the way they guide the approach used by the teacher. The textbook is the most important single item in the foreign-language curriculum.

A good textbook requires more than the services of a linguist, whether direct or by way of some previously written contrast grammar. The requirements of psychology, pedagogy, and style are almost as great as those of grammar. In the past decade it has come to be realized that if speaking a language is the most complex skill we possess, teaching it is complex too and requires a cooperative effort. The concept of team writing has gained ground, and most of the better textbooks represent the joint efforts of several persons.

The ideal textbook will never be written and therefore cannot be described; but we know enough about the faults of our present less than ideal books to describe it partially in terms of what it would not be like:

1. It would not boast of its "method." There is no one approach to language.

2. It would express itself, whether in English or in the target language, without stiffness or formality. Students must be made to feel that the foreign language is as much alive as their own. Language material is to teach language, not to instruct in elevated diction, morals, or polite behavior. (Needless to say, a book that tries to be cute or to curry favor by using an overabundance of slang is not good either, but this is hardly a temptation to most textbook writers).

3. It would not try to cover a year's work in a hundred pages. There must be adequate exercise materials and accessories of various sorts. A short book may be a good one in the hands of a highly skilled teacher who supplements it; but in the hands of such a teacher almost any text can be made to work (and usually wastes too much of his time).

4. It would not rely excessively on straight text without diagrams, charts, or other visual aids. Nor would it trick itself out in scientific-looking formulas with a terminology and notation invented for the purpose or borrowed from technical monographs.

5. It would include little if any translation from the target language to English. To do otherwise puts the emphasis on the wrong skill: how to compose sentences in English. It would also restrict the amount of translating from English to the target language, espe-

cially in long passages or in collections of sentences that have no relationship to one another. As much material as possible would be in the target language, and grammatically or topically organized.

6. The grammatical explanations would be careful, clear, and detailed. Most outright claims to "simplified grammar" are worthless. The textbook can carry most of the burden of grammatical teaching, leaving the classroom free for practice and conversation.

7. The factual materials would be culturally authentic but as close as possible to the student's range of interests.

These are some of the hedges on the ideal as we see it in terms of our present philosophy. It is difficult to say more: the goals of education are never permanent, and philosophies change.

Conditions for learning a second language

The prime condition for learning a second language is the relationship between teacher and learner. It can be formal—master teaching pupil— or informal—friend learning from friend. If formal, it can be in the setting of a tutorial session in which the master sits with one pupil; or in that of the classroom, where he sits (or better *stands*) among many; or even, in these impersonal times, where the pupil sits with a machine on whose records or tapes an absentee master has recorded the lesson. There is no space to discuss all these relationships, so we shall pick the one that fits the average learner best, that of the classroom, and describe it in ideal terms. We shall assume (1) that the learner is motivated, (2) that the teacher is skilled and interested in his subject, (3) that a good grammar is available, (4) that the school system allows adequate time and provides adequate physical facilities, (5) that classes are not too large, and (6) that the goal is proficiency in the language rather than knowledge about the language or its speakers or its literature. Translating these provisions into concrete conditions, and inferring other conditions from them, the student could expect to find his foreign-language class characterized by the following:

1. Conversation groups will be small enough for him to be heard from frequently. This means not more than fifteen or twenty students—large enough to stimulate a lively exchange of words (language is, after all, a social activity), but not so large that the teacher cannot make several circuits during each period.

2. He will be occupied every working day. Daily contact with the teacher and with other students is as important as daily practice in football, and for the same reason: both have to do with getting and maintaining skills.

3. The teacher will be trained for his job. He will not be a native speaker of the target language casually appointed on the theory that a person with a healthy digestion makes a good dietitian, nor a regular teacher of journalism who happens to have a free period at the time the foreign-language class is scheduled. But though he need not be a native speaker, his training will have given him a native or near-native command of the target language so as to serve as a proper model for his students, and though he need not know English natively either, he will have made the comparisons between the two languages that will enable him to foresee the problems his students must face. And, whether as a result of training or simple temperament, his style will be as mettlesome and as full of give-and-take as that of a dancing master or an athletic coach. He will not monopolize the class session with his own talk but will make each word of his draw several from his students. He will know how to make every minute count.

4. The norm in the class will be practice. Patterns will not only be recognized but be used. Here it is essential to understand the difference between language (or football or piano-playing) and sociology (or history or philosophy). As *skills*, the former must be practiced as well as understood. For the child, the practice and the understanding are one; he infers what he understands from what he does, and he practices all day long. In second-language learning the linguist makes up for the adult's lack of time by working out the grammatical principles beforehand and presenting them for intellectual understanding, along with examples and drills. Drilling is as essential in language as in athletics. For the learner, a grammatical rule is only a set of directions, like those for a particular stroke in swimming: understanding it—that is, being able to repeat it and seeing its relevance in the total scheme of things—does not insure performance. Nor does mere performance—going through the motions of a single stroke under the direct supervision of the teacher—insure understanding, which is the student's support when he is trying on his own. Understanding and performance are inseparable; it is one of the anomalies of foreign-language teaching that some persons still view them not as companions but as opposites. Old-fashioned teachers over-intellectualized, explaining too much and practicing too little. As

a reaction to this and with the support of behaviorist psychology, for which speech is a response triggered automatically, some recent teaching has overemphasized mechanical drill. This has provoked a second reaction that has close ties with recent theories of grammar and with the notion of the innateness of language: if language is intricately patterned we can scarcely keep our bearings well enough to perform at all unless we are permitted an insight into the structure.[21]

5. There will be a language laboratory or some other arrangement (ideally it would be in the student's own room) with positions for listening and recording, plus a library of lessons, drills, and programs based on the materials of the course, which the student is free to use outside of class. The classroom will not be used for practice with machines. Class time is needed for the live interchange between teacher and students.

6. The class will be homogeneous. Students will have been selected by placement examination or otherwise, so that all are at approximately the same level of preparation.

7. The language material will be presented within as nearly authentic a cultural setting as can be managed, but the language and the setting will not be confused. There is no cultural determinism in the fact that French uses the place-activity construction *I'm going to class* (no article, as against *I'm going to the class* for straight location) very sparingly, while English uses it rather freely. On the other hand, gestures and bodily attitudes are equally a part of communication and a part of the total culture and have a definite place in the language course. The colorful externals of costume, folk dance, architecture, transportation and the like may help to motivate a few students toward more serious study but can easily be overemphasized.

If it seems curious that homogeneous groups, interested teachers, adequate facilities, and so on are even mentioned, the reason is that things as obviously necessary as these have not always been the rule. Schools have the faults of all large institutions: they throw a protective shell around organs that have outlived their usefulness and fail to develop new ones that are needed in getting about. Fortunately so much has been happening to focus attention on languages that lack of good teaching and ade-

---

[21] See Wilga M. Rivers, *The Psychologist and the Foreign Language Teacher* (Chicago: University of Chicago Press, 1964), p. 30.

quate facilities is harder to conceal than it was in the past, and government financing has wiped out most excuses for not having them.

LANGUAGE AND EMPATHY

The uses of money have their robber barons and philanthropists, capitalists and day laborers, conservatives and socialists, bearers of the gold standard and coiners of free silver, all concerned in one way or another with how the prime medium of exchange in society is to be managed and distributed. The economy is a material fact with an ethical side, for it concerns who shall have comfort and who shall not, who is to wield power and who is to submit.

Language also has its ethic, though for some reason we seldom pose it to ourselves in the ordinary terms of power and prestige or of good conduct and bad. We feel that we have a right to regulate the use of money in ways that will spread its benefits, for it is the creature of society and must respond to society's needs. But language is no less a medium of exchange and like money was created by and for society. And like money it is subject to abuse.

The exchange of language is the sharing of experience. If we regard as the highest mark of civilization an ability to project ourselves into the mental and physical world of others, to share their thoughts, feelings, and visions, to sense their angers and encounter the same walls that shut them in and the same escapes to freedom, we must ask how language is to be used if we are to be civilized.

Though laws forbid the undue concentration of economic power, the only laws against the misuse of language have to do with the content of messages: obscenity, perjury, sedition, and defamation in its various forms of libel and slander. There are no laws against the unfair exploitation of language as language, in its essence. The individual may carry as many concealed verbal weapons as he likes and strike with them as he pleases— far from being censured for it, he will be admired and applauded as a clever fellow. Perhaps because we feel that language is everyone's birthright and that being born with it means that all have equal access to its storehouse, we have never seen fit to limit even by custom the ways it is used. Custom frowns on the liar, sometimes, but lies again are content, not essence. The only part of the essence that suffers from the slightest disfavor is that small segment of the vocabulary that is affected by taboo, and even that is partly content.

In a small, unstratified society the rule of equal access perhaps applies. No one is excessively rich in either material or verbal goods. In more complex societies it does not apply, because language, like wealth and color, is a weapon of *de facto* segregation. With the disappearance of the less visible tokens of birth and breeding, language has in some areas taken over their function of opening or closing the doors to membership in a ruling caste. There is no question that the Received Pronunciation of Southern British has been just such a badge of admission—this was the theme of Bernard Shaw's *Pygmalion* and its musical version, *My Fair Lady*. The lines are not so clearly drawn in America, but a rustic accent is enough to preclude employment in certain jobs, and even a person with a markedly foreign accent may have an easier time renting an apartment by telephone than someone who exhibits a particular variety of Southern speech.

Society recognizes the problem of equal access only through the unequal efforts of the schools. They are unequal because alongside of schools striving for an ethic of equality there are others striving for an ethic of chivalry that, for all its good intentions, only deepens class lines. The *public* effort for equal access must be toward the elimination of every sort of verbal snobbery. There is nothing intrinsically bad about words as such, and by excluding another man's forms of speech we exclude him. The task of democratizing a society includes far more than speech forms, of course, but headway will be that much more difficult if we overlook the intricate ties of speech with everything else that spells privilege.

Public cures may be long in coming, but meanwhile some of the ills of unequal access can be avoided if we recognize our personal responsibility toward the sharing of experience through language. We can discharge it by trying as hard to meet our neighbor on his dialectal terms as we would try to meet a foreigner on the terms of his language. This means never using our superior verbal skill, if we have it, or our inheritance of a prestige dialect for which we never worked a day, to browbeat or establish a difference in status between our neighbor and us. It means remembering that language is the most public of all public domains, to be kept free at all costs of claims that would turn any part of it into the property of some exclusive club, whether of scientists, artisans, or the socially elect. The virtue of language is in being ordinary.

ADDITIONAL REMARKS
AND APPLICATIONS

1. Discuss laughter as a weapon of conformity. It is no longer considered good taste to laugh at racial jokes, and it long since ceased to be good taste to laugh at the behavior of the crippled and feeble-minded. Consider to what extent we still laugh at linguistic nonconformity, for instance as the basis for stage humor.

2. Linguistic nonconformity in adult speakers usually takes one of two forms: the lapse or accidental slip of the tongue and the use of non-standard dialectal forms. An instance of the former is the spoonerism, for example *Is the bean dizzy?* for *Is the dean busy?* Does our tendency to laugh at them make any distinction between the two?

3. A study of *shall* and *will*[22] showed that *will* has always predominated in sentences of the *I will go* type, with *shall* only in recent times gaining a special favor in England. The effort to impose *shall* when the subject is *I* or *we* is now seen as a classic instance of pedantry. See if you can describe your own uses of *shall* and *will,* and compare them with the recommendations of any reference grammar or hand-book that you can readily consult.

4. One scapegoat achieved fame in the slogan for a brand of cigarette: *Winston tastes good like a cigarette should.* This way of using *like* has long been common among English writers, including Shakespeare, but nowadays stirs feelings of guilt in many speakers. For those who would also feel uncomfortably formal if they replaced *Do it like I do it* with *Do it as I do it,* what is the two-word substitute for *like?*

5. Would you regard the following as mistakes? *Tell him to kindly leave; a more perfect union; I'll explain whatever you ask about; Whenever Mary or John is at home, they answer the phone.* Decide how you would express any that you would reject.

---

[22] C. C. Fries, "The Periphrastic Uses of *Shall* and *Will* in Modern English," *Language Learning* 7:1–2.38–99 (1956–57).

6. In 1966 the United States Supreme Court validated a New York law permitting the literacy test for voting to be given in Spanish as well as English. Was this law a step in the right direction? (The "low IQ's" that have condemned many children of minority groups to second-rate educations have often turned out to be the result of a compulsory use of an unfamiliar language. In Mexico one of the first steps toward the acculturation of Indians has been to teach them to read and write in their own language, then in the national language.)

7. Government intervention in the teaching of language to civilians was rare in the United States until 1958, when the National Defense Education Act made funds available for training teachers in foreign languages. It was extended in 1963 to cover teachers of English, and more and more support has been given in various forms, especially to the teaching of English in other countries. What economic reasons prompted this? Though the government supports the teaching of language it makes no rules for what shall be taught such as a national academy might make. Is this as it should be?

8. If it is assumed that the function of the dictionary is to constitute a record but not to rate acceptability, does there nevertheless remain a place for the guide to usage? Consider such a book as H. W. Fowler's *A Dictionary of Modern English Usage* (revised by Ernest Gowers [New York: Oxford University Press, 1965]). Is there also a place for the debunking book, such as H. L. Mencken's *American Language* (Fourth Edition, New York: Alfred A. Knopf, 1955)?

9. One pernicious fallacy about foreign language learning is that it ought to be possible to find word-for-word equivalents between one language and another. How does a grammar that gives word lists to be memorized with their meanings encourage this notion?

10. How do you react to a person who says *He don't, I won't go there no more, Who did they see?, Me, I wouldn't do it*? If you react unfavorably, what is the basis for your dislike? How does one strike a balance between the opposing demands of uniformity in language and the equal right of each dialect to consideration?

INDEX

Boldface numbers refer to illustrations.